MW00459723

Letters of

RAINER MARIA RILKE

RAINER MARIA RILKE

In Translations by M. D. HERTER NORTON
Letters to a Young Poet
Sonnets to Orpheus
Wartime Letters to Rainer Maria Rilke
Translations from the Poetry of Rainer Maria Rilke
The Lay of the Love and Death of Cornet Christopher Rilke
The Notebooks of Malte Laurids Brigge
Stories of God

Translated by STEPHEN SPENDER and J. B. LEISHMAN
Duino Elegies

Translated by JANE BANNARD GREENE and M. D. HERTER NORTON
Letters of Rainer Maria Rilke
Volume One, 1892–1910   Volume Two, 1910–1926

Translated by DAVID YOUNG
Duino Elegies

In Various Translations
Rilke on Love and Other Difficulties
Translations and Considerations of Rainer Maria Rilke
Compiled by JOHN J. L. MOOD

RILKE was born in Prague in 1875, the son of a conventional army-officer father and a religious-fanatical mother, who first sent him, most unsuitably, to military school. After that, largely autodidact, he studied philosophy, history, literature, art, in Prague, Munich, Berlin. From his earliest years he wrote verse. In the '90s both *Erste* and *Frühe Gedichte* appeared, short stories, plays. Much of his early work he declined to include in his collected works. In 1899 (which saw the *Cornet*, first version) came the first of two trips to Russia with Lou Andreas-Salomé (*Vom lieben Gott und Anderes*, later to be called *Geschichten vom Lieben Gott*, appeared in December 1900). He married Clara Westhoff in 1901, lived in Worpswede till the birth of their only child, Ruth, moving to Paris in 1902, Clara to work with Rodin, Rilke to write his monograph on him. Between travels in Germany, France, Italy, Spain, Egypt, Scandinavia, and his prodigious letter-writing, the twelve years with Paris as base were productive: *Stundenbuch, Buch der Bilder, Neue Gedichte, Notebooks of M. L. Brigge,* translations of E. B. Browning, Gide, de Guérin. After the outbreak of World War I he lived mostly in Munich, served briefly in army office work in Vienna, and in 1919 went to Switzerland. Here, in the small stone tower of Muzot, he achieved in 1922 the *Duineser Elegien* and the *Sonette an Orpheus*, followed by poems in French and translations of Valéry and others. He died at Valmont near Glion on December 29, 1926, and is buried beside the little church of Raron overlooking the Rhone Valley.

In the Living Room of the Westerwede House

1902

Letters of
RAINER MARIA RILKE

1892 — 1910

Translated by

JANE BANNARD GREENE

and

M. D. HERTER NORTON

W · W · NORTON & COMPANY

New York · London

Copyright 1945 by W. W. Norton & Company, Inc.
First published in the Norton Library 1969

Copyright renewed 1972 by M. D. Herter Norton

Books That Live
The Norton imprint on a book means that in the publisher's
estimation it is a book not for a single season but for the years.
W. W. Norton & Company, Inc.

W. W. Norton & Company, Inc., 500 Fifth Avenue, New York, N.Y. 10110

ISBN 0-393-00476-7

PRINTED IN THE UNITED STATES OF AMERICA

7 8 9 0

CONTENTS

TRANSLATORS' NOTE   7

INTRODUCTION   9

THE LETTERS   15

NOTES   365

LIST OF CORRESPONDENTS   400

ILLUSTRATIONS

IN THE LIVING ROOM OF THE WESTERWEDE HOUSE (1902)
From *Rainer Maria Rilke* by Lou Andreas-Salomé   *Frontispiece*

FACSIMILE OF LETTER TO HUGO VON HOFMANNSTHAL
Reproduced from that in the first edition of the *Briefe*   270–1

FACSIMILE OF LETTER TO DR. MARTIN ZICKEL
From the collection of Richard von Mises, Cambridge, Mass.   290–1

TRANSLATORS' NOTE

UNLESS otherwise indicated in the Notes, all these letters have been taken from the two editions of the general collection of Rilke's *Letters*, edited by his daughter and son-in-law, Ruth Sieber-Rilke and Carl Sieber, and published by Insel-Verlag, which differ not greatly yet enough to make them complementary.

Our thanks go to Richard von Mises, of Harvard University and the Massachusetts Institute of Technology, for his generous interest and help, and to Paul Graham, of Smith College, who kindly read much of the text.

We owe particular gratitude to Herbert Steiner, formerly editor of *Corona*, who has been for us a keen critic in the larger sense, giving many patient hours to discussion of difficult passages in the translation, and allowing us to draw for guidance in points of interpretation upon his knowledge of the background of Rilke's life and creative activity.

INTRODUCTION

MANY of the letters in Rilke's extraordinary correspondence have an artistic validity of their own and are to be enjoyed for themselves, even by one unacquainted with his poetry or with his life. While the letters in this volume have been chosen principally for their intrinsic beauty or wisdom, others have been included because they are psychologically revealing in a more personal sense, or because, like those of the very young Rilke, they contain a first statement of characteristic themes, or because they give the continuity that helps to make of the collection a kind of spiritual autobiography. To piece together a complete biographical story would not have been possible at this time. Rilke made it clear in his will that since a part of his creative energy had gone into his letters there would be no objection to their being published; but many people who were closest to him are still alive and much of a personal nature has inevitably been left out of the two editions of the *Letters*, prepared by his daughter and son-in-law, which still remain the principal source we have to draw on.

Both in his life and in his artistic development, 1910, when he had finished the *Notebooks of Malte Laurids Brigge*, offers a logical year in which to close this first of two volumes of Rilke's letters. The period from his seventeenth year until this time embraces all the great experiences of his early adult life, and these, save for his friendship with Lou Andreas-Salomé which was lifelong, were rounded out by now or just entering upon a new phase. Russia no longer dominated his conscious thinking but had become embedded, as he was to put it, in the substructure of his life; there are later few letters to his wife, the sculptress Clara Westhoff, to whom so many of the present pages are addressed; Paris, with which he had wrestled so desperately, had become the stern but benevolent guardian of his work; the overwhelming impact of Rodin's art and personality had passed over the rapids and come down to a quiet stream, and he had made his discovery of Cézanne and his paintings. With all this, the springs of his own inspiration, while they did not go dry, seemed to disappear underground; he became prey to a distressing inner restlessness that was to outlast even the war years and not again be overcome by the great flow of his creative genius until 1922, the year of the *Duino Elegies* and the *Sonnets to Orpheus*.

These strands of experience wove significant patterns in the poet's art. "In reality," he wrote in 1899, "one seeks in everything new (country or person or thing) only an expression to help some personal confession to greater power or maturity. All things are there in order that they may become pictures for us." So Russia gave him pictures for the *Stories of God*, the *Book of Pictures*, and the *Book of Hours;* Paris gave him pictures (many of them painful) for the *Book of Pictures*, the third part of the *Book of Hours*, the *New Poems*, and the *Notebooks*.

Only his approach to the pictures changed. "Nature," he had written of the time before he met Rodin, "was still a general stimulation for me, an evocation, an instrument on whose strings my fingers found themselves again; I did not sit before her; I let myself be carried away by the soul that went out of me; she came over me with her great immense existence, as prophecy came over Saul, just that way. I went along with her and saw, not Nature, but the faces she inspired in me." Already in his contact with the Worpswede painters he had been made aware of a different relationship to Nature, "this daily attentiveness, alertness, and readiness of the out-turned senses, this thousandfold looking and always looking away from oneself . . . this being-only-eye," as he noted in his journal. Rodin too believed in looking, observing, seeing, in drinking things in with his eyes and letting them speak for themselves—in a word, in objectivity. This Rilke set himself to learn in his own field, and the effort involved in fixing his attention on an external object, in keeping the music within him so muted that, as it were, the thing itself could speak and be heard, proved to be a rigorous discipline for himself and his art. The *New Poems*, the product of this new seeing, are firmer, more plastic than anything he had written hitherto.

Rodin gave him more than pictures and more than an understanding of observation plastically rendered. Rodin, through incessant work, was always in touch with the unconscious sources of his creative power. Rilke, subject to spells of inspiration interrupted by arid periods when he was burdened with the uneasiness of living—the *Cornet* was written in a single night, the three sections of the *Book of Hours* in twenty-four, ten, and eight days, respectively, in three different years—, learned the value of this "always working" and tried hard to attain it himself. That he never did, his correspondence is there to testify, as well as the completing of the *Elegies* and the coming of the *Sonnets*, again all in a few days' hurricane. His nearest approach to it was perhaps between May, 1908, and January, 1910, a time spent almost continuously in Paris, when he wrote *New Poems II*, the *Requiems*, and the *Notebooks*.

After the *New Poems* he was no longer so consciously preoccupied with seeing.

> Work of sight is done,
> now for some heartwork
> on those pictures within you . . .

he wrote in a poem called "Turning," in a letter to Lou Andreas-Salomé. In the *Notebooks* he rid himself of many fears; for it is a book of fear, of the fears of his childhood, of great cities, of loneliness, of death, of love, of losing himself. And in 1910, the ordeal of that writing over, he was able to declare that "almost all songs are possible."

Letters were to Rilke at once a means of communication and a channel for artistic expression. Like Donne, he found that

> . . . more than kisses, letters mingle Soules;
> For thus friends absent speake. This ease controules
> The tediousness of my life: But for these
> I could ideate nothing, which could please,
> But I should wither in one day, and passe
> To'a bottle'of Hay, that am a locke of Grasse.

To those who knew him his presence and conversation were unforgettable, but he himself was easily exhausted by personal contacts. His aloofness, his constant insistence upon solitude should not mislead one into believing that he was by nature cold or indifferent; he was, on the contrary, too responsive for his own peace of mind. The letters may fail to give the whole picture of his personality, in that the lighter side—the humor of which all his friends speak, the courtesy that sometimes hid a cutting wit—is not in evidence. But they are a monument not only to his capacity for friendship but also to his great need of imparting the life within him to those he loved.

He took pains with his letters, not only with their content but with their appearance as well. The pages are exquisitely neat, for he wrote naturally in a regular, elegant, calligraphic hand. Often he would patiently recopy an entire page rather than mar it by a change of word or phrase; and if he regarded a letter as important, he would copy it down for his own reference before sending it.

Rilke must have derived from letter-writing some of the same satisfaction that came from his work. In the *Requiem* for Count Kalckreuth he speaks of fate passing into verses and not returning, implying that once an experience has been poured into an artistic mold, the weight and pain of it leave the artist. Letters provided a release of the same sort, a means of easing the pressure of life; but the release would have been only partial, the expression provisional. To find out why this was so would take one to the heart of that strange necessity that inhabits an artist's soul. Perhaps in letters his experiences had not finally come to rest, had not passed totally into the picture beyond, into the pure image they became in verse. Perhaps fate could still return to him from the letters.

Particularly when inspiration lagged he turned to his correspondence, for in it he "could ideate" much that pressed for release. It became his handicraft, the tool that could keep him at work in constant preparation for the creative moments. One feels he could scarcely have survived the unproductive periods without it. The best of the letters, indeed, were written in these times.

Revealing his mind as they do, it is natural that the letters should illuminate and enrich one's interpretation of Rilke's poetry. The interplay between the two is active at almost every level of experience. Over and over again, as our Notes attempt in some measure to indicate, the letters tell of some incident, of something seen or read, which became also the subject of a poem. The fresh transcript of the experience, or his revival of the memory, enhances one's appreciation of the heightened and universalized reality of the verse. For the *Notebooks*, further-more, he seems to have used the letters as a kind of proving ground, particularly those to Lou Andreas-Salomé about Paris, which startlingly resemble certain pages of the book.

Since the drama of Rilke's life was largely an inner one, it lent itself well to this kind of record. For the letters reflect the emotional and spiritual struggles he underwent, and a compre-hension of them often gives a key to the poems which are, in a sense, the resolution of those tensions. In them one constantly meets with Rilke's exceedingly individual ideas—those ideas on love, on death, on art that are familiar from the poetry—and be-comes acquainted with the soil from which they grew.

Rilke has said many profound things about living, yet the words of Euripides come to mind:

> Wisdom is full of pity, and thereby
> men pay for too much wisdom with much pain.

The letters show that the springs of Rilke's wisdom lay not in cool detachment but in deep anguish of spirit. They reveal the tangled root as well as the tranquil flower, and they are evi-dence that his words are spoken in the deepest humility. "Who speaks of victory? To endure is everything."

The Letters

To Franz Keim　　　　　　　　15b/I Wassergasse, Prague
[1892]

I deem it my duty, upon receipt of your friendly lines, to thank you immediately for your great kindness. I prize your opinion most highly and learn it the more gladly as it is a good one.—So with all my heart, thanks for your kind letter.

Today I must only add the request that you will always keep the good will and the kind friendliness you have shown me, for more distant days as well.

Severe with myself, as you, most esteemed master, advise, I want always to be and to remain. A firm, beautiful, and shining goal before my eyes, striving toward that goal; not on the road along which ordinary people senselessly stagger, not on the broad-trodden highway of the millions!—to press upward on roads one has oneself laid, to the one unclouded light on high!—

For my view is:

>　A genius, so noble observers of men suppose,
>　Is often doomed to ruin.—
>　No!—*If the period creates no great men for itself,*
>　*Then the man will create himself a great period!—* . . .

To Valery David-Rhonfeld　　　　　December 4, 1894
before midnight

Vally mine, mine, mine!

Over there in the dining room my aunt is sitting at her evening meal; I renounced my share of supper, withdrew from the to me dismal atmosphere into my room and there, not from need, rather to have a certain taste—frankly, from a mortal craving for sweets ate three pieces of the cake in question. My heart was oppressed and out of sorts without my knowing the reason at first. Then, as I sat across from Tante G. in the dining room for a few minutes, it became evident to me that the abrupt exchange of the light-flooded sphere of your presence for the dreary, humdrum atmosphere of my so infinitely remote relatives was the weighty cause of that bad mood. But that has vanished now. My heart is light and my mind is clear. Your letter, your dear letter, has banished the clouds. It is bright. The heaven of our love shines out of the quiet flooding of my soul. Sweet sensations murmur softly like strong reeds, and longing like a rustling tree in blossom spreads out its arms within me. I don't know how often I have read your lines. I don't know what so overwhelms me. Is it alone the consciousness that they come from you, or is it rather the aroma of a deep, warm feeling that is wafting toward me, that intoxicates me. Vally, your dear words have poured a holy magic into my soul, yes, in it glimmers that worshipful, trembling earnestness that must have pervaded the hearts of the oracle-questioning Greeks when they awaited at the temple gate, half in hope, half in trepidation, the answer of the mysterious god. For to me too it is as though my eyes were seeing farther than usual—as though the dimming walls of the cramped little room were betaking themselves away—, as though today I were permitted to take a look into the future! But before I look out into that colorful rolling sea of mists, let me first of all gaze within myself. In this night, about half past eleven, it will be exactly nineteen years that I have been alive. You know the lack-luster story of my frustrated childhood and you know those persons who are to blame for my being able to note nothing or little that is joyous in those days of growth. You know that for the greater part of the day I was entrusted to a serving-girl, immoral and of few scruples, and that the woman whose first and most immediate care I should have been loved me only when it came to bringing me out in a new little dress before a few marveling acquaintances. You know how I acquitted myself with varying success at the Primary School of the Piarists and—a stupid boy—in the main avenue of the Baumgarten decided my own fate with a childish word. If in my father's house love was shown me with both care and concern only by my papa, I was in general thrown entirely upon my own resources and for the most part could not share with anyone my little sufferings and blisses, in the new phase of my young life I was very well acquainted with that cowardly, undisguised heartlessness which does not shrink even from being brutal out of pure bestial lust for murder (the expression is not too strong). My heart, apart from this inclined through the loneliness of my earliest days to quiet endurance and courageous resignation, trembled at the sight of these injustices, and bore with a submission not proper to its years the torments of that treatment. Yes, bore them—. You often call me idealistic. Dearest Vally, if I am still that now, think what pure feeling must have shone in that little soul which, always lost in itself, was averse even to the simple, gay, innocent games of rowdy boys in the Primary School, and consider further, my love, how frightfully the onslaught of such wild, undeserved crudities must have echoed in the undefiled sanctuary of that childish spirit. What I suffered in those days may be compared to the worst pain in the world, although I was a child, or rather because I was one. Because neither the strength of resistance nor the fullness of enlightened reason were mine, with which to recognize in it common knavishness and nothing more. I endured blows without ever having returned a blow or so much as repaying it with an angry word, I suffered and bore. I believed the will of an infinite, unalterable destiny required of me this heroic endurance—had I known, recognized, that instead of this inevitable fate it was only the whim of a pitiful, pleasure-seeking creature— —(Mother). How was I to suspect that!—By the same necessity by which I saw day yield to night, I believed my torments to exist and took a certain pride in bearing them. In my childish mind I believed myself through my patience near to the virtues of Jesus Christ, and once when I received a hard blow in the face, so that my knees shook, I said to my unjust assailant in a quiet voice—I still hear it today—: "I suffer it because Christ suffered it, silently and without complaint, and while you were hitting me, I prayed my good God to forgive you." For a while the pitiable coward stood there, dumb and motionless, then he broke out into the derisive laughter with which all to whom he imparted my outcry of desperation chimed in howling. And I always fled back then into the farthest window niche, bit back my tears which would then break out violent and hot only in the the night, when the regular breathing of the boys sounded through the wide dormitory. And it was in the very night in which I was arriving at I don't know which anniversary of my birth that I knelt on my bed and with clasped hands prayed for death. A sickness at that time would have appeared to me a sure sign of response, only it didn't come. To compensate, there developed at that time the urge to write, which even in its childish beginnings provided me consolation. "Maritana," a tale of a heroically courageous maiden whose character resembled that of Jeanne d'Arc was, after several poems I no longer remember, the first work of any size. "The war horse rears and the trumpets sound." That was the end of a fiery monologue from this remarkable fantasy. That that period was filled above all with religious songs, which thanks to Providence have all been lost, needs no confirmation in view of the above-mentioned soulful frame of mind. Isn't that so?—You also know how furthermore it became ever clearer to me that to remain in the hated military school was no longer possible and, only too often already, have I told you of the years of hesitation and the final development of the decision.—During this time, which for the most part I spent in the sickroom more spiritually exhausted than physically ill, my poetic attempts developed greater clarity and independence, and I mention especially the two thoughts, "Satan on the Ruins of Rome" and "Exorcism," with joyful recollection. So in these troubled days for the first time the often stifled urge for consolation shot up freely; simultaneously, however, my mind growing older, my heart growing lighter, felt the chilling emptiness of isolation. After all, it had never, never yet met with friendly response, let alone love, and yet seemed to be demanding love. Once more I became deeply attached to a comrade, by the name of Fried. This time my heart should not go empty away.

There developed a truly brotherly affection based on mutual sympathy, and with kiss and handclasp we sealed a bond for life. As children do. We understood each other well, and I blossomed out in the knowledge that the scarcely varied events of my soul were sounding and ringing on in the like-tuned soul of my friend. I was jealous, as he was of me; he admired my poetic thoughts and I begged him to try his hand too, and heartily rejoiced in the timid success of his stories. Fried's grandmother, for whom he had a tremendous admiration, died suddenly, he went to her funeral, and I spent two tearful nights tortured by worry, knowing my beloved friend far away. He returned at last, longingly awaited by me and—was another. Later I learned that fellow pupils had dragged our pure bond into the mud and besides this Fried had received orders from higher up not to associate so much with the fool. After that my heart never became attached to anyone again. But even the friend who had so easily fallen away I did not shun and spoke officially with him, without ever reproaching him, but I did reject the offer of reconciliation he made me once more, without pride, but with earnest firmness; and my heart went on being orphaned. It seems perhaps to be the confession of a weakling. Yet I shall never be ashamed that my heart was empty before I found you, Vally, and leave the shame to those who had scorned to earn a place in it. Then came the time that you know (Linz Commercial School), whose bitter disillusionments and errors are buried in your forgiveness. Then came the fourth big division of my existence: the period of study. I was already prepared to renounce my scholastic future, weary of the everlasting, unsuccessful and aimless work, when I met you, beloved, dearest Vally, when you strengthened, healed, comforted me and gave me life, existence, hope, and future. On December 4th of the year in which I entered upon my high-school career in Schönfeld, I renounced this plan and, exhausted with work, wanted to fling myself into the arms of destiny's stream, to go under or to land somewhere or other. But that today I am not straying through the world a purposeless wanderer, but rather as a confident fighter —my breast full of love, gratitude, and hope—am striding toward our happiness, our union, could I thank anyone but you for that, my divine Vally? My whole previous life seems to me a road to you, like a long unlighted journey at the end of which my reward is to strive toward you and to know you will be *all* mine in the near future. And now, as that spirit, that oracular courage wafting from your letter proclaims: this future is ours. Is ours under the protection of our dear, loved dead, of your good grandmama, and under the shielding power of our own strength and the steadfastness of our love. Let us still, dearest heart, with the help of your noble grandmama, whom I so honor and esteem, survive well this year's troubles as also the extraordinary things of next year—then will come, if all goes off according to plan and hope, the university years which grant us much more time still and will besides lead us so blissfully near to our happiness. Then let us found the longed-for household on whose solid foundation our inner contentment is to rest as on a strong substructure.— Then let us create, industrious in the practice of our arts, helping each other, taking counsel like two sturdy, blissful human beings— who over their love and their work forget the world and pity or despise people.—Then in six years, in the first year of the twentieth century, probably in the first or second of our official engagement, you will get, my much beloved *panička*, another letter like this which will contain a little backward glance over the worse times surmounted and a prophecy for better ones!

Eleven o'clock at night it has already struck out there, and before I complete and read over this letter, nineteen years will certainly be full.—When I look briefly over them once more, the brightest point is that you stepped into my orbit and for life, as long as it beats, have given my poor heart, a stranger to love, the most worthy object of adoring, grateful devotion—in yourself!

René

[3]

To Dr. Bauschinger 15b/I Wassergasse, Prague
December 2, 1895

. . . Is it not strange that almost all great philosophers and
psychologists have always devoted their attention to the earth
and to the earth only? Would it not be more sublime to turn one's
eyes away from the little clod and to consider not a tiny grain
of dust in the universe but the universe itself?—Think, dear sir,
how small and insignificant earthly hardships would appear the
moment our earth had to shrivel up to the tiniest, whirling, will-
less little part of an endless world! And how man would have
to grow on his "little earth"!—

Strange. Every bird that makes its dwelling under the shelter
of the roof beams first investigates the place it has chosen and
over which a part of its diminutive life is now to trickle away.
And man is quite content to know the earth halfway and scantily,
and lets the faraway worlds above wander and roam. Does it not
seem as if we were very deep down still, since our gaze clings so
persistently to the ground?—Could not that be the only true
philosophy which claws its strong roots into infinity instead of
into the slime of the earth?! . . .

[4]

To Bodo Wildberg
(*H. von Dickinson-Wildberg*) March 7, 1896

. . . Thiel develops his strictly German patriotic idea as op-
posed to my world enthusiasm, and it seems to me the story of
our two philosophies of life is that of the two parallel lines that
cross at infinity! For in the end they are running toward the same
goal. Only Thiel thinks that this goal will be reached by a tight
closing together of each nation and hostile severing of that nation from the outside world, because this eternal battling and
worrying wakens and exercises their powers, while I am of the
opinion that this natural and paltry advance takes place of itself

and needs at most the help of workers but not the power of kings. Those who tower clear-eyed above the tumult should not look toward the way stations where our weary successors will rest, but should marvel freely and proudly at the golden sun-goal beyond, which late grandchildren will enjoy in full radiance. Even Moses was permitted to gaze on the Promised Land—and before his failing eyes lay its blossoming splendor and not the thousandfold danger through which his people had to wrestle its way!

Hence Thiel seems not to want to dedicate his powers for the present to the "League of Genuine Moderns," which is much to be deplored. I like the idea very well, and I should be glad if it would take shape in reality.—In that case one should not beat the advertising drum, one would have to search quietly for like-minded and like-feeling people . . . wouldn't one? . . .

[5]

To Bodo Wildberg
  (H. von Dickinson-Wildberg)   15b/I Wassergasse, Prague II
                                     [1896]

. . . Your opinion of Thiel's letter which, for lack of time, I still haven't answered certainly agrees more or less with mine.— A *league* does not, after all, bear the stamp of a perfect herdlike similarity among its members, as Thiel seems to suppose. On the contrary: the more different its individual components, the more full-toned and rich will be the result of their combined sound, if only they are tuned to *one* fundamental tone,—that of genuine, deep, true feeling for art. One should not confuse league with school. While it is the tendency of the latter to narrow the course of the creator by certain rigid norms, the league enables each, according to his own peculiarity, to express himself without concern for petty interests and advantages. . . .

[6]

To Karl Baron Du Prel   8/I Blütenstrasse, Munich
                                       February 16, 1897

It may be an awkward token of my respect, if I offer you my latest book of poems.—

But I can give my feelings no other expression. You are the most significant investigator in the domain of hypnotism and will pardon an interested layman the following request, which is: by what road does one become a worthy initiate?—There are plenty of pamphlets which deceive and mislead the novice by their charlatanish falsehood, and the unpracticed eye does not know how to differentiate them from those genuine guides which direct one intelligently into the dark lands of clarity and of the future.

Apart from the charm of the mysterious, the domains of spiritualism have for me an important power of attraction because in the recognition of the many idle forces and in the subjugation of their power I see the great liberation of our remote descendants and believe that in particular every artist must struggle through the misty fumes of crass materialism to those spiritual intimations that build for him the golden bridge into shoreless eternities.

If I may penetrate into the nature of your science, it will perhaps be vouchsafed me sometime to become with word and pen one of the adherents of the new faith that towers high above church-steeple crosses and shines like the first hint of morning on the princeliest peaks.

Please give me your advice, my dear Baron. What works should I go through and where can I (who am not in a position to buy them) get hold of them?

Do not let this be a burden to you; it seems to me that in my "Visions of Christ," appearing this year, I shall come a big step nearer to your group. . . .

[7]

To Ludwig Ganghofer   8/I Blütenstrasse, Munich
                                                April 16, 1897

. . . Dearest, much honored master, when one has a very dark childhood behind one, in which the everyday resembles walking in dank cold streets and a holiday is like a resting in some narrow, gray, inner court, one becomes diffident. And even more diffident if, at the age of ten, from these troubled and yet enervated days one is deposited in the rough activity of a military institution where, above the longing for love that has scarcely come to consciousness, an icy, wild duty rages away like a winter storm, and where the lonely, helpless heart after unhealthy coddling experiences unreasonable brutality. Then comes the crisis: the child becomes either indifferent or unhappy. I became the latter. A strong disposition toward excessive piety grew to a kind of madness under the influence of the spiritual loneliness and the coercion of an odious duty hard as fate. The blows I often endured from mischievous comrades or coarse superiors I felt as happiness and went in for the idea of a false martyrdom. The continual excitement of this almost ecstatic joy in torment, the passing of the hours of recovery in the institution chapel, the excruciating sleeplessness of nights frantic with dreams—all that together was bound finally to exercise a detrimental influence upon my resistless growing organism. After an added inflammation of the lungs, I was sent for six weeks as "highly nervous" (!) to Salzburg for a salt cure. Had I been allowed to leave then! But everybody thought it perfectly natural that, having borne it four years, I should remain for the six to come, which would be better, in order to become a lieutenant and—to provide for myself.

In the fifth year of my military training (the fifteenth of my life) I finally forced my departure. Things didn't get much better. They put me in a commercial school in Linz, where I saw a cheerless office future darkening before me.—After scarcely a year's time, I tore myself away against everyone's will by an act of violence and have since been accounted a kind of prodigal son.

They wanted to try the last resort. Since in both previous institutions and in my family it was noticed with scorn and uneasiness that I "made poems," they wanted to make college possible for me. At that time it was my father's brother, who played a considerable role in Prague as lawyer and deputy to the assembly of Bohemia, who put in a good word for me and with generous financial assistance made possible the costly private study my father could never have afforded. For that I thank him far beyond the grave. After three years of serious but joyous work I had gone through the entire eight-grade grammar school so well, even after the thoroughly defective preparatory training of the military school, that in the summer of '95 I passed my entrance examination with distinction. Unfortunately my uncle could no longer look upon this success . . . and he probably took with him under the earth the opinion that I would not amount to much. He left no stipulations of any kind in his will save that his daughters, my cousins, should allow me to study up to the entrance examination and, under certain circumstances, the university years.

Now it seems to me that all people do not give alike. And in the two years of my university study I have got the feeling rather strongly that I am a burdensome duty to the two ladies. Much more burdensome to me is the feeling of slavery in such helpless dependence at my age when others may already support their parents. And then: on this road I have *no objective at all.* For I keep costing more and more money, and if I become a doctor and do not want to pine away as a high-school instructor—then I shall be costing money again until I get some professorship or other which, however, I do not in the least desire.

With every day it becomes clearer to me that I was right in setting myself from the start against the phrase my relatives like: Art is something one just cultivates on the side in free hours, when one leaves the government office, etc.—That to me is a fearful sentence. I feel that this is my belief: Whoever does not consecrate himself wholly to art with all his wishes and values can never reach the highest goal. He is not an artist at all. And now it can be no presumption if I confess that I feel myself to be an artist, weak and wavering in strength and boldness, yet aware of bright goals, and hence to me every creative activity is serious, glorious, and true. Not as martyrdom do I regard art—but as a battle the chosen one has to wage with himself and his environment in order to go forward with a pure heart to the greatest goal, the one day of celebration, and with full hands to give to all successors of the rich reconciliation finally achieved. But that needs a whole man! Not a few weary leisure hours.

I do not know, dearest master, in how far you agree with me and whether you are perhaps wisely smiling at the impetuousness of this youthful resentment; then you will forgive too.— Now I am free of the university.—The time has come. Dear sir, you yourself once offered to give me help if I needed it. Now then: today I have come to you.

I would like through agreement with a publisher or some steady engagement on a newspaper to earn enough to be able to live soon and well on my own. I would like to spare my cousins their wanting-to-give-gladly and, by grateful renunciation of my monthly allowance, to enable my dear father, who is somewhat ailing, to allow more for his health. I cannot work in peace before that happens.—I myself, of course, need little. . . .

Full of profoundest trust I lay this whole avowal in your kind hands and sincerely beg you: counsel me, help me. . . . Be assured that I shall never and nowhere bring discredit upon your recommendation . . . and to you all the gratitude I can prove to you through deeds for a lifetime.

[*8*]

To Frieda von Bülow   Munich
                                                  August 13, 1897

. . . We are reading in the most various books on Italian Renaissance art and seeking an opportunity to get as independent a judgment as possible on this interesting period. From the early golden age of Florence we want to push forward by degrees to the Caraccis. As a matter of fact, I am especially fascinated by one Florentine master of the quattrocento—Sandro Botticelli, whom I now want to go into somewhat more deeply and personally. His Madonnas with their weary sadness, their great eyes asking for release and fulfillment, those women who dread growing old without a holy youth, stand at the heart of the longing of our time. I do not know whether you had the opportunity to see Botticelli and how you stand toward his works. It is interesting in any case to meet this man in a period when the Bible and the holy legends constituted the subject matter for all painters and each was seeking to do as much justice as possible to the religious motif, to narrate the legendary version without wanting anything for himself in so doing—save at most the solution of some problem of color technique or of pure form; along comes Sandro Botticelli and in his naïve longing for God perceives that the Madonna, in her deep sympathy ennobled and sanctified by her strange motherhood, can quite well become the herald of his own sadness and of his weariness. And in fact all his Madonnas look as if they were still under the spell of a melancholy story, quite bare of hope, that Sandro has been telling them; but they are utterly tender in feeling and keep his avowals in confessional sanctity and meditate on their obscurities and gaze on much, much misery and have nothing but that little playing boy upon their laps who wants to become the Redeemer. . . .

[9]

To Adolf Bonz   Im Rheingau, Berlin-Wilmersdorf
                                [December] 25, 1897

. . . I want to speak to you in all sincerity now . . . about the poems. You see, my view on this point is purely subjective, and it must be and must remain so. It is not my way to write poems of epic or lyric style that can stand five to ten years of desk air without becoming deathly sick. Short stories and dramas are results that do not age for me,—poems, which accompany every phase of my spiritual longing, are experiences through which I ripen. Short stories are chapters, poems are continuations, short stories are an appeal to the public, courtings of its favor and interest, poems are gifts to everyone, presents, bounties; with a short-story book in my hand, I am a petitioner before those who are empty,—with poems in my heart, I am king of those who feel. A king, however, who would tell his subjects in ten years how he felt ten years ago, is a sham. Seven sketchbooks full of things I am burning to utter await my choice, and they must be said either *now* or never. But because I knew that I would want to say them, I have undertaken to mark each lyric period by a book. Since the *Dreamcrowned* period seven sketchbooks have come into being and an eighth is begun which seems to me to indicate an entirely new stage.—So it is my plain duty to settle accounts with these ripe riches, that is, to commit what is good in them either to the fire or to the book trade. I prefer the latter, for my books have had success, that is, they have awakened here a smile, there a love, there a longing, and have given me an echo of that love, the reflection of that smile and the dream of that longing and have thereby made me richer and riper and purer. Please understand me, I grow up by them, they are my link with the outside, my compromise with the world. Now I can defend the verses as episodes, as little moments of a great becoming, as real, deep spring: if ever I have a name, they would be misunderstood as final products, as maturities, mistaken for summer.—I cannot keep my springtime silent in order to give it out some day in summer, old and faded, and were I untrue to my resolve, which for four years has been fulfilled in *Life and Songs*, *Wild Chicory*, *Offerings to the Lares*, *Dreamcrowned*, all further publication, seeming to me a betrayal then, would probably cease too. But I am earnestly sworn to persevere, and this whole attitude is so bound up with my life that I cannot dismiss it. Quite the contrary, if I ever have a name, that is, *have become* (and the becoming is much too glorious for me to long for that), then the poems will be entirely superfluous; a selection can then be made, a complete edition which will then also have something about it of a comprehensive result—but *then* they will be blossoms, memories of spring, lovely and warm with the summer that lies over their stillness. Until then is further than from today until tomorrow. What I am saying today is nothing but the word "heart's need" of the other day, a rocket sent into the air, bursting into these thousand words of my innermost conviction. And valued and dear as your advice is to me, you will now not take it amiss any more if I do not follow it, but do everything to consecrate a new book of poems, *Days of Celebration,* to young '98.

I cannot do otherwise, so help me God. . . .

[*10*]

To Frieda von Bülow   Ligowka 35, St. Petersburg
                                         May 27 (June ·7), 1899

An intention to write never turns into a letter. A letter must happen to one like a surprise, and one may not know where in the day there was room for it to come into being. So it is that my daily intentions have nothing to do with this fulfillment of today. They were concerned with much that I am now saving up to tell personally. For the many experiences and impressions are still heaped up in me in such disorder and chaos that I do not want to touch them. Like a fisherman who comes home late at night, I can guess only vaguely at my catch from the burden of the nets and must wait for the morrow in order to count it and enjoy it like a new discovery. As I think over the immediate future, it seems to me it will be in Meiningen that the sun will first rise on my wealth. Accordingly you will be able to witness my greater or lesser prosperity, and I do well to be silent about it before I can show it fully.

Only this much: I feel my stay in Russia as a strange complement to that Florentine spring of whose influence and success I have told you. A friendly Providence led me to the next thing, further into the depths, into a greater simplicity and toward an ingenuousness that is finer. Florence seems to me now like a kind of prefiguration of and preparation for Moscow, and I am thankful that I was permitted to see Fra Angelico before the beg-

gars and supplicants of the Iberian Madonna, who all create their
God with the same kneeling power, again and again, presenting
him and singling him out with their sorrow and with their joy
(little indefinite feelings), raising him in the morning with their
eyelids, and quietly releasing him in the evening when weariness
breaks the thread of their prayers like rosaries. At bottom one
seeks in everything new (country or person or thing) only an
expression that helps some personal confession to greater power
and maturity. All things are there in order that they may, in
some sense, become pictures for us. And they do not suffer from
it, for while they are expressing us more and more clearly, our
souls close over them in the same measure. And I feel in these days
that *Russian* things will give me the names for those most timid
devoutnesses of my nature which, since my childhood, have been
longing to enter into my art! . . .

In the old book of which you so kindly wrote me, there are
already weak attempts at it. And I believe the goal is worthy of not
growing weary in the attempt. . . .

[*11*]

To Frieda von Bülow   Villa Waldfrieden
                                Schmargendorf bei Berlin
                                September 14, 1899

Neither from you nor from our dear house, nor from Troll,
the black, have I really and truly taken leave: read this letter,
therefore, as audibly as possible.

My leave-taking is a great and warm gratitude for everything
in that homelike house in which so much that was joyous and industrious happened to me; in which I was physically so peaceful
and lived full of a new health and won a new courage through
definite study. The Bibersberg days—will be for me the expression for a past that will long influence all the happenings and in-
cidents and successes of my day and that will endure in my feeling
more and more richly (not through reflection) but because of *its
having been.*

The high park, the quiet, listening house in the midst of its broad rustlings, the gentle lamp-lit evenings in the living room —all of that willingly unites with my dearest thoughts. I still recall the first evening when the high, red lilies were so vigilant before the Gothic door, and the park grew so deep with the night, and the cellar lay there distant and uncertain like an entrance into something new, visible only in premonition; and I remember with pleasure how much like a guest of a hundred secrets I felt then, and I rejoice that the feeling of the first evening somehow always hung over the known things, so that even now I must lay my gratitude before many closed doors.

But in any case to you, the finder and discoverer of that house, I am thankful for many things. Had we come to your house as brief visitors for idleness and enjoyment, you would have received more visible signs of our gratitude. But since we came as fellow inhabitants, occupied with a life of our own, with the purpose of completing (as we actually did) something very definite in that country summer, we accepted the good in simple, quiet enjoyment—which also means a form of thanks (the best perhaps!).

Anyway you will be moving down to Meiningen soon now; the weather makes the park sad and the otherwise so sunny house seem strange: but then go with a good feeling for the things that were really dear and common to us in many a deep sense. You will have time to take your leave; we were prevented from doing that by the sudden necessity of returning home. Greet, therefore, in our name too all the rooms and the Bibersberg sun that goes down behind the great hall! . . .

[*12*]

To Sofia Nikolaevna Schill   Villa Waldfrieden
                                        Schmargendorf bei Berlin
                                            March 5, 1900

. . . The translation of the *Chaika* is finished. I have enjoyed working on it and learned a great deal in the process. A week ago

Sunday I read the play aloud at Frau Lou's, and now for the first time I can look at it clearly and cannot help seeing that its performance here is not without danger, for many characters are brought right to the verge of exaggeration, and it is quite possible that the public here would take them for caricatures, although they are intended and felt seriously. It is also striking that the three acts with the long conversations contain scarcely any progress and that during the course of them the characters involved are lightly sketched in the style of a comedy, in weak suggestive contours,—until in the last act the stirring action appears as the closing catastrophe of events in the storms of which persons *other* than those of whom we know something from the first three acts must have stood. If one takes the characters in the sense of the first act, namely as comedy, they are incapable of setting foot in the fourth act; on the other hand, I scarcely believe one will be able to come through the hesitant scenes of that first part with a serious conception.

I am saying all this because it seems to me important that we should introduce Chekhov in the theater with a *sure* success—for which *Uncle Vanya* (so far as I know its content) is perhaps more suited. . . .

. . . Russian people seem to live fragments of endlessly long and powerful life-spans, and even if they linger in them only a moment, there still lie over these minutes the dimensions of gigantic intentions and unhurried developments. . . . And just that it is which out of all their lives affects us as so eternal and of the future. . . .

[*13*]

To Sofia Nikolaevna Schill   Villa Waldfrieden
                                     Schmargendorf bei Berlin
                                     March 16, 1900

. . . I simply cannot tell you how much I look forward to seeing Russian pictures, wandering through the Tretiakov Gallery, and catching up on everything I had to lose a year ago because of haste and strangeness.

That is all so sympathetic and familiar to me, and awakens in me—as things never have before—good feelings of home. Also you must not think that the *Chaika* has become distasteful to me or that I have regretted having taken pains with it. I am convinced that the impression you describe would be very similar to mine, had I had a chance to see the play at the Moscow theater. There it certainly had a strong effect, and all its merits were in any case brought out by an understanding interpretation, in such a way that its defects had no room to make themselves apparent. I entirely agree with you that Chekhov is in every case a modern artist when he has the intention of portraying in artistic form the tragedies of the commonplace with their banal breadth, behind which the great catastrophes develop. To our dramatic artists too it is quite clear that all catastrophes have a relatively smaller effect amid great events and highly emotional people, while they tower terribly high above the commonplace and collapse over it with endless din.

But if it is necessary to portray everyday life on the stage with all its trivialities and conventional gestures, empty words, tedious give-and-take and the stale falsities of daily intercourse, all these manifestations on the stage must be differentiated by the tempo of their development from the actual examples from which they are copied. Just consider: everyday living as it really happens counts on *one life* and gives itself time,—everyday living on the stage must be completed in *one evening*. All the proportions must be shifted accordingly. The scenes on the stage may under no circumstances be as long as the scenes in reality which are their prototypes, and the public ought not to receive from the stage the feeling of *this* reality, since this reality is, after all, accessible to everyone anyhow. The sensation of tedium, for example, is evoked *not* by scenes which *are* actually tedious, but only by *those* highly interesting moments in which the characteristics of tedium occur in a condensed form: through these then is conveyed to the spectator not the feeling of tedium well known to him but a superlative of this feeling which excites and surprises him. And similarly with all portrayed emotions. As also, for example, from a picture, ugliness may not be experienced by the beholder as ugliness, but rather as the new expression, wrung from beauty, for an indecisiveness of form, for a necessary transition to another possibility of beauty as yet unexperienced by us. Before the portrait of an ugly man, we ought to have only the impression that his features were unfinished, on their way to a new unity which we can sense through the disorder of his face. And as the artist, through his absorption in the details of this face, experienced nothing of its ugliness, so the ordered relationship of this detail must transfigure the whole in such a way that the beholder takes it in with satisfaction and no thought of ugliness. Artist and beholder behave toward each other in this case like two children who tell each other in whispers about an event grownups think is sinful. They tell about it, and it is beautiful and pure: between them is no knowledge of sin. And that is what I have against Chekhov's first three acts, that he gives the everyday at the tempo of the everyday, without artistic recasting, without force. The artist who succeeds in showing us the tones of long, empty days *all* in one hour on the stage will evoke in us the suffering of a dreary eternity, while the chance section of the everyday simply transferred to the stage has merely the effect of the original—tedious and unpleasant.—A great deal may be said about it, since this tempo of events is of great importance in every art. What makes *Resurrection*, for example, so wonderful is that in an hour on the march or in prison, we review the outline of many days, and involuntarily through the nature of the events mentioned (superfluous ones are never enumerated) feel that we are experiencing centuries of human development.—Moreover, *Resurrection* is a very significant book, full of artistic values; and when one reflects that it did not arise from his putting to use this great art of his, but progresses in a constant battle *against* it, then one can measure the superhuman power of this artistic force which, despite all resistance on the part of the aged Tolstoy, still so wonderfully controls individual parts of the work.—We have just come to know it from the only complete German (but alas, very bad) translation. I shall order the complete London edition (Russian) for you and bring it to you with great pleasure. . . .

[*14*]

To Lou Andreas-Salomé   St. Petersburg, 1900
                                                          Saturday morning

I have your letter, your dear letter that does me good with every word, that touches me as with a wave, so strong and surging, that surrounds me as with gardens and builds up heavens about me, that makes me able and happy to say to you what struggled stupidly with my last difficult letter: that I long for you and that it was namelessly dismaying to live these days without any news, after that unexpected and quick farewell and among the almost hostile impressions of this difficult city, in which you could not speak to me out of the distance through any thing at all. So it came to that ugly letter of recently which could scarcely find its way out of the isolation, out of the unaccustomed and intolerable aloneness of my experiences and was only a hurrying, a perplexity and confusedness, something that must be alien to you in the beauty to which your life has immediately rounded itself out again under the new circumstances.

Now I can scarcely bear it that in the great song around you, in which you are finding again little childrens' voices, my voice should have been the strange, the only banal one, the voice of the world among those holy words and stillnesses of which days about you are woven. Wasn't it so? I fear it must have been so. What shall I do? Can I drown out the other letter with this one? In this one your words echo, the other is built upon your being away, of which I learned nothing, and now that I am informed no longer has the right to exist . . . but *does,* doesn't it?

Will you say a word to me? That in spite of it, everything is as you write; that no squirrel has died of it and nothing, nothing has darkened under it or even remained in shadow behind it.

You know, I have often told you of my squirrels that I raised in Italy, as a child, and for which I bought long, long chains so that their freedom might come to an end only in the very high treetops. It was certainly very wrong to force oneself at all as a power into their light lives (when they had already grown up, that is, and no longer needed me), but it was also a little their intention to go on reckoning with me too, for they often came running after me, so that at the time it seemed to me as if they wanted a chain.

How they will miss you, the good youngsters! And will they be mature enough to go without you into wood and world? High up in the firs of Rongac their childhood will sometimes occur to them, and on a branch that is still rocking from the burden of the leap, you will be thought of. And though they are only three little squirrels, in whose little eyes you have no room, still somewhere in them it is so big that you can be in their lives. You dear one.

Come back soon, come back as soon as you can leave them. Lead them out into the wood, tell them with your voice how beautiful it is, and they will be the happiest little squirrels and the most beautiful wood.

Yes, please, be here by Sunday! You won't believe how long the days in Petersburg can be. And at that not much goes into them. Life here is a continuous being underway, whereby all destinations suffer. One walks, walks, rides, rides, and wherever one arrives the first impression is that of one's own weariness. To add to this, one almost always makes the longest excursions for nothing. Nevertheless I already know this much, that we still have a few beautiful things to see when you come. In any case for two weeks everything I have thought has ended with: when you come.—

The moonlight night of Wednesday to Thursday I also love. I went along the Neva quite late, by my favorite place, across from St. Isaac's Cathedral, where the city is simplest and greatest. There I too (and indeed quite unexpectedly) felt peaceful, happy, and serious, as now since having your letter. I hasten to send off these lines so that what you send me Monday (and you will surely send one or two words by your brother? Only a few words, I shall understand them all!) is already an answer to *this*. Answer to the one question: are you happy? I am, behind all that bothers me, so fundamentally, so full of trust, so unconquerably happy. And thank you for it. Come soon! . . .

[*15*]

To Sofia Nikolaevna Schill   Tula
                                                      May 20, 1900

The lovely hour with you was the last little stone in the gay mosaic of our Moscow days. Next day everything was colored by the haste of departure, and Moscow, dear as it is to us, paled before the anticipation of the many things ahead. We had no idea how close our dearest fulfillment was to us. On the train, we found Professor Pasternak who was traveling to Odessa, and when we spoke to him of our indecision as to whether we should after all try to see Tolstoy now, he informed us that there should be on the train a good acquaintance of the Tolstoy house, a Mr. Bulanshe, who should be apprised of the present whereabouts of the Count. And it was actually Mr. Bulanshe who was most kindly willing to advise us. We decided to remain in Tula, and to go next morning to Lasarevo, and thence by carriage to the estate of the Obolenskys at Pirogovo where, in all likelihood, Mr. Bulanshe thought, the Count must still be. Two days before, Mr. Bulanshe had accompanied the Countess to Yasnaia, and so the possibility was at any rate good that one of these days he might ride to Yasnaia. Therefore Mr. Bulanshe sent a telegram to the Countess from Serpukhov inquiring where the Count would be on Friday. The answer was to come by telegram to our hotel in Tula. We waited for it in vain and went on, as had been agreed, early yesterday to Lasarevo, completely at a loss. There we found a station employee who informed us that the Count had accompanied Tatiana Lvovna to the station yesterday, and had then departed with his luggage for Koslovka. So it became a question for us of reaching as quickly as possible (by freight train) a place from which Yasnaia was accessible. We drove back to Yasinki, hired a carriage there, and raced with breathless bells to the rim of the hill on which stand the poor huts of Yasnaia, driven together into a village, yet without coherence, like a herd standing about sadly on exhausted pastureland. Groups of women and children are only sunny, red spots in the even gray covering ground, roofs and walls like a very luxuriant kind of moss that has been growing over everything undisturbed for centuries. Then the hardly discernible street dips down, forever flowing past empty places, and its gray streamer glides gently into a green valley foamy with treetops, in which two little round towers on the left, topped with green cupolas, mark the entrance to the old, overgrown park in which lies hidden the simple house of Yasnaia Poliana. Before this gate we dismount and go quietly like pilgrims up the still woodland road, until the house emerges gradually whiter and longer. A servant takes in our cards. And in a while we see behind the door in the dusky front room of the house the figure of the Count. The eldest son opens the glass door, and we are in the vestibule facing the Count, the aged man, to whom one always comes like a son, even when one does not want to remain under the sway of his fatherliness. He seems to have become smaller, more bent, whiter, and his shadowlessly clear eyes, as though independent of his aged body, await the strangers and deliberately scrutinize them and bless them involuntarily with some inexpressible blessing. The Count recognizes Frau Lou at once and greets her very cordially. He excuses himself and promises to be with us from two o'clock on. We have reached our goal, and, minds at ease, we remain behind in the great hall in the son's company; with him we roam through the spacious wild park and return after two hours to the house. There in the front room is the Countess, busy putting away books. Reluctantly, with surprise, and inhospitably she turns to us for a moment and explains briefly that the Count is unwell. . . . Now it is fortunate that we can say we have already seen him. That disarms the Countess somewhat. She doesn't come in with us, however, throws the books about in the front room, and shouts to someone in an angry voice: We have only just moved in! . . . Then while we are waiting in the little room, a young lady arrives too, voices are heard, violent weeping, soothing words from the old Count who comes in to us, distraught, and excitedly asks a few questions, and leaves us again. You can imagine, we stay behind in the little room, in great fear of having come at the wrong time. But after a while the Count comes in again, this time alert, turning his entire attention upon us, encompassing us with his great gaze. Just think, Sofia Nikolaevna,—he proposes a walk through the park. Instead of the general meal, which we had dreaded and at most hoped for, he gives us the opportunity of being alone with him in the beautiful countryside through which he carried the heavy thoughts of his great life. He doesn't participate in the meals, because, indisposed again for the last two days, he takes almost nothing but café au lait, and so this is the hour he can easily withdraw from the others in order to lay it in our hands like an unexpected gift. We go slowly along the long, thickly overgrown paths, in rich conversation which, as formerly, receives warmth and animation from the Count. He speaks Russian, and when the wind doesn't cover up the words for me, I understand every syllable. He has thrust his left hand under his wool jacket in his belt, his right rests on the head of his walking stick without leaning on it heavily, and he bends down now and then to pick some herb, with a gesture as if he wanted to capture a flower with the fragrance surrounding it; from his cupped hand he drinks in the aroma, and then, as he talks, heedlessly lets fall the empty flower into the great profusion of the wild spring, which has become no poorer thereby.—The talk passes over many things. But all the words do not pass by *in front* of them, along externals, they penetrate the darkness behind the things. And the deep value of each is not its color in the light, but the feeling that it comes out of the obscurities and mysteries out of which we all live. And every time something not-shared became apparent in the tone of the talk, a view opened up somewhere on to light backgrounds of deep unity.

And so the walk was a good walk. Sometimes in the wind the

figure of the Count grew; his great beard fluttered, but the grave face, marked by solitude, remained quiet, as though untouched by the storm.

As soon as we had entered the house, we took leave of the Count with a feeling of childlike thankfulness and rich with gifts of his being. We did not want to see anyone else on that day. As we went back on foot to Koslovka, we enjoyed and understood the country of Tula in which wealth and poverty are side by side, not like contrasts, but like different, very sisterly words for one and the same life, jubilantly and carelessly fulfilling itself in a hundred forms. . . .

[*16*]

To Clara Westhoff   Schmargendorf bei Berlin
                                       October 18, 1900

Do you remember, dear Clara Westhoff, the evening in the little blue dining room? You told me then about those days that piled up before your journey to Paris.

At your father's wish you had to delay your departure and try to model his mother.—Your eyes, full of presentiment, already caught up in distances and new beauties, had to turn back and accustom themselves to the very near face of a grave, dignified, old lady, and every day go weary ways over furrows and wrinkles. The quiet work subdued your hands, already outstretched, ready for all there was to grasp. And instead of changing amid the many great chance happenings of a foreign land, you grew, rising by the daily work. Instead of your art, thirsty for the friendly strangeness of new things,—your human feeling and trust unfolded in these unexpected days, your love gathered itself together and went out to meet the quiet, peaceful face that offered itself to you, enigmatically rich, as though it were the countenance of many, having neither expression, nor head, nor hands. As though things sometimes joined together to lift a collective face as if it were theirs and hold it before a beholder . . . and before a creator! You see, I was so struck then by your humility:

suddenly your eye, which was already preparing itself for larger dimensions, goes about willingly with little, hesitating, hearkening steps over the many overgrown paths of a long dead experience and stands still by all its landmarks reverently and respectfully. And has forgotten the world, and has no world but a face.

I know exactly everything you said then. The figure of the old lady who speaks rarely and reservedly, who hides her hands when a gesture of tenderness would move them, and who only with rare caresses builds bridges to a few people, bridges that no longer exist when she draws back her arm and lies again like an island fantastically repeated on all sides in the mirror of motionless waters. —My eyes too were already caught up in the radiance and bound to great and deep beauties. Your home was for me, from the first moment, more than just a kindly foreign place. Was simply home, *the first home in which I saw people living* (otherwise everyone lives abroad, but all homes stand empty . . .). That struck me so. I wanted at first to be a brother beside you all, and your home is rich enough to love me too and to uphold me, and you are so kind and take me in as a real member of the family, and initiate me trustfully into the abundance of your work weeks and holidays. And I am entirely devoted to the great beauty of which I am, after all, only an enjoyer (I did not join in the work of contemplating this beauty) . . . : So I all but forgot it, the quiet face of life, which waits for me and which I must shape with humble, serving hands. I was all the time looking out beyond it into radiance and greatness and am only now accustoming myself again to the near and solemn sternness of the great face which must have been shaped by me before I may receive something more distant, new. You worked for a month; I shall perhaps have to work for years before I may devote myself to something which down deep is friendly, and yet is unexpected and full of surprise. Much of the mood of those weeks of work, of which you told, is in me. For a while now, I have felt myself to be in the presence of the stillest hour, but only when I resolved to stay here, to study, to make full use of all the means Berlin offers for my plans, and merely to serve, then only did I begin to model. I still think much and with longing of Worpswede, of the little house in which there will be black evenings, day in, day out, and cold lonely days . . . of our Sundays and of unexpected hours so full of unforgettable beauty that one can only bear them with both hands,—only behind me, my work is already growing in the great sea of the background like a wandering wave that will soon seize me and envelop me—utterly, utterly. . . .

That is what, above all, I must let happen. You will understand it, since I began with your little story and yet from the first moment have spoken only of myself, as is justifiable in a letter which comes to you in my stead. I myself cannot go away from the "face." I am arranging my whole winter to make the most of every day, and perhaps as early as January 1901 I shall go to Russia again. There all the features of life become clearer and strangely simplified for me; there I can more easily work ahead, improve, complete. . . .

I have always known that one of the events which you told me about would be especially significant for me . . . now your November days of last winter stand almost symbolically over me. And if I had not received this wonderfully beautiful picture out of your memory and out of your feeling, I should not have known *what* I am now living through, and that what I am now living through is good.

It is good, isn't it?

I am not saying farewell to you. I feel gratefully near to you, and it does me good not to have taken leave. . . . Leave-takings are a burden on feeling. Distance remains stressed behind them, acts and grows and becomes mighty beyond all that is shared, which should be spontaneous even between those who are widely separated.

How beautiful your letter was! It was very full of you and it is wonderful that you write as you are. Very few can do that, and many who only write never learn it (what a bad word "learning" is for it!) as long as they live. And with you writing isn't even the main thing. I could readily believe that it is. With your pen too, you would create people.

Before what little figure are you sitting by your warm stove? Before the stiffly standing child that you separated from the cowering girl? And the boy with the tightly drawn-up knees that I like so much,—is he all finished? Whenever you write of such things, and of everything you want to, you do me good.

I thank you so much and think of you in connection with only nice things.

(half past one at night)

[*17*]

To Paula Becker   Schmargendorf
                                                    October 18, 1900

Your letter . . . found me here, and it would still have done so after two weeks and even after four weeks; for I cannot begin the Worpswede winter about which I was so happy day after day. Here it has become clear to me: my studies require me to stay here in the neighborhood of the big city, in communication with all the helps and helpers, like one intent on a single purpose, who is serving.

You know what these studies, which I have set up beside my most personal work, mean to me; the everyday, the enduring, the path on which I return from every flight, the life above which one can raise oneself only when one has and rules it, the stillness and the shore of all my waves and words. To me Russia has really become that which your landscape means to you: home and heaven. About you, in tangible form, stands all that is yours; reality and warmth are about you, with clouds and winds and waters all love of life lives toward you and surrounds you with sympathy and ennobles the least detail of your everyday life. *My* surroundings are *not* placed about me. Far away on distant paths I have seen the cities in which I dwell, and the gardens that rustle over me are many rivers away from me. Churches that stand by the Volga and are repeated in the rolling stream in softer white and with duller gold on their cupolas, ring out to me morning and evening with their great standing bells, and songs that blind men and children sing move about me like lost spirits and touch my cheeks and my hair. Such is my landscape, dear friend. And I may not desire to supplant these surroundings, which are like fragrance and sound about me, by a broader reality; for I want indeed to live and create in such a way that that which, half memory, half intuition, surrounds me now, may gradually rhyme itself into space and really encircle me, still and sure, like something that has existed forever and for which my eyes have only just become sufficiently strong. Do you understand that it is an infidelity if I behave as though I had found hearth and home already fully realized elsewhere? As yet I may have no little house, may not yet dwell. Wandering and waiting is mine.

That somewhere there is a home about fine growing people, so that one can feel and grasp it with all one's senses, that what to me is remote and accessible only with extended senses somewhere became reality for grateful people, this it was that strongly swayed me and so impressed me that I resolved to stay. Every home has a warm and good influence, like every mother. Only I must seek my mother, mustn't I? . . .

It is an evening hour as I write to you. No great golden one. One that is hemmed in on all sides by rain, and I am not yet in my own home, which is still being fitted out,—but still I have a warm feeling, as sometimes in your beautiful twilight that is unforgettably dear to me. We haven't taken leave, so really we are still together whenever we meet anywhere in related thoughts or my gratitude otherwise seeks you out among the dear figures of my recent past. . . .

[*18*]

To Clara Westhoff   Schmargendorf
                                       October 23, 1900

That evening, as we sat together in the little blue dining room, we also spoke of other things: In the cottage there would be light, a soft, veiled lamp, and I would stand at my stove and prepare a supper for you: a fine vegetable or cereal dish,—and heavy honey would gleam on a glass plate, and cold, ivory-pure butter would form a gentle contrast to the gaiety of a Russian table-cloth. Bread would have had to be there, strong, coarse-grained bread and zwieback, and on a long narrow dish somewhat pale Westphalian ham, streaked with bands of white fat like an evening sky with long-drawn-out clouds. Tea would stand ready for the drinking, gold-yellow tea in glasses with silver holders, exhaling a delicate fragrance, that fragrance which blended with the Hamburg rose and which would also blend with white carnations or fresh pineapple. . . . Great lemons, cut in disks, would sink like suns into the golden dusk of the tea, dimly shining through it with the radiant flesh of their fruit, and its clear, glassy surface would tremble from the sour, rising juices. Red mandarins should be there, in which a summer is folded up very small like an Italian silk handkerchief in a nutshell. And roses would be about us, tall ones, nodding on their stems, and reclining ones, gently raising their heads, and the kind that wander from hand to hand, like girls in the figure of a dance. So I dreamed. Premature dreams; the cottage is empty and cold, and my apartment here too is empty and cold: God knows how it is to become habitable.— But even so I cannot believe that reality is not to achieve some relation to what I dreamed. I sent you yesterday a little package of a very excellent oat cereal to try. Directions on the package. Only it is good to let it cook somewhat longer than the fifteen minutes prescribed. Before eating put a piece of butter in it, or take applesauce with it. I like best to eat it with butter, day in and day out. In fifteen minutes, the whole meal is ready, that is, boiling water must already have been made; it is put on hot then, and cooks fifteen to twenty minutes. If you send for a patent "all purpose" double boiler from a big household-goods store, you hardly need to stir it; the danger of burning is very slight then. Try it, give me a report. The big California firm has other glorious preparations also.—I will send the catalogue shortly.— For the rest, you know that I imagined an industrious day before that richly dreamed of supper. Isn't that so?

[19]

To Otto Modersohn   Schmargendorf bei Berlin
                                        October 23, 1900

. . . when winter comes, I shall have memories, gentler, richer, and more splendid than ever. I feel that. As if I had costly fabrics in chests that I cannot open because days not yet in order stand like heavy vessels on their lids. Sometime there will be order, and I shall raise the lids and reach through heavy scent for the materials which it is a festival to unfold.

I do not know now what is woven into these cloths; what destinies had to come to pass in what landscapes so that pictures should be there for this manifoldness of threads and folds . . . but I have the dark feeling of an age of greatness and goodness whose days are preserved therein, interwoven and well turned to use.

Dear Herr Modersohn, I have such a beautiful and good time behind me, and I turn to all who came so strangely close to me in that time, with thanks. I am not trying to say what I am thanking for, indeed, to explain that I am saying thank you is already too much, is something else altogether. I want to *do thanks* to all of you and to your country and your art.—Remember that afternoon when you showed me the confidence of which I am just a little proud: you showed me the little evening pages, and I feel how from each sketch, in black and red, more than reality grew out toward me; that being, which only the deepest art is able to produce in deep hours, was fulfilled in these sketches before which I had the feeling that in each one, veiled by the flight of the strokes, was everything one can experience and become in that mood. It thrilled me so to hold those brimming little pages in my hands, to look into their secret as into creation itself: I was like one who steps into many darkening rooms and recognizes that there before his slowly accustoming eyes stands everything beautiful that he had ever thought up or remembered. So it must be for a child that goes in a dream from room to room and in each keeps finding its mother again, who apparently has entered everywhere a moment before it. The child has the comforting feeling: she is preceding me, she is everywhere. There is no picture without her. So in every page there was that warm and eternal quality, that atmosphere which is about young mothers in the evening. That most peaceful thing in the world, that one thing which is not chance, that moment of eternity about which everything we think and do circles like birds about clock towers. . . .

Then I thought: sometime I would like to have hours like these pages. Dark and yet more than clear, with rich, not countable things and figures around which lovely patience flows. Now I know that I am living toward such hours, toward such poems.— Almost every day in Worpswede brought an experience for me— I often told you so: but I have only been as pious and reverent as before your little pictures two or three other times in my life; for it doesn't often happen that what is very great is crowded together into a thing that one can hold all in one's hand, in one's own powerless hand. As when one finds a little bird that is thirsty. One takes it away from the verge of death, and its little heart beats increasingly against the warm, trembling hand like the very last wave of a gigantic sea whose shore you are. And you know suddenly, with this little creature that is recovering, life is recovering from death. And you are holding it up. Generations of birds and all the woods over which they fly and all the heavens to which they will ascend. And is all that so easy? No: you are very strong to carry the heaviest in such an hour. . . .

[20]

To Frieda von Bülow   Schmargendorf
                                          October 24, 1900

. . . in order not to alienate peaceful, sober daily work, I have given up in these autumn days a very dear plan. I had rented a little house in Worpswede (where I was for five weeks) . . . it turned out, however, that I would really be too far away from all the helpers and helps which my labors need (particularly the

Russian ones) and would run the danger of losing all touch with my laboriously achieved study.

Added to that is the fact that Worpswede has too strong an influence: its colors and people are overwhelmingly big, rich, and capable of dominating every other mood. But although my stay there momentarily took me away from Russian things, I still do not regret it; I am even thinking with some homesickness of my little deserted house and of the dear people there to whom I must seem faithless somehow. I have lots to tell you. . . .

[21]

To Paula Becker   Schmargendorf
                                               November 5, 1900

How splendid it has become in my rooms. Just think, dear Paula Becker, I had a copper pitcher on my desk, in it dahlias the color of old ivory, slightly yellowing dahlias, are standing in just such a way that it needed only the fantastic, wonderful leaves of the cabbage stuck in with them for a miracle to happen. It has happened and is operating.—On the bench built onto the bookcase a tall slender glass with a few branches of dog rose had been set, and there the heavy umbels of the mountain-ash berries worked in, and fir branches harmonized with the big yellow and gold leaves, those great chestnut leaves that are like outspread hands of autumn wanting to grasp sunrays. But now, when sunrays no longer walk but have wings, no chestnut leaf catches a sunray. Everything in my place (I mean to say with this enumeration) was prepared to receive the autumn with which you surprised and presented me. For every bit of your rich autumn a place was already destined, predestined by Providence. For the chestnut chain too. Only here it doesn't always hang on the wall, but I get it sometimes and let it slide through my fingers like a rosary (you know those Catholic prayer-chains, don't you?). At every bead of those rosaries one must repeat a certain prayer; I imitate this pious rule by thinking at every chestnut of something nice that has to do with you and Clara Westhoff. Only then it turns out there are too few chestnuts.

These first November days are always Catholic days for me. The second day of November is All Souls' Day which, until my sixteenth or seventeenth year, wherever I may have been living, I always spent in graveyards, by unknown graves often and often by the graves of relatives and ancestors, by graves which I couldn't explain and upon which I had to meditate in the growing winter nights. It was probably then that the thought first came to me that every hour we live is an hour of death for someone, and that there are probably even more hours of death than hours of the living. Death has a dial with infinitely many figures. . . . For years now I have visited no more graves on All Souls'. These days it is my custom to drive out only to Heinrich von Kleist in Wannsee. Late in November he died out there; at a time when many shots are falling in the empty wood, there fell also the two fateful shots from his weapon. They were hardly distinguished from the others, perhaps they were somewhat more violent, shorter, more breathless. . . . But in the oppressive air, noises all become alike and are dulled by the many soft leaves that are sinking everywhere.

But I see this is no letter for you and not really one for me either. I am full of longing, my friend. Farewell!

[22]

To Clara Westhoff   Schmargendorf
                                       Sunday, November 18, 1900

. . . I am not ashamed that, as already once before, it is *your* pictures, your words almost, with which I am trying to express myself, as if I wanted to present you with your own possessions. But so it is, Clara Westhoff, we receive many of our riches only when they come to meet us borne by the voice of another; and had this winter become as I dreamed it, my daily duty would have been to lade my speeches with your possessions and to send my sentences to you, like heavy, swaying caravans, to fill all the rooms of your soul with the beauties and treasures of your unopened mines and treasure chambers.

Do you remember . . . (doesn't that appear in each of my letters?), do you remember that you spoke of how eagerly you experienced that period when for the first time autumn and winter were to meet you not in the city, but among the trees whose happiness you knew, whose spring and summer rang in your earliest memories and were mingled with everything warm and dear and tender and with the infinitely blissful melancholies of summer evenings and of long, yearning nights of spring. You knew just as much of them as of the dear people in your surroundings, among whom also summer and spring, kindness and happiness were dedicated to you and whose influence held sway above your growing up and maturing, and whose other experiences would touch you only by report and rarely like a shot in the wood of which superstitious folk tell for a long time. But now you were to remain out in the country house that was growing lonely and were to see the beloved trees suffer in the rising wind, and were to see how the dense park is torn apart before the windows and becomes spacious and everywhere, even in very deep places, discloses the sky which, with infinite weariness, lets itself rain and strikes with heavy drops on the aging leaves that are dying in touching humility. And you were to see suffering where until now was only rapture and anticipation, and were to learn to endure dying in the very place where the heart of life had beaten most loudly upon yours. And you were to behave like the grownups who all at once may know everything, yes, who become grown up just because of the fact that even the darkest and saddest things do not have to be hidden from them, that one does not cover up the dead when they enter, nor hide those whose faces are sawed and torn by a sharp pain. And you, Clara Westhoff, how simply and well you endured, lived through the experience, and made it a forward step in your young existence! So great was your love that it was able to forgive the great dying, and your eye was so sure, even then, that it conceived beauty in all the new colors, feelings, and gestures of the earth, and that all coming to an end seemed for your feeling only a pretext under which Nature wanted to unfold beauties yet unrevealed. Just as the eyes of angels rest on a dying child, delighting in the similar transfiguration of its half-released little face, so without concern you saw in the dying earth the smile and the beauty and the trust in eternity.

Dear Clara Westhoff, if autumnal things or wintry come in your life, or a dread like that which ushers in springs: be comforted: it will be like that time in Oberneuland. You will only receive new beauties, the beauties of pain and of greatness, and you will enter more richly into the summer days which sound their hymns once more behind all troubled heavens. Bless you! Amen. . . .

[23]

To Paula Becker   Schmargendorf
                                    Night, (De . . .) January 24, 1901

Twenty-fourth of December I was about to write up there! That is how I feel, just like that. Now I need not go on wooing words and pictures for what I wanted to tell you right away, my dear friend: I have had a present, and you were wrong when you wrote that at the time you were sending flowers to Worpswede you wanted to send me something too—although, as you said, only something borrowed.—But nevertheless in reading your journals I couldn't help taking from the shells of your words a great deal that I cannot return. It is like strings of pearls breaking. The pearls weren't counted, and although one thinks one has found them all again,—in the most secret corners some remain that have rolled away, a silent, if you will—illegitimate treasure of the room in which the string broke. I am room and culprit alike. Seeker of all pearls that were scattered through my impatient seizing of the beautiful ornament, finder and unconscious concealer of those that were not recovered. What to do? Admit it and beg for mercy. Am I doing it? Well, I promise that any part of your jewel garland I happen to find here, I shall give back, set in the hour in which the discovering light makes the rolled-away pearl smile. Set in the joy of the finding. That is how it really was in Worpswede too. It seems to be a way of mine, to hide pearls and sometime in a good hour to forge a beautiful ornament in which I can secretly bring back the hidden one, lost in the procession of richly clad words that accompany the homecomer with a thousand triumphs.—I feel Christmassy. From all the light too that I have looked at. For in the end all the anxieties of this book are only like those final anxious moments before the doors open to the decorated and gift-filled room which the strong radiant tree makes bigger, deeper, and more festive than one knows it. And always on the next page the doors are open into a Christmas or into a landscape, into something simple, dear, big that one may trust. Even in Paris that is so. And that isn't just temperament. You have made that out of yourself, or the things into whose hands you have put yourself with such quiet and reverent patience have helped you to it. Life has helped you to life, to your life. That that, your life, is something apart, something that stands in roots of its own and has its fragrance and its blossom— that I did know (and I feel as if I had known it a long time already). But now I know more than the *one* spring in which I see you; I know of the earlier springs and of the winters in which they were prepared. I see better into the past. Into your childhood that is still like yesterday, or again like yesterday. Your glad and joyous colors repeat themselves in the later pages, applied to the new things and possessions that come to you, as the light of the sun repeats itself over every new little child that was born in the night.—I couldn't help thinking again (as so often and on various occasions) of the Worpswede evenings, when such a glad and grateful feeling awoke in me through the certainty with which you loved life, took delight in it, and greeted it, without becoming confused by it; now I have felt intuitively the rising shaft of that certainty with whose quiet, eye-dark blossom I was acquainted, and know how gently and slowly, imperiled rather than protected by you (Maria Bashkirtseff!), it has grown in

lovely slenderness, brought up by winds that wished it well.—
"Life": Often, on the margin of your simply animated verse-
pictures and rhythmic consolations, this word stands, alone, as a
slender figure stands against the sky, against which you understand and love things. It speaks to you, it means to you the
reality toward which all fairy tales (may their effect be never so
rich and fantastic) really do yearn, as toward the something
higher, toward the greater miracle that still surpasses them, because it happens so simply and in such variety and to human beings! What a growth from the fairy tale at the end of the first
book to the reality of the second. And within this reality: how
much motion, will, warmth, longing and—take it in your own
sense—how much reverence! It is as in my *Stories of God.* God
appears everywhere; I found him in it, and children would find
him too!—

And to you, the artist, I also came. Here a regret comes to me:
in Worpswede I was always at your house in the evening, and
then here and there in the conversation I did see a sketch (a canal
with a bridge and sky still stands clearly before my memory),
until words came from you that I *also* wanted to see, so that I
forbade my glances the walls and followed your words and saw
the vibrations of your silence that seemed to gather about Dante's
brow above the lily, in its concentrated fragrance, when twilight was falling. So I saw almost nothing of yours; for you yourself never showed me anything, and I didn't want to ask you to
because such things must come from an inner necessity, independent of asking and being asked. And I did think that I would
be in Worpswede for a long time, long enough to wait for the
hour in which this suppressed wish (for that matter I did express
it softly two or three times in the beginning) would be fulfilled.
Now I suddenly lack much, and who knows whether later in
life I shall not ask for many things for fear of their passing me
by without having spoken to me? Luckily I remember quite accurately the ring of girls about the big tree. Even before the
color. But already completely finished as to movement. I can
recall almost every figure (as movement) in this garland of

girls which, lightly wound, came out of the hands of joy into
those of the wind and now draws flickering circles about the big
quiet trunk. And with this single memory I don't seem poor
to myself; it is wonderful and good to think that my eyes, unconsciously almost, drank in this picture once while you were
getting tea ready, and that it was perhaps at work in me when
we spoke later of something dear and of—life.

You haven't lost your "first twenty years," dear and serious
friend. You have lost nothing that you could ever miss. You didn't
let yourself be bewildered by the eyes in the veils of the Schlachtensee that look out of the space which is not water and not sky.
You went home and created. Only a great deal later will you
feel how much. In your art you will feel it. And someone is going
to feel it in your life, the person who receives and enlarges it and
will lift it into new and broader harmonies with his ripe, rich,
understanding hands.

Such was my evening tonight. So it ends as though in prayer.
I thank you for it, today and always.

Midnight

[24]

To Emanuel von Bodman   Westerwede bei Bremen
                                     August 17, 1901

I thank you for your letter and for the verses, those marks of
affectionate and genuine confidence. I can indeed appreciate your
being able to write to me out of such serious days, and you will
not feel it importunate if from this I assume the right to impart
to you something of my own thought about struggles of this
kind.

In a case like this, the thing is (in my own opinion) to draw
back upon oneself, and not to strive after any other being, not
to relate the suffering, occasioned by both, to the cause of the
suffering (which lies so far outside) but to make it fruitful for
oneself. If you transfer what goes on in your emotion into soli-

tude and do not bring your vacillating and tremulous feeling into the dangerous proximity of magnetic forces, it will, through its inherent flexibility, assume of its own accord the position that is natural and necessary to it.—In any case, it helps to remind one-self very often that over everything that exists there are laws which never fail to operate, which come rushing, rather, to manifest and prove themseves upon every stone and upon every feather we let fall.

So all erring consists simply in the failure to recognize the natural laws to which we are subject in the given instance, and every solution begins with our alertness and concentration, which gently draw us into the chain of events and restore to our will its balancing counterweights.

For the rest, I am of the opinion that "marriage" as such does not deserve as much emphasis as it has acquired through the conventional development of its nature. It does not occur to anyone to expect a single person to be "happy,"—but if he marries, people are much surprised if he *isn't!* (And for that matter it really isn't at all important to be happy, whether single or married.) Marriage is, in many respects, a simplification of one's way of life, and the union naturally combines the forces and wills of two young people so that, together, they seem to reach farther into the future than before.—Only, those are sensations by which one cannot live. Above all, marriage is a new task and a new seriousness,—a new challenge to and questioning of the strength and generosity of each partner and a great new danger for both.

It is a question in marriage, to my feeling, not of creating a quick community of spirit by tearing down and destroying all boundaries, but rather a good marriage is that in which each appoints the other guardian of his solitude, and shows him this confidence, the greatest in his power to bestow. A *togetherness* between two people is an impossibility, and where it seems, nevertheless, to exist, it is a narrowing, a reciprocal agreement which robs either one party or both of his fullest freedom and development. But, once the realization is accepted that even between the *closest* human beings infinite distances continue to exist, a wonderful living side by side can grow up, if they succeed in loving the distance between them which makes it possible for each to see the other whole and against a wide sky!

Therefore this too must be the standard for rejection or choice: whether one is willing to stand guard over the solitude of a person and whether one is inclined to set this same person at the gate of one's own solitude, of which he learns only through that which steps, festively clothed, out of the great darkness.

This is my opinion and my law. And, if it is possible, let me soon again hear good and courageous things from you.

[25]

To Helmuth Westhoff   [Westerwede
                                          November 12, 1901]

You wrote me a very fine letter and thought of me so kindly, although I still hadn't sent you the poem about the "Peacock-feather" I promised you long ago; but see, now I will go right away and copy it neatly out of the book in which it is printed. I composed this little poem several (it must have been at least five), several years ago in the city of Munich where in October there is something like your free market. A whole field of booths. And while the other people went about laughing and teasing each other and trying to touch and tickle each other with the long peacockfeathers (which amused them very much), I went about alone with my peacockfeather which was much too proud to tickle anybody, and the longer I carried it about with me thus, the more the slenderness of its form engaged me as it balanced on its elastic shaft, and the beauty of its head from which the "pea-cock eye" looked out at me dark and mysterious. It was as though I were seeing such a feather for the very first time, and it seemed to me to hold a whole wealth of beauties that no one was noticing but I. And out of this feeling came the little poem that I dedicated at that time to a dear friend, a painter, who I knew loved peacockfeathers too. You can imagine what a peacockfeather means to a painter, who has a different, far more intimate relationship with colors than we have, how much he can learn from it and how much the harmony in the variety, and the multitude of colors all together there on such a little spot, can give him.

But do you know what the principal thing was for me, dear Helmuth: that I saw once again that most people hold things in their hands to do something stupid with them (as, for example, tickling each other with peacockfeathers), instead of looking carefully at each thing and asking each about the beauty it possesses. So it comes to pass that most people don't know at all how beautiful the world is and how much splendor is revealed in the smallest things, in some flower, a stone, the bark of a tree, or a birch leaf. Grown-up people, who have business and cares and worry about a lot of trifles, gradually lose their eye entirely for these riches which children, when they are alert and good children, soon notice and love with all their hearts. And yet the finest thing would be if all people would always stay in this relationship like alert and good children, with simple and reverent feelings, and if they would not lose the power to rejoice as deeply in a birch leaf or in the feather of a peacock or the pinion of a hooded crow as in a great mountain range or a splendid palace. The small is as little small as the big—is big. There is a great and eternal beauty throughout the world, and it is scattered justly over the small things and the big; for in the important and essential there is no injustice on the whole earth.

This, dear Helmuth, all hangs together somewhat with the poem of the peacockfeather in which I could only express badly what I meant. I was still very young then. But now I know it better every year and can tell people better all the time that there is a great deal of beauty in the world—almost nothing but beauty.

That you know as well as I, dear Helmuth. And now, thank you again, dear Helmuth. It doesn't matter that today isn't my birthday but only my name day, which you really don't celebrate at all. With us in Austria that is a festive day. There everyone has a saint whose name has been given to him, and on the day that is dedicated to that saint, he receives

—for him, wishes and words and gifts which he may keep for himself, and doesn't have to pass on to the saint. It is quite a beautiful and sympathetic custom.

Yes, it is too bad you aren't with us, with Friedrich and your parents, for then I would be able to talk to you and tell you something nice, and what is more, I could offer you the cake I got—a very beautiful cake—, which without help the two of us alone can finish up only with great difficulty.

I gave our black dog your greeting. Then he stood up, settled himself on his hind legs, laid his front paws on my shoulders and tried to give me a big, black kiss—which I naturally don't allow.

He is strong and has a voice that rings out fearfully if one hasn't a good conscience. But we always have one.

Clara sends you many affectionate greetings, but above all, dear Helmuth, greetings, and thanks from

Your faithful
Rainer

Peacockfeather

[from the book *Advent*]

Matchless in your delicacy,
how I loved you even as a child.
I held you for a lovetoken
which by silver-silent pools
elves in cool night hand each other
when children all are sleeping.

And because good little Granny
often read to me of wishing-wands,
so it was I dreamt: frail spirit,
in your delicate fibers flows
the cunning power of the enchanted rod—
and sought you in the summer grass. . . .

[*26*]

To Gustav Pauli   Westerwede bei Bremen
                                     January 8, 1902

. . . In the middle of 1902, through family circumstances, I shall lose an allowance from home which is not large but on which we have lived remarkably well and are living (under various difficulties). What will happen then, I don't know. For weeks I haven't had a single moment of peace under the pressure of this colossal new fear. At first I kept hoping I could take on something that would enable me to remain out here with my dear ones in the quiet home we have scarcely established, of whose quiet I am not to be able to take full advantage for my work. The interest of a publisher who made possible for me a year of quiet work would have sufficed to offer me the opportunity for that progress which I know I could now make if my powers might remain concentrated and my senses within the quiet world that has been rounded out in such a wonderfully beautiful way by the dear child. For me, marriage, which from the ordinary point of view was an act of great foolishness, was a necessity. My world, which has so little connection with mundane existence, was, in my bachelor room, abandoned to every wind, unprotected, and needed for its development this quiet house of its own under the wide skies of solitude. Also I read in Michelet that life for two is simpler and cheaper than the life open to betrayal on all sides, the exploited existence of the single person—and I gladly believed the belief of that dear child Michelet. . . .

It is an extremely cruel fate that now, when I am surrounded by all the conditions that were as desirable and necessary to my art as bread,—I must probably leave everything in midstream (for what other way out remains!), to go away from all that is dear to all that is alien. I am trying daily to accustom myself to the thought of the approaching departure by taking it every evening in stronger and stronger doses. But where am I to go? Of what work am I capable? Where can I be used and *so* used that that which, in the end, remains and *must* remain my life, my task, even my duty, is not destroyed! My father, in his remote generosity, wants to procure for me the post of an official at a bank in Prague,—but that means giving up everything, making an end, renouncing, returning to the conditions from the proximity of which I fled even as a child. From the spiritual point of view alone, that is a sort of resignation, a frost, in which everything would have to die. This my good father, who was always an official, does not sense, and thinks anyway that beside an art like mine there is room for any occupation. If it were a question of a painter, he would understand that such a position would mean the ruin of his art,—*my* activity I could still pursue satisfactorily (so he thinks) in a few evening hours. And moreover, I especially, who haven't too much strength at my disposal, must live out of a unified and collected state and avoid every hindrance and division which diverts the resultant in the parallelogram of forces from its direction,—if I want to reach my objectives (so unexplainable to others, even to my dear father). And that I want that, and that I want it although the objectives are great, is not arrogance and worldly vanity which I am choosing for myself; it is imposed on me like a task, like a mission—and in everything in which I succeed, I am, more than anyone, the willing and humble executor of lofty commands, whose device in his finest hours, may read, "I serve." And finally it would, after all, be irresponsible, at the moment when the necessity of earning my own living presents itself close at hand and energetically, to forsake the path which, obeying urges and longings of my own, I have trod since boyhood, and to leave lying on the old building site the hewn building stones of a life which bear only the traces of my chisel,—in order, with no heart for the work, to help build with manufactured bricks, in the pay of a little man, someone else's house next door, to which I am indifferent.

Wouldn't that mean jumping out of my own skiff, which will perhaps touch on my own shore after a few strong strokes of the oar (if I may be permitted to give them), and continuing on a big steamer, lost among hundreds of people, to a common place, as indifferent and banal as a coffeehouse garden on Sunday afternoon?

I would rather starve with my family than take this step, which is like a death without the grandeur of death.

Isn't it much more to the point to draw practical results from what I have already done, to make out of a poetic art a literary art-craft which would support its follower? This literary art-craft *could* be journalism, but isn't. The roads to it are closed, or at least made very difficult for me by my own disinclination. But there must be other points at which my honest powers could get started; to be sure, I am the last to find these points—I don't even know whom I could ask about such points. . . .

If nothing presents itself anywhere (a collaboration of a regular kind or something of the sort) I shall probably have to leave Westerwede in the course of this year, and I wonder if in Bremen, where as a stranger I have found such a kind and trusting reception, there wouldn't be some position in which I could prove myself useful. Doesn't the enlarging of the Art Museum necessitate any filling out of the personnel, or isn't there some other collection or an institution in which I could work? I haven't got my doctorate, and now there isn't any money to go on studying; I think that title (which I have gladly avoided like all titles) couldn't help me anyway at this moment! If I succeeded in giving a series of lectures yearly, and if my wife were to take over the school, perhaps it would then be possible to survive the first, most difficult years, as each could live on his own earnings. With the inexpensive requirements of our farmhouse, and the trifling needs we both have, an income of about 250 marks monthly would suffice us together, so that each would have to earn about 125 marks.

Shouldn't that be possible somehow?

If, without disturbing our own work, we could last out a year in this way, I am convinced that that work would have grown strong enough during this year to take us on its shoulders and carry us along.—But if you think this cannot be managed by any means, may I beg of you to give me, for some city in which you have connections, be it Munich or Dresden or another, some advice or a good word which I can use when the time comes?

Forgive me for writing this presumptuous letter. Since the fall, all my days and nights have been a continual, anxious battle with the morrow, and in the face of your generosity it seems to me dishonest to hide from you a situation which everyone really should know who wishes me well. And I know that you do, my dear doctor.

Should my disclosures be a burden to you, take no further notice of them, without therefore changing your friendly attitude toward me; I know that it is inconsiderate to take someone into one's confidence so forcibly at the eleventh hour, but I am at the point where I think that for once I may be inconsiderate of people I trust: as when one's clothes are burning, or someone is dying, one would certainly awaken a friend whose sleep one would otherwise never have dared to disturb. . . .

[27]

To Paula Modersohn-Becker
Bremen
February 12, 1902

Permit me to say a few words about your letter to my dear wife: it concerns me very closely as you know, and if I were not in Bremen, I would seek an opportunity to discuss the matter with you in person,—the . . . indeed, what matter? Will you believe me that it is hard for me to understand what you are actually talking about? Nothing has happened really—or rather: much that is good has happened, and the misunderstanding is based on the fact that you do not want to grant what has happened. Everything is supposed to be as it was, and yet everything is different from what it has been. If your love for Clara Westhoff wants to do something now, then its work and task is this: to catch up with what it has missed. For it has failed to see whither this person has gone, it has failed to accompany her in her broadest development, it has failed to spread itself out over the new distances this person embraces, and it hasn't ceased looking for her at a *certain* point in her growth, it wants obstinately to hold fast to a definite beauty beyond which she has passed, instead of persevering, confident of new shared beauties to come.

The confidence you proved to me, dear friend, when you vouchsafed me a little glance into the pages of your journal, entitles me (as I believe) to remind you how strange and distant and incomparable Clara Westhoff's nature seemed to you in the beginning, how surrounded by a solitude whose doors you didn't know. . . . And this first important impression you have been able so far to forget as to accompany only with blame and warning the entering of this person, whom you began to love because of her differentness and solitude, into a new solitude, the reasons for which you are even better able to examine than the reasons for that first seclusion, which you certainly didn't regard with reproach then, but rather with a certain admiring recognition. If your love has remained vigilant, then it must have seen that the experiences which came to Clara Westhoff derived their worth from the very fact that they were tightly and indissolubly bound up with the inner being of the house in which the future is to find us: we had to burn all the wood on our own hearth in order to warm up our house for the first time and make it livable. Do I have to tell you that we had cares, heavy and anxious cares, which might not be carried outside any more than the few hours of deep happiness? . . . Does it surprise you that the centers of gravity have shifted, and is your love and friendship so distrustful that it wants constantly to see and grasp what it possesses? You will continually have to experience disappointments if you expect to find the old relationship; but why don't you rejoice in the new one that will begin when someday the gates of Clara Westhoff's new solitude are opened to receive you? I too am standing quietly and full of deep trust *before* the gates of this solitude, because I hold this to be the highest task of a bond between two people: that each should stand guard over the solitude of the other. For, if it lies in the nature of indifference and of the crowd to recognize no solitude, then love and friendship are there for the purpose of continually providing the opportunity for solitude. And only those are the true sharings which rhythmically interrupt periods of deep isolation. . . . Think of the time when you came to know Clara Westhoff: then your love waited patiently for an opening gate, the same love which now raps impatiently on the walls behind which things are being accomplished of which we have no cognizance, of which I know just as little as you,—only that I have faith that they will touch me deeply and closely when they reveal themselves to me someday. And cannot your love grasp a similar faith? Out of this faith alone will joys come to it by which it will live without starving.—

[28]

To Countess Franziska Reventlow   Westerwede bei Worpswede
April 11, 1902

I haven't written you, my very dear friend, for such an endlessly long time; there were so many external living worries,—earning, earning, earning, and that isn't at all easy from Westerwede. I had to write and do a lot of things in order to help my outward circumstances,—and since they have not been basically helped yet, I shall have to write and do much more still,—if it does any good anyway. . . . But things are going well with my family, and little Ruth is growing wonderfully well, already has quite incredibly serious and thoughtful hours which alternate harmoniously with very happy and few crying ones. My wife is growing with her, rejoicing in the charming example of the dear little creature! And so my house is standing upright as never before in the spring that wants to come. . . . And if it weren't for those daily worries. . . .

[29]

To Oskar Zwintscher   Westerwede
                                          April 24, 1902

. . . Yes, it has become spring, and this time, since we see a
little garden coming up under our hands, we feel in some near
degree related to it. Tulips and narcissus, beside a big peony, are
already growing, two little arbors are already hung with the
twigs of young birches as with green lace veils, and a few tall-
stemmed roses are already sprouting, something one can't forget
at all and feels as a most delightful promise.

On the neighbors' roof a stork appeared recently and the minute
investigation of the roof in which he was engaged permits the
hope that he is thinking of settling there: that naturally would be
a great joy.

Very beautiful is the spring here in its coming. In the morning the day is released from thousands of bird voices, and the
evenings deepen at the beginning of the first sound of the
nightingale, which makes the stillness stiller and more full of
portent. And the moonlight nights are unusually bright, and if
they darken, a rain begins to fall; tender, soft, and warm, idle
like a dream and yet full of veiled happening. . . .

[30]

To Clara Rilke   Schloss Haseldorf in Holstein
                                          June 5, 1902

Dearest and best, I thank you for your big letter. I can imagine
that the day of travel was difficult and oppressive and the night
in the Amsterdam hotel not pleasant; on that day, Hamburg
(where I had indeed about two hours) didn't appeal to me at all
either; it was as hot and airless as any inland city. . . . And my
first night in Haseldorf was no less sultry than yours at the Van
Gelder. And since then, there have been a lot of such days,
burning, breathless days that sometimes dissolved only toward
evening in the slowly darkening air. Today (for the first time)

there is a cloudy sky and some rain. The park is beautiful. It is especially entrancing to stand at one of the tall windows of the dining hall. There one sees the high stretches of lawn that are growing wild and are already so high that a few rosebushes almost disappear in the green billows. In these meadows stand two infinitely beautiful blossoming trees, resembling apple trees. They call them Crataegus (thornless Crataegus); I don't know what that is,—but anyway it won't be unfamiliar to you. Otherwise, when I walk in the garden, I always enjoy recognizing one or another of the flowers or a bush which you have named for me. The loveliest are the paths along the castle moat. There the old chestnuts now stand, built up like mountains, with their branches all the way down to the earth and with a whole world of shadows under the thousand hands of their leaves. They are blossoming now. And it is quite wonderful the way those blossom-cones rise up at rhythmic intervals to the highest branches. By day that is all rather too green, but recently, in the evening about ten-thirty (it was still twilight), these old trees were like dark mantles with embroidered, regularly recurring patterns. The white of the blossoms became wonderfully mysterious and sometimes one of the blossom-pyramids had the appearance of raised, clasped hands coming out of a dark cloak. Unfortunately the murky, sluggish moat gave back no reflection of these wonderful trees. Lilacs and rhododendrons also grow at a similar height on ancient bushes that suddenly display rich blooms somewhere high up in the treecrowns. Flesh-colored azaleas stretch out their fragrance, and the magnolias already have leaves beside the great water-lily-like blossoms. Today I also discovered a tall tree covered with broad cool green leaves and strange silver-gray closed buds that were very dignified. I take it to be a nut tree . . . but I am not very often in this garden, because the heat makes it heavy and being shut in by the dike evokes a kind of close sadness. Also, there are so many black, houseless wood snails on the paths that one goes about in continual fear of crushing one.

I am a great deal in my room where it is warmest and pleasantest and where I feel tolerably alone. . . . Now I go over sometimes into the archives, rummage in old books and read a few lines here and there: whether I shall find something I can use is questionable. The letters I had in mind are so impossible to glance through that one would have to read for a year to get any insight into them, and in addition the difficult old script, the bad air, and the dust in the archives are no encouragement to it. So in this connection too I must confine myself to what is already printed; I am browsing in the histories of the von Ahlefeldt and von Oppen-Schilden families who formerly resided at Haseldorf, and it is not impossible that I will run into some interesting biography there, although I lack talent and practice as a discoverer of good book passages. What interests me very much meanwhile is looking through old editions just for the sake of their type and their frontispieces, rummaging through old portfolios with engravings from the end of the eighteenth century and smiling a little at the long, almost inquisitive profiles of deceased chamberlains and knights of the Danebrog. In somewhat cooler weather I would certainly have been disposed to somewhat more activity, but certainly too it is a reaction from my recent work period which won't allow me to get at anything real. There is no harm; and the weeks here still have their sense, even if they consist merely in the reading of a few books I wouldn't otherwise have laid hands on. . . .

[*31*]

To Frau Julie Weinmann   for the present
Schloss Haseldorf (Holstein)
June 25, 1902

. . . The last time I wrote (somewhat over a year ago) I announced to you my marriage. The person who is so fondly bound up with and indispensable to my life is a young sculptress who has worked with Rodin in Paris, a girl full of power and artistic ability, an artist, from whose growth I expect the greatest conceivable results. That and a limitless, mutual faith brought us together. Since December we have a dear little daughter, Ruth, and life has become much richer with her.—For the woman— according to my conviction—a child is a completion and a liberation from all strangeness and insecurity: it is, spiritually too, the mark of maturity; and I am filled with the conviction that the woman artist, who has had and has and loves a child, is, no less than the mature man, capable of reaching all the artistic heights the man can reach under the same conditions, that is, if he is an artist. In a word, I consider the woman in whom lives deep artistic striving the equal of the masculine artist from the moment of her maturity and fulfillment on, entitled and summoned to the same ambitious goals in which he in his best hours may solitarily believe. I am saying this only so that I may now say that the meaning of my marriage lies in helping this dear young person to find herself, her greatness and depths, in so far as one human being can help another. Clara Westhoff has for a long time been no beginner: she has proved by my portrait-bust, by the bust of Heinrich Vogeler (which was purchased by the Bremen Art Museum) and several smaller works that have been exhibited, that she can hardly be mistaken for anyone else now and can be seen beside the best.—All this, however, is not the matter about which I want to speak, although it leads me to the subject of this letter, to myself.

It is clear to me that I need help in order to continue on my way. I need the opportunity to be allowed to absorb quietly, to learn for a year or two, without having to write. The course of my education was broken by a variety of accidents, and in the end that is not a misfortune; for in those years one has not really the ability to *choose* one's education, which later makes the winning of knowledge and truth so precious. Now I know what I need; two great journeys to Russia which I have taken in recent years have given me wide ranges and tasks and have strengthened and confirmed me in myself. And now in the fall I want to go to Paris, in order, guided by the connoisseur of Russian things, the Vicomte de Vogué, to work in the libraries, to collect myself, and to write about Rodin whom I have loved and revered for a long time. That is the external side of what I want for the immediate future, a little portion of that deep wanting which goes toward my work and toward its continuous realization.

What can one who wants a great deal say of this wanting without betraying it and becoming a boaster? Here every word involves a false note and an affront to what it means. One can only say that one comes more and more to protect this wanting which goes toward deep and important things, that one longs more and more sincerely and wholeheartedly to give it all one's strength and all one's love and to experience worries through it and not through the little harassing accidents of which life in poverty is full. I am very poor. I do not suffer from poverty because at bottom it refuses me nothing. But this winter, for the first time, it stood before me for months like a specter, and I lost myself and all my beloved aims and all the light out of my heart and came near taking some little official post, and that would have meant: dying and setting out on a spiritual transmigration full of homelessness and madness.—I deliberated at the last moment and clung to what, even as a child, I had begun dimly and longingly to want. I am indeed no longer a beginner who throws himself at random into the future. I have worked, for years, and if I have worked out anything for myself, it is the belief in the right to raise the best I have in me and the awareness of the treasures in the sesame of my soul which I can no longer forget. And after all I know that my pen will be strong enough to carry me: only I may not misuse it too early and must give it time to attain its full growth.

My dear lady, I am speaking to you because I know of no one who could understand and feel the meaning of words like this, despite all the omissions, no one who would be generous enough to pardon them, and kind enough to see what lies behind them. I am gathering all my confidence together and begging you to accept it, because my memory of you, of your husband and of the spirit of your kindly house brings before me people who do not consider the striving for artistic fulfillment as something superfluous, but rather as a great law which awakens in those who love life most deeply.

Perhaps you remember me: perhaps one of my verses will excuse me for approaching you out of my distance, perhaps something in your heart will believe that I am not presuming too much when I beg for my best, as for a child that I do not want to let die.

In the past year I have had a little household with my wife (in a little village near Worpswede); but the household consumed too much, and so we have promised each other to live for our work, each as a bachelor of limited means, as before. That also gives to each the possibility of being wherever his work happens to require. For, since work must be quite uppermost, we are also prepared to bear a geographical separation from time to time if it is necessary. We have lost a good deal of time, but this year must take us both further along. Will you help me to my goal, dear lady? Will you and your husband make it possible for me to work on myself this year in Paris, in quiet and peace of mind, without this continual fear that insinuates itself into all thoughts and into every quiet of my heart? Not without poverty, only without fear! —And only for a year?

I have never begged from anyone; you see I don't know how it is done, nor do I know whether I can thank: but I believe I can.

My wife will probably obtain an artist-fellowship and only accept a very small subsidy from me which I can easily afford from what I earn on the side. What I desire so ardently, however, and consider so important for my development, is what I have never actually had: a single year of quiet, fear-free work. A little peace and composure from which so much future can come.

I know of no fellowship for which I could apply, no person whom I may really ask. And so I come to you, quite unashamed, as to old friends.

Perhaps, dear lady, none of the books I have written in recent years has come to your notice. Fortunately a new book of poems is coming out in the next few weeks, so that I can at least tell you where I stand and whither I have gone in these years; that I will do at all events.

I am writing this letter in a still, lonely evening hour and not reading it over because perhaps then I wouldn't send it off. Not that I am ashamed of it; but I am afraid, dear lady, of losing or offending you the moment the picture you have of me shifts under its influence. If it could have such an effect, then—please—let it be nothing, let it not have been, for beyond everything the assurance is precious to me that you still think kindly of me and that I may kiss your hand in unaltered respect.

[32]

To Friedrich Huch Schloss Haseldorf in Holstein
[July 6, 1902]

. . . I rejoice in all the activity that lies before you, in the new position you will have in Lodz, which is so wonderful, so fine and human in the most forward-looking sense, that I cannot congratulate you enthusiastically enough on it. Congratulate, unfortunately not envy; for although I quite share your knowledge and feeling that the world belongs to young youth, the world in its breadth and reality, there is nevertheless between me and every young person a perpetual embarrassment which does not allow a mutual influencing and relationship to arise. I suffer under this ban which sometimes makes my great solitude (which since early boyhood I have otherwise borne so gladly and thankfully) raw at the borders; but that is why my *Stories of God* also had the subtitle: told to grownups for children, because I knew that only over those swaying bridges and through those dark ravines can I get to the dear creatures who can understand me if I try to say something about God. . . .

But alas, this burden of the monograph has been demanding and has used up or dulled the strength and joy for thousands of things. I am so little made to write for money, and otherwise nothing remains for me but to take an obscure little official post in Prague, with a killing monotony. Which really would be death for me. I don't believe I would still be permitted then to think of writing anything, although the unsaid stands weeping about me. An official's life is an official's life.

To my verses, to the health of soul out of which they rise,

belongs the country, long roads, walking barefoot in the soft grass, on hard roads or in the clean snow, deep breathing, listening, stillness, and the reverence of wide evenings. Without that: shut up in a writing room with other people and stale air and condemned to a senseless manual work consisting of inanity and habit, I would never again venture to write down a word, distrustful of the altered voice of my lazy, misused blood, deaf to the dearest words of my soul whose truth I would no longer be allowed to feel and live.

For months already, dear Friedrich Huch, I have been resisting this fate, this death without an hour of dying. I have looked about for everything possible, but nowhere is there anyone who can use me as I am. Not being able to say what I "can do," I have difficulty in making what I am looking for intelligible to people. I hoped, asked, waited for some correspondence, but in vain. Now, with difficulty enough, we have already made the decision to dissolve our little household, because it became evident that it (this so-called household) was sitting as a third at our table and taking from our plates what we wanted to eat. In so doing we enable each to live better for his work, for our marriage was made in order that each might better help the other to his work and to himself. I hope it will be possible for us to settle not too far from one another. But Clara Westhoff (of whose art I expect the greatest things!) has to think of Ruth as well as of herself and her development, think, that is, with concern and care, and must not in any way suffer in poverty as one of the concomitants of a marriage. Next winter then is somehow to be arranged accordingly. Clara Westhoff (she and our dear little child, who are still in Westerwede now) must choose for herself the place to stay which she considers good and useful for her work, and I hope very much she will obtain a fellowship which will help her to peace and composure. (She had, by the way, quite a good deal of success at the exhibitions: the portrait bust of Heinrich Vogeler—a very good work—was purchased twice in bronze.) If then the dearest person I have in the world again has her life and her work, I too may think seriously of myself and make one more attempt to come to terms with circumstances.

I want first (at the beginning of September perhaps) to go to Paris; for I have undertaken to write the book on Rodin in the new publications instigated by Muther. At first I thought I might perhaps be able to keep myself there somehow, but now I scarcely believe any more in this possibility.—I urgently need besides my most intimate work, which is gift and miracle every time it happens, something I can *always* do in order to live over the in-between times to new work hours to come. My Russian study was welcome to me for that; but now the necessity of earning continually comes over both, wipes out the boundaries, makes one as well as the other vain, and imposes a third thing on me and fear and suffocation. To change this at last, I am thinking of going to a university, to Muther, who is a friend of mine, of working for a while quite objectively, of writing something only now and then (enough to be able to study, no more), of doing my doctorate as soon as may be . . . and? . . . The title is of some help after all, but I believe that above all the quiet, objective work will make me of more use for taking some position later that will not make me too miserable. I know so little, and I lack the magic word at which books open. I would like so much to read and learn many things, some need in me runs parallel to that plan of study.—I have done three or four semesters at various universities, in which I could give a satisfactory account of myself, so ought surely to be able (circumstances being what they are) to obtain the "doctorate" in a year to a year and a half. Do you understand how I mean that? It seems to me not so completely hopeless: externally the way to a title that does after all help, inwardly: work. . . . Tell me, dear Friedrich Huch, what you think of this decision. Can I in my situation look for anything different or better? Advise me as you would advise a child, for I deserve to be thus advised. Here in the still summer days my plan grew up out of a great deal of anxiety, and besides you only Muther, whom it closely concerns, knows of it.—But when your kind letter came today, I decided to tell you how things are with me. That is how they are, if I see correctly. And now tell me, do I see correctly? . . .

[33]

To Arthur Holitscher   Westerwede bei Worpswede
                                              July 31, 1902

. . . I am . . . utterly absorbed in Rodin who is growing and growing for me the more I hear and see of his works. Does anyone exist, I wonder, who is as great as he and yet is still living; (it often seems to me that death and greatness are only one word; I remember how, when I read *Niels Lyhne* for the first time years ago in Munich, I planned to look for the person who had written• it . . . later I heard him spoken of as of one long dead . . .) and Rodin is still living. I have the feeling that, quite aside from his art, he is a synthesis of greatness and power, a future century, a man without contemporaries. Under such circumstances, you can imagine that I am impatiently awaiting the first of September, the day when I shall go to Paris. . . .

[34]

To Auguste Rodin   Worpswede bei Bremen
    [in French]   August 1, 1902
My Master,

. . . I wrote you from Haseldorf that in September I shall be in Paris to prepare myself for the book consecrated to your work. But what I have not yet told you is that for me, for my work (the work of a writer or rather of a poet), it will be a great event to come 'near you. Your art is such (I have felt it for a long time) that it knows how to give bread and gold to painters, to poets, to sculptors: to all artists who go their way of suffering, desiring nothing but that ray of eternity which is the supreme goal of the creative life.

I began to write (when still quite young) and there are already eight or nine books of mine: verses, prose, and a few dramas which, played in Berlin, found only irony in this public which loves the opportunity of showing its disdain for the solitary man.

To my sorrow there exists no translation of my books so that I could ask you to give them just one glance; nevertheless I shall bring you, when I come, one or another in the original language, for I need to know some of my confessions among your things, in your possession, near you,—as one puts a silver heart on the altar of a miraculous martyr.

All my life has changed since I know that you exist, my Master, and that the day when I shall see you is one (and perhaps the happiest) of my days.

. . . It is the most tragic fate of young people who sense that it will be impossible for them to live without being poets or painters or sculptors, that they do not find true counsel, all plunged in an abyss of forsakenness as they are; for in seeking a powerful master, they seek neither words, nor information: they ask for an example, a fervent heart, hands that make greatness. It is for you that they ask.

[35]

To Clara Rilke   11 rue Toullier, Paris
                                     Tuesday, September 2, 1902

. . . Yesterday, Monday afternoon at three o'clock, I was at Rodin's for the first time. Atelier 182 rue de l'Université. I went down the Seine. He had a model, a girl. Had a little plaster object in his hand on which he was scraping about. He simply quit work, offered me a chair, and we talked. He was kind and gentle. And it seemed to me that I had always known him. That I was only seeing him again; I found him smaller, and yet more powerful, more kindly, and more noble. That forehead, the relationship it bears to his nose which rides out of it like a ship out of harbor . . . that is very remarkable. Character of stone is in that forehead and that nose. And his mouth has a speech whose ring is good, intimate, and full of youth. So also is his laugh, that em-

barrassed and at the same time joyful laugh of a child that has been given lovely presents. He is very dear to me. That I knew at once. We spoke of many things—(as far as my queer language and his time permitted). . . . Then he went on working and begged me to inspect everything that is in the studio. That is not a little. The "hand" is there. C'est une main comme-ça (he said and made with his own so powerful a gesture of holding and shaping that one seemed to see things growing out of it).—C'est une main comme-ça, qui tient un morceau de terre glaise avec des . . . And indicating the two figures united in such a wonderfully deep and mysterious fashion: c'est une création ça, une création. . . . He said that in a marvelous way. . . . The French word lost its graciousness and didn't take on the pompous heaviness of the German word *Schöpfung* . . . it had loosed itself, redeemed itself from all language . . . was alone in the world:
création . . .

A bas-relief is there; "Morning Star" he calls it. A head of a very young girl with a wonderfully young forehead, clear, delightful, bright, and simple; and deep down in the stone, a hand emerges which protects from the brightness the eyes of a man, of one who is awakening. Almost those eyes are still in the stone (so marvellously is the not-yet-having-waked expressed here—so plastically): One sees only the mouth and the beard.—There is a woman's portrait. There is more than one can say, and everything small has so much bigness that the space in studio H seems to stretch into the immeasurable in order to include everything.

And now today: I took the train at nine o'clock this morning to Meudon (Gare Montparnasse, a twenty-minute ride from there). The villa, which he himself called un petit château Louis XIII—is not beautiful—. It has a three-window façade, red brick with yellowish framework, a steep gray roof, tall chimneys. All the "picturesque" disorder of Val Fleury spreads out before it, a narrow valley in which the houses are poor and look like those in Italian vineyards. (And there are probably vineyards here too, for the steep dirty village street through which one passes is called rue de la Vigne . . .); then one walks over a bridge, along another stretch of road past a little osteria, also quite Italian in appearance. To the left is the door. First, a long avenue of chestnuts, strewn with coarse gravel. Then a little wooden latticed door. Another little latticed door. Then one rounds the corner of the little red-yellow house and stands—before a miracle—before a garden of stone and plaster figures. His big pavilion, the same one that was in the exposition at the Pont Alma, has now been transported into his garden which it apparently fills completely, along with several more studios in which are stonecutters and in which he himself works. Then there are in addition rooms for baking clay and for all kinds of manual work. It is an immensely great and strange impression, this great, light hall with all its white, dazzling figures looking out of the many high glass doors like the inhabitants of an aquarium. The impression is great, colossal. One sees, even before one has entered, that all these hundreds of lives are *one* life,—vibrations of *one* power and *one* will. What a lot is there—everything, everything. The marble of La Prière; plaster casts of almost everything.—Like the work of a century . . . an army of work. There are gigantic showcases, entirely filled with wonderful fragments of the Porte de l'Enfer. It is indescribable. There it lies, yard upon yard, only fragments, one beside the other. Figures the size of my hand and larger . . . but only pieces, hardly one that is whole: often only a piece of arm, a piece of leg, as they happen to go along beside each other, and the piece of body that belongs right near them. Once the torso of a figure with the head of another pressed against it, with the arm of a third . . . as if an unspeakable storm, an unparalleled destruction had passed over this work. And yet, the more closely one looks, the more deeply one feels that all this would be less of a whole if the individual bodies were whole. Each of these bits is of such an eminent, striking unity, so possible by itself, so not at all needing completion, that one forgets they are only *parts*, and often *parts* of *different* bodies that cling to each other so passionately there. One feels suddenly that it is rather the business of the scholar to conceive of the body as a whole—and much more that of the artist to create from the parts new relationships, new unities, greater, more logical . . . more eternal. . . . And this wealth, this endless, continual invention, this poise, purity, and vehemence of expression, this inexhaustibleness, this youth, this still having something, still having the best to say . . . this is without parallel in the history of men. Then there are tables, model-stands, chests of drawers . . . completely covered with little figures—golden-brown and yellow-ochre baked clay. Arms no bigger than my little finger, but filled with a life that makes one's heart pound. Hands one can cover with a ten-pfennig piece and yet filled with an abundance of wisdom, quite exactly worked out and yet not trivial . . . as if a giant had made them immeasurably big:—so this man makes them to his proportions. He is so great; when he makes them very small, as small as he can, they are still even bigger than people . . . among these little things which are all about and which one can take into one's hand, I felt the way I did that time in Petersburg before the little Venus from the excavations. . . . There are hundreds and hundreds of them there, no one little piece like another—each a feeling, each a bit of love, devotion, kindness, and searching. I was in Meudon until about three o'clock. Rodin came to me from time to time, asked and said many things, nothing important. The barrier of language is too great. I brought him my poems today—if he could only read them. . . . I think now that the "Last Judgment" would mean something to him. He leafed through them very attentively. The format surprised him, I think, especially in the *Book of Pictures*. And there stand those stupid languages, helpless as two bridges that go over the same river side by side but are separated from each other by an abyss. It is a mere bagatelle, an accident, and yet it separates. . . .

After twelve Rodin invited me to déjeuner, which was served out of doors; it was very odd. Madame Rodin (I had already seen her before—he did *not* introduce me) looked tired, irritable, nervous, and inattentive. Across from me sat a French gentleman with a red nose to whom I was also not introduced.—Beside me a very sweet little girl of about ten (I didn't learn who she is either . . .). Hardly were we seated,—when Rodin complained of the tardiness of the meal; he was already dressed to go to the city. Whereupon Mme. Rodin became very nervous. Comment puis-je être partout? she said. Disez-le à Madelaine (probably the cook), and then out of her mouth came a flood of hasty and violent words which didn't sound really malicious, not disagreeable, but as though they came from a deeply injured person whose nerves will all snap in a minute. An agitation came over her whole body—she began to shove everything about a bit on the table, so that it looked as if dinner were already over. Everything that had been laid out so neatly was left, as after a meal, lying scattered about anywhere. This scene was *not* painful, *only sad*. Rodin was quite quiet, went on saying very calmly *why* he was complaining, gave very exact reasons for his complaint, spoke at once gently and firmly. Finally, a rather dirty person came, brought a few things (which were well cooked), carried them around and, in a very good-natured way, *forced* me to help myself when I didn't want to: he apparently thought me extremely shy. I have hardly ever been present at such a singular déjeuner. Rodin was fairly talkative,—spoke sometimes very rapidly, so that I didn't understand, but on the whole clearly. I told about Worpswede—about the painters (of whom he knew nothing); he knew, as far as I could see, only Liebermann and Lenbach—as illustrator. . . . The conversation was not conventional, also not out of the ordinary, just soso. Sometimes Madame also took part, always speaking very nervously and passionately. She has gray curls, dark, deep-set eyes, looks thin, listless, tired, and old, tormented by something. After lunch she spoke to me in a very friendly manner—only now as housekeeper—, invited me always to have déjeuner whenever I am in Meudon etc. Tomorrow just as early I am going out again and perhaps a few days more: there is a very great deal. But it is fearfully taxing—in the first place because of the quantity, secondly, because everything is white; one goes about among the many dazzling plaster casts in the very bright pavilion as through snow. My eyes are hurting me, my hands too. . . . Forgive this smudged letter. You can surely read it. I had to write down for you just quickly all that I have lived today. It is important. Farewell, my dear! dear and good one. I am glad that there is so much greatness and that we have found our way to it through the wide dismayed world. The two of us. Kiss our Ruth with my kisses.

[36]

To Clara Rilke   11 rue Toullier, Paris
                                                  September 5, 1902

. . . I believe much has now been revealed to me at Rodin's recently. After a déjeuner that passed no less uneasily and strangely than the one I last mentioned, I went with Rodin into the garden, and we sat down on a bench which looked out wonderfully far over Paris. It was still and beautiful. The little girl (it is probably Rodin's daughter), the little girl had come with us without Rodin's having noticed her. Nor did the child seem to expect it. She sat down not far from us on the path and looked slowly and sadly for curious stones in the gravel. Sometimes she came over and looked at Rodin's mouth when he spoke, or at mine, if I happened to be saying something. Once she also brought a violet. She laid it bashfully with her little hand on that of Rodin and wanted to put it in his hand somehow, to fasten it somehow to that hand. But the hand was as though made of stone, Rodin only looked at it fleetingly, looked past it, past the shy little hand, past the violet, past the child, past this whole little moment of love, with a look that clung to the things that seemed continually to be taking shape in him.

He spoke of art, of art dealers, of his lonely position and said a great deal that was beautiful which I rather sensed than understood, because he often spoke very indistinctly and very rapidly. He kept coming back to beauty which is everywhere for him who rightly understands and wants it, to things, to the life of these things—de regarder une pierre, le torse d'une femme. . . . And again and again to work. Since physical, really difficult manual labor has come to count as something inferior—he said, work has stopped altogether. I know five, six people in Paris who really work, perhaps a few more. There in the schools, what are they doing year after year—they are "composing." In so doing they learn nothing at all of the nature of things. Le modelé (ask your Berlitz French woman sometime how one could translate that, perhaps it is in her dictionary). I know what it means: it is the character of the surfaces, more or less in contrast to the contour, that which fills out all the contours. It is the law and the relationship of these surfaces. Do you understand, for him there is *only* le modelé . . . in all things, in all bodies; he detaches it from them, makes it, after he has learned it from them, into an independent thing, that is, into sculpture, into a plastic work of art. For this reason, a piece of arm and leg and body is for him a whole, an entity, because he no longer thinks of arm, leg, body (that would seem to him too like subject matter, do you see, too—novelistic, so to speak), but only of a modelé which completes itself, which is, in a certain sense, finished, rounded off. The following was extraordinarily illuminating in this respect. The little girl brought the shell of a small snail she had found in the gravel. The flower he hadn't noticed,—this he noticed immediately. He took it in his hand, smiled, admired it, examined it and said suddenly: Voilà le modelé grec. I understood at once. He said further: Vous savez, ce n'est pas la forme de l'objet, mais: le modelé. . . . Then still another snail shell came to light, broken and crushed . . . :—C'est le modelé gothique-renaissance, said Rodin with his sweet, pure smile! . . . And what he meant was more or less: It is a question for me, that is for the sculptor par excellence, of seeing or studying not the colors or the contours but that which constitutes the plastic, the surfaces. The character of these, whether they are rough or smooth, shiny or dull (not in color but in character!). Things are infallible here. This little snail recalls the greatest works of Greek art: it has the same simplicity, the same smoothness, the same inner radiance, the same cheerful and festive sort of surface. . . . And herein things are infallible! They contain laws in their purest form. Even the *breaks* in such a shell will again be of the same kind, will again be modelé grec. This snail will always remain a whole, as regards its modelé, and

the smallest piece of snail shell is still always modelé grec. . . .
Now one notices for the first time what an advance his sculpture is.
What must it have meant to him when he first felt that no one had
ever yet looked for this basic element of plasticity! He had to
find it: a thousand things offered it to him: above all the nude
body. He had to transpose it, that is to make it into *his* expression,
to become accustomed to saying *everything* through the modelé
and *not otherwise*. Here, do you see, is the second point in this
great artist's life. The first was that he had discovered a new
basic element of his art, the second, that he wanted nothing more
of life than to express himself fully and all that is his through
this element. He married, parce qu'il faut avoir une femme, as
he said to me (in another connection, namely when I spoke of
groups who join together, of friends, and said I thought that only
from solitary striving does anything result anyway, then he said
it, said: Non, c'est vrai, il n'est pas bien de faire des groupes,
les amis s'empêchent. Il est mieux d'être seul. Peut-être avoir une
femme—parcequ'il faut avoir une femme) . . . something like
that.—Then I spoke of you, of Ruth, of how sad it is that you
must leave her,—he was silent for a while and said then, with
wonderful seriousness he said it: . . . Oui, il faut travailler, rien
que travailler. Et il faut avoir patience. One should not think of
wanting to make something, one should try only to build up one's
own medium of expression and to say everything. One should
work and have patience. Not look to right nor left. Should draw
all of life into this circle, have *nothing* outside of this life. Rodin
has done so. J'ai y donné ma jeunesse, he said. It is certainly so.
One must sacrifice the other. Tolstoy's unedifying household,
the discomfort of Rodin's rooms: it all points to the same thing:
that one must choose either this or that. Either happiness or art.
On doit trouver le bonheur dans son art . . . R. too expressed it
something like that. And indeed that is all so clear, so clear. The
great men have all let their lives become overgrown like an old
road and have carried everything into their art. Their lives are
stunted like an organ they no longer need.

. . . You see, Rodin has lived nothing that is not in his work.

Thus it grew around him. Thus he did not lose himself; even in the years when lack of money forced him to unworthy work, he did not lose himself, because what he experienced did not remain a plan, because in the evenings he immediately made real what he had wanted during the day. Thus everything always became real. That is the principal thing—not to remain with the dream, with the intention, with the being-in-the-mood, but always forcibly to convert it all into things. As Rodin did. Why has he prevailed? Not because he found approbation. His friends are few, and he is, as he says, on the Index. But his work was there, an enormous, grandiose reality, which one cannot get away from. With it he wrested room and right for himself. One can imagine a man who had felt, wanted all that in himself, and had waited for better times to do it. Who would respect him; he would be an aging fool who had nothing more to hope for. But to make, to make is the thing. And once something is there, ten or twelve things are there, sixty or seventy little records about one, all made now out of this, now out of that impulse, then one has already won a piece of ground on which one can stand upright. Then one no longer loses oneself. When Rodin goes about among his things, one feels how youth, security, and new work flow into him continually from them. He cannot be confused. His work stands like a great angel beside him and protects him . . . his great work! . . .

[37]

To Clara Rilke   Paris, 11 rue Toullier
                                                   September 11, 1902

. . . [in Meudon] I sat all day in the garden in a quiet spot before which the distance is magnificently opened up, had a box of newspapers in front of me, and read the marked passages about Rodin. He has this whole material together, but it doesn't contain much, no more than was finally collected in *La Plume*. We again took déjeuner together, and afterward there was a good hour of serious conversation when the others had risen. It is quite wonderfully reassuring when he speaks, answers, judges. He is so tremendously balanced, his words go so confidently, and even those that come all alone don't falter and hesitate. Then I stayed on until after five in the garden over my work and then went into the Meudon wood where it was cool and lonely. When I came out again, the houses were shining on the slopes, the green of the vineyards was undulating and dark, and the skies were wide and filled with stillness. The bells were ringing and spreading out high up and nestling into the narrow Val Fleury and were everywhere in every stone and in the hand of every child. For a long time I haven't felt land, sky, and distance thus. As if I had sat for a year in a city or in a prison—that is how I was thankful to these things for their loneliness and moved by every little leaf that took part, subservient and still, as the smallest member in the greatness of this evening. Very, very near I was to you. I went on for a long time looking over at the house with the steep roof and at the hall beside it in which lives an ineffable world, a world that has many hours like this evening. Then I rode heavily back into the city. Oh, these heavy summer evenings! They aren't at all as in the open any more: walled up in odors and respirations. Heavy and fearful as under heavy earth. I sometimes press my face against the grating of the Luxembourg in order to feel a little distance, stillness, and moonlight—but there too is the same heavy air, heavier still from the scents of the many too many flowers they have crowded together into the constraint of the beds. . . . All that can make one very fearful. . . . And if you are glad now and happy at the liberation, *never* forget that you are going toward difficult days and that there will perhaps be no hour for a long time when you will have the courage to buy yourself a rose. This city is very big and full to the brim of sadness. And you will be alone and poor in it and very unhappy unless from the first hour on you cultivate through your work a happiness, a stillness, a strength. . . . Heavy your life will be. . . . But it is true: it will then be your *own* heaviness that you have to carry, the heaviness of your heart, of your longing, the burden of your work. And therefore be happy, deep inside, behind words and thoughts rejoice . . .

[38]

To Auguste Rodin
[in French]

11 rue Toullier, Paris
September 11, 1902

My dear Master,

It doubtless seems somewhat strange that I am writing you, since (in the greatness of your generosity) you have given me the possibility of seeing you so often. But always in your presence I feel the imperfection of my language like a sickness that separates me from you even at the moment when I am very near.

Therefore in the solitude of my room I spend my time preparing the words I want to say to you next day, but then, when the time comes, they are dead and, beset by new sensations, I lose all means of expressing myself.

Sometimes I feel the spirit of the French language, and one evening, walking in the Luxembourg Gardens I composed the following verses which are not translated from German, and which came to me by I don't know what secret path, in this form:

Ce sont les jours où les fontaines vides
mortes de faim retombent de l'automne,
et on devine de toutes les cloches qui sonnent,
les lèvres faites des métaux timides.

Les capitales sont indifférentes.
Mais les soirs inattendus qui viennent
font dans le parc un crépuscule ardent,
et aux canaux avec les eaux si lentes
ils donnent une rêve vénitienne . . .
et une solitude aux amants . . .

Why do I write you these verses? Not because I dare to believe that they are good; but it is the desire to draw near to you that guides my hand. You are the only man in the world who, full of equilibrium and force, is building himself in harmony with his work. And if that work, which is so great, so just, has for me become an event which I could tell of only in a voice trembling with awe and homage, it is also, like you yourself, an example given to my life, to my art, to all that is most pure in the depths of my soul.

It was not only to do a study that I came to be with you,—it was to ask you: how must one live? And you replied: by working. And I well understand. I feel that to work is to live without dying. I am full of gratitude and joy. For since my earliest youth I have wanted nothing but that. And I have tried it. But my work, *because I loved it so much*, has become during these years something solemn, a festival connected with rare inspirations; and there were weeks when I did nothing but wait with infinite sadness for the creative hour. It was a life full of abysses. I anxiously avoided every artificial means of evoking the inspirations, I began to abstain from wine (which I have done for several years), I tried to bring my life close to Nature itself. . . . But in all this which was doubtless reasonable, I didn't have the courage to bring back the distant inspirations by working. Now I know that it is the only way of keeping them.—And it is the great rebirth of my life and of my hope that you have given me. And that is also the case with my wife; last year we had rather serious financial worries, and they haven't yet been removed: but I think now that diligent work can disarm even the anxieties of poverty. My wife has to leave our little child, and yet she thinks more calmly and impartially of that necessity since I wrote her what you said: "Travail et patience." I am very happy that she will be near you, near your great work. One cannot lose oneself near you. . . .

I want to see if I can find a living in some form here in Paris, —(I need only a little for that). If it is possible, I shall stay. And it would be a great happiness for me. Otherwise, if I cannot succeed, I beg you to help my wife as you helped me by your work and by your word and by all the eternal forces of which you are the Master.

It was yesterday in the silence of your garden that I found

myself. And now the noise of the immense city has become more remote and there is a deep stillness about my heart where your words stand like statues. . . .

[*39*]

To Clara Rilke

. . . This last week, every day from ten o'clock until five in the afternoon, I have been in the Bibliothèque Nationale and have read many books and seen many reproductions of cathedrals of the twelfth and thirteenth centuries. My dear, that was a great, great art. The more one concerns oneself with its creations, the more deeply one feels the value and exquisiteness of the work: for these cathedrals, these mountains and mountain ranges of the Middle Ages, would never have been finished if they had had to grow out of inspirations. One day had to come like another and set to work, and if each one wasn't an inspiration, still each was a road to it. Everything has already been said about these great churches; Victor Hugo has written a few wonderful pages about Notre-Dame de Paris, and yet these cathedrals still have their effect, strangely alive, unbetrayed, mysterious—an effect greater than words can tell. . . . I think they are in the midst of this great city like a forest or like the sea; a bit of Nature in this city in which the gardens are Art. They are solitude and stillness, refuge and quiet in the change and jumble of these streets. They are the future as they are the past; everything else runs, flows, races and falls . . . they tower and wait. Notre Dame grows with every day; the more often one returns to it, the greater one finds it. At sunset almost every day I go past there at the hour when the Seine is like gray silk into which the lights are falling like polished gems.—Then I am also looking for paths to antiquity. I have seen wonderfully beautiful things in the Louvre, and many I understand better now, although I am just at the very, very beginning.

The Venus of Milo is too modern for me. But the Nike of

Samothrace, the Goddess of Victory on the ship's hull with the wonderful movement and wide sea-wind in her garment is a miracle to me and like a whole world. That is Greece. That is shore, sea and light, courage and victory. Then on the gravestones, there are modelings of a wonderful kind, profiles and hands, hands, groups of hands which are felt quite incomparably deeply and artistically and almost: wisely. And then Tanagra. That is a spring of imperishable life!

And with all this, Botticelli, the glorious frescoes opposite the Nike of Samothrace,—and Leonardo; again and again Leonardo. —Rodin I haven't seen for a long time. He is working on a portrait, is very deep in this work, does everything else as though in a dream. And I have the feeling that one disturbs him even on his Saturday. . . . Of the journey he doesn't speak, so you will probably still find him when you come. And now you are coming soon, aren't you? I am waiting.

[*40*]

To Clara Rilke   11 rue Toullier, Paris
                                    September 27, morning [1902]
    . . . One can learn much here, I think, but one must have a certain maturity, otherwise one sees nothing, on the one hand because there is too much here, and then because such a variety of things speak simultaneously. From all sides.—I have already told you that I am trying to get closer in feeling to antiquity and am even succeeding now and then in finding a new and deep joy in its things. Rodin has a tiny plaster cast, a tiger (antique), in his studio in the rue de l'Université, which he values very highly: C'est beau, c'est tout . . . he says of it. And from this little plaster cast I saw what he means, what antiquity is and what links him to it. There, in this animal, is the same lively feeling in the modeling, this little thing (it is no higher than my hand is wide, and no longer than my hand) has hundreds of thousands of sides like a very big object, hundreds of thousands of sides which are all alive, animated, and different. And that in plaster! And with

this the expression of the prowling stride is intensified to the highest degree, the powerful planting of the broad paws, and at the same time, that caution in which all strength is wrapped, that noiselessness. . . . You will see this little thing, and we mustn't fail to pay a visit to the original either (a little bronze), which is in the medal cabinet of the Bibliothèque Nationale.—When one comes from such things to the sculpture of the twelfth and thirteenth centuries, one often misses there that peaceful and quiet completedness and animation of the surface and finds only the same force of expression and something new, conscientious, and thorough that seeks for types and generalizes the model. And yet the surface here in these things has become, through the influence of time, of the wind and the rain, the sun and the night of centuries, just as alive, just as plastic, and without the slightest emptiness.

The Trocadero Museum is very interesting; it contains tolerably good plaster casts and copies of old portals from Provence, from Chartres, from Rouen and other cities, fragments, details, columns, in which one can see how the whole of life with all its things and figures passed through the hand of the sculptor into the stone, as if it belonged there. One feels, even more than in the Renaissance, how people's eyes were opened, how they suddenly saw everything and tried their hand at everything. And Rodin has many connections with that too. I am convinced, for example, that the flowers on the pedestal of the woman's bust in the Luxembourg came into his sculpture the way they came into the works of the masters of the twelfth century. As a thing that was also an experience for him, also driven along in the great stream that is perpetually pouring into his art.

Today I will try again to see him. Then I go mostly by the little steamer on the Seine as far as the Pont de Jena (opposite the Trocadero), that is the shortest way from whatever quarter I happen to be in.—The afternoons now are often beautiful and just slightly veiled and withdrawn; and then it has such a gentle way of becoming evening. One might say there is a moment when the hours cease going, one no longer feels their step, they mount upon some animal which carries them along on its broad back. So quietly they bear themselves, and only beneath them is something big and dark that moves, slips away, takes them with it.— Until five o'clock I am for the most part in the Bibliothèque Nationale, then they close there, and I go and experience this growing into evening somewhere on the Seine bridge, or on the Quai; sometimes I get as far as the Luxembourg Gardens, which even then are beginning to grow dusky, gently warding off the darkness with their many red flowers. Then suddenly from somewhere a drum-roll begins, rolling up and down, a soldier all in red passes through the avenues. And then everywhere people emerge, happy, laughing, high-spirited people, serious, sad, silent, and lonely people, people of all kinds, of today, of yesterday and day before yesterday. Some who have sat for many hours on a remote bench, like people who wait—and into whose brains it is now being drummed that they have nothing to wait for, and then some who, as long as it is day, live, eat, sleep, and read a newspaper on the benches: all manner of people, faces, and hands —many hands pass by then. It is something like a Last Judgment. And behind those who pass, the garden grows ever bigger: big. And Paris becomes close, light, noisy, and begins again one of its insatiable nights stimulated by spice, wine, music, and the clothes of women. . . .

[41]

To Otto Modersohn   Paris
                                    New Year's Eve, 1902

My dear Otto Modersohn, my intention of laying the monograph on your Christmas table has been badly thwarted. Two days before the twenty-fourth, I learned that the publishers of this book (because of technical difficulties unknown to me) will not finish printing before January. I am very sorry about this, for I had long been looking forward with joy to sending you the monograph for the Christmas celebration in your dear lonely country. Even to the last minute I hoped to, and now I miss the joy this gift would have given me, everywhere. I have in mind your birthday and wish Velhagen may have finished by then.

So we did nothing further on Christmas; for it was no proper, valid festival for us either,—only a kind of quiet day of remembrance that passed gently away for us in solitude. Of our dear child very good news comes to us: that made our hours bright and gave them a good confidence.—But of you two also we thought with warm wishes, on this holiday eve, and again today as a multifarious year finally dies out. We wish you and your dear wife may in these hours begin a good year well, a rich year for your art so full of future, dear Otto Modersohn, for each of you and for your life together,—in short: in every sense and by every standard a good year.

When on this last dying day I look over the past, I am impelled to say to you, dear Otto Modersohn, that to the best memories and attainments it has brought and vouchsafed belongs the close relationship I have found with your art. I have received so much that is good and great from you that my gratitude will not fade; the path through your work led me at many places nearer to myself, much became clear to me through it, much is thereby linked together for me forever, and I can well say when I recognized it in those spring days: I grew along with it for a stretch. All the blessing of my loyal trust upon your further path!

In the meantime my little book dealing with Rodin's work has also been finished. It may even come out in the first half of 1903. I was deep in work—that is why I simply haven't written. I really wanted to tell you about Paris. Dear Otto Modersohn, stick to your country! Paris (we say it to each other daily) is a difficult, difficult, anxious city. And the beautiful things there are here do not quite compensate, even with their radiant eternity, for what one must suffer from the cruelty and confusion of the streets and the monstrosity of the gardens, people, and things. To my anguished feeling, Paris has something unspeakably dismaying. It has lost itself utterly, it is tearing like a star off its course toward some dreadful collision. So must the cities have been of which the Bible tells that the wrath of God rose up behind them to overwhelm them and to shatter them. To all that, Rodin is a great, quiet, powerful contradiction. Time flows off him, and as he works thus, all, all the days of his long life, he seems inviolable, sacrosanct, and almost anonymous. He and his work are of the same nature and essence as the old cathedrals, as the things in the Louvre and: as the days with you, Otto Modersohn, in your big, simple, grand country that you have earned for yourself with lively love. I always feel, when I think of you, that you have everything there and that if sometime you come again to Paris, it will be only for a short time. For whoever really has a home must care for it and love it, and he should go from it but rarely. The world is not outside for him; he must wait in patience and work for it to come to him from all distances and to fill the things of his home with all manifoldness, greatness, and splendor. . . .

[*42*]

To Clara Rilke   Hotel Florence, Viareggio presso Pisa
                                     March 27, 1903

. . . I want and need these days only for rest. When I have that, something heavy begins to fall off me, very slowly; but if I move too soon, it quickly climbs back up on me again.

And yet gently, very gently I am already beginning sometimes to feel a benefit I haven't known in years . . . no, no, dear, I will *not* worry and will think only good things. When anxious, uneasy and bad thoughts come, I go to the sea, and the sea drowns them out with its great wide sounds, cleanses me with its noise and imposes a rhythm upon everything in me that is bewildered and confused. And much is so. I feel that I must build my powers anew from the ground up, but I feel too that this difficult thing is possible here, if I have patience and faith. . . .

[43]

To Friedrich Huch   (Hotel Florence)
Viareggio presso Pisa (Italy)
April 1, 1903

. . . Dear Friedrich Huch, there is something in me that gladly
lets itself be spoiled; and spoiled (perhaps in the not good sense)
I was by your *Peter Michel*, which was so entirely joy and
pleasure to me, along with all the fine shocks of surprise. And
this softening must have made me sensitive to any other air, so
that I at once cried draught when the healthy winds of some
transition blew in your new book. I am no critic, and I will not,
will not (for heaven's sake, for heaven's very great sake!) will
not be one; I measure a work of art by the happiness it gives me,
and because I believe that my understanding of happiness (of real
happiness, that broadens) is ripening with life, becoming greater,
more ambitious and at the same time more grateful, I am of the
opinion that this measure for works of art could in time acquire
something just and clarifying, if I grow. And perhaps it is so.
But you see (since the book drifted into your hands) how even
to the Worpswede artists I came not as a critic but by the paths
of a personal and cautious love that was happy in being allowed
to go to all those places where before it lonely joys of growing
blossomed, smiled, and lived. But in my long letter to you, Friedrich Huch, there was something (now I believe I know it in my
heart's core), something, perhaps a trifle only, of the critic's in-
solence, rashness, and hypocrisy, something that doesn't belong
to me and that, even if it should look brilliant and of value, I
would want to reject in any case. And that made mischief. Had I
the letter now, I could indicate the place where it got in, that
little grain of foreignness that spread its poisonous smell over the
whole letter. But how it could have got in? Perhaps I wrote the
letter too soon, it ran along, so to speak, ahead of my own words
which were not yet done; perhaps the reason lies in the bad state
of mind I was in this winter in Paris (with the heaviest of all cities
on my heart). Finally, almost simultaneously with the new year,

influenzalike torments began to set in that kept me for months equally far removed from sickness and from health, upon a narrow strip of dizzy discomfort, to walk on which was a continual anxiety and a desperate impatience. In the end (although it was difficult to accomplish this with my always too limited means) I came via Turin and Genoa to this little place, which, from bygone happy days, I have honored with something like filial love, adorning it in my grateful memory from year to year with all the jewelry of my wishes and all the treasures of my remembrance. So that it was not without danger to come and to make clear to an unsuspecting reality here that it would have to raise itself to the high level of my grateful imagination. Meanwhile the disappointment has not been too violent, no greater than with almost any seeing-again, and if I cannot yet rejoice as I once rejoiced in the wideness of the woods, in the size of the sea, and the grace of all this glory, that is because of my hesitant health, which still lacks the strength for joy, that superabundance that is necessary in order to take heart, beyond the little hindrances, in the great glories. . . .

[44]

To Ellen Key　　　　　Hotel Florence, Viareggio presso Pisa (Italy)
April 3, 1903

How shall I thank you, dear Ellen Key, for your two so inexpressibly loving letters? I would like most to write you a long, long letter, a whole book, and tell you how everything was, how my childhood was, my difficult, difficult childhood. But I *cannot* now!—Finally after a difficult decision I have left Paris, wanted first to stay on the Riviera di Levante which, however, I found overcrowded like a full close room. So I pushed still farther to this quiet village, which lies between Pisa and the marble mountains of Carrara, by a lively, spirited sea. In summer it is a big society seaside resort—but now nothing more than a little town with empty streets, enclosed by pine woods, and wide open before a mighty sea. I was here once five years ago, and those were days full of benefit that were given me here then, days of sun, that were the advent of many songs. That is why I trust this place and want to try to live here for a while.

You too are under way in the meantime, carrying your dear, towering and summoning word to many who hunger for it. My thoughts and wishes accompany you on this trip, and I send this letter after you and: the Rodin book that now at last has come out. May it give you joy. You won't believe how happy I am about your understanding, your encouragement, and your love, and how I return all this to you from out of my deepest depths, dear friend. I feel as if my books had never, never yet been so well off as with you. Rarely has anyone received them thus, so spoiled them with warmth.

I thank you!

Your second letter was sent after me here from Paris. I had already gone when it came. But my wife opened it there and conveyed everything to the Bojers that you wanted to have known. She sees the Bojers often, is very busy, and I have good news of her.

Yes, dear Frau Ellen Key, you shall have pictures of us as soon as possible; we have, I believe, a few more copies to give away, and we also want you to know us soon! Ruth's little picture will naturally come too. Should there be no more copies of the last pictures, I shall have some taken: then you must be patient a few more weeks.

It will be harder with the old books; I believe that of most of them I myself have no more copies, and the publishers no longer exist! And those of the old books that I may possess are still lying in boxes in Worpswede, and I cannot get at them. But Wilhelm Michel who wrote the article in *Zeit* has some more material; and I will look and see to it that in time you come to know everything; I am *so glad and happy* that you want to.

Oh, and to tell you otherwise who I am; that is difficult. I have a hope that we will meet sometime soon (and perhaps it will be in Italy!): then I will tell you much about myself, to make up, in a way, for what you really should have known long ago: for I feel as if you had always been close to me!

Yes, my family is old. As early as 1376 it belonged to the ancient Carinthian nobility, later it emigrated (at least in part) to Saxony and Brandenburg, and in the seventeenth and in the first decades of the eighteenth century it blossoms richly into three powerful branches. Then comes the decline, lawsuits that wipe out the entire fortune and loss of all estates and lands and: poverty, almost obscurity. After almost a century, which passed in darkness, my great-grandfather again came into power. He was lord of Kamenitz an der Linde (a castle in Bohemia, whither the family had emigrated in the anxious transition period). He collected the old traditions, he rescued from oblivion what was on the point of dying away, the family's ancient name. But immediately behind him the depths close again. My grandfather, who still spent his childhood at Kamenitz, was later steward of someone else's estate. My father began the career of officer (following a family tradition) but then switched over to that of official. He is a railroad official, holds a fairly high post in a private railroad, which he has earned with infinite conscientiousness. He lives in Prague. *There* I was born. Twenty-seven years ago. (In the Catholic baptism I received the name René Maria.) Of my mother's family I know nothing. Her father was a wealthy merchant whose fortune went to pieces on a prodigal son. My childhood home was a cramped rented apartment in Prague; it was very sad. My parents' marriage was already faded when I was born. When I was nine years old, the discord broke out openly, and my mother left her husband. She was a very nervous, slender, dark woman, who wanted something indefinite of life. And so she remained. Actually these two people ought to have understood each other better, for they both attach an infinite amount of value to externals; our little household, which was in reality middle class, was supposed to have the appearance of plenty, our clothes were supposed to deceive people, and certain lies passed as a matter of course. I don't know how it was with me. I had to wear very beautiful clothes and went about until school years like a little girl; I believe my mother played with me as with a big doll. For the rest, she was always proud when she was called "Miss." She wanted to pass for young, sickly, and unhappy. And unhappy she probably was too. I believe we all were.

Soon after she left the house, I was put in one of our big officers' training establishments. I was ten years old. After the worst coddling, I (who had never known brothers, sisters, or playmates hitherto) found myself among fifty boys who all met me with the same scornful hostility. Noncommissioned officers trained us. What I suffered in those five years (for I remained that long in spite of sickness, in spite of opposition in the place) is a life in itself: a long, difficult life. Even today, my parents still suspect nothing of it. They could not understand it. When I came out and took off the uniform, I knew that they were quite remote from me. And that now manifested itself over and over again. They put me in a commercial school, in circumstances that nearly brought about my downfall, until a brother of my father (I was already sixteen years old then) had me take school studies privately. By expending all my powers, I got over the eight classes in three years and passed the final examination. Then I was tired. There came a time when I hated my parents, especially my mother. Over the years I got rid of this error. I see my mother sometimes and feel beyond all strangeness that she is very unhappy and very alone. And to my father I would like to show a great, great deal of love. He is of an inexpressible kindness, and my life, which he cannot understand, is a subject of touching, daily anxiety for him. I know that he has an infinite longing to know who I am and what I am doing, but, as we are poor, he sees above all only the one thing: that I cannot earn my own bread, and therefore he holds no confidence in my ability or has to keep giving it up. And I am suffering, suffering more and more from the fact that I still have to live on him, although I know that it is difficult for him: but I find no other expedient.

For what is mine no one gives me bread, and I know that I haven't powers enough to divide myself into one who earns and one who creates. And even if I had all the powers in the world, I would have to give *all* my powers to the important thing in me: it has a right to that. Isn't that so?! Tell me, my friend! The last two years since my marriage I really have tried to earn, continually, day by day: not much has come of it on the one hand, and on the other hand in so doing I have forfeited *so much*. Do you know, I am sometimes afraid that I have lost everything in the process!—I did know that I can write *only* out of deepest necessity but, when I wanted to earn by my writing, I counted on this deepest necessity coming over me *often*. But, will you believe me, dear Ellen Key: since there has been an external compulsion, this necessity has come more and more rarely, and recently it has left off almost entirely. You cannot imagine *what* I am suffering and what I have suffered all these last months; I know I am not exhausted; but the little and continual thoughts of every day and its most unimportant things confuse me so that I can no longer recollect my own. How shall I say that to you: Before I used to hear all my voices in me; now it is as if someone had closed the window toward the garden in which my songs live: far, far away I hear something and listen and can no longer distinguish it. My head is full of ridiculous additions. And hardly have I been paid for one job and am thinking that I may now collect myself for my own work, when it is already time again to think of the *next* and of where it is to be found and by what efforts obtained. On that my nervous strength is slipping away, my time, my courage, and I fail to catch up with myself day after day, and am somewhere out of reach, full of flowers past their bloom, whose fading scents fill me with dead weight.—It isn't so new for me, indeed, this feeling. My whole art has grown up from its first day against opposition: against the laughter and scorn of the noncommissioned officers, against my father, against all about me; but this time it is more dangerous than before. For, with this idea and necessity of earning, the opposition, which until now always came from others, *from outside*, has come *into me myself*, I carry it with me everywhere, I cannot elude it, and that is why I am so fearful for everything important in me. Boundlessly fearful. Now I have journeyed here in order to recover and collect myself, in order perhaps to come to myself again in this lovely place which is protected by a good past; two weeks have now passed here, I am not yet well—and yet already I ought really to begin to think, to be concerned again about the future. . . . And the thought of money, which used not to exist so isolatedly for me, has conjured up other worries: this, for example, that all of a sudden I know now that my education is not sufficient for a single, definite position, scarcely for a journalistic occupation. And of *that* particularly I have a nameless horror! I feel too clearly the apparent kinship between literature and journalism, of which one is an art and so looks to eternity, and the other a trade in the midst of the times: more in the times than any other. And I am so far away from the times, from all their wishes and all their successes; I *cannot* participate in them. I have nothing *in* them, not even a home. I live not in dreams but in contemplation of a reality that is perhaps the future. Only in Russia, on my two extensive journeys through that land, have I felt home; there I was somehow at home, perhaps, because there one notices so little of the times, of the temporal, because there it is always future already and every passing hour closer to eternity. I always thought I would have to live there sometime. . . .

But now I scarcely have plans any more; now it seems to me an infinite presumption to have plans, when the very next stage is so dismaying, so dark, and so full of tiniest questions. It seems as if I were in the midst of nets; I feel these nets on my hands with every gesture that would arise freely.

One day I think I must make this gesture in order at last to be able to live; the next day I believe I should somehow finish off my studies; then again I look for some person who will understand my need without taking me for a beggar: which I most fear. And finally no time is left for anything, and when an indisposition comes I have scarcely enough resistance left to avert it among all these pursuing cares, and so everything draws in about me and sets itself against the flowers in me. . . .

How is that to get better? I have written eleven or twelve

books and have received almost nothing for them, only four of them were paid for at all. The rest of the publishers took my books *without* paying. The Worpswede monograph was a commission that was well paid,—but the Rodin book, in which I have lived for months, brought only 150 marks! And still there is something in my innermost soul that does not at all want these books to become known; a longing to remain nameless fills me to the brim, and I would gladly get lost behind my songs like some bygone people. . . . But that again is—"imprudent," as my father would say. . . .

Why am I saying all this to you, dear, dear Frau Ellen Key? *To whom* am I to say it? My dear young wife knows it and is bearing it loyally with me and in addition is bearing her own lot which is similar and is bearing the separation from our little child for the sake of her serious work.—But the burden over me has become so great, and I would like so much to speak of it to a near person and ask this person, who understands and loves me: do you think there is a way out? Must a miracle happen for me to find quiet a while and hear what is mine ringing again;—and if a miracle is necessary for it: shall I live and believe that it will come? Or what shall I do? Am I wrong to be galled by longing day and night for what is important in me, since the unimportant is calling me with the voice of life? But no, I believe that is not the voice of life. For I wanted to tell you *this* too, dear friend: I love life, and I believe in it! Everything in me believes in it. You have felt that my letters lie in the shadow of some bitter sorrow, and that is why there are in your last letter those beautiful, good, bell-pure words affirming life. As a child, when everyone was always unkind to me, when I felt so infinitely forsaken, so utterly astray in an alien world, there may have been a time when I longed to be gone. But then, when people remained alien to me, I was drawn to things, and from them a joy breathed upon me, a joy in being that has always remained equally quiet and strong and in which there was never a hesitation or a doubt. In the military school, after long fearful battles, I abandoned the violent Catholic piety of childhood, made myself free of it in order to be even more, even more comfortlessly alone; but from things, from their patient bearing and enduring, a new, greater and more devout love came to me later, some kind of faith that knows no fear and no bounds. In this faith life is also a part. Oh, how I believe in it, in life. Not that which makes up our time, but that other, the life of little things, the life of animals and of the great plains. That life which endures through the millenniums, apparently without interest, and yet in the balance of its powers full of motion and growth and warmth. That is why cities weigh on me so. That is why I love to take long walks barefoot, in order to miss no grain of sand and to give my body the whole world in many forms as feeling, as event, as kinship. That is why I live on vegetables, where possible, to be close to what is simple, to an awareness of life intensified by nothing foreign; that is why no wine goes into me: because I desire that only my own juices shall speak and stir and shall have bliss, as in children and animals, from deep within themselves! . . . And that is why I also want to put all pride far from me, not to raise myself above the very least animal and not to hold myself grander than a stone. But to be what I am, to live what was set for me to live, to want to voice what no one else can voice, to bear the blossoms that are commanded of my heart: that I want—and surely that *cannot* be presumption.

Dear friend, I have such difficult, such difficult days. But also it cannot become more difficult, and perhaps, when you read all this, you will find some word on which I can raise myself up a tiny bit.—My father in his dear, ready kindness, has held out the prospect, if it just won't work any longer, of procuring me an official position in Prague. Of course, he doesn't sense that it would be a new "military school" for me. But I am afraid of this rescue as of a prison. I know I shall die if I have to write figures more than three-fourths of the day in cold office rooms; I know that all, all will then be over and forever. And I am namelessly afraid of it!

So often I cannot help thinking of Ellen Ljunggren. Will she put through what she wanted? (Have you news of her?) Ought I

too to do something of the sort? For two or three years, *only*
earn and then . . . but it seems to me that I have already been
away much, much too long from what is mine: there was so
much that still wanted to come! . . .

Now you know much of me, dear Frau Ellen Key, more than
you wanted to know: forgive the presumption that lies in this
confidence; I didn't know, when I began this letter, that I would
tell you all this; it came over me in a way, it dragged me with it;
where was I to leave off?

And then, too, you would continually have felt on each of my
letters the pressure, the shadow of some strange thing you didn't
know about. Now you will understand everything, and that
you should.

In one of your good letters, you pictured my mother as a
beautiful and distinguished woman whose hands came to her
child from among flowers; how often have I longed for such
a woman; for a mother who is greatness, kindness, quietude, and
beneficence . . . in my family's past there must have been such
women, for at times I feel something of their presence, like the
light of a distant star, like a dark glance, resting on me. But to
you I have written as I would have written to a mother like that,
or to an older sister who knows more of life and of people than I.

Accept it in your great, great kindness!

And take at the same time the Rodin book. And along with it
one more request; I am putting in a second copy of the Rodin
book; will you, *if it does not cause you any inconvenience at all,*
see that it reaches the hands of Georg Brandes? I do not know
his address, and I would like so much to have him *surely* get it.
(My two last books Juncker, I think, sent him, but I do not
know whether he received them.) But *only* if it is no trouble
to do so. And thank you!

Are you still having snow and winter now? And how will
Easter morning break then? When does spring begin in your
homeland?—I think of you, full of love, full of gratitude, full of
trust.

[45]

To Clara Rilke Hôtel de Florence, Viareggio presso Pisa (Italy)
Wednesday, April 8, 1903

. . . here it is again a day full of unrest and violence. Storm
against storm over the sea. Fugitive light. Night in the wood.
And the great noise over all. I was in the wood all morning, and,
after four or five glaring days, the darkness that lived there was
pleasing to all the senses and the coolness and the almost sharp
wind. You must imagine this wood as very, very tall-trunked,
dark, straight pine trunks and high overhead their spreading
branches. The ground all dark with needles and covered with very
tall prickly broom bushes that are all full of yellow blossoms,
blossom upon blossom. And today this yellow shone in the cool,
almost nightlike dusk and swayed and nodded, and the wood
was lit from below and very lonely. I walked (after I had taken
my sun bath and gone barefoot a little) back and forth there
for hours and thought a great deal. . . . I can't say what it will
come to, or whether the Spanish plan will materialize or some
other, perhaps not yet mentionable at all. Nor is there any use
talking about it now; I think someday it will be known and done.
And knowing and doing will be one. So much is certain, that
first of all I shall return to Paris, perhaps to write the Carrière
book; it still seems to me that Paris must give me one more
work. . . . Everyone must be able to find in his work the center
of his life and from there be able to grow out in radiate form
as far as he can. And in this no other person may watch him, his
nearest and dearest particularly: for he may not even do so himself. There is a kind of purity and virginity in it, in this looking
away from oneself; it is as when one is drawing, one's gaze riveted
on the object, interwoven with Nature, and the hand goes its
way alone somewhere below, goes and goes, takes fright, falters,
is happy again, goes and goes far below the face that stands above
it like a star, not looking, only *shining*. It seems to me as if I
had always created like that: my face gazing at far-off things,

my hands alone. And so it must certainly be. So I shall again become in time; but for that I must remain as lonely as I am now, my loneliness must first be firm and secure again like an untrodden wood that is not afraid of footsteps. It must lose all emphasis, every exceptional value, and every obligation. It must become everyday, the natural and daily; the thoughts that come, even the most fleeting, must find me all alone, then they will again make up their minds to trust me; there is nothing worse for me than to become unaccustomed to loneliness: and I almost was. That is why I have long ways to go now, day and night, back through all that is past and confused. And then, if I come to the crossroads and find again the place where I began to go astray, then I will begin work and way again, simply and seriously, like the beginner that I am. It is very big and festive in my heart when I think that we understand each other in this now and are of one mind in these dark riddles. I feel . . . as if we had gone together through endless developments, through worlds, and worlds through us. . . .

. . . today a very dear letter came from Rodin (dictated), very warm and full of interest. . . . I shall be so happy to see his new things: Oh how he grows and grows!—(Hokusai, the great Japanese painter, said somewhere in speaking of the hundred views he painted of the mountain Fujiyama: "C'est à l'âge de soixante-treize ans que j'ai compris à peu près la forme et la nature vraie des oiseaux, des poissons et des plantes"). . . .

[46]

To Clara Rilke   Hôtel de Florence, Viareggio presso Pisa (Italy)
April 24, 1903 (Friday)

. . . It was well I didn't leave on Wednesday, for the weather these days has been so unspeakable, so unruly with storms and downpours that fell thick as webs, half days and whole nights long, that I would not like to have been in a foreign city and particularly in one that derives its beauty from the sun and that, all adjusted to southern days, wants to stand by a blue sea, but not by one that fetches all its deepest, oldest, and most forgotten colors out of the depths, spreads them out and then indignantly, from enormous wave bellies, throws over them the yellow-white sheepskins of their foam.—Nor is it good to be on the train in such days of upheaval, when, instead of at least staying always in one rain, one must ride through the rains of all those many little stations which stand there dripping so peevishly and looking twice as dirty as usual.

So it was all right, although I am a little impatient and would gladly be gone already, particularly since with this storm it isn't comfortable even here, and is variable and noisy; not even in the wood was it still today, the sea has come much closer, and the wind snatches its noise in by the hair and winds it about the trees, which are themselves full of rushing and excitement, and as if they had already had to watch and blow like that all night.

Yes, it is time to come home. . . .

Here I am still, now in *Niels Lyhne*, now in the Bible, and much in your dear, dear letters that are for me the dearest of all. In my own books, too, I am finding much; am going about in the *Stories of God* and rejoice in much and forgive them what doesn't seem good to me for the sake of the rest which is essential and beautiful and which also will never be different. Isn't it as if no one had ever read the book? I would it were all as good as the best in it; then it could be found later sometime like a beautiful old object. There wasn't enough patience in me when I shaped it, that is why it has so many blurred and uncertain places; but perhaps I shall come soon again to such a book, and then I will build it with all the reverence I have in my hands, and will not let go of any passage as long as it is less than I myself, and will make each into an angel and will let myself be overcome by him and force him to bend me although I have made him. . . .

[47]

To Lou Andreas-Salomé   Worpswede bei Bremen
                                                July 18, 1903

I would like to tell you, dear Lou, that Paris was for me an experience similar to the military school; as a great fearful astonishment seized me then, so now again terror assailed me at everything that, as in an unspeakable confusion, is called life. Then, when I was a boy among boys, I was alone among them; and how alone I was this time among these people, how perpetually disowned by all I met; the carts drove right through me, and those that were hurrying made no detour around me but ran over me full of contempt, as over a bad place in which stagnant water has collected. And often before going to sleep, I read the thirtieth chapter in the Book of Job, and it was all true of me, word for word. And in the night I got up and looked for my favorite volume of Baudelaire, the petits poèmes en prose, and read aloud the most beautiful poem that bears the title: "A une heure du matin." Do you know it? It begins: Enfin! seul! on n'entend plus que le roulement de quelques fiacres attardés et éreintés. Pendant quelques heures nous posséderons le silence, sinon le repos. Enfin! la tyrannie de la face humaine a disparu, et je ne souffrirai plus que par moi-même. . . . And it ends grandly; stands up, stands and finishes like a prayer. A prayer of Baudelaire's; a real, simple prayer, made with his hands, awkward and beautiful as the prayer of a Russian.—He had a long road to go to get there, Baudelaire, and he went on his knees and crawling. How far away from me he was in everything, one of the most alien to me; often I can scarcely understand him, and yet sometimes deep in the night when I said his words after him like a child, then he was the person closest to me and lived beside me and stood pale behind the thin wall and listened to my voice falling. What a strange companionship was between us then, a sharing of everything, the same poverty and perhaps the same fear.

Oh a thousand hands have been building at my fear, and out of a remote village it has become a city, a big city, in which unspeakable things happen. It grew all the time and took the quiet green out of my feeling that no longer bears fruit. Even in Westerwede it was growing, and houses and streets arose out of the fearful circumstances and hours that passed there. And when Paris came, it quickly became very big. In August of last year I arrived there. It was the time when the trees in the city are withered without autumn, when the burning streets, expanded by the heat, will not end and one goes through smells as through many sad rooms. Then I went past the long hospitals whose gates stood wide open with a gesture of impatient and greedy compassion. When I passed by the Hôtel Dieu for the first time, an open carriage was just driving in, in which a person hung, swaying with every movement, askew like a broken marionette, and with a bad sore on his long, gray, dangling neck. And what people I met after that, almost every day; fragments of caryatids on whom the whole pain still lay, the entire structure of a pain, under which they were living slow as tortoises. And they were passers-by among passers-by, left alone and undisturbed in their fate. At most one took them in as an impression and looked at them with calm, detached curiosity like a new kind of animal in whom want had developed special organs, organs of hunger and death. And they were wearing the comfortless, discolored mimicry of the too great cities, and were holding out under the foot of each day that trod on them, like tough beetles, were enduring as if they still had to wait for something, twitching like bits of a big chopped-up fish that is already rotting but still alive. They were living, living on nothing, on dust, on soot, and on the filth on their surfaces, on what falls from the teeth of dogs, on any senselessly broken thing that anyone might still buy for some inexplicable purpose. Oh what kind of a world is that! Pieces, pieces of people, parts of animals, leftovers of things that have been, and everything still agitated, as though driven about helter-skelter in an eerie wind, carried and carrying, falling and overtaking each other as they fall.

There were old women who set down a heavy basket on the

ledge of some wall (very little women whose eyes were drying up like puddles), and when they wanted to grasp it again, out of their sleeves shoved forth slowly and ceremoniously a long, rusty hook instead of a hand, and it went straight and surely out to the handle of the basket. And there were other old women who went about with the drawers of an old night stand in their hands, showing everyone that twenty rusty pins were rolling around inside which they must sell. And once of an evening late in the fall, a little old woman stood next me in the light of a store window. She stood very still, and I thought that like me she was busy looking at the objects displayed and hardly noticed her. Finally, however, her proximity made me uneasy, and I don't know why, I suddenly looked at her peculiarly clasped, worn-out hands. Very, very slowly an old, long, thin pencil rose out of those hands, it grew and grew, and it took a very long time until it was entirely visible, visible in all its wretchedness. I cannot say what produced such a terrible effect in this scene, but it seemed to me as if a whole destiny were being played out before me, a long destiny, a catastrophe that was working up frightfully to the moment when the pencil no longer grew and, slightly trembling, jutted out of the loneliness of those empty hands. I understood at last that I was supposed to buy it. . . .

And then those women who pass by one quickly in long velvet cloaks of the eighties, with paper roses on antiquated hats under which their hair hangs down looking as though it were melted together. And all those people, men and women, who are in some transition, perhaps from madness to healing, perhaps also toward insanity; all with something infinitely fine in their faces, with a love, a knowledge, a joy, as with a light that is burning only a very little bit troubled and uneasy and could certainly be made clear again if someone would look and help. . . . But there is no one to help. No one to help those who are only just a very little bit perplexed, frightened, and intimidated; those who are just beginning to read things differently from the way they are meant; those who are still living in quite the same world, only that they walk just a little obliquely and therefore sometimes think that things are hanging over them; those who aren't at home in cities and lose themselves in them as in an evil wood without end—; all those to whom pain is happening every day, all those who can no longer hear their wills going in the noise, all those over whom fear has grown,—why does no one help them in the big cities?

Where are they going when they come so quickly through the streets? Where do they sleep, and if they cannot sleep, what goes on then before their sad eyes? What do they think about when they sit all day long in the open gardens, their heads sunk over their hands which have come together as from afar, each to hide itself in the other? And what kind of words do they say to themselves when their lips summon up their strength and work? Do they still weave real words? . . . Are those still sentences they say, or is everything already crowding out of them pell-mell as out of a burning theater, everything that was spectator in them and actor, audience and hero? Does no one think of the fact that there is a childhood in them that is being lost, a strength that is sickening, a love that is falling?

O Lou, I was so tormented day after day. For I understood all those people, and although I went around them in a wide arc, they had no secret from me. I was torn out of myself into their lives, right through all their lives, through all their burdened lives. I often had to say aloud to myself that I was not one of them, that I would go away again from that horrible city in which they will die; I said it to myself and felt that it was no deception. And yet, when I noticed how my clothes were becoming worse and heavier from week to week, and saw how they were slit in many places, I was frightened and felt that I would belong irretrievably to the lost if some passer-by merely looked at me and half unconsciously counted me with them. Anyone could push me down to them with the cursory judgment of a disparaging glance. And wasn't I really one of them, since I was poor like them and full of opposition to everything that occupied and rejoiced and deluded and deceived other people? Was I not denying everything that was valid about me,—and was I not actually homeless in spite of the semblance of a room in which I was as much a stranger as if I were sharing it with someone unknown? Did I not starve, like them, at tables on which stood food that I did not touch because it was not pure and not simple like that which I loved? And did I not already differ, like them, from the majority about me by the fact that no wine was in me nor any other deluding drink? Was I not clear like those lonely ones who were misted over only on the outside by the fumes and heaviness of the city and the laughter that comes like smoke out of the evil fires that it keeps going? Nothing was so little laughter as the laughter of those estranged creatures: when they laughed, it sounded as though something were falling in them, falling and being dashed to pieces and filling them up with broken bits. They were serious; and their seriousness reached out for me like the force of gravity and drew me deep down into the center of their misery.

What did it avail that on many mornings I got up happier and went out with more courage and capable of a quiet industrious day. . . . Once (it was rather early in the day) I came thus down the Boulevard St. Michel with the intention of going to the Bibliothèque Nationale, where I used to spend a great deal of time. I was walking along rejoicing in all that morning and the beginning of a new day dispenses, even in a city, of freshness, brightness, and courage. The red on the wagon wheels that was as moist and cold as on flower petals gladdened me, and I was glad that somewhere at the end of the street a person was wearing something light green without my thinking what it might be. Slowly the water wagons drove uphill, and the water sprang young and light out of their pipes and made the street dark, so that it no longer dazzled. Horses came by in shimmering harness, and their hooves struck like a hundred hammers. The cries of the vendors had a different ring: rose up more lightly and echoed high above. And the vegetables on their handcarts were stirring like a little field and had a free morning of their own above them, and in them darkness, green, and dew. And when it was still for a moment, one heard overhead the noise of windows being flung open. . . .

Then I was suddenly struck by the peculiar behavior of the people coming toward me; most of them walked for a while with heads turned to look back, so that I had to be careful not to collide with them; there were also some who had stopped, and by following their gaze I arrived, among the people walking ahead of me, at a slender man dressed in black, who, as he went along, was using both hands to turn down his overcoat collar which apparently kept standing up in an annoying way. Because of this exertion which was visibly taxing him, he repeatedly forgot to pay attention to the walk, stumbled or sprang hastily over some little obstacle. When this had happened several times in quick succession, he did turn his attention to the walk, but it was remarkable that nevertheless, after two or three steps, he again faltered and then hopped over something. I had involuntarily quickened my step and now found myself close enough behind the man to see that the movements of his feet had nothing at all to do with the sidewalk, which was smooth and even, and that he only wanted to deceive those he met when he turned about after each stumble as if to call some guilty object to account. In reality there was nothing to be seen. In the meantime the awkwardness of his gait slowly diminished, and he hurried on quite quickly now and remained for a while unnoticed. But suddenly the restlessness began again in his shoulders, drew them up twice and then let them fall, so that they hung quite slantwise from him as he went on. But how amazed I was when I suddenly had to admit having seen how his left hand moved with indescribable speed to his coat collar, almost unnoticeably seized it and stood it up, whereupon he attempted with a great deal of trouble to lay the collar down with both hands, seeming, just like the first time, to succeed only with great difficulty. In so doing he nodded to the front and to the left, stretched his neck and nodded, nodded, nodded behind his busy upraised hands, as though the shirt collar too were beginning to trouble him, and as if there were work to be done up there for a long time yet. Finally everything seemed to be in order again. He went some ten steps completely unnoticed, when quite suddenly the rise and fall of his shoulders began again; simultaneously, a waiter, who was cleaning up in front of a coffeehouse, stood and looked with curiosity at the passer-by, who unexpectedly shook himself, stopped and then took up his walk again in little jumps. The waiter laughed and shouted something into the store, whereat a few more faces became visible behind the windowpanes. But the strange man had in the meantime hung his cane with its crooked handle on his collar from behind, and now, as he went on, he held it thus, vertically, just over his spine; there was nothing startling about this, and it supported him. The new position calmed him considerably, and he went along for a moment quite relieved. No one paid any attention to him; but I, who couldn't keep my eyes off him even for a second, knew how gradually the restlessness was returning, how it became stronger and stronger, how it tried now here, now there to express itself, how it shook at his shoulders, how it clung to his head to tear it out of balance, and how suddenly it quite unexpectedly overcame and broke up his walk. As yet one hardly saw all this; it was enacted at short intervals imperceptibly and almost secretly, but it was really there already, and it was growing. I felt how this whole man was filling up with restlessness, how this restlessness which couldn't find an outlet increased, and how it mounted, and I saw his will, his fear, and the desperate expression of his convulsive hands pressing the cane against his spine as though they wanted to make it a part of this helpless body, in which lay the incitement to a thousand dances. And I experienced how this cane became something, something important, on which much depended; all the strength of the man and his whole will went into it and made it into a power, into a being that could perhaps help and to which the sick man clung with wild faith. A god came into being here, and a world rose up against him. But while this battle was being waged, the man who bore it was trying to go ahead, and he succeeded for moments in appearing innocent and ordinary. Now he was crossing the Place St. Michel, and although the avoiding of carriages and pedestrians, which were very numerous, might have offered him the pretext for unusual motions, he remained quite still, and there was even a strange, stiff quiet in his whole body as he stepped on to the sidewalk of the bridge beyond. I was now close behind him, will-less, drawn along by his fear that was no longer distinguishable from mine. Suddenly the cane gave way, in the middle of the bridge. The man stood; extraordinarily still and rigid he stood there and didn't move. Now he was waiting; but it was as though the enemy in him didn't yet trust this submission; he hesitated—only a minute, to be sure. Then he broke out like a fire, out of all the windows at once. And there began a dance. . . . A dense circle of people that had quickly formed, gradually pushed me back, and I could see no more. My knees shook, and everything had been taken out of me. I stood for a while leaning against the bridge railing, and finally I went back to my room; there would no longer have been any sense in going to the library. Where is there a book that would be strong enough to help me out over what was in me? I was as though used up; as though another person's fear had been nourished out of me and had exhausted me, that is how I was.

And many mornings were like that one—and evenings were like that. Had I been able to *make* the fears I experienced thus, had I been able to shape things out of them, real, still things that it is serenity and freedom to create and from which, when they exist, reassurance emanates, then nothing would have happened to me. But these fears that fell to my lot out of every day stirred a hundred other fears, and they stood up in me against me and agreed among themselves, and I couldn't get beyond them. In striving to form them, I came to work creatively on *them*; instead of making them into things of my will, I only gave them a life of their own which they turned against me and with which they pursued me far into the night. Had things been better with me, more quiet and friendly, had my room stood by me, and had I remained well, perhaps I would have been able to do it even so: to make things out of fear.

Once I succeeded, though only for a short time. When I was in Viareggio the fears broke loose there, to be sure, more than before and overwhelmed me. And the sea that was never silent was too much for me and drenched me with the noise of its spring waves. But it came nevertheless. Prayers came into being there, Lou, a book of prayers. To you I must tell it because in your hands are resting my first prayers of which I have so often thought and to which I have so often clung out of the distance. Because their ring is so great and because they are so peaceful with you (and because no one besides you and me knows of them)—that is why I could cling to them. And sometime I would like to be allowed to come and lay the prayers, the others that have since come into being, with the others, with you, in your hands, in your quiet house.

For, see, I am a stranger and a poor man. And I shall pass; but in your hands shall be everything that might sometime have been my home, had I been stronger.

[48]

To Ellen Key   for the present, Oberneuland bei Bremen
                                              July 25, 1903

We have come over from Worpswede to Oberneuland for a few days for a reunion with little Ruth. And now we are about her day and night and are getting to know her; and she is good to us. In the morning when she wakes up, she tells us about herself in her self-constructed, expressive language and herself initiates us into her little life; and it is as if memories in her were helping her to overcome all strangeness that was between us at first. She came to us herself, and all at once it was natural to her to say "Mother," and me she calls "Man," and sometimes "Good Man," and rejoices every morning that I am still there. And the garden around the quiet house is so beautiful, and we know definitely now that she is well off and we are drawing a great peace and strength for ourselves out of these days. . . .

[49]

Worpswede bei Bremen
                              August 1, 1903

. . . Only now that our summer really makes so little sense and has become so restless, we want to think of leaving before the end of August. First a reunion with my father is to take place in Leipzig, and then we shall travel via Munich, Venice, and Florence to Rome where my wife (at Rodin's wish) is to work during the next year. I myself will then remain a month or two in Rome also, for I am most anxious to see antiquity, which I really don't know at all yet, especially its little things that are of such full-grown beauty. With them and with Gothic carving Rodin's work, through which I have gone so deeply and patiently, has connected me, and I feel an Italian sojourn now as a natural continuation of the best that Paris gave me to learn. But I do not want to stay too long in Rome and after a while will go on alone to some remote place that has a good winter. Where I shall live then, I do not yet know. The Tuscan country is dear to me, and I would certainly like to be where St. Francis opened up his radiant poverty like a cloak into which all the animals came: in Subiaco or in Assisi; but it is a mountainous country and perhaps too wild in winter. And I may have to go southward from Rome, perhaps to the little town of Ravello that lies near Amalfi, high above the blue gulfs of that happy coast. Perhaps solitude will come over me there and the great quiet that everything in me longs for; then I will live quietly in the company of things and be thankful for everything that keeps the all-too-commonplace from me. . . . The little book on Rodin's work that I am sending you today will tell you much . . . ; it is sheer personal experience, a testimonial of that first time in Paris, when in the shelter of an overgreat impression, I felt somewhat hidden from the thousandfold fear that came later. . . .

[50]

To Lou Andreas-Salomé   Oberneuland bei Bremen
                                                    August 8, 1903

. . . When I first came to Rodin and lunched with him out there in Meudon with people to whom one was not introduced, at the same table with strangers, I knew that his house was nothing to him, a paltry little necessity perhaps, a roof for time of rain and sleep; and that it was no care to him and no weight upon his solitude and composure. Deep in himself he bore the darkness, shelter, and peace of a house, and he himself had become sky above it, and wood around it and distance and great stream always flowing by. Oh what a lonely person is this aged man who, sunk in himself, stands full of sap like an old tree in autumn! He has become deep; he has dug a deep place for his heart, and its beat comes from afar off as from the center of a mountain. His thoughts go about in him and fill him with heaviness and sweetness and do not lose themselves on the surface. He has become blunt and hard toward the unimportant, and he stands among people as though surrounded by old bark. But to what is important he throws himself open, and he is wholly open when he is among things or where animals and people touch him quietly and like things. There he is learner and beginner and spectator and imitator of beauties that otherwise have always passed away among the sleeping, among the absent-minded and unsympathetic. There he is the attentive one whom nothing escapes, the lover who continually receives, the patient one who does not count his time and does not think of wanting the next thing. For him what he gazes at and surrounds with gazing is always the only thing, the world in which everything happens; when he fashions a hand, it is alone in space, and there is nothing besides a hand; and in six days God made only a hand and poured out the waters around it and bent the heavens above it; and rested over it when all was finished, and it was a glory and a hand.

And this way of looking and of living is so fixed in him because he acquired it as a handworker: at that time when he attained the element of his art which is so infinitely simple and unrelated to subject matter, he attained that great justice, that equilibrium in the face of the world which wavers before no name. Since it was granted him to see things in everything, he made his own the opportunity to build things; for that is his great art. Now no movement can confuse him any more, since he knows that even in the rise and fall of a quiet surface there is movement, and since he sees only surfaces and systems of surfaces which define forms accurately and clearly. For there is nothing uncertain for him in an object that serves him as a model: there a thousand little surface elements are fitted into the space, and it is his task, when he creates a work of art after it, to fit the thing still more intimately, more firmly, a thousand times better into the breadth of space, so that, as it were, it will not move if it is jolted. The object is definite, the art object must be even more definite; withdrawn from all chance, removed from all obscurity, lifted out of time and given to space, it has become lasting, capable of eternity. The model *seems*, the art object *is*. Thus the one is an inexpressible advance over the other, the calm and rising realization of the wish to be that emanates from everything in Nature. And by this the error is confounded that would make of art the most arbitrary and most vain of occupations; it is the most humble service and entirely founded on law. But of this error all creators and all arts are full, and a very powerful man had to rise up against it; and it had to be a doer who doesn't talk and who does things unceasingly. His art was from the very beginning realization (and the opposite of music, which transforms the apparent realities of the everyday world and renders them still more unreal as easy, gliding appearance. For which reason too this antithesis of art, this noncondensation, this temptation to flow out has so many friends and listeners and henchmen, so many who are unfree and bound to pleasure, who do not take increase out of themselves and are charmed from the outside . . .). Rodin, born in poverty and low estate, saw better than anyone that all beauty in people and animals and things is endangered by relationships and time, that it is a moment, a youth that comes and goes in all ages, but does not last. What troubled him was just the *semblance* of that which he considered indispensable, necessary, and good: the semblance of beauty. He wanted it to *be*, and he saw his task in fitting things (for things endured) into the less menaced, more peaceful and more eternal world of space; and unconsciously he applied to his work all the laws of adaptation, so that it developed organically and became capable of life. Already very early he tried to make nothing "on the basis of appearance"; there was no stepping back with him, but a perpetual being close to and being bent over what was coming into being. And today this characteristic has become so strong in him that one could almost say the appearance of his things is a matter of indifference to him: so much does he experience their *being*, their reality, their release on all sides from the uncertain, their completedness and goodness, their independence; they do not stand on the earth, they circle about it.

And as his great work arose from handwork, from the almost unintending and humble will to make better and better things, so he stands even today, untouched and free of intent and matter, one of the simplest among his grown-up things. The great thoughts, the lofty significances have come to them like laws consummated in something good, complete; he didn't summon them. He didn't desire them; humbly as a servant he went his way and made a world, a hundred worlds. But each world that lives radiates its heaven outward and flings starry nights far out into eternity. This: that he invented nothing, gives to his work that striking immediacy and purity. The groups of figures, the larger relationships of forms he did not put together in advance while they were still ideas; (for the idea is one thing—and almost nothing—but the realization is another and everything). He promptly made things, many things, and only out of them did he form or let grow up the new unity, and so his relationships have become intimate and logical, because not ideas but things have bound themselves together.—And this work could only come from a worker, and he who has built it can calmly deny inspiration; it doesn't come upon him, because it is *in* him, day and night, occasioned by each looking, a warmth generated by every gesture of his hand. And the more the things about him grew, the rarer were the disturbances that reached him; for all noises broke off against the realities that stood about him. His very work has protected him; he has lived in it as in a wood, and his life must have lasted a long time already, for what he himself planted has become a tall forest. And when one goes about among the things with which he dwells and lives, which he sees again every day and every day completes, then his house and the sounds in it are something unspeakably trivial and incidental, and one sees it only as in a dream, strangely distorted and filled with an assortment of pale memories. His daily life and the people that belong in it lie there like an empty stream-bed through which he no longer flows; but there is nothing sad in that; for near by one hears the great roar and the powerful flow of the stream that would not divide into two arms. . . .

And I believe, Lou, that it must be so. . . . O Lou, in one of my poems that is successful, there is much more reality than in any relationship or affection that I feel; where I create, I am true, and I would like to find the strength to base my life entirely on this truth, on this infinite simplicity and joy that is sometimes given to me. Even when I went to Rodin, I was seeking that; for I had had a presentiment for years of the endless example and model of his work. Now, since I have come from him, I know that I too may ask and seek for no other realizations than those of my work; there my house is, there are the women I need, and the children that will grow up and live a long time. But how shall I begin to go this road—where is the handwork of my art, its deepest and lowest point at which I might begin to be proficient? I shall go back over every path to that beginning, and all that I have done shall be nothing, less than the sweeping of a doorstep to which the next guest brings traces of the road again. I have patience for centuries in me and will live as though my time were very big. I will collect myself out of all distractions, and I will bring back and save up what is mine from too quick applications. But I hear voices that bode well, and steps that are coming nearer, and my doors are opening. . . . And when I seek out people, they do not counsel me and don't know what I mean. And toward books I am just the same (so clumsy), and they do not help me either, as though even they were still too human. . . . Only things speak to me. Rodin's things, the things on the Gothic cathedrals, the things of antiquity—all things that are complete things. They directed me to the models; to the animated, living world, seen simply and without interpretation as the occasion for things. I am beginning to see something new: already flowers are often so infinitely much to me, and excitements of a strange kind have come to me from animals. And already I am sometimes experiencing even people in this way, hands are living somewhere, mouths are speaking, and I look at everything more quietly and with greater justness.

But I still lack the discipline, the being able to work, and the being compelled to work, for which I have longed for years. Do I lack the strength? Is my will sick? Is it the dream in me that hinders all action? Days go by and sometimes I hear life going. And still nothing has happened, still there is nothing real about me; and I divide again and again and flow apart,—and yet would like so much to run in *one* bed and grow big. For, it's true, isn't it, Lou, it ought to be this way: we should be like one stream and not enter canals and lead water to the pastures? It's true, isn't it, that we must hold ourselves together and go surging on? Perhaps when we are very old, sometime, at the very end, we may give in, spread ourselves out and flow into a delta. . . . *Dear* Lou!

[*51*]

To Lou Andreas-Salomé   Oberneuland bei Bremen
                                            August 10, 1903

To learn that my little Rodin book means a lot to you, Lou, was an unspeakable joy to me. Nothing could fill me so with certainty and with hope as this yea-saying of yours to the most full-grown of my works. Now for the first time it *stands* for me, now for the first time it is completed, acknowledged by reality, upright and good.

And what your letter contained besides of elucidation illumined me infinitely helpfully and brightly with quiet light; my letter of Saturday (which you have surely received) attempted to find similar ways and to trace the event Rodin was for me. He is one of the most important, a sign high above the times, an uncommon example, a miracle visible far and wide—and yet nothing but an unspeakably lonely old man, lonely in a great old age. See, he has lost nothing, he has collected and gathered about him for a great life long; he has left nothing in uncertainty and has given reality to everything; out of the flight of a frightened feeling, out of a dream's fragments, out of the beginning of a presentiment even, he has made things and has placed them about him, things and things; so a reality grew around him, a wide calm relationship of things that linked him with other and older things, until he himself seemed to stem from a dynasty of great things; his quiet and his patience comes from thence, his fearless, enduring age, his superiority over people who are much too mobile, too vacillating, playing too much with the equilibriums in which, almost unconsciously, he rests.

You are so wonderfully right, Lou: I suffered from the too great example which my art offered no means of following directly; the impossibility of fashioning things physically became pain in my own body, and even that fearfulness (whose substance was the close proximity of something too hard, too stony, too big) arose from the impossibility of uniting two worlds of art: the way you feel it and clarify it with your great knowledge of the human: you prophetess . . .

But just because you have helped me with this lighting up, with this indescribably helpful, pertinent understanding, it is becoming apparent to me that I must follow him, Rodin: not in a sculptural reshaping of my creative work, but in the inner disposition of the artistic process; I must learn from him not how to fashion but deep composure for the sake of the fashioning. I must learn to work, to work, Lou, I am so lacking in that! Il faut toujours travailler—toujours—he said to me once, when I spoke to him of the frightening abysses that open up between my good days; he could hardly understand it any longer; he, who has become all work (so much so that his gestures are homely movements taken from manual work!).—Perhaps it is only a kind of clumsiness that hinders me from working, that is, from accumulating from all that happens; for I am equally perplexed when it comes to taking what is mine from books or from contacts; I scarcely recognize it: external circumstances disguise and conceal it from me, and I no longer know how to separate the important from the superfluous and am bewildered and intimidated by all there is. For weeks I sat in Paris in the Bibliothèque Nationale and read books I had long wished for; but the notes I made then help me to nothing; for while I read, everything seemed extraordinarily new and important to me, and I was strongly tempted to copy out the whole book since I couldn't take it with me; inexperienced with books, I go about in them like a country boy, in continual, stupid admiration and come out confused, laden with the most superfluous objects. And I am similarly clumsy about events that come and go, without the gift of selection, without the calmness for reception, a mirror turned this way and that, out of which all images fall . . . that is why it is so frightfully necessary for me to find the tool of my art, the hammer, my hammer, so that it may become master and may grow above all noises. There must be a handwork beneath this art too; a loyal, daily work that makes use of everything must after all be possible here too! Oh that I had workdays, Lou, that my most secret heart chamber were a workroom and cell and refuge for me; that all this monkishness in me might become cloister-building for the sake of my work and reverence. That I might lose nothing more and might set up everything about me according to kinship and importance. That I might rise again, Lou! For I am scattered like some dead man in an old grave. . . .

Somehow I too must manage to make things; written, not plastic things,—realities that proceed from handwork. Somehow I too must discover the smallest basic element, the cell of *my* art, the tangible medium of presentation for everything, irrespective of subject matter: then the clear strong consciousness of the tremendous work that lay before me would coerce and bend me to it: then I would have so infinitely much to do that one work-day would resemble another, and I would have work that would always be successful because it would begin with the attainable and small and yet from the beginning would be in the great. Then everything would suddenly be distant, disturbance and voices, and even what is hostile would fit in with the work as sounds pass into a dream, gently guiding it to the unexpected. The subject matter would lose still more of its importance and weight and would be nothing but pretext; but just this apparent indifference to it would make me capable of shaping all subject matter, to find and to form pretexts for everything with the right and disinterested means.

Does the handwork lie perhaps in the language itself, in a better recognition of its inner life and will, its development and past? (The big Grimm dictionary, which I once saw in Paris, put me on to this possibility.) Does it lie in some specific study, in the more exact knowledge of a matter? (For many this is certainly so without their knowing it, and the subject is the daily task, the handwork for them.) Or does it lie in a certain well-inherited and well-increased culture? (Hofmannsthal would speak for that. . . .) But with me it is different; toward everything inherited I have to be hostile, and what I have acquired is so slight; I am almost without culture. My continually renewed attempts to begin a definite course of study broke down pitifully; for exterior reasons, and because of the strange feeling that always surprised me during it: as if I were having to come back from an inborn knowledge by a wearisome road that again led to it by many windings. Perhaps the sciences at which I tried my hand were too abstract, and perhaps new things will come out of others? . . . But I lack books for all that and guides for the books.—But my *knowing* so little often distresses me; perhaps only my knowing so little of flowers and of animals and of simple procedures. . . .

[52]

To Lou Andreas-Salomé   Oberneuland bei Bremen
                                          August 11, 1903 (Tuesday)

. . . Even I do not want to tear art and life apart; I know that
sometime and somewhere they have the same meaning. But I am
a clumsy fellow at life, and that is why, as it closes in about me,
it is so often a stopping place for me, a delay that makes me lose
a great deal; rather as in a dream sometimes when one cannot
finish dressing and on account of two obstinate shoe buttons
misses something important that will never come again. And it is
indeed true, too, that life goes by and really doesn't grant time for
experiences missed and for many losses; especially for one who
wants to have an art. For art is far too great and too difficult and
too long a thing for one life, and those who are of a very great
age are only just beginners in it. "C'est à l'âge de soixante-treize
ans que j'ai compris à peu près la forme et la nature vraie des
oiseaux, des poissons et des plantes," wrote Hokusai, and Rodin
feels the same way, and one can also think of Leonardo who grew
very old. And they always lived in their art and, concentrated on
the one thing, let all the rest become overgrown. But how then
is a man not to become anxious who only rarely comes into
his sanctuary because outside in refractory life he gets caught in
every snare and bumps himself stupid against all obstacles. That
is why I want so ardently and so impatiently to find work, the
workday, because life, if only it has first become work, can become art. I know that I cannot cut my life out of the destinies
with which it has become intertwined; but I must find the strength
to lift it up wholly, as it is, with everything, into a peace, into a
solitude, into the stillness of deep workdays: only there will
everything find me that you have prophesied for me, and you too,
Lou, will be looking for me there. Be indulgent with me if I keep
you waiting; you have gone like a wise man, but I move as animals move when the closed season is over.

[53]

To Lou Andreas-Salomé   Oberneuland bei Bremen
                                           August 15, 1903

Dear Lou, behind the park that surrounds this house the fast
Hamburg trains go by, and their noise is great and drowns out all
the wind in the trees; and it becomes daily more meaningful, for
already the leaves are falling from the little bit of peace that has
surrounded us, and one can see through to the impending journey, and feels approaching, mingled with hardships to come, the
promises of distant cities and the spirit of remote regions, the
New. Next Friday perhaps, or Saturday, we start on our journey;
the first stop is Marienbad (where a meeting with my father has
been agreed upon), and then we stop in Munich to admire a
great picture of a friend we made in Paris. It is the family of a
bullfighter which Ignacio Zuloaga has painted, and the Spanish
painter as a person too impressed us as so big and simple that
we look forward to seeing this picture, into which he put much
of himself, as eagerly as to a reunion. In Venice also (which
means the next pause in our journey) we shall see pictures of his;
perhaps as the only reality in that dreamlike city whose existence is like a reflection. Then, after a short stay, we travel toward
Florence, toward the bright and lovely country that called forth
so much adoration, praise, and joy. Even there we shall be given
only a few days' respite, for: Rome is imminent, the great, summoning Rome that is still only a name to us, but soon to be a thing
made of a hundred things, a great shattered vessel out of which
much past has trickled into the ground, Rome the ruin we want to
build up again. Not the way she may once have been, but as
seekers of the inner future in that past in which was included much
of the eternal. As descendants of those solitary things, lost out
of their time, about which science errs when it burdens them with
names and periods, to which admiration does injustice when it
sees in them a specific and describable beauty; for they held their
faces into the earth and shed all name and meaning; and when
they were found, they rose up, light, over the earth and became

almost as the birds, so very much beings of space and standing like stars above inconstant time. Therein, I believe, lies the incomparable value of these rediscovered things, that one can look at them so entirely as things unknown; one does not know their intention, and no subject matter attaches itself to them (at least for the unscientific), no unessential voice breaks the stillness of their concentrated existence, and their permanence is without retrospect and fear. The masters from whom they derive are nothing, no misunderstood fame colors their forms which are pure, no history overshadows their naked clarity—: they are. And that is all. That is how I imagine the art of antiquity. That little tiger at Rodin's is like that, and the many fragments and broken pieces in the museums (that one carelessly passes by for a long time, until someday one reveals itself, shows itself, shines like a first star beside which suddenly, when one notices it, hundreds arrive, breathless, from out of the depths of the sky—) are like that, and so is the very great Nike, standing on its driving ship-fragment in the Louvre like a sail full of joyful winds,— and much that seems trivial to one who is still mistaken in looking for sculpture in the subject matter, in the pretext, lives in this lofty perfection among men, broken off and sketchy as they are. Of like greatness are of course the Gothic things which, although they stand much nearer in time, are just as remote, just as anonymous, just as independent in their solitude, without origin, like the things in Nature. These, and what came from Rodin's hands, led us to the most distant works of art, to the pre-Greek, in whose nature lies a sculptured ruthlessness, a thing-likeness, heavy as lead, mountainlike and hard. Relationships were uncovered which no one at all had yet felt, connections formed and closed the streams that go through the ages, and the history of endless generations of things could be divined beneath human history, like a stratum of slower and more peaceful developments that come about more deeply, more intimately, and more unconfusedly. Into this history, Lou, the Russian will perhaps fit sometime, who, as one becoming and enduring, is descended from things and related to them, the way Rodin is as a creator, related by blood. The biding quality in the character of the Russian (which the German's self-important busyness with the unimportant calls indolence—) would thus receive a new and sure enlightenment: perhaps the Russian was made to let the history of mankind pass by in order later to chime into the harmony of things with his singing heart. He has only to endure, to hold out and like the violinist, to whom no signal has yet been given, to sit in the orchestra, carefully holding his instrument so that nothing may happen to it. . . . More and more, and filled with a deeper and deeper sympathy, I bear within me my affection for this wide, holy land; as a new ground for solitude, and as a high hindrance against others . . .—: I always fall right away with the whole burden of my love to the very bottom of the sea and frighten people, as with a too quick (almost awkward) confidence, when I begin at once to tell of what is deepest and most secret; toward people that is a mistake, a rudeness almost, which astonishes them, and in me it is a lack, a mania, that makes real (that is, fruitful and useful) association with people impossible; for me it is difficult to the point of unbearableness to believe that a conversation that begins somewhere in the insignificant can end in the important; some accident will certainly intervene or a diversion or a misunderstanding unimportant in itself, on which further continuance of course breaks off: that is why everything in me continually plunges toward the final, ultimate, most important, and my interlocutor of the moment no longer attempts to keep step with me at all; superior to my impoliteness, he remains behind, and when I look around breathless at the end of my course, I see him far off, very small, but smiling in a friendly way and wholly occupied with acting as if nothing had happened. . . .

But it is not from any wisdom in me that this economy of the important springs. It is a defect in my nature to forget all roads that lead anywhere, yes, even all arrivings, up to whatever is the latest arriving, of which alone I am then able to speak. Does that happen perhaps because I fly to so many destinations or reach them walking blindfold, so that with its end I am not likewise given the way? Or is it simply a negligence of my memory, which retains only the results, letting slip the advancing steps of calculation from which they flow? From this defective tendency comes my continual poverty, my possessions, so slight in proportion to the daily intake, the emptiness and inactivity of many days; for since I carry nothing in me but some last-acquired product, while the calculation itself, in which this again becomes a factor, goes on illegibly in me,—waiting period after waiting period occurs from one result to another. And also, that so often I seem to open disproportionately wide to people who are more or less strangers is not alone a weakness of the spiritual closing muscles, as I long thought; there is only *one thing* in me, and I must either stay locked up (that is, be silent or prattle—) or else open myself, whereupon my sole inhabitant becomes visible. This inner constitution of mine, which is faulty, really shuts me off from all association, since in this form it leads only to disparities and misunderstanding and pushes me into unwanted relationships in which I suffer and from which many a dangerous repercussion can come. It is characteristic that I have acquired all my "friends" in this dishonest way, for which reason also I possess them only badly and without a good conscience. Only thus is it possible (as for example in the pre-Worpswede period three years ago) that I should have acquired a whole crowd of friends who could give nothing in return for my continual expenditure, and that no one can respond to me anyway, because I give ruthlessly and brutally, without regard to others, unloading at this place and that, instead of offering, of showing and bestowing with fine selection from an ordered store. In these past years I have been coming to a better and better insight into my illnesses, even into this one; and I now touch people with greater caution and intend, for my part, each time to be the one to wait, wherever possible the one to respond and not the one to take the initiative. On this new foundation a few relationships have been formed in which I can more honorably rejoice than in the earlier ones; on it is based a correspondence with Ellen Key (who wants to help me in a practical way), a cordial association with Gerhart

Hauptmann which has brought me beautiful letters from the heart of his creative activity, the contact with Zuloaga and the great acquisition of Rodin; in both the latter cases I feel it especially good that no too-impetuous and too-blind opening up on my side can have been the cause of one disappointment after another; for the language stood in the way of that. In both cases only a rather laborious understanding through French was possible, yes, even my books (to which I would so gladly have entrusted it) were deprived of the chance to speak for me and about me;— and that in spite of all resistance, inherent in the circumstances, quiet relationships with these solitary people grew up, relationships which perhaps need not be put to work at all because they rest on an already conclusive knowledge of a few great common experiences, gives me somewhat more confidence with people. But a tendency like mine is a danger, especially when it is accompanied by a practical clumsiness toward others and by the intimidating feeling of being among a lot of people who are superior at life; such tendencies aren't easily overthrown, and the highest one can achieve is to use them more generously and more diffidently, to apply them more maturely and with more experience. Even in the innermost processes of my creative activity there are traces of this tendency; in the extremely unscientific developments which every subject matter and every provocation to work experiences in me anyway, whenever the synthesis, the thing that is last and most remote appears as the point of departure, going backward from which I must invent precedents and paths, utterly uncertain of their course and initiated only into the goal, into the ultimate, final summation and apotheosis.

And this ignorance of the way, this being sure only in the most extreme and most remote, makes all going so difficult for me and scatters over me all the sadness of those who have got lost, even while I am in the process of finding myself. That Russia is my home is one of the great and mysterious certainties out of which I live,—but my attempts to go there, through journeys, through books, through people are as nothing and are more a putting to use than a getting closer. My efforts are like the crawling of a snail and yet there are moments when the unutterably distant goal is reflected in me as in a near-by mirror. I live and learn in so much distraction that I often cannot see at all to what purpose it will all sometime have been. In Paris I didn't get appreciably nearer to Russia, and yet somehow I think that even now in Rome, in the presence of antique things, I'll be preparing for things Russian and for returning thither. If I didn't know that all developments pursue circular paths, I should become anxious, knowing myself again sent out into the temptation of a foreign land that calls, that will speak to me of its own in an intoxicating language. More than once already Italian life has enraptured me and misled me into ascents from which I painfully fell; but for that reason it is perhaps good that this young artist will be beside me now, this woman who neither as a creator nor for the sake of life has ever longed for this southern land, because her northern feeling mistrusted the too open quality of its radiant splendor and her receptivity, already overladen with the taciturn accent of the serious moors, had no need of more loquacious persuasion. Now, at a mature point in her art, she is attempting this journey on Rodin's advice, after acquaintance with antique remains in Paris has inspired her with a certain need to see Italy, not Italy as it presses about any particular idler or an art student indiscriminately abandoned to all impressions, but Italy as it is about one quietly trying to carry on his work there, in order to raise his eyes in the pauses to the new that surrounds him. In these pauses we shall see many things together; but I, in any case, shall first learn to live entirely for looking and for the receiving of many things; for in Rome (where Clara Rilke will work the entire winter) I want to hold out only a little while and, before I feel the pressure of the city, to find a lonely little place (perhaps by the sea) which has both a gentle winter and an early spring. If only the days would come there, Lou, in which I would learn to work deeply and collectedly; if only I might find a high room, a terrace, an avenue in which no one walks, and nights without a neighbor; and if the worry about the everyday would vouchsafe me only for a little while this life for which I cry out,—then I will never again permit a complaint to escape me, whatever may come later.

Out of this stillness, if it is given to me, I will sometimes raise myself to you, as to the saint of that far-off home that I cannot reach, deeply moved that you, bright star that you are, stand right over the place where I am darkest and most fearful.

[54]

To Lou Andreas-Salomé   Via del Campidoglio, Rome
                                           November 3, 1903

Do you still remember Rome, dear Lou? How is it in your memory? In mine sometime there will be only its waters, those clear, exquisite, animated waters that live in its squares; its steps, built on the pattern of falling water, so strangely thrusting stair out of stair like wave out of wave; its gardens' festiveness and the splendor of great terraces; its nights that last so long, still and filled to overflowing with great constellations.

Of the past that laboriously holds itself erect, I shall perhaps know nothing more; nothing of its museums full of meaningless statues, and little of its pictures; the bronze statue of Marcus Aurelius on the Capitol square I shall remember, a beautiful marble thing in the Ludovisi Museum (the throne of Aphrodite), a pillar in some little, forgotten church, some quite unknown things, a view out over the poor Campagna, a lovely walk toward evening and much sadness in which I was living.

In which I am living.

For I am dissatisfied with myself, because I am without daily work, tired, although not sick, but in anxiety. When, Lou, when will this miserable life begin to be effective, when will it grow out over inability, inertia, and opacity to the simple, reverent joyousness for which it longs? Is it growing at all? I scarcely dare ask about my advancing steps, because I am afraid (like that man in Tolstóy) to find that their tracks run in a circle, keep coming back to that notorious disconsolate spot from which I have already so often started out.

From which even now I want to start out again, under unspeakable effort and with only a little courage.

So begins the Roman winter. I shall try to see much, want to go to the libraries and read; and then, when it begins to grow a little lighter in me, I want to be much at home and to collect myself around the best that I have not yet lost. For my time and my strength, as things stand with me, can have but one task, but this one: to find the road on which I shall come to quiet, daily work in which I can dwell with more security and stability than in this uncertain sickly world that is collapsing behind me and before me does not exist. The question whether I shall find such a road is not new—but the years are passing, and it has become urgent, and I must be able to answer. . . . You do know too from my Oberneuland letters how things stand. They are not good.

From the middle of November on, I have a very quiet place to live: the last, furthermost house deep in a big old garden of Porta del Popolo, beside the Villa Borghese; built as a summerhouse, it contains just one single simple high-windowed room, and from its flat roof one looks out over the garden to countryside and mountains. There I will try to arrange my life on the pattern of my Schmargendorf Woodpeace days; to be as quiet, as patient, as turned away from everything external, as in that good, expectant, joyous time: so that they may become days of garden-peace. . . .

But now I am utterly without books and being so clumsy in dealing with libraries, I cannot easily get on; so I come asking you for something: Can you recall a modern, scientifically good German translation of the Bible of which you once spoke, and if possible, give me the name of the translator and publisher so that I can try to get the book here? And if I am not asking too much of you: perhaps give me the name of some new book or other that you have read: it might help me very much now.

But above all I need a letter from you, Lou.

I have thought of you so much during the journey and here and with many wishes have wanted you to return healthy from the mountains. For of all my thoughts that of you is the only one in which I find repose, and sometimes I lie in it wholly and sleep in it and get up out of it. . . .

Now it is autumn with you, and you walk in the wood, in the big wood into which one can already see so far, in the wind that is transforming the world. I think of the little pool, to the left of the Dahlem road, that always grew very big and lonely about this time. I think of the evenings after which comes the stormy night, taking all that is withered from the trees, and think of the storm itself, of the night flying past the stars into the morning. Into the empty, new, clear, stormed-out morning. . . . But here nothing alters; only a few trees are changing, as if they were coming into yellowish blossom. And the laurel stays.

[55]

To Arthur Holitscher 5 via del Campidoglio, Rome
November 5, 1903

. . . We have been in Tre Fontane, we have stood before the Tartarughe Fountain and seen in the churches the beautiful mosaics you love. To us too the Borghese Gardens were a familiar place of refuge even in the first days—and we had need of a retreat, as the museums especially, with their many wretched statues, made us desolate, so to speak tore hope and home from our bodies. Perhaps that will change, but I have the feeling now that the Romans had very excellent painting but quite second-rate, decorative, superficial sculpture; that the Greeks were great sculptors I learned in the Louvre and from Rodin,—not here; apart from the throne of Aphrodite and a few little fragments, there seems to me to be nothing more here that speaks of them, and what a lack of paintings of the good period there is here, where everything is full of Renis and Guercinos. . . .

But the sadness that arises from the fact that Rome is, for the most part, a bad museum you felt too and predicted to me; naturally there still remains enough to live on here; the fountains alone in all the squares, those bright, youthful fountains, and the steps that are so wonderfully built, as if on the pattern of waters.

The ascent to the Capitol (when, in motion like one riding, the beautiful, simple bronze statue of Marcus Aurelius mounts, from step to step, from stair to stair) is among my favorites here; I make it every day, for I am still living now in the Via del Campidoglio, in the last house on the little terrace that faces the Forum. Only until the middle of this month; then I shall move into a little house, the last and most remote in the great wild garden of the Villa Strohl-Fern (where for several weeks already my wife too has had her studio and apartment). I don't know whether you know this garden? Perhaps. Very deep within it behind high laurel bushes, there lies a little red building on the arch of a bridge that spans the main path of the garden, before it drops steeply for the descent (to Villa di Papa Giulio). Built years ago as a summerhouse, it contains a single simple high-windowed room and has a flat roof from which one can see Roman landscape far and wide. There I shall live, and I rejoice at the prospect of such great and remote solitude deep in the wide park. It is a kind Providence that permitted me to discover this room, and I think I shall rejoice in it, in the evenings that can pass there, in the great open nights with the noise of animals moving, fruits falling, winds stirring. . . . The most important thing for me will be as soon as possible to get to some kind of work there whose regular, daily return I must simply force in case it won't establish itself of its own accord. I will then get into the city relatively seldom, will be out there often for days, and will myself prepare my little meals in my hermitage and be all alone with my hands.

Thus I will try to build a winter for myself. . . .

[56]

To Ellen Key   Villa Strohl-Fern, Rome
                                  December 22, 1903

After many long rainy days with heavy, falling skies, a kind of spring is beginning here; fragrance comes from the bushes, and the laurel trees, warmed by noonday, smell of first summer days. There are shrubs from which the long catkins are hanging, and other shrubs that will blossom tomorrow, if the night is as gentle as these last nights that have passed slowly and mildly in the waxing moon. And yet Christmas is near; so people say at least, and if one happens of an evening into the too bright streets of the city, the crowd is big, and the display windows glitter. But here in the big garden in which we live, it will not be Christmas; a day will come, bright and shining, and will pass, and there will be a spring evening—an evening with distant, darkening skies out of which all the stars break suddenly, all the many stars that live over southern gardens.

But for us this evening will be only a quiet hour, nothing more; we shall sit in the remote little gardenhouse and think of those who are having Christmas; of our dear little Ruth and of ourselves, as if somewhere we were still the children we once were, —the waiting, joy-frightened Christmas children, whom great surprises approach like angels from within and without; like children who feared and loved the darkness of those evenings that preceded the one evening; who felt how small, in those December days that prepared the festival, was the circle of lamplight and how more and more mysteriously the room round about was lost, so that one couldn't say at all where its walls were, and whether one were not sitting at a round table in the middle of the woods. . . . Until all the dark was changed into radiance, so that one could see even the least things shining.

But for all this to happen, there must have been great winds; one must have lived through long nights in which the storm was everything—nights and days that were veiled, half-lit and faint, like a delaying of the morning merely until early evening, everything, even to that great, still snowfall that fell and fell and caused the world to move more gently, the day to pass more noiselessly, and night to come more secretly— . . .

[57]

To Lou Andreas-Salomé

Lou, dear Lou, I am writing the date of your last letter over mine,—only because I want to know that nothing you have written has been lost; the Italian postal service continually and in every possible way lends support to such distrust.

Now, dear Lou, I am in my little gardenhouse, and after much unrest it is the first quiet hour in it; now everything in the simple room has its place, dwells and lives and lets day and night befall it; and outside, where there was so much rain, is a spring afternoon, are the hours of some spring that tomorrow perhaps will no longer be, but that now seems to come from eternity: so very poised is the light slender wind whose motion the leaves follow, the laurel's shiny leaves and the modest leaf-bundles on the scrub-oak bushes, so confident are the little reddish buds on the scarcely emptied trees, and so great is the fragrance that arises from the light grey-green narcissus field in my quiet garden valley that the arch of an old bridge meditatively spans. I have swept the heavy dregs of the rain from my flat roof and cleared withered oak leaves off to one side and that has made me warm, and now, after the little real work, my blood is ringing as in a tree. And for the very first time in a long while I feel just a tiny bit free and festive and as if you might walk into my home. . . . This happy feeling too will pass again, and who knows whether, behind the distant mountains, a rainy night is not in preparation that will again flood over my roof, and a wrenching wind that will again fill my ways with clouds.—

But that this hour may not pass without my having written you I do feel; for the few moments when I can write to you, when I am peaceful, clear, and lonely enough to draw near you, I may not lose, because I have much, much to say. In Paris, at Durand-Ruel, once in the spring of last year, antique paintings were exhibited, murals from a villa near Boscoreale being shown once again in their fragmentary, interrupted continuity before the hazard of auction tore them quite apart; they were the first antique pictures I had seen, and I have seen no more beautiful ones here, and they say that even the museum of Naples has no better paintings of that almost completely vanished time which must have had such great painters. Of these picture fragments one was preserved whole and undisturbed, although it was the biggest and perhaps the most sensitive; in this a woman was portrayed quietly sitting with serious, calm countenance, listening to a man who was speaking softly and lost in thought, speaking to himself and to her with that dark voice in which destinies that have been are reflected like shores at dusk; this man, if I remember rightly, had laid his hands on a staff, folded them on the staff, with which he had long walked through distant lands; they were resting while he spoke (as dogs lie down to sleep when their master begins his tale and they see that it will last a long time—); but although this man was already deep in his tale, probably had a great stretch of memory before him still (level memory in which, however, the path often turned unexpectedly), yet one knew even at first glance that he was the one who had come, the traveler to this quiet, stately woman, the stranger to this tall, home-filled woman: so much was the quality of coming still in him, as it is in a wave upon the beach, still, even when it is already withdrawing, flat, shining like bright glass; the haste from which even a riper wanderer is not quite free had not yet fallen entirely from him; his feeling was still focused upon the unexpected and changing, and the blood was still *going* in his feet which, more excited than his hands, couldn't go to sleep. Thus were rest and movement juxtaposed in this picture, not as contrast, rather as an allegory, as a final unity that was slowly closing like a healing wound; for even the movement was already rest, laying itself down as quietly falling snow lies down, becoming landscape, as snow does when it spreads itself over the shapes of distance, and now the past, as it returned, took on the aspect of the eternal, resembling those events that comprised and transfigured the life of the woman.

I shall always know the way in which that great simple picture gripped me, that picture which was so very much painting because it contained only two figures, and was so significant because those two figures were filled with themselves, heavy with themselves, and joined together by an unparalleled necessity. As the content of traditional legends is self-evident in good pictures, so I understood the meaning of this picture at the first moment. In that so thoroughly confused Paris time, when every painful and difficult impression fell into my soul as from a great height, the meeting with that beautiful picture acquired its decisive accent; as if, beyond all that was impending, I had been permitted to look at something final, thus did the sight of it affect me and uphold me. Then the courage to write you, dear Lou, came into being; for it seemed to me as if every path, even the most confused, could acquire sense through such a final return to a woman, to the one woman dwelling in maturity and quiet, who is big and, like a summer night, knows how to hear everything: the little noises frightened of themselves and calls and bells. . . .

But I, Lou, your somehow lost son, for a long, long time to come I can be no teller of tales, no soothsayer of my way, no describer of my past fortunes; what you hear is only the sound of my step, still going on, still on undefined ways retreating, I do not know from what, and whether it is drawing near to anyone I do not know. Only that my mouth, when it has become a great river, may sometime flow into you, into your hearing and into the stillness of your opened depths—that is my prayer, which I say to every hour that is powerful, to every anxiety, longing, or joy that can guard and grant anything. If my life is insignificant even now and often and often seems to me like an untilled field on which the weed is master and the birds of chance that search fastidiously through its untended seed,—it will *be* only when I can tell it to you, and will be as you hear it!

[58]

To Lou Andreas-Salomé
Villa Strohl-Fern, Rome
March 17, 1904

. . . I cannot help wondering every day whether the Russian war has not brought terror and danger to your family: your nephews, your mother, and you. That this evil had to come, this burden, this suffering for thousands who all feel war the way Garshin felt it: as calamity inflicted.

God, had I strength, strength-savings—were I not living, as I am, meagerly and fearfully enough even in this quiet, remote life, on the daily bread of strength,—had I become something real (a doctor, which fundamentally I should have been—), nowhere but in those dressing stations where Russians are grievously and terribly dying would be the place and the calling now for one who might use and bow himself. . . .

[59]

To Lou Andreas-Salomé
Villa Strohl-Fern, Rome
Last day of March, 1904

Christos voskres! . . .

Ivanov and Gogol once wrote those words from here, and many are still writing them now from here into their eastern homeland. But alas, this is no Easter city and no country that knows how to lie beneath great bells. It is all display without reverence, festival performance without festival.

For me it was Easter just once; that was the time in that long, extraordinary, uncommon, excited night when people were all milling about, and when Ivan Veliky struck me in the darkness, stroke after stroke. That was my Easter, and I believe it will suffice for a whole life; the message was given to me writ strangely large in those Moscow nights, given into my blood and into my heart. I know it now:

Christos voskres!

Yesterday they sang Palestrina in Saint Peter's. But it was nothing. Everything dwindles away in that haughtily big, empty house that is like a hollow chrysalis out of which a dark giant butterfly has crept. But today for many hours, I was in a little Greek church; a patriarch was there in a great robe, and through the imperial door of the iconostas in a long file they brought him his ornaments: his great crown, his staff of ivory, gold and mother-of-pearl, a vessel with holy wafers and a golden chalice. And he accepted everything and kissed the bearers, and they were all old men who brought him those things. And later one saw them, those old men with their golden mantles and their beards, standing in the holy of holies about the great, simple, stone table reading for a long time. And outside, before the wall of pictures stood to right and left, facing one another, young convent pupils singing to each other with heads uplifted and throats stretched, like black-birds on spring nights.

Then, dear Lou, I said Christos voskres to you.

And then right afterward, when I came home, your card was there on which it was written. I thank you.

And for the letter I thank you and for the dear picture. Much more was fulfilled by them than the one request; past things that were lost, and things to come that could not come, hold on to them and climb up by them, dear Lou.

The war—our war—is almost like a physical unrest in me—but I read little about it because I am quite unused to newspapers and they are abhorrent to me and because they do distort every-thing. In the *Zeit* (daily sheet of the *Zeit*) there was a few days ago the letter of a Russian officer which I am enclosing; of course they didn't even have the tact to print this simple, tremulous piece of news without an annoying introduction. Once I read too that the war would probably last for years; Kuropatkin was supposed to have said so; but that cannot really be possible! . . .

It is good that you are in your house with the flowers that want to come; you are so near to your family too, and are after all at home and having the spring of the winter that you have lived. But your having been ill . . . ?

Be well, dear Lou,—for yourself and for those who need you.

[60]

To Ellen Key   Villa Strohl-Fern, Rome
                                          Easter Saturday, 1904 [April 2]

I am answering all in one your good letter to Clara Rilke and
the list of questions; I would like to have done it even earlier,
two days ago, but the changeable warm-cold beginning of spring
has, despite all precautions, again brought health disturbances, a
cold and pains, so that I couldn't write.

First, of the fact that to both of us, to Frau Clara and to me,
your dear letter was a great joy; it was in every respect full of the
way you are always and always so sweet and kind in thinking of
us—did us good with every word.

You were sweet, so sweet to have had that thought about little
Ruth, my dear friend. We have pondered much over it and
spoken about it, and although we have finally had to see that the
carrying out of such a plan would be impossible for us and for
our feeling . . . still it was a joy to feel that you and your help
are always near and alert! *Thank* you!

It would be impossible, for one thing, on account of our now
being able to use *only* space, peace, and work and not being far
enough along even for a joy, not yet. But also on the little girl's
account this daring change would not be possible. In the end
it is really above all a question of her, of Ruth, of the growth of
her little life being as untransplanted and quiet as possible, and
not of us, of our joy in her. And we feel that in her present home
in the quiet country house and the big garden she has *everything*
that she needs and that we would give her if we could. There she
has the healthful and vegetarian way of life that suits her well;
as circumstances have now shaped themselves she has, over and
above the most necessary, the precious abundance of quiet country life, summer and winter, has my wife's little fourteen-year-
old brother for friend and playmate, and lastly is not in the
strangest of hands with my mother-in-law (a sensible and energetic woman who loves her above everything). We believe too
that her little existence has already struck root in this ground and

in the people who are about her, that one may not transplant her, not for the sake of bringing her into more uncertain circumstances and to strangers. If Ruth were here, she would also have to be entirely with us,—and since that is impossible for both parties, we must believe in that distant time when that will somehow happen of itself which would now seem premature and imprudent because, while it would indeed be the fulfillment of our wish and our longing, it would not correspond to our reality and to the necessary things that must now be done.

We may now think *only* of work, not of other things, not of joy. Work itself must be the way that sometime will quietly and naturally bring the three of us together again, through it everything must happen, little by little and in long patience. For the present the knowledge that our dear little girl has everything her life needs for its best growth must make us happy and peaceful, and so it does to a certain degree. . . . That is the way we think and feel, dear Ellen Key, about all this, and you will understand how we have to live it and carry it through.—But we thank you from our hearts for the care and love of your thought, which does us good even by itself, through its mere effect. . . .

Now I will answer the question list:

I first read Jacobsen in 1896–97 in Munich. I was very immature then and read sensing rather than observing, first *Niels Lyhne*, later *Maria Grubbe*. Since then these books, to which were added in 1898 the "six short stories" and the letters, have been influential in all my developments; and even today my experience with them is that, wherever I may be standing, always, every time I want to go on, I find the next, the next higher, the approaching stage of my growth sketched out and already created in them. In these books much of what the best people are seeking even today is already found, derived from one life, at least. Jacobsen and Rodin, to me they are the two inexhaustible ones, the masters. Those who can do what I would sometime like to be able to do. Both have that penetrating, devoted observation of Nature, both the power to transform what they have seen into reality enhanced a thousandfold. Both have made things, things

with many sure boundaries and countless intersections and profiles: that is how I feel their art and their influence. . . .

Immortality? I believe that nothing *that is real can pass away*.
But I believe that many people are not *real*. Many people and
many things. But that is hard to say, and I would like to avoid
stating that I share this or that opinion, because in every such
finished view something conclusive lies,—whereas I nowhere feel
myself concluded and finished, am rather nothing but change.
I would like sometime to have an expression *of my very own* for
all that and, as long as I cannot yet find it, to attach myself to no
opinion but simply to be silent and say: I do not know.

Similar is the answer with regard to the black monk in the
"White Princess." I meant nothing definite by him,—I just
wanted to make a black monk in the landscape, against the sea;
I believe that the best figures are those which come into being
for their creator without ulterior motive, simply as figures. The
interpretation always rests with the reader and must be free and
unlimited by any preconceived name; with Rodin's figures, for
example, it is always so. He says: I make men and women, and
that is how it must be. One must, I believe, make men and women
without bothering about what they mean; the more meanings
there is room for in them, the broader and more real they are.
. . . I cannot say *more;* I felt that I had to have a figure for
something inexpressible,—for the stage needs a figure where
otherwise perhaps words, verses, pauses might be—: the figure
came and was the black monk, because once years ago in Viareggio I had been deeply affected by the appearance of a begging
black monk. I was standing at the window, and when he stepped
into the garden, with his back toward the sea, a singular fear
came over me; it seemed to me that I must not move because,
having noticed me, he would interpret any movement as a beck-
oning, as a call, and would come—. . . .

It is not impossible that among the women of my house were
also some of Slavic blood; though not in recent times. Since the
family settled in Bohemia, it was emphatically German in consequence of the situation there which compels a clear distinc-

tion. But in earlier days at any rate (I still don't know enough about it) a number of alliances may very well have taken place through marriage with families of Bohemian stock. Much in me speaks for it. The Czechs, it is true, are not close to me, nor are the Poles (the union of Slavdom with the Catholic element has for me something intolerable in it—). But you do know what Russia is to me; what an event it was, finding it! And when I first came to Moscow everything there was known and long familiar; around Easter it was. And it touched me like *my* Easter, my spring, my bells. It was the city of my oldest and deepest memories, it was a continual meeting again and greeting: it was home. . . .

All, all kind things to you on your kind journey, dear friend. Tell people that I need patience and forbearance, but that I am all longing to do something good and important, something in the deepest sense necessary! . . .

[*61*]

To Lou Andreas-Salomé   Villa Strohl-Fern, Rome
                                        April 15, 1904

When—as sometimes happens—you are in a dream of mine, then that dream and its afterring on the following day are more real than all daily reality, are world and happening. I am thinking about it because the night before the eleventh and that day (the same on which you wrote your card) passed thus: in your presence which makes me peaceful, patient, and good.

There has been a lot of disturbance lately, and I had a presentiment too that disturbance after disturbance would come when I began my new work on the eighth of February; it became apparent then that my mode of working (as well as my much more receptive observation) had altered, so that I shall probably never again manage to write a book in ten days (or evenings), shall rather need for each a long and uncounted time; that is good, it is an advance toward the always-working that I want to achieve at any price; perhaps a first preliminary step in it. But in this change lies also a new danger; to hold off all external disturbances for eight or ten days is possible—: but for weeks, for months? This fear oppressed me, and perhaps that in itself was primarily to blame for my work faltering and early in March breaking off. And what I took for a little disconnection and pause has, in spite of me, become a burdensome vacation that is still going on.

My mother came to Rome and is still here. I see her only rarely, but—as you know—every meeting with her is a kind of setback. When I have to see this lost, unreal woman who is connected with nothing, who cannot grow old, I feel how even as a child I struggled to get away from her, and fear deep within me lest after years and years of running and walking I am still not far enough from her, that somewhere inwardly I still make movements that are the other half of her embittered gestures, bits of memories that she carries about broken within her; then I have a horror of her distraught pieties, of her obstinate faith, of all those distorted and perverted things to which she has clung, herself empty as a dress, ghostly and terrible. And that still I am her child; that some scarcely recognizable wallpaper door in this faded wall that doesn't belong to anything was my entrance into the world—(if indeed such an entrance can lead into the world at all . . .)!

That is difficult and confusing for me who have so much to make up and keep losing my courage. But there were other things too. People, who were coming to Rome and (though I have no social relations at all) expressed the intention of seeing me or making my acquaintance. A few even had introductions to me, and it cost me letters and apologies on all sides to hold them off. . . . At the same time the spring was growing in abrupt shifts of wind, and every day rose steeply from the frosty morning to its noon overheated by the sun, in such a way that naturally I did not escape a cold and the influenza-feeling. Ants in swarms broke out of all the walls of my little house and attempted invasion upon invasion. The first scorpions appeared, unusually big and early. And finally the painter came from whom we had taken over furniture in the fall (as a loan, unfortunately with only a verbal and not sufficiently explicit understanding, according to which we would be able to buy it later if necessary), this painter returned to Rome and without further ado, forgetting any agreement, wanted his property back, so that now my little house, at one stroke, is almost empty. And after all I had looked out for those things all winter, they were my family, and I already had little roots in them. Now I am comforting myself with the fact that for the present I have been allowed to keep a bookcase and a bed, that my standing desk belongs to me and that it fits with summer not to have many things about me.

For what is going on here, heaven knows, has for three or four days not been spring any more, has been dense, young summer. The hyacinths in my little bed, which have long been hesitating, are flinging open their blossom eyes like one hammered awake by an alarm clock, and have already been standing there quite long and straight. The elms and oaks by my house are full, the Judas tree has shed its blossoms, and all its leaves will be ready overnight; and a syringa tree that stretched out its clusters only three days ago is already in process of fading and scorching. The nights are scarcely cool any more, and the busy clamor of frogs is their voice. The owls call less often, and the nightingale still hasn't begun. Will she still sing now that it is summer?

Summer in Rome. That is a new misery. I thought it was still far off and was longing, now when my mother will be gone again, to have one or two not too oppressive months of work. And I am still hoping that it is possible, that it will still be spring again after a few trial summer days. (Moreover I shall probably have to stay on here in summer too, for I have scarcely any possibility of going away, wouldn't know where to go, either. But that will only be the question after next; the next is about work and composure and I want to see that it is soon decided.)

It is beautiful here in the big garden, even though not much is blooming there and though what is peculiarly Roman is perhaps too loud, too penetrating, to be called spring. Even these meadows full of anemones and daisies are too dense, too heavy, too tight-meshed, and in the skies are none of those gray days behind still

empty trees, those wide, transforming winds and the softly falling rains that are for me the depth of all spring. It is, alas, a spring
for foreigners who have only a little time, obvious and loud and
exaggerated. But still there is a tree in the garden that might also
be standing in the Tuscan scene, in an old cloister: a tall old
cypress, all interleaved with a trail of wisteria that is now letting
its light blue-violet pendants climb and fall everywhere, even to
way up, out of the darkness of the tree;—that is joy. That and
the glorious fig trees, like altar candlesticks out of the Old Testament standing there with their upward-curving branches and
slowly opening their light-green leaves.

And that I can now observe and learn all this calmly and patiently is, I feel, a kind of progress and preparation; but, you
know, my progress is somehow like the faint steps of a convalescent, uncommonly weightless, tottering, and beyond measure
needing help. And the help is lacking. A help it would be to talk
to you of many things and to see you listening and keeping silent;
to read you something sometime. . . . But that writing you is
also a help, dear Lou, I know if I think of the years when I did
not have this refuge.—

Please: And now do get well!

[*62*]

To Friedrich Westhoff   Villa Strohl-Fern, Rome
                                April 29, 1904

Through Mother we have heard of you often lately, and without knowing anything more specific about you, we nevertheless
feel that you are having a hard time. Mother will not be able to
help you, for at bottom no one in life can help anyone else in life;
this one experiences over and over in every conflict and every
perplexity: that one is alone.

That isn't as bad as it may at first glance appear; and again it
is the best thing in life that each should have everything in himself: his fate, his future, his whole expanse and world. There
are moments, to be sure, when it is difficult to be in oneself and

to persist within one's own ego; it happens that at the very instants when one should hold faster and—one would almost have to say—more obstinately than ever to oneself, one attaches oneself to something external, during important events transfers one's own center out of oneself into something alien, into another person. That goes against the very simplest laws of equilibrium, and only difficulty can come of it.

Clara and I, dear Friedrich, have found ourselves and come to an understanding in the very fact that all companionship can consist only in the strengthening of two neighboring solitudes, whereas everything that one is wont to call giving oneself is by nature harmful to companionship: for when a person abandons himself, he is no longer anything, and when two people both give themselves up in order to come close to each other, there is no longer any ground beneath them and their being together is a continual falling.—We have learned such things, my dear Friedrich, not without great pain, have learned what everyone who wants his own life gets to know somehow or other.

Sometime when I am older and more mature I shall perhaps get around to writing a book, a book for young people; not by any means because I think I have been able to do anything better than others. On the contrary, because from childhood on and during my entire youth everything became so much more difficult for me than for other young people.

So I learned over and over again that there is scarcely anything more difficult than to love one another. That it is work, day labor, Friedrich, day labor; God knows there is no other word for it. And look, added to this is the fact that young people are not prepared for such difficult loving; for convention has tried to make this most complicated and ultimate relationship into something easy and frivolous, has given it the appearance of everyone's being able to do it. It is not so. Love is something difficult and it is more difficult than other things because in other conflicts Nature herself enjoins men to collect themselves, to take themselves firmly in hand with all their strength, while in the heightening of love the impulse is to give oneself wholly away.

But just think, can that be anything beautiful, to give oneself away not as something whole and ordered, but haphazard rather, bit by bit, as it comes? Can such giving away, that looks so like a throwing away and dismemberment, be anything good, can it be happiness, joy, progress? No, it cannot. . . . When you give someone flowers, you arrange them beforehand, don't you? But young people who love each other fling themselves to each other in the impatience and haste of their passion, and they don't notice at all what a lack of mutual esteem lies in this disordered giving of themselves, they notice it with astonishment and indignation only from the dissension that arises between them out of all this disorder. And once there is disunity between them, the confusion grows with every day; neither of the two has anything unbroken, pure, and unspoiled about him any longer, and amid the disconsolateness of a break they try to hold fast to the semblance of their happiness (for all that was really supposed to be for the sake of happiness). Alas, they are scarcely able to recall any more what they meant by happiness. In his uncertainty each becomes more and more unjust toward the other; they who wanted to do each other good are now handling one another in an imperious and intolerant manner, and in the struggle somehow to get out of their untenable and unbearable state of confusion, they commit the greatest fault that can happen to human relationships: they become impatient. They hurry to a conclusion, to come, as they believe, to a final decision, they try once and for all to establish their relationship, whose surprising changes have frightened them, in order to remain the same now and *forever* (as they say). That is only the last error in this long chain of errings linked fast to one another. What is dead cannot even be clung to (for it crumbles and changes its character); how much less can what is living and alive be treated definitively, once and for all. Self-transformation is precisely what life is, and human relationships, which are an extract of life, are the most changeable of all, rising and falling from minute to minute, and lovers are those in whose relationship and contact no one moment resembles another. People between whom nothing accustomed, nothing that has already been present before ever takes place, but many new, unexpected, unprecedented things. There are such relationships which must be a very great, almost unbearable happiness, but they can occur only between very rich natures and between those who, each for himself, are richly ordered and composed; they can unite only two wide, deep, individual worlds.—Young people—it is obvious—cannot achieve such a relationship, but they can, if they understand their life properly, grow up slowly to such happiness and prepare themselves for it. They must not forget, when they love, that they are beginners, bunglers of life, apprentices in love,—must *learn* love, and that (like *all* learning) wants peace, patience, and composure!

To take love seriously and to bear and to learn it like a task, this it is, Friedrich, that young people need.—Like so much else, people have also misunderstood the place of love in life, they have made it into play and pleasure because they thought that play and pleasure were more blissful than work; but there is nothing happier than work, and love, just because it is the extreme happiness, can be nothing else but work.—So whoever loves must try to act as if he had a great work: he must be much alone and go into himself and collect himself and hold fast to himself; he must work; he must become something!

For, Friedrich, believe me, the more one is, the richer is all that one experiences. And whoever wants to have a deep love in his life must collect and save for it and gather honey.

One must never despair if something is lost to one, a person or a joy or a happiness; everything comes back again more gloriously. What *must* fall away, falls away; what belongs to us remains with us, for everything proceeds according to laws that are greater than our insight and with which we are only apparently at variance. One must live in oneself and think of the *whole* of life, of all its millions of possibilities, expanses, and futures, in the face of which there is nothing past and lost.—

We think so much about you, dear Friedrich; our conviction is this: that in the confusion of events you would long ago, by yourself, have found your own solitary way out, which alone can help, were not the whole burden of your year of military service still lying upon you. . . . I remember that after my locked-up military school period my craving for freedom and my distorted consciousness of self (that had to recover only gradually from the bendings and bruises that had been administered to it) would drive me into perplexities and desires that do not belong at all to my life, and it was my good fortune to have my work: in it I found myself and I am finding myself in it daily and am no longer looking for myself elsewhere. That is what we both do; that is Clara's life and mine. And you will also come to that, very certainly. Be of good courage, all is before you, and time passed in the difficult is never lost. . . .

[63]

To Ellen Key   Villa Strohl-Fern, Rome
                                                April 29, 1904

My friend, is it very indiscreet of me to long so much to hear from you again? Please, when a more quiet hour comes for you, write me a few words about how it was in Göteborg and in Copenhagen—what it meant to you and how people received it. You did send me a newspaper, but in the first place, it is in Swedish, and in spite of industrious spelling out and guessing, we did not grasp much of its account,—and in the second place, I would like to know not about the external course of your lectures, rather about the inner life that was in you, dear Ellen Key, and that you felt in those to whom you spoke. How did you feel it? How was it? Is it indiscreet of me to ask about it?—

In the meantime I have received through the Insel publishing house the proofs of that translated fragment of your lecture that was to go in front of the book about God. Let me tell you first of all that those loving words which so delicately trace out my delicate seeking touched me infinitely; if now (in agreement with the publishers) I nevertheless do *not* want to place this fragment in front of the *Stories of God*, it happens from the following feeling:

Those words, which are built up over passages from my recent letters like a quiet little church, lead and point too far out *beyond* the God book, which came into being four years before, clarify it *too* much, are keys to all its doors. Now I believe that this book, in which everything is anticipation (anticipated fear and anticipated joy), cannot well stand such an elucidation, that it must remain as it is, in all its darkness, that it must be alone with itself. The more so as with those words that point out beyond it not only is the old storybook about God placed in too bright a light (so that one sees its cracks and defects) but also a new book I am writing and with which I shall perhaps have to wrestle for a long time yet would appear too soon given away and discussed. All of a sudden it seems to me dangerous to see my newer letter passage beside the clumsier, shyer words of the book about God; just because they stem from a so much further stage of development of the same thought cycle, they are hostile to the earlier transitions and do not look well beside them, rather the way with many plants it hurts to see blossoms and fruits side by side on the same stem.—Above all then, for the sake of *those words of mine* I shall *not* use that fragment as introduction to the new edition of the storybook;—the book about God will come out alone, *without* a foreword, as it did the first time!—You will understand my reasons no differently than as I mean and say them, dear Ellen Key, and you did also give me the right to tie and loosen and be master of the words that were destined for this purpose.—

Remarkably strongly the words of that fragment point to my growing book which will also be a book about God; this came about in part through the letters I wrote you from the midst of work, but also your kind and deep understanding of those passages led you close to the ways that, laboriously and with difficulty, I am now trying to go.—Again I have had bad weeks, from indisposition, hindrances, scribbling of all sorts and from the sudden high midsummer heat that broke in upon us with full force about ten days ago, crippling and destructive, heavy as lava.

Now it has turned cooler again and I hope to become capable

of work and effective again; for I *long* to get on with my work which is dear to me above everything, and to get through at least a section before the big Roman heat comes and with it the necessity of going away from here. . . .

My wife sends you, dear Ellen Key, the most cordial of greetings. We rejoice in the good news of you and both think of you a great deal, gratefully and with love!

Postscript:

My wife is very depressed by the climate, and (in spite of the fact that Italy has its benefits) I believe we (I too) do need the north soon again, distance, wind! It is sad for us to see this rapid, redundant, galloping spring that is a continual fading and burning up,—and all our longing is with the slow, hesitant coming of northern spring days, with the great and heavy transformations of northern Nature in whose existence each little flower is a life, a world, a beginning, a destiny: a great deal. What is one little flower here where there are millions of blossoms! . . .

[64]

To Lou Andreas-Salomé   Villa Strohl-Fern, Rome
                                           May 12, 1904

Your letter, dear Lou, I have read often; it was just and good. When it came there was a great, quiet evening over the garden, and I read it slowly on the flat roof of my little house and pondered over it a long time. Perhaps, said something in me, I shall begin something good tomorrow morning, perhaps. And amid much suppressed hope there was a little bit of gladness in me—:

That was not to blossom; for the burden of my vacation time increased with every day. It had gradually grown cooler, and the disturbances had receded, and nevertheless things wouldn't begin to get better in me. . . .

With this clear experience is linked the necessity for new decisions, and before I set about making one or another, I would like to tell you, dear Lou, a few things about myself, as well as I am able in these ineffectual days. Perhaps you will say something to me in connection with this or that; which would mean a great deal to me; you know how much. (But if you are now in work, at your beloved work, put this letter aside, because it comes from a restless man; he can wait; he can wait as long as you want.)

And then see:

I have rented my little gardenhouse in the park of the Villa Strohl-Fern until fall (until October). I hoped to be able to stay on in it all summer (or at least the greater part of it); now I know that is not to be thought of. But I had the further intention of keeping the house for still a year more: for where should I ever find such another? A tiny little house, all to myself, with big windows and flat roof-terrace, containing a spacious bright simple room, and situated deep, deep in a private garden, inaccessible and secluded, and far removed from traffic and noise—a feeling advised me to hold on to this place where all that can be mine, as long as the otherwise so uncertain and intolerable external circumstances of life in any way permit it; but now this same feeling tells me that I might persist in such favorable living possibilities only if it all lay under a healthier sky, under which one may live all year without fear and dread. The fall was bad here, the winter, with so much sirocco and the long rain, oppressive, and the spring everybody extols so is only a hastening into the dangerous summer, like a descent without a stopping place. What is more, people who live here maintain that one gets along with the Roman climate best as a novice, later worse and worse from year to year, and that one becomes more and more defense-less against the seasickness-mood of the sirocco days.

And in addition (something that I already felt a year ago in Viareggio,—where I attributed it to other circumstances—) I must in the past years have got far, far away from things Italian. My feeling everything so differently now from formerly is per-haps contributed to by my being in Rome and not in the Tuscan country which, with Botticelli and the Robbias, with marble-white and sky-blue, with gardens, villas, roses, bells, and foreign girls, spoke so intimately to me—: but speak it did (and Rome speaks too), it did not keep silent and did not bluster: it spoke. It talked until my cheeks glowed—(and I sometimes wonder whether that was the good and important thing for me and whether my first Viareggio, which closed with so great an expenditure into nothing, with such fireworks, was not already a proof that Italian influence is not among the things that really advance me).

However that may be,—in any case more northern and more serious countries have since educated my senses to the subdued and simple, so that they now feel what is glaring and strong, schematic and uninflected in Italian things as a relapse into picture-book instruction. It came about quite of itself that I received and learned this very obvious and showy spring from a purely botanical point of view, with the objective and quiet attentiveness which my observation is more and more assuming, that its movements and voices and the upward flight and course of its birds interested me quite objectively, without my ever sensing it as something entire, living, mysterious, as soul alive and bordering on my soul. I noted details, and since I have heretofore observed so little and in mere looking, as in so much, am a beginner—I was content with such occupation, making progress in it. But if once it happened that I expected or needed something from the whole, I opened up and shut again, empty, and hungered deeply. As it would for a lung in a stuffy room, so it became difficult for my soul in an exhausted world into which nothing new comes with the spring, nothing distant and incalculable. I felt the great poverty that lies in richness: how with us a flower, a little first flower that struggles and comes, is a world, a happiness, to participate in which is infinitely satisfying,— and how here herds of flowers come without anything stirring in one, without anything participating and feeling akin and sensing its own beginning in other things. Here everything is given over to the easy, to the easiest side of the easy. Flowers come and blossoms, anemones bloom and wisteria, and one says it to oneself and says it again, as to someone hard of hearing. But it is all so ensnaringly sham and make-believe; colors are there, to be sure, but they always sub-

ordinate themselves lazily to some cheap shade and do not develop from out of themselves. The Judas tree bloomed, bloomed,
and bloomed, its redundant, unfruitful bloom welling even out
of its trunk like blood-sodden mesentery, and in a few weeks
everything: anemones and clover and syringas and starflowers,
everything was purple with its purple, for God knows what reasons—from laziness, from accommodation, from lack of original
ideas. And even now the red roses, fading, are taking on this
corpselike purple, and the strawberries have it if they stand for
a day, and the sunsets puff it out, and it appears in the clouds in the
evening and in the morning. And the skies in which such cheap
plays of color take place are shallow and as if choked with sand;
they are not everywhere, they do not play about things like the
skies of the moor, of the sea, and of the plains, are not endless
beginning of distance, are finish, curtain, end;—and behind the
last trees, which stand flat like theater wings against this indifferent photographic background,—everything ceases. It is indeed a
sky over something past; drained, empty, forsaken sky, sky-shell
from which the last sweetness has long ago been drunk. And as
the sky is, so are the nights, and as the nights are, so is the voice
of the nightingales. Where nights are vast, their tone is deep, and
they bring it from infinitely far away and carry it to the end.
Here the nightingale is really just a little lustful bird with a
shallow song and an easily satisfied longing. In two nights even
one becomes accustomed to its call, and one notes it with an inner reserve, as if fearing to hurt one's own memories by any
more interest, the memories of nightingale-nights that are quite,
quite different.

Exhibition atmosphere, so typical of the city, is also the most
obvious characteristic of the Roman spring: it is spring exhibition that takes place here, not spring. The foreigners indeed enjoy it and feel themselves honored like little sovereigns in whose
honor everything is shined up; for these respectable Germans,
Italy must always have been a kind of royal journey with tri-
umphal arches, flowers, and fireworks. But, in a certain sense, they
are right: they come down here, weary of having winter, of

making fires and of darkness, and find ready-made here all that is sunny and comfortable. More they do not ask. And of this sort too was probably the effect I sometimes used to get from Arco or from Florence and the benefit connected with it. But if as a native one has seen the whole winter here (full of the morose persistence of that which cannot die), then the miracle that is supposed to come fails. One knows that that isn't a spring, for one has seen none *coming*, that these blossoms have had as little difficulty in appearing at this place or that as decorations, for instance, have in being put up somewhere. And one comprehends so well the illusory life of this past people, the empty phrases of its descendant-art, the garden-flower-beauty of D'Annunzio's verses.

It is good that I have experienced all this so slowly and so concretely, for Italy had still been a summons for me and an unfinished episode. But now I can leave it, comforted, for the end is here.

It will be hard for me, to be sure, because this little house stands on this spot and cannot be taken along and set up again in another, more northern garden; hard, because the new break comes unexpectedly and leads into the uncertain; hard—because I am tired anyway of breaking off and starting again.

. . . As to the question of earning a living, which bobs up again, threatening and demanding, with every change, there is this to say: that I am not closing my eyes to it and am not putting it off until it returns more urgently; I see it and always know that it is there. If nevertheless in the present choice of place I do not give it the most important voice, this is from the ever-growing conviction that my bread must one day come to me out of my work; for it is work and as such necessary, and it must be possible (or become possible) to do it and to live, if only it is done well. Art is indeed a longest life-path, and when I think how trifling and elementary is what I have heretofore done, it does not surprise me that this achievement (which resembles a foot-wide strip of half-tilled land) does not nourish me. Plans do not bear, and what is prematurely sown does not come up. But patience and work are real and can change at any moment into bread. . . .

That is why, everything else aside, I want to decide on my next place of sojourn by my work and only by it. . . .

The works I have in mind and which are to occupy me in turn are:

1. The "Prayers," which I want to continue.

2. My new book (whose firm, close-knit prose is a schooling for me and an advance that had to come so that later sometime I could write everything else—the military novel too).

3. An attempt at a drama.

4. Two monographs:
   The Poet: Jens Peter Jacobsen.
   The Painter: Ignacio Zuloaga.

Both of these necessitate trips. The first a trip to Thisted and a stay in Copenhagen, the second a trip through Spain. (Zuloaga was, beside Rodin, the only person with whom I was closely and long in contact during my stay in Paris and whose importance and worth I feel and can say. Or shall be able to say. Sometime I will tell you about him.)

But there is no hurry about these travels and books; probably I shall get first to Jacobsen. You can't imagine how necessary he has become to me; by always new paths I have gone to him, often alone, often with my wife (who reads him so well and so lovingly); indeed, it is even true that when one goes anywhere in the important one can be sure of coming out at a place where he too is (if one goes far enough); and how singular it is to find that his and Rodin's words agree often to the point of congruity: then one has that crystal-clear feeling one gets in mathematical demonstrations the moment two distant lines, as if out of eternity, meet at one point, or when two big complex numbers, that do not resemble each other, simultaneously withdraw in order, jointly, to acknowledge a single simple symbol as the thing that matters.—Singularly untouched joy comes from experience of that sort.

Besides these works, to accompany and supplement them, I have in mind several studies. I am already beginning to learn

Danish, chiefly so that I can read Jacobsen and various things of Kierkegaard in the original.

Then I began something in Paris that I would like to continue: reading in the big German dictionary of the Grimm brothers, from which, it seemed to me, a writer can derive much wealth and instruction. For indeed one really ought to know and be able to use everything that has once entered into the language and is there, instead of trying to get along with the chance supply that is meager enough and offers no choice. It would be good if a pursuit like this led me now and then to read a medieval poet; that Gothic, which architecturally had so much to give that is unforgettable and vast, shouldn't it also have had and worked on a plastic language, words like statues and sentences like rows of pillars? I know nothing, nothing of it. Nothing, I feel, of all that I would like to know.—There are so many things some old man should tell one about while one is little; for when one has grown up, knowing them would be a matter of course. There are the starry heavens, and I don't know what people have already learned about them,—why, not even the order of the stars do I know. And so it is with flowers, with animals, with the simplest laws that are operative here and there and go through the world in a few strides from beginning to end. How life comes into being, how it functions in lower animals, how it branches and unfolds, how life blossoms, how it bears: all that I long to learn. Through participation in it all to bind myself more firmly to the reality that so often denies me,—*to exist*, not only through feeling but also through knowledge, always and always: this it is, I believe, that I need in order to become more secure and less homeless. You will feel that I do not want sciences, for any one of them require a lifetime, and no life is long enough for its beginning; but I would like to stop being a person shut out, one who cannot read the deeper tidings of his time, that point further on and reach further back, a prisoner who senses everything but hasn't the little certainty of whether it is at the moment day or evening, spring or winter. I would like, somewhere where it can be done, to learn that which I probably would know if I had had a chance to grow up in the country and among more essential people, and that which an impersonal and hasty schooling failed to tell me, and the rest, since discovered and recognized and belonging to it. It is not art history and other histories, not the nature of philosophic systems that I would like to learn,—I want a chance to get and earn for myself just a few great and simple certainties that are there for everyone; I want a chance to ask a few questions, questions such as children ask, unrelated for those outside, but full of family likeness for me who know their birth and genealogy to the tenth generation.

May 13, 1904

Up to now universities have given me so little every time; I seem to feel such an aversion to their ways. But it lies also with my clumsiness which never and nowhere understands how to take; with my not having the presence of mind to recognize what I need; and of course one thing I haven't yet had either, the most important: patience. Perhaps that has all improved now; I shall no longer lack patience, at least, in anything. And if I don't attempt as before to hear disciplines read, in which one can be of this or that opinion—words about words, conceptions of conceptions—, but hear something real said, something new, to which all that is premonition in me says yes, I shall not even notice any unpleasantness in the external conditions or shall quietly endure it for the sake of what is important. I miss a learning-time of that sort more than anything else, not only because I do not know so much that is simple and essential, but also because I always imagine that for me it must be the path on which I shall finally be able to help myself alone to what I shall later need in each case. That I am unable to do this, that I am helpless when left alone among books, a child whom one must lead out again, continually holds me up, dismays me, makes me sad, perplexed. If the pursuit of some scientific study were slowly to result in my learning to survey a subject, to sift and read the existing bibliography (not even to mention the finding), if I were to make my own the ability to study older books and old manuscripts too—in short, if I might acquire on the side a little of the historian's craft and the archivist's patience and might hear spoken a few real truths and perceptions—, then any place would suit me which would afford me such. It seems to me that without acquisitions of this kind I cannot take my next forward steps; after the Rodin monograph I thought of one on Carpaccio, later of one on Leonardo: what I lack for these is not an art historian's knowledge (which is just what I would like to avoid), but rather the simple craft of the research worker, the technical assurance and practice for which I must often envy quite young people; to the great libraries here and in Paris I lacked the key, the inner directions for use (to put it tritely), and my reading was fortuitous reading because, for want of preparation, it couldn't turn into work. With my education, over which no plan lay, and with the intimidation in which I grew up (everywhere running into laughter and superiority and pushed back by everybody into my own clumsiness), it came about that I never got to learn at all much preparatory matter and most of the technical material of life, which later are effortless for everyone; my feeling is full to the brim of memories of moments when everyone about me knew and could do something and did it mechanically without thinking, while I, embarrassed, didn't know how to go about anything, wasn't even capable of watching and copying others. Like one who finds himself in a game the rules of which he doesn't know—, I feel like a knot in the thread on thousands of occasions. Then I am a hindrance to others and a cause of annoyance —but the same deficiencies hold me back myself and disconcert me.

Once I sat a whole summer on the Schönaich's estate, alone in the family library whose archives are crammed with old correspondence and records and documents; I felt in every nerve the immediate proximity of destinies, the stirring and rising of figures from which nothing separated me but the foolish inability to read and decipher old symbols and to bring order into the unsifted confusion of those papers. What a good, industrious summer that could have been had I understood a little of the archivist's craft; something like a *Maria Grubbe* would perhaps have been given me in substance; at any rate I would have learned and gathered much from such close contact with the still untold happenings—while as it was I only got new proof every day of my unfitness, of that being shut out, which life keeps making me experience whenever I want to approach it anywhere.

And not for work on monographs alone, for every work I do, I shall more and more miss such preparation and perspective; for my plans connected with things Russian, for instance, it has always been a hindrance and the reason why I progress so slowly in them. But wouldn't a schooling such as I have in mind (without being able to picture it exactly) enable me more surely to attack and hold on to all my work, wouldn't it too be a means of reaching that "toujours travailler" which is what matters?

So in sum my study projects read thus:

1. I want to read books on natural sciences and biology and hear lectures that will stimulate the reading and learning of such things. (See experiments and preparations.)

2. I want to learn work with archives and history, in so far as this is technique and craft.

3. I want to read the Grimm brothers' dictionary, simultaneously with medieval writings.

4. I want to learn Danish.

5. To continue reading Russian and now and then to translate from the Russian.

6. To translate from the French a book of the poet Francis Jammes.

And to read carefully the following books: Michelet's natural-history studies and his history of France; the Eighteenth Century of the Goncourts . . . and other things.—

I thought for a while of attempting all this in Copenhagen; of going there in the fall and working there.

But against it is

—the fact that I make my projected studies more difficult for myself if I go into a country with a foreign language, where hearing lectures has less sense and everything practical (such as the use of libraries, collections, and laboratories) also becomes complicated.

—The fact that Copenhagen is a very big city and perhaps not beneficial to my health.

. . . Do you know besides that just now in Copenhagen (in the Student Club, before a very full hall) someone spoke about my books? Yes, it really came about that Ellen Key, with a big lecture manuscript dealing only with my works, traveled to Stockholm, to Copenhagen and into God knows what Swedish cities—on my account! There she told people about me, and now, she writes me, many are beginning to buy and read my books; and through this it was that she wanted to be useful and to help me. But not satisfied with that, she wants to have published in a Swedish periodical, and (translated) in a German one, a big essay which grew out of those lectures. She is a dear and capable person and has gradually become an indispensable friend to both of us, to my wife and to me (yes, even to little Ruth). I understand well and with heartfelt gratitude the nature of her help and activity, although I distinctly feel that such intercession for me is in no way justifiable; just now, while it is going on, I am watching her undertaking (confidentially speaking) with terror—: for in reality and to less charitable eyes, nothing has actually been done, nothing demonstrable. A few things in the *Book about God*, in *In My Honor* and in *The Book of Pictures* (of the "Prayers" she knows nothing) could speak for me; but I am afraid she has presented all that as much less mixed and has given everything a semblance of conclusiveness which it doesn't possess and in which people will feel cheated when they buy my books now. Also she has based much of what she said (as it seems —I am not acquainted with the essay yet, only a small fragment of it) on passages from my letters of recent years and has found out the sort of things that cannot be deduced from my thus far published works.—And over and above all this I feel: if anybody needs seclusion, it is I. (Every line and every perplexity of this

letter, but also that in which it is determined, speaks for it—.)
Nevertheless, I do see that I must agree to everything that can
support my existence and prolong the possibility of remaining
at my work. And for that such a being named and proclaimed is
surely good. Furthermore that has all come through the lips of
a refined and discreet person and (even if it has happened much
too early) can have no bad consequences. It also turned out in
due course that there were young people here and there in Sweden
who already knew about me, even some who could recite verses
from my books by heart; and it came to light incidentally that
one of the young Swedish writers was just in the process (in-
dependently and without knowledge of Ellen Key's intention)
of collecting material for an essay on my work. . . .

Dear Lou, if it were possible to meet you this summer, do,
please, let it be possible. I see for miles around no thought, no
confidence, in which I believe so much that they would help me.

Meantime comes this letter, running through two days with
its length and making many presumptuous demands upon you;
be very indulgent toward it. The writing of it has helped me
infinitely; it has been like an activity after all these weeks of im-
mobile inner numbness.—There are, as I come to think of it,
certain little animals, beetles, and insects, that fall into such states
of arrested life if one touches them or comes near them; often I
have watched them, have noticed that they let themselves be
rolled along like things, that they do everything to be as like
things as possible: they do this when they see a danger's bigness
coming toward them—and want to save themselves. Has my
condition like causes? Is this becoming numb and keeping still
that goes to my very core, up to the very entrance of my heart's
chambers, an instinctive defense by which something that can
annihilate me is to be deceived? Who knows?

I will trust and not count the time and will wait for it to pass.
But *then* bestir myself, for nothing has yet been done. . . .

[65]

To Clara Rilke   Borgeby gård, Flädie
                                                    Province of Skåne, Sweden
                                                    July 9, 1904

. . . a big wind is coming over from the Sund, the garden is foaming, and when one looks up, one sees very bright little patches of distant meadows appearing and vanishing behind the flickering leaves of the bushes. In the beds the roses are beginning to blossom, rather stunted roses for which no one really has time, blossom and fade, very quickly it seems to me. Today's storm is casting off many that yesterday were not yet there, and now they lie in the grass like torn-up letters. In the wallflower bed a spray of blossoms has been open for days, but big mallows, dahlias, and many other things are all still to come. In the many-branched, wonderfully drooping laburnum tree, are hanging the little grey-violet pod-bundles of its fruits and their pallor permeates the whole tree and withdraws it from all the rest, makes it recede, veils it almost. In the round, tower-high haw-thorn shrub the little rose-blossom bouquets have turned brown, but behind it the white jasmine is still blooming in single dense-white blossoms, visible from way off, that are grouped together like constellations, far apart for all their nearness. And very large, like the beginnings of some piece of yellowish Brussels lace, lie the large, flat blossom-patches of the elder bushes in their taffeta-dull foliage. And their smell on still mornings (when their scent is not torn and can collect and concentrate itself) is like the strong scent of the sweat of young girls who have chased each other and have run over meadows and are now arriving hot and disheveled, with a strained, almost angry seriousness in their faces and quite exhausted laughter.—But today, in the blow, every scent is thin, fluid, passes by, comes back weak and mingled with distance and again goes by. From the walnut tree and from the big full chestnuts, torn-off fruits strike with a hard, startling clang, and down below the little river is all combed up on its surface and ruffling up against the Sund that pushes it back into its mouth.

The bulls, far away on the westward pasture, are quiet, multi-colored, massive things, but the calves yonder are merry and play-ful, and sweep along with them the horses that suddenly come gal-loping up, turn, trot and assemble with sturdy action. And above, sky in misty, distant, transparent white that has slowly formed out of mounting clouds, while the sun kept breaking through and disappearing, so that the day already seems very long.—

Fräulein Larsson went to Lund this morning, and I am sitting under the big walnut tree (as long as it isn't raining yet) and am quite alone at Borgeby gård, of whose history and inhabitants I already know a great deal now; much from old descriptions la-boriously picked out in Swedish, still more that is conjecture and much that I merely sense. Before me stands Bishop Birger's tower, quite spoiled by the restoration of the next to last owner, but still his tower, a thing known and discussed among the people of all Skåne. In the church, under the bell-loft, is preserved (care-lessly enough) a triptych portraying Hans Spegel, knight and chamberlain of Frederick II, and the two so very dissimilar mis-tresses of his house. And in the narrow, prisonlike crypt, under the nave, three skulls and a few strong masculine bones lie be-tween crumbled bits of coffin and belong perhaps to the picture under the bells. And on the western gable of the house, simply wrought like iron fastenings, are still the initials of Hans Spegel's heirs: Φ "Otto Lindenow and his wife F Elsa Juel 1638." Then came owner after owner, many from Sweden's greatest families, Counts von Trolle, von Bonde, Barons von Ramel, von Hastfer, Counts De Geer and von Wachtmeister (from whom Hanna Larsson acquired the castle). It passed from name to name, be-cause it was always handed down as an inherited estate on the maternal side from daughter to daughter and with each of their husbands got a new master. Nevertheless the women were always the real proprietors, whether it was that they were more indus-trious and more often in residence than the foreign lords to whom they gave themselves, whether (as happened mostly) it was that they outlived them, long outlasted them: for they were all of an upright, sturdy house that bore aging. Of all these no sign nor evidence has remained here; it is to be assumed that the last counts who were its lords, allied by marriage to those old families, took off everything in any way relating to them. Only for that one lady of the house of Hastfer there are two old, weather-beaten memorial stones in the park that speak gently of a life gently passed. The one stone was erected by Colonel Carl Bergenstråhle for Brita Sophie Hastfer who, after a long maidenhood, became his wife at the age of 43, and also records her death, which took place 13 years later. The other stone (without date) comes from the son of a sister of Brita Sophie (who was childless) and only says once more that she was dear and good and that they cannot forget her.—

So it was always women's destinies that passed away at Borgeby gård, flowed along, or hesitated to pass on. And strangely: again (after Fräulein Larsson's father bought it) it has come into a daughter's hands; again, as five and six centuries ago, a strong, prudent woman is residing at Borgeby, of an old peasant family, energetic and good and capable of outliving perhaps many suitors.

And in the tops of the old beech trees dwell the tribes of ravens, hundreds and hundreds of them; and when in the evening they fly in, in flocks, screaming, the treetops grow small under them; and when swarm upon swarm goes up once more and mounts and circles, there is a noise as of many dresses and fans, only much louder. And surely there is one among them, an old one with a good memory for tradition, who in his thoughts is continuing the chronicle of Borgeby and (in the foreshortening in which he sees her) comparing Hanna Larsson with Brita Sophie, with Vivika Bonde, and with Elsa Maltesdotter Juel! . . .

[66]

To Clara Rilke
Borgeby gård, Flädie
Province of Skåne, Sweden
July 19, 1904

. . . Saturday toward eight, we drove in the carriage to Bjerred (station for the train to Lund), which is at the same time a little seaside resort, and from a wooden bridge built far out into the quiet sea watched the evening dying away in many cloudy and watery grays. Yesterday, Monday, I was in Lund and on the way home in the evening spent another hour alone on that wooden bridge. It was the evening of a very windy day, and the broad storm thrust a tremendous night-gray cloud-continent over the sky and set free the sun that was sinking—, so that two seas lay beneath it, separated by a strip of dazzling radiance: a wholly shadowed, gray, restrained, heavy one and a light, animated, shiny one that quivered far and wide and without ceasing and whispered excitedly to itself.

After two days of great warmth we are having a big, powerful wind; unfortunately one doesn't feel it in the windows because the house stands behind its walls of tree and bush as in a room. But outside, on the road that forms the margin of the park toward the meadows, it is very big, and the rustling and shaking of the trees is full of passion.

Today, toward morning, a little horse was born in the pasture. I think I on my early walk was the first to see it. Little, light brown, scrubby, with a short neck, slightly dizzy head motions, narrow little body bound about the ribs, it stood on four stiff, much too long legs very close by its brown, relieved mother who slowly and cautiously began to graze. . . .

[67]

To Clara Rilke
Borgeby gård, Flädie
Province of Skåne, Sweden
July 24, 1904, Sunday, toward evening

. . . I am not idle, and there is nothing lazy in me; all sorts of currents and a stirring that through depth and surface is the same. A very good stirring. I am not even writing a journal, just keep hoping to get through all sorts of letters yet to be written and to read my way through all sorts of books yet to be read. That I am making attempts to read Danish, three to four hours a day, is something too and wants time and gets it, and wants strength.—In spite of all this it seems to me that I am building; at the invisible, at the most invisible, at some foundation; no that is too much; but that I am breaking ground for something that is to be erected there sometime; a perfectly inconspicuous activity for which day laborers and hod carriers suffice (one thinks).

That is only to say how matters stand here; it is said without complaint and without regret. Perhaps it would be best if I christened this time recreation, and lived it that way (one shouldn't mix recreation and work, half and half, as is always happening out of faintheartedness and failing strength), but for that I do lack the zest, lack something or other that I ought to have done beforehand. A point of departure, a testimonial, an examination passed before myself.

Well, even so, the way it is and is going, this time will be good for me, if not in collecting, still in preparing to collect myself. Summer was really never and nowhere my high time. Always and everywhere the point was to live through it; but the autumn this year should be mine again. If I were then living in a quiet room among great autumnal broadleaved trees, near the sea, alone and well and left in peace (and this might all by most fortunate chance be found near Copenhagen and the Sund), a great deal could alter in my life, much good could then be brought into the world.—

. . . Petri. Yes, I too remember an excellent conversation with him about Edgar Allan Poe. A lot in it was vital, though in a temperamental direction especially there were disagreements we did not clear away. He is growing without doubt, which is why he is in great straits too, and that is the sympathetic thing about him: that he remains in great straits. For years in continually new straits, in genuine (even if perhaps self-sought, invoked) straits. May he never find his way out of them: musicians are full of ways out, corresponding to the easy solutions their art puts at their disposal. Only when they despise and reject solution after solution, as Beethoven did in his living or Bach in his praying, do they grow. Otherwise they simply increase in circumference.—

. . . Taken absolutely, without regard to the inferior conversation that fills up the whole world, even the most admirable conversation now seems to me like a dissipation. I thought this recently of an evening here when (in French to boot) I was talked into saying a few important things, felt it after the exhausting conversations with Norlind at the beginning of my stay here. What a bitter taste, what a spent feeling, what a morning-after-the-night-before mood remains! And how guilty one feels! I always used to believe it came from a regret that one had given oneself out to someone not quite fine, mature; but no, it comes simply from the fact that giving oneself out is sin, is music, is surrender. At bottom one must lock oneself up before one's best words and go into solitude. For the word must become flesh. That is the world's secret! . . .

[68]

To Clara Rilke

Borgeby gård, Flädie
Province of Skåne, Sweden
July 27, 1904, evening

. . . For a while at least, I have begged out of having to take supper; so near bedtime it is one meal too many for me and then: for the most part we end by staying together afterward, going out together, talking; good for one who by evening has had his day's work—(although for him too silence and solitary celebration would be more important than the wearier ring of words), but bad for me, to whom the evening means the core, the fruit and fullness of the day. To have to talk in the evening, not to be alone in the evening, to laugh in the evening—: to me that means unraveling a day thread by thread, seam by seam; the whole pattern dissolves into long threads, all the work pours back into my hands, and I begin a difficult, a reproachful night. For that reason and in order to use this time here, as much as I can, for my soul's best hunger—, I have taken the evenings for myself.

. . . Now it is . . . Thursday morning, there are still torn

night clouds in the light sky, little bird-sounds are stirring everywhere; perhaps rain is coming. (They want it very much, that is,
the people connected with the land need it. For three weeks there
has been sunny dryness, and the corn that promised such good
things is spoiling; it is ripening, ripening, but without quite developing inside, which is indeed a misfortune.)

. . . Thanks for Kappus' letter. He is having a hard time. And
that is just the beginning. And he is right in this: in childhood
we have used up too much strength, too much strength from
grownups,—that is perhaps true of a whole generation. Or is
true over and over again for individuals. What is one to say to
this? That life has infinite possibilities of renewal? Yes, but this
too: that the using up of strength is in a certain sense still an
increase of strength; for fundamentally it is only a matter of a
wide circle: all the strength we give away comes back over us
again, experienced and transformed. It is so in prayer. And what
is there that, truly done, would not be prayer? . . .

And one more thing with reference to the thoughts of recovery. There are here, in among the field-kingdoms, spots of
dark, untilled land. They are empty, and yet they lie there as if the
light stalks round about were there for their sake, rows of pickets
for their protection. I asked what these dark strips of land were
all about. They told me: c'est de la terre en repos. So beautiful,
you see, can resting be, and that is how it looks alongside work.
Not disquieting, but such that one acquires a deep trust and the
feeling of a big time. . . .

[69]

To Clara Rilke   Borgeby gård, Flädie
                                     Province of Skåne, Sweden
                                        July 29, 1904, Friday

. . . So it didn't rain yesterday; toward evening a blow came
up; high above, inaccessible and destined for another earth, clouds
passed by, cloud after cloud, and by nightfall everything far and

wide was free again, almost empty in its clarity, like a maneuver field after the review. Then the moon rose again, and I went once more through the park, over whose great silence flocks of crows were describing their last circles . . . I walked and didn't stop until the edge of the park, before the dark grazing-meadows, from which through the great stillness comes the crunch of chewing and warm, subdued munching. And powerful fragrance and distance and absence of human beings. . . . Every moment I see something. I have also learned a lot from Hokusai in this looking through the *Mangwa*. A path, the ground dark, rhythmically strewn with the twin fruits of a maple tree—: that would have become one of his thousand prints. The laburnum bush with its fruit husks hanging there like old-fashioned earrings, the jasmine that won't stop blooming and whose stars form whole milky ways in the darkening green; and the fruit trees, these above all, with their work-boughs that give one to see their overburdened existence and the laborious summer; and the meadows on which their shadows unfold like plays with many disguises. And farther on the flowers in the bed that have nothing to bear, that are only lighted for a while and burn like candles . . .(it occurs to me, don't night butterflies think lights are flowers?). And the ornamental trees that have been growing for ever and ever, the chestnuts that have space for whole halls under them, and the one old blooming linden opposite the entrance, whose round cupola is the last gold of the evening when everything grows dark—: there is enough to look at, for there is much more still. The world is like that, but here and there are painters searching for motifs, painters who break five little stones out of the great mosaic in order to combine them in some harmony. And perhaps it is not only painters who are like that (for then they would be the most Godforsaken people alive), perhaps people in general are like that—: haven't they made even life out of little motifs, aren't their joys and their troubles, their professions and riches merely motifs? Alas! and real life is like the real world. And lies there like a pasture from which, in the evening, comes warm breath and scent and absence of human beings. . . .

[70]

To Tora Holmström
Borgeby gård
August 2, 1904

That you, Fräulein Holmström, thought of me with kind regards does me a lot of good; I have sometimes thought, since you left us, that our talks might have troubled and disturbed rather than refreshed you; for the things we said were fragments, detached at random from large contexts, without beginning and without conclusions, without issue.

So I am glad that yesterday in Lund I found a little book, which (seems to me) carefully takes up many threads that we let fall and weaves them into a lovely pattern. That it is by Hugo von Hofmannsthal, whom you wanted to read, and can serve very well as introduction to Stephan George's poetry, is an added agreeable circumstance.

But what also quite especially makes me want to put this book in your hands is the way in which in both its essays the figure of Goethe as a poet has been treated. Through its being *I* who am allowed to transmit to you these distinguished words of great admiration for Goethe, I hope to tear up, like a letter that has become worthless, the memory of a certain evening talk that must be irksome to you. You must ascribe it to my loneliness, to my small experience in expressing myself in conversation, that I was able to carry on so absurdly that time; for I have no right to say *more* than this: that I lack the organ for receiving from Goethe; more I really do not know.

And that I respectfully acknowledge what life has taught you to call Goethe, the breadth and clarity that begin for you with this name,—that is what I should have said (as I knew immediately afterward) instead of all those childish words.

If the little book becomes acceptable to you in the days by the sea, I beg you to keep it. It is against Nature to part from books with which one has an understanding, just as it is important in similar case not to keep people too long. . . .

[71]

To Clara Rilke

Borgeby gård, Flädie
Province of Skåne, Sweden
August 10, 1904

. . . We are again amidst wind which is almost cold and without limit. (What skies it built yesterday evening!)

I walk about a great deal in this bluster, only sometimes I stand by the wallflowers, by the mallows (many have already opened . . .) or in the scent of the phlox. And am thoughtful . . .

[72]

To Clara Rilke

Borgeby gård, Flädie
Province of Skåne, Sweden
August 12, [1904] Friday

. . . see the wind is so big and wide and does not cease; it roars all night and only quiets down when a rain falls, and the rain grows heavier and heavier and roars too. Autumn? Why not; for everything is ready, the fruit is big, and the little storks are no longer distinguishable from the big ones. And along by the highway there is a part of the park that is not swept and not raked on Saturday; there are weeds there, all burned and drooping, and the half-grown chestnuts have many yellow leaves and are shedding them one by one; not when it storms: then they summon up their strength and hold on as tight as they can; but afterward, when it becomes so expectantly still, then they scatter, leaf by leaf, a lot of great, yellow, twisted leaves. There are decayed thistles there with sad little purple heads, thistles that have grown tall like that without thinking; birches are there that are all tremulous, and perhaps they have been so all summer—, but now it looks as if they were intentionally and joyfully so, and the clouds pass behind them, and one can see right through them everything that happens in the skies. And a kind of pensive, faded fragrance goes about, as from flowers the sun has dried and the wind has pressed, and it is autumn. And so I often walk up and down there now and avoid the place under the walnut tree and all my summery paths; for I want the autumn! Doesn't it seem as if autumn were the real creator, more creative than spring, which all at once *is*, more creative, when it comes with its will to change and destroys the much too finished, much too satisfied, indeed almost bourgeois-comfortable picture of summer? This great glorious wind that builds sky upon sky; into its land I would like to go, and along its roads. And perhaps you have it about you too in your own home garden and see its image of a morning in the trees it stirs. . . .

[73]

To Lou Andreas-Salomé   Borgeby gård, Flädie
Province of Skåne, Sweden
August 16, 1904

. . . I haven't done much; I have learned to read a little Danish from books by Jacobsen and Hermann Bang and from the letters Sören Kierkegaard wrote to his fiancée; translating these letters has been almost my only work. . . . I feel as if I had had much too much summer and too much sun. Everything in me is waiting for the trees to strip themselves and for the distance beyond them to become visible with its empty fields and with the long roads into winter. . . .

[74]

To Arthur Holitscher   Borgeby gård, Flädie
Province of Skåne, Sweden
August 17, 1904

. . . You must not upset the Roman plan for my sake, dear friend; it has in it so much that is good. The other, concerning London, I cannot judge. Everything English is far away and foreign to me; I don't know the language of that country, almost nothing of its art, none of its poets; and London I imagine as something very distressing. You know my fear of very big cities;

also I shall probably never go farther west, since after all everything keeps calling me to Russia. If sometime, somewhere, anything like home could be given me, it will be there in that wide sorrowful land. . . .

[75]

To Clara Rilke   Borgeby gård, Flädie
                                                Province of Skåne, Sweden
                                                August 17, 1904

. . . it is Wednesday today, and I think a letter will come from you, written Monday; have been thinking so since getting up and look forward to it.

Here the big storm is still on; in the park on the quieter private paths one can hear it, and when one rounds a corner into the open, the whole country rushes upon one, the roads come running, and the little river comes back all ruffled from the sea, instead of going toward it. It is strange then, in all this activity, to see the calm of the grazing animals; the grass blows under their feeding and stirs, but they are calm and dark and self-absorbed. Even the little foal is out on the windiest meadow with its brown mother (who is nourishing herself vigorously); already it is a regular little rocking horse, when it jumps up and down with its long stiff legs and rejoices. But mostly it lies in the grass, flat on its side and motionless. Only its thin tail flips from time to time across its flank. From the distance one sees only its body in the green, and then it looks, in form and color, like a very large, ripe hazelnut.

Torsten Holmström, the student, is here again now; he goes hunting with Norlind, and last evening they shot a seagull. A big seagull. You ought to see it . . . maybe you would draw one of its wings. They are magnificently constructed, so sure and compact and all of gray silk; but you should draw the under side which is more beautiful by far; everything is more delicate there and as ineffably untouched as a young cloud. And those contours: so sure and necessary, feather upon feather, and yet as delicate as in a Rodin drawing. Or in Japanese prints; of them the color of the whole too reminds one. There is white and gray. But from the last white to the gray's first beginning there is still a world of color, a thousand transitions that have no name. There is hesitant white that, hard before the gray, turns back into itself again, and gray that flashes and wants to turn white. There is the gray of fish scales and the gray of water and the tremulous gray of damp air—: as though the mirror of this outspread pinion had preserved everything that happened below it.

It is the time anyway when one sees many things flying: as though the great wind were drawing the birds with it, so they come up sometimes in its current and drift away off over the park.—

[76]

To Tora Holmström   Borgeby gård, Flädie
August 24, 1904

. . . I have so often asked myself whether the days on which we are compelled to be idle aren't the very ones we spend in the deepest activity? Whether our actions themselves, when they come later, are not merely the last afterring of a great movement that takes place in us on inactive days?

In any case it is very important to be idle with trust, wholeheartedly, if possible with joy. The days when even our hands do not stir are so uncommonly still that it is scarcely possible to live them without hearing a great deal. . . .

[77]

To Lou Andreas-Salomé   Furuborg, Jonsered
October 19, 1904

. . . I see that I can't get on with my work this way; that I must open up new tributaries to it, not because the tributaries of all happening and existence are too meager,—only: because I cannot order, cannot combine them. I must learn to grasp and hold: I must learn to work. I have been telling myself that for years and yet go bungling on. Hence the guilty conscience; all the guiltier when others have confidence in me. My immediate family; my father, who is patient with me now in such a sad way; Ellen Key; the people here in the house. I cannot be happy in my own eyes, and that is why I am never happy.

I lack perhaps just a few knacks and helps. If only the first door were opened to me, then I think I would know all right how to handle the mechanism of the others. And if water now, a great deal of water, suddenly came over my wheels, some tributary that knows how to plunge and roar, perhaps the whole misery of this sluggish milling would be over forever. . . .

[78]

To Clara Rilke
Furuborg, Jonsered
October 28, 1904 (Friday)

. . . Only now is the big birch bare that one saw from the windows of Furuborg hanging against the lake-distance; only now are all the paths quite covered with leaves, only now does one see the white house from afar. Everything is brown, reddish-brown, and brown in brown. At intervals one sees pale green strips of meadow, and the firs and pines are a dense dark winter-dress green. Only now and then a quite golden birch is held up high above everything, like a monstrance, into the sunset. . . .

[79]

To a young girl
November 20, 1904

My greeting you with only a few words, out of much occupied days, will seem ungrateful to you; since you managed to find time to tell me such nice things?

Your words were a welcome message to me. I will write you only that. I am happy to know about you, in order to imagine you sometimes and to surround you with wishes: may life open up to you, door by door; may you find in yourself the ability to trust it, and the courage to give to the difficult most confidence of all. To *young people* I would always like to say just this one thing (it is almost the only thing I know for certain up to now)—that we must always hold to the *difficult;* that is our part. We must go so deep into life that it lies upon us and is *burden:* not pleasure should be about us, but life.

Think: isn't childhood difficult in all its unexplained connection? Aren't girlhood years difficult—do they not like long heavy hair pull your head into the depths of great sadness? And it *must* not become otherwise; if for many life suddenly becomes easier, lighterhearted and gayer, that is only because they have ceased to take it seriously, really to carry it and feel it and fill it with their own entity.—That is no progress in the meaning of life. That is a renunciation of all its breadths and possibilities. What is required of us is that we *love the difficult* and learn to deal with it. In the difficult are the friendly forces, the hands that work on us. Right in the difficult we must have our joys, our happiness, our dreams: there, against the depth of this background they stand out, there for the first time we see how beautiful they are. And only in the darkness of the difficult does our smile, so precious, have a meaning; only there does it glow with its deep, dreamy light, and in the brightness it for a moment diffuses we see the wonders and treasures with which we are surrounded. That is all I know how to say and to advise. Whatever else I have known or grasped beyond all knowing is in my verses, which you read with so much affection.

It is so natural for me *to understand girls and women;* the deepest experience of the creator is feminine—: for it is experience of receiving and bearing. The poet Obstfelder once wrote, when describing the face of a strange man: "it was" (when he began to speak) "as if there were a woman in him—"; it seems to me that would fit every poet who begins to speak. . . .

[80]

To Clara Rilke

Furuborg, Jonsered
Thursday, December 1, [1904], evening

. . . now for the first time I really know what winter is and winter-joy. And think you must have it someday, this real winter gladness, white in white and soft and fresh. Or we must both have it together, here in this dear northern land or in Russia sometime. Must sit in a little, completely fur-covered sleigh, just like the one in which I drove out today with Frau Lizzi. Only two people in that little gliding seat and before us one of the tall horses with a three-belled chime on the harness and connected by a white, wide-meshed, protecting net trimmed with tufts of wool to the dashboard of the little sleigh-seat (so that the snow tossed up by the horse's hoofs won't fall into the sleigh). And behind us, in front of his little seat, the good Strandberg standing on the runner, and the reins above us, and high over us now and then the flick of a whip. And white, white country roundabout, up and down and again high up and into the distance, shadowy and radiant white in variously inclined planes as far as the dark near-by wood and farther on again to the distant, gray-blue wooded hills, behind which an early, yellow-green sunset is going on at a place where the dense gray of approaching snow is torn. And here and there in the skies are other such opened places. And it is blue behind, gray thin blue, or else a light glassy green in which the pink of a cloud is slowly turning to white.—That was my farewell to Furuborg,—for today is my last evening in the golden room which has not become confused even by trunks and boxes and still has so much space and peace that I could work in the midst of all this packing. Tomorrow I shall be on the way to Copenhagen. I shall get out in Charlottenlund and live there. . . .

[81]

To Lou Andreas-Salomé   Villa Charlottenlund
                                    Charlottenlund near Copenhagen
                                    December 4, 1904

Dear Lou, now at last I am on the way back after a long, good
time at Furuborg; long: for it seems to me as if I had had summer,
autumn, and winter there and each one wholly; for the last summer days with which it began were so thoroughly summery, and
then each autumn day was an autumn festival, and finally, it also
became regular deep winter with sleigh rides into the soft country, in which everything had become distance, along the cold
lake, over toward strange blue-darkening mountains. And there
came a whole journey, white in white, seven hours on the train
into Småland, and it changed into a sleigh ride through a sound-
lessly snowing afternoon and ended in the early dusk on a lonely
estate. Amid the ringing of ten little bells we went through a
long, old avenue of linden trees—the sleigh swung out and there
was the castle yard, enclosed by the little side wings of the
castle. But there, where four steps rose with weary effort out of
the snow of the yard to the terrace and where this terrace,
bounded by a vase-ornamented railing, thought it was preparing
for the castle, there was nothing, nothing but a few snow-sunken
bushes, and sky, gray, trembling sky, out of whose twilight falling flakes were being loosed. One had to say to oneself, no, there
is no castle there; one did remember too having heard that it was
burned down years ago, but one felt nevertheless that something
was there, one had somehow the sensation that the air behind
that terrace had not yet become one with the rest, that it was
still divided into passages and rooms and in the middle still formed
a hall, an empty, high, deserted, darkening hall.—But at that moment, out of the side wing to the left, stepped the lord of the
manor, big, broad, with a blond mustache, and rebuked the four
long dachshunds for their sharp barking;—the sleigh drove past
him in the curve up to the tiny little right wing, and out of its
little door stepped the good Ellen Key, a modest figure in black,

but all joyous under her white hair. For it was Oby, her brother's estate, and in this right wing is the old-fashioned room where, sitting on a red sofa of her grandmother's, she is writing the second part of her *Lifslinjer* and answering her countless letters to a lot of young girls and young women and young men, who want to know from her where life begins. . . .

[*82*]

To Countess Luise Schwerin   Worpswede bei Bremen
                                                June 5, 1905

It happens, dear and kind Countess, that your generous letter found me still here in Worpswede, where all sorts of circumstances (my still hesitant health too) have held me fast week after week; spring week after spring week, and now for the last few days it has been summer, flung open, like a quickly unfolded fan that now waves gently with its many-colored surface, stirring air and fragrance. The old chestnuts are holding up their towers of blossom, black alder and lilac have thrown out their fragrances like nets, and here and there a little golden laburnum rain falls across the path. And the houses, which a while ago were everything, are now nothing, now that they stand withdrawn so far back in the clear, transparent shadow of trees and tree groups.

So much has happened to overtake me here, while I lagged behind it all; I had to sacrifice to my weariness so much time which with idle hands it plucked to bits and scattered; but the few hours in which I was collected, I was so to good purpose—about Meister Eckehart's purple darkness, collected by his words that are so penetrating. How I thank you, dear friend, for this book; how gladly I owe it to you, how fitting it is that this master should have been shown me by you and that it happened at just this moment in my development, when I needed his sanction and his blessing in much. You will someday see . . . how much I, without knowing about him, have for years been his pupil and proclaimer. Somewhere (I feel it in all humility) I have grown out beyond him: at the places where he established, stood still, gave definitive form; but where he flowed, torrential, and fell down in great waterfalls to God, there I am only a small piece, torn along by him, the stream that with the broad delta of the Trinity moves out into eternity. . . .

That such a human being ever spoke to humanity, to the needy and the helpless—that is an inexpressibly beautiful thing. And yet no consolation, when one thinks that centuries have gone out from this man, not (as might be possible) out beyond him, but passing away under him, passing him by.

Just last evening (while a thunderstorm was slowly coming up) I read Clara my two favorite sermons: the homily on St. Luke "The Kingdom of God Is at Hand" and the sermon "On the Going Forth and Returning Home of the Spirit," which I would like to call that of the never-said. It was solemn and wide about us. We thought of just a few people: of you, of two or three others; and this being alone was full of vision and distance.

Clara Rilke, who is all day in her studio, charges me with affectionate messages for you, dear Countess. I am also to say that the material, which we chose together at the time, . . . pleases her very much (there is so much summeriness in its light-and-dark harmony, something soft and unspoken, as it should be in summer dresses, whose beauty lies in their being more unreal than flower petals and the whole background of summer which seems long to outlast their fluttering fugitiveness).

We are so glad you are enjoying things and resting, as your dear letter so well tells. I am glad, my kind friend, of every word and happy to hear from your sister too, so that I may now think of and write to both of you. The promised account of a festival on your island I would very much like to have, if it is not too presumptuous to expect something beyond your letter which is wholly what you, in an enhanced and fulfilled sense, called "stimulating."

I expect to go from here after Whitsuntide; first to Göttingen to an experienced and dear friend, with whom I want to discuss the Berlin plan again. . . . Of all decisions and arrangements I will keep you informed; for what I don't want to miss in anything important are your and your sister's sympathetic thoughts and the helpful kindness of your generous feeling.

[83]

To Clara Rilke
Göttingen auf dem Hainberg
June 16, 1905

. . . Your dear letter with the pinks brought me something dear and quiet from you. . . . With all the good I have here your words joined in like consent. Thanks. . . . I will not tell you much about it all, how I am living now, how I am being given strength here and composure and encouragement. Often we wish you were with us when we sit in the garden and read or speak of all the things with which I have often bothered you and which are now becoming so much easier or at least more bearable in their difficulty; yesterday especially, you were so much missed when I showed Lou the throne of Venus from the Ludovisi collection; she gets such inexpressible joy, so much happiness from it; without being in any way prepared for looking at such things, she enjoyed from within herself by some path of her very own the glory of the antique piece, and exactly as she enjoyed my "Rodin" and a few days ago, the "Panther."—

How good . . . it was that I came here. It is so much more beautiful than I could ever have divined, because it had an even greater necessity than I thought. And if everything here rejoices and helps me now, there is among the most real joys a confidence scarcely to be suppressed any longer: that to *you* too this dear person here, with her breadth of soul, can someday become dear; that the possibility of it is there, I feel every moment now, and all that is needed is that the aimless paths of life shall sometime lead to the necessity, to the place where it becomes a matter of course for this person, who plays such a big part in my inner history, to be (and not only for my sake) indispensable and essential to you too. Without this hope I could not be entirely here nor become entirely happy; but this way I am so, and I believe it will be noticeable for a long time to come that I once was so.

I love my little room with a few books that I know, with a few things from which memories emanate, with the little wooden platform and the steps into the long, narrow garden that goes gliding down the hillside into a dense field of fruit trees. And the landscape is friendly too: to the one side, the wide valley with the tiny, quite factory-free city of learning, to the other, beyond a wooded hill's rim, valleys, and hills in broad, large, green waves, from forest to forest right up into the Harz. Avenues and quiet paths everywhere, up and down which I walk for hours alone (Lou cannot take much exercise), sunk in my own thoughts, like one of the *Hainbund* poets perhaps, and yet quite different, without allies, in far wider alliances. . . .

[*84*]

To Clara Rilke   Marburg a.d. Lahn
                                                    July 27, 1905

. . . I have been in Marburg now since eleven-thirty; have walked up and down the little crooked town as far up as the castle and as far down as St. Elizabeth's, built around and over the miracles of the sainted countess.—Delightful German Gothic enacted in the way a hand is held, in the way a head is bent, in a fold drawing up slender and steep along a narrow figure. And in the one side wing, stone tombs of the fourteenth and fifteenth centuries,—men lying in iron, the right leg slightly retracted, the iron gloves laid one upon the other. And the face deep within between hauberk and visor, shadowed and shone upon by both. . . .

[*85*]

To Clara Rilke   Friedelhausen, Lollar, Hesse
                                                    August 23, 1905

. . . Yesterday, on a glorious, full summer's day with many radiant and colorful hours, we drove out again as before, the lunch basket on the box—: first to the Rabenau and from there,

almost without a stop, on to Appenborn, the old family seat of
the one main Rabenau line. A little rustic-seignorial manor with
an outside staircase and old, oaken pillars; the farmyard round
about, so that one overlooks it from the hall, and with an old,
terraced garden sloping down toward the house, in which the
tenant-farmer's wife raises all kinds of flowers. And the phlox
stands tall beside the old shored-up apple trees and, dahlias and
asters and gladioli and the tobacco's blossom star that is closed
by day. . . . On the drive back Hassan struck again, which re-
sulted in our having an evening and a nightfall in "Grandfather's
garden," in the old Londorf pavilion, where the chandelier was
burning, shimmering out with a radiant festiveness into the garden walks from which, as if from many sides, came the noise of
the fountain. Those hours were very beautiful and full of memories that came and went without being ours.—In the wood by
the Rabenau family vault, I saw a fox that sprang past me slender
and wild, his face with the quick eyes turned full upon me. . . .

[86]

To Clara Rilke   Schloss Friedelhausen, Lollar, Hesse
                                    September 7, 1905

. . . I shall live at Rodin's in Meudon. Just think. For day before yesterday afternoon came the following letter (written by
his secretary): "Monsieur Rodin me charge de vous faire savoir
qu'il sera heureux de vous voir; Monsieur Rodin vous attendra
à Paris à partir du 7 courant. Monsieur Rodin me charge en outre
de vous faire savoir que vous pourrez demeurer chez lui, à Meudon, pendant la durée de votre séjour à Paris. Agréez Monsieur
etc . . ." (signed by the secretary and underneath: Aug. Rodin
in his own hand.)—Then, on the back, a postscript by the secretary with his signature once again, reading: "Monsieur Rodin
tient à ce que vous restiez chez lui pour pouvoir parler." Isn't
that kind, that further corroboration and confirmation Rodin had
him add? In answer I wrote yesterday: j'accepte, for he does
mean it that way, it is his will, and it will be good. For the moment,

as I wrote, I accepted only for a few days, because I was afraid of causing Madame Rodin too much trouble; but it will become apparent in the simplest way how long I can stay with him out there without anyone's suffering from it. Of the great nearness and intimacy of his daily life I think with deep joy, and as gladly of the little Villa des Brillants and its garden looking out far and wide. . . .

[87]

To Countess Luise Schwerin
Wacholderhöhe, Godesberg
September 10, 1905

. . . out of the last swift days in the dear gray castle many thoughts came to you from me; a letter would gladly have come; but there was so much, outside and in; life had to go on in its own way: that was the surest means of being close to you. We had to sit at breakfast as though you might at any moment walk in, and at noon gather in your high workroom and evenings be quietly together in your dear name. And in between were various things; the first two proof signatures of my *Book of Hours* came and insisted on being read, and the afternoon brought our Kant hour, which on the last day too led to finishing the book that we had undertaken. Two most beautiful drives we made; each into a different world and country, with distant views over bright fields and the shining river and on beyond to the quietly full contours of dense wooded hills—: to Salzböden first through the village as far as a big mill and then across a bridge and circling back through Odenhausen, and the second drive, to the Neh bridge, from which one sees Marburg, medieval and as if with the light of another star, on a gray afternoon, when everything distant was wonderfully gently toned down within the grayness. And then I tried to achieve now and then an hour of quiet in which I did nothing but walk up and down on the terrace below, with eyes that really contemplated and found repose in everything, with which I sought to take once more, and deep in the taking to hold, all the dearness, all the reality that I so gladly owe to your daily giving. How often, I feel, how often in all that is to come, picture after picture out of it all will return to me, the castle, that moment or some particular movement that took place in one of the rooms grown dear: and when such a return comes toward me out of deep-sunk recollection full of memories, it will be significant every time and related to much and evoking the future with a new noble name. My life, everything that I am, has gone through Friedelhausen the way a whole river goes through the warmth of a sunny countryside, wider spread and broader as it were and gleaming with all its waves.

And yesterday, on the journey, I saw Weilburg for an instant, built up on its mildly commanding mountain,—and when that was past, nothing came for a long time save forests and curved forest valleys like long-echoing afterrings of the tone it had awakened in me. Past robust Limburg too we went and past a steep strong castle of Runkel and past ruins that went on looking with but a single arched window out of the forests, as though they had gone down to destruction in their green, agitated darkness.

And are now amid the von der Heydts' cordial, quietly generous hospitality.

Tomorrow I go on, far from all this, but still not out of the nearness that includes and holds me with you and your dear ones. And I shall come to the great man, dear as a father, the Master, of whom I shall still tell you much. He wants me to live with him, and I could not do otherwise than accept; so I shall be allowed to share all his days, and my nights will be surrounded by the same things as his. And I shall not have the city about me with its voices and violence, but him and the stillness of his house in the country that from the heights of Meudon overlooks with quiet eyes distant Paris and the near valley of Sèvres. Thence my affectionate thoughts will seek you and bless you. . . .

[88]

To Clara Rilke

Rodin, Meudon
September 15, 1905

. . . he received me, but it means nothing if I say cordially; in the way a beloved place receives one, to which one returns by paths that have become more overgrown: a spring that, while one was away, has sung and lived and mirrored, day and night,—a grove above which birds of passage have flown back and forth, spreading shadows over its tracery,—a path lined with roses that hasn't ceased leading to those remote places; and like a big dog he greeted me, recognizing me with exploring eyes, contented and quiet; and like an eastern god enthroned, moved only within his sublime repose and pleasure and with the smile of a woman and with a child's grasping gesture. And led me about. Now things are well with him; much more world has grown about him; he has built several little houses from the museum downward on the garden slope. And everything, houses, passages, and studios and gardens: everything is full of the most wonderful antiquities that associate with his dear things as with relatives, the only ones they have, happy, when the thousand eyes in their bodies open, not to be looking out into an unfamiliar world. And he is happy and strokes their beautiful shoulders and cheeks and from afar reads on their lips the inexpressible. And with him everything is in blossom. How all that has grown! And how one understands and loves all the new as that which had to come, the most necessary, most inward, decreed, destiny! He moves like a star. He is beyond all measure. About my book, which was carefully translated for him only recently, he said the greatest things one can say: placed it beside his things, very big. . . . I have a little cottage all to myself: three rooms: bedroom, workroom, dressing room, with enchanting things, full of dignity, and the main window with all the glories of the Sèvres valley, the bridge, the distances with their villages and objects. . . .

[*89*]

To Clara Rilke   Chez Rodin, Meudon-Val-Fleury
                                    Wednesday, September 20 [1905]

. . . what are all times of rest, all days in wood and sea, all attempts to live healthily, and the thoughts of all this: what are they against this wood, against this sea, against the indescribably confident repose in his holding and carrying glance, against the contemplation of his health and assurance. There is a rush of forces streaming into one, there comes over one a joy in living, an ability to live, of which I had no idea. His example is so without equal, his greatness rises up before one like a very near tower, and at the same time his kindness, when it comes, is like a white bird that circles, shimmering about one, until it lights trustfully upon one's shoulder. He is everything, everything far and wide. We speak of many, many things. It is good for him to talk about many things, and though I can't always keep up with him very well, being hindered by the language, still I am doing better and better every day with the listening. And just imagine the last three mornings: we got up very early at five-thirty, yesterday even at five o'clock, and went out to Versailles; at the Versailles station we take a carriage and drive into the park, and in the park we walk for hours. And then he shows one everything: a distance, a motion, a flower, and everything he evokes is so beautiful, so understood, so startled and young, that the world is all one with the youth of this day that begins in mists, almost in soft rain, and quite gradually becomes sunny, warm, and weightless. Then he tells a great deal about Brussels where he had his best years. The model for the "Age d'airain" was a soldier and he used to come quite irregularly, sometimes at five o'clock in the morning, sometimes at six o'clock in the evening; [Rodin's] colleague on the other works forced him out from jealousy, and so he was left with almost all his time to himself. And he spent it in the environs of Brussels, always on the move with Madame Rodin (who is a good, loyal person), in the woods, always wandering. At first he would set up his paintbox somewhere and paint. But

he soon noticed that in doing this he missed everything, everything alive, the distances, the changes, the rising trees and the
sinking mist, all that thousandfold happening and coming-to-
pass; he noticed that, painting, he confronted all this like a hunter,
while as observer he was a piece of it, acknowledged by it,
wholly absorbed, dissolved, was landscape. And this being landscape, for years,—this rising with the sun and this having a part
in all that is great, gave him everything he needed: that knowledge, that capacity for joy, that dewy, untouched youthfulness
of his strength, that unison with the important and that quiet
understanding with life. His insight comes from that, his sensitivity to every beauty, his conviction that in big and small there
can be the same immeasurable greatness that lives in Nature in millions of metamorphoses.—"And if today I were to paint from
Nature again, I would do it just as I do my sculptures, a very
quickly sketched contour that I would improve at home, but
otherwise I would only gaze and unite with and be the same as
everything about us." And while we speak thus of many things,
Madame Rodin picks flowers and brings them to us: autumn
crocuses or leaves, or she draws our attention to pheasants, par-
tridges, magpies (one day we had to go home earlier because she
had found a sick partridge that she took with her to care for),
or she collects mushrooms for the coachman, who is sometimes
consulted too when it appears that none of us knows a tree. That
was in the elm avenues that go around by the edge of the Versailles
park outside the Trianon. A twig was broken off: Rodin looked
at it for a long time, felt its plastic, strong-veined leaves and finally
said: so, I know that forever now: c'est l'orme. Thus in everything
he is receptive as a goblet, and everything becomes wellspring,
wherever he proffers himself and shines and mirrors.—Yesterday I lunched in the city with him and Carrière and an author,
Charles Morice; but usually I see no one but him. In the evening,
at twilight, when he comes back from the rue de l'Université,
we sit at the rim of the pool near his three young swans and look
at them and talk of many and serious things. Also of you.—It is
beautiful the way Rodin lives his life, wonderfully beautiful. We

were to meet Carrière at the studio in the rue de l'Université; we were there promptly at twelve o'clock. Carrière kept us waiting. Rodin looked at the clock a few times while he was attending to some of the mail he had found there, but when I looked up again, I found him deep in his work. That is how he spends his waiting times! . . .

Soon after supper I retire, am in my little house by eight-thirty at the latest. Then the wide blossoming starry night is before me, and below, before the window, the gravel walk goes up a little hill on which, in fanatic silence, an effigy of Buddha rests, dispensing with quiet reserve the inexpressible self-containedness of his gesture beneath all the skies of day and night. C'est le centre du monde, I said to Rodin. And then he looks at one so kindly, so wholly a friend. That is very beautiful and a great deal. . . .

[90]

To Karl von der Heydt   Villa des Brillants
                                  Meudon-Val-Fleury (Seine et Oise)
                                  November 20, 1905

 . . . only the very great *are* artists in that strict yet only true sense, that art has become a way of life for them—: all the others, all of us who are still only just busying ourselves with art, meet on the same wide roads and greet each other in the same silent hope and long for the same distant mastery. . . .

[91]

To Clara Rilke   Villa des Brillants
                                  Meudon-Val-Fleury (Seine et Oise)
                                  November 24, 1905

 . . . yesterday in the great storm, read Verhaeren whom I visited Wednesday with Ellen's greetings and found sweet and simple, reminding me somehow of Otto Modersohn,— . . . nevertheless I await the Master with impatience; he is work and nourishment, and when he is here, the day has many more hours and sleep more industry.

[*92*]

To Clara Rilke   Villa des Brillants
                              Meudon-Val-Fleury (Seine et Oise)
                                   December 2, 1905

. . . yesterday it was like this: the Master and I went early to Versailles (for the first time again, though it was raining) and walked about slowly two gray, gentle hours in the garden of the Grand Trianon which belonged entirely to us and was so new and odd, with a row of palaces and pavilions which even the Master had never seen like this, and courts overgrown with grass and forgotten, and water mirrors of big darkened panes against which a hand of chestnut leaves held itself now and then, while the misty rain approached it all from afar.—Then we returned quickly for lunch (Madame Rodin had not been with us) and went right afterward into the city and up to Notre Dame, entering on the dot of two o'clock with the petitioners of the first Advent Sunday. There Madame Rodin set in place two chairs for us by a pillar near the big left-hand grillwork gate that leads into the middle between main nave and high altar, . . . there we sat still, quite still for two hours on end, and there was a singing over us and for us and for God, singing and booming and roaring in the dark treetops of the organ, out of which now and then, scared up by voices, the soprano flew up like a white bird and mounted and mounted.

And Rodin was as though he had once done all that five hundred years ago; became so lost and was yet so much there and so initiated into everything and so recognized by the shadows that stepped up to him out of the pillars and reverently accompanied him.

Later we walked slowly, the three of us, in the falling mist and light, first past the antique dealers, then against the stream of all the Sunday strollers (as we often did too) up the Boul^d Saint-Michel, bought cakes at the little pointed corner of the rue Racine and its sister street on the right side of the Boulevard,— the very cakes that Rodin showed us from outside through the bright windows, walked the rue Racine, through under the Odéon, into the already quite dense-gray Luxembourg, stopped a while before the Fontaine Médicis and finally came through the Avenue de l'Observatoire on to the B^d Montparnasse, which also for Rodin and Madame Rodin is full of memories of their very early days. . . . That was Sunday and already quite a birthday, altogether. . . .

[93]

To Arthur Holitscher   Villa des Brillants, Meudon-Val-Fleury
                                          December 13, 1905

. . . a constellation of dear people stands above me and above all this that makes me light and heavy, and again and again heavy; they are the people from whom I do not often hear, about whom I rarely ask (I am so sure of them), and when I look up, they are always in the same place, always above me: you are of these people, dear friend. All the silence is like space between us, but not like time: it does not separate us, it only determines the extent of what we have in common and makes it very wide. Isn't that so?—Where did you last leave me? Now you find me again in a little cottage that belongs to Rodin and stands in his garden on the slopes of Meudon, facing the skies, before which, far, far off, Saint-Cloud rises, with the window always on that part of the Seine which through the Pont de Sèvres has become a stanza. And there my life is. A little as Rodin's secretary, writing very reprehensible French letters, but above all among his grown-up things and in his great serene friendship learning, slowly learning this: to live, to have patience, to work, and never to miss an inducement to joy. For this wise and great man knows how to find joy, friend; a joy as nameless as that one remembers from childhood, and yet full to the brim with the deepest inducement; the smallest things come to him and open up to him; a chestnut that we find, a stone, a shell in the gravel, everything speaks as though it had been in the wilderness and had meditated and fasted. And we have almost nothing to do but listen; for work itself comes out of this listening; one must lift it out with both arms, for it is heavy. My strength often fails, but Rodin lifts everything and lifts it out beyond himself and sets it down in space. And that is a nameless example. I believe in age, dear friend. To work and to grow old, this it is that life expects of us. And then someday *to be old* and still not by any means to understand everything, no, but to begin, but to love, but to sense, but to link up with what is distant and inexpressible, even into the stars. I say to myself: how good, how precious life must be, when I hear this old man so grand in his speaking of it, so torrential in his silence.

Often indeed we do not know this, we who are in the difficult, up over our knees, up to our chests, up to our chins. But are we then happy in the easy, aren't we almost embarrassed in the easy? Our hearts lie deep, but if we are not pressed down into them, we never go all the way to the bottom. And yet it is necessary to have been to the bottom. That is the point.

Bon courage, Rodin says to me sometimes, for no apparent reason, when we part in the evening, even when we have been talking of very good things; he knows how necessary that is, every day, when one is young:—

[94]

To Clara Rilke   Villa des Brillants
                              Meudon-Val-Fleury (Seine et Oise)
                    [postmarked January 26, 1906] Friday morning

. . . We came home tired, the weather was too much against us, after brisk cold rawness and then snow and right after that thaw and east wind and glare ice; all in one day and on this particular one, and the most impracticable weather for our road from the station. So we arrived tired. Perhaps also because it is saddening to see all that ruin and that bad restoration which is even more intolerable, in its stiffness and hardness and ugliness, than the loss of a beautiful thing. Chartres seems to me much more ravaged even than Notre-Dame de Paris. Much more hopeless; much more abandoned to those who destroy. Just the first impression, the way it rises up, as in a great cloak, and the first detail, a slim weatherbeaten angel holding out a sundial exposed to the day's whole round of hours, and above it one sees, infinitely beautiful still in its fading, the deep smile of his joyfully serving face, like sky mirroring itself. . . . But that is nearly all. And the Master is the only one (it seems) to whom all that still comes and speaks. (If it spoke to others even a little, how could they, one wonders, how would they be allowed to miss it?) He was quiet as in Notre Dame, fitting in, infinitely recognized and received. Speaking softly of his art and confirmed in it by the great principles that reveal themselves to him wherever he looks. And it was very beautiful; from the station we got to the cathedral about nine-thirty; there was no longer any sun, there was gray frost, but it was still quiet. But when we arrived at the cathedral, around the angel's corner a wind came suddenly, like some very large person, and went pitilessly right through us, sharp and cutting. "Oh," I said, "here's a storm suddenly coming up." "Mais vous ne savez pas," said the Master, "il y a toujours un vent, ce vent-là autour des grandes cathédrales. Elles sont toujours entourées d'un vent mauvais agité, tourmenté de leur grandeur. C'est l'air qui tombe le long des contreforts, et qui tombe de cette hauteur et erre autour de l'église. . . ." Something like that the Master said it, briefer, somewhat less elaborate, more Gothic too. But something of the sort was the sense of what he meant. And in this vent errant we stood like damned souls compared with the angel holding out his dial so blissfully to a sun that he always saw. . . .

[95]

To Clara Rilke   Villa des Brillants
Meudon-Val-Fleury (Seine et Oise) (France)
February 8, 1906, Thursday, toward evening

. . . I am writing, I should say, a hundred letters every day, morning for the Master and afternoon for myself, and if anything is then left over that isn't yet night, I hearken to my poems that still want to go into the *Book of Pictures*. Slowly I listen to each one and let it die away into its farthest echo. Few will stand up in the stillness in which I place them, several will recast themselves, of many only a piece will be left and will wait until, one day perhaps, something joins it. . . .

[96]

To Clara Rilke   Villa des Brillants
Meudon-Val-Fleury (Seine et Oise)
Thursday evening, February 15, 1906

. . . yesterday we lunched once more at Troubetzkoi's (three vegetarian lunches in succession), and afterward (he lives in Boulogne-sur-Seine) we walked to the Jardin d'Acclimatation through a more quiet part of the Bois de Boulogne, out of whose depths now and then a light deer face had been looking at us for a while; we landed first in a kind of exhibition, the way you and I once did too, beside which is an enclosure with monkeys; the fearful hamadryads were furious as before, bit into their hands, and beat themselves against the wall, as if out of their minds over the unspeakable ugliness in which cruel Nature had left them, as it passed on to the next. (All this she had to make, continually trying new combinations, in order to get to us, said the Master.) In the same enclosure, in a cage opposite, were three monkeys the size of little dogs, with pale sick faces and the great dreamy eyes of consumptives. Infinitely forlorn and hopeless, they had joined fast together in a sad merging-into-each-other, each expecting comfort from the warmth of the other, the three faces, each separate, each different, set into the whole, as sometimes in Minne's woodcuts, or less firmly drawn and given over to the total effect, as sometimes in Carrière. But then we stepped out again under the afternoon skies that were wintry, and into the wind that came off snow, and it was almost painful in that air to see the rose and red flamingos blooming. Rodin lingered for the most part near the precious Chinese pheasants that seemed to be of enamel and finished with so much care that it was surprising to find on one or another a gray head, as if only in underpainting and never carried out. (How often Nature has probably gone on thus to the next thing, driven by what comes to her mind and by the joy of beginning that next thing!) The last we saw was a marabou, holy, but ugly, full of wilderness in his feeling and utterly hopeless in his meditation: (first sketch perhaps for a hermit, abandoned and not taken up again until much later). . . . There is so much now for the Master to do; we are already at a "discours" again; he sent one as a letter for the opening of the first exhibition, at the time of my return; now he has to speak himself at his banquet on the twenty-first, and he has a lot of nice and fruitful ideas, of which he wants to hand over all that is best. I must only see to it that each idea is glad to stay beside the other; I may add noth-ing, but just that is not easy. And letters upon letters. . . .

[97]

To Clara Rilke

Villa des Brillants
Meudon-Val-Fleury (Seine et Oise)
February 22, 1906

. . . With this letter I ought to bring bread into the house for you, into the new one; but again my fields are not yet that far along. There is scarcely a shimmer even of what is to come next, and the sun is still hidden behind the gray of my activities and can almost never shine on it, on the little green. Alas . . . I could copy out your long letters with all their questions about what life wants of us, I could copy them out and they would be my letters, word for word.

There are mornings, all the birds call so specially, and a singular agitation is in the air, and I can scarcely contain myself with yearning to be long alone, for anything that is so absolutely mine as those Roman days, of which I often cannot help thinking because in the garden now it sounds so like that sometimes. And mornings, and afternoons with the Bible on the reading desk, and boundless evenings, and nights that seem to rise up out of one's own heart,—and all mine. And tomorrow another day. I have thought what to do, but the time here is already as good as up, Sunday I leave and — —. But life wills it thus, your life and mine . . . our life, to which we have always had to give way: its way. . . .

I am thinking of so much now, and the practical jostles with the limitless in me as in dreams sometimes. Everything that insists on being thought of and attended to, and all the rest that wants to be beside some sea and wants to sing, days on end, nights on end. . . .

[98]

To Clara Rilke   Thursday, April 5, morning
                                    [postmarked April 5, 1906]

. . . Here it is spring. There is only the one word for it. And already it is no longer premature to say so. The violets are past their bloom, the blue periwinkle looks large-eyed out of its dark green (the pervenche Francis Jammes loves so), the primroses are standing side by side in big groups, as though they had run together from everywhere, and the wallflower (giroflé) is as if darkened by its own heavy perfume. All that is full of memory, but it is a memory without heaviness, that rises up and away from the things into the sky. And against the skies stand the bearing gestures of the plum trees, as if ashamed of the easiness of their blossoms that will open fully tomorrow by the hundreds. And yet as in wisdom already bearing this ease, as later the burden. And the little valley is beautiful and as though it lay further away from the house than usual, being so set into the spring. And the antiquities standing out there are as if they too were to put forth, so full, so full of rising life.

Day before yesterday we were in the woods, toward Jouy-en-Josas and Vélisy, and there everything was full of little white anemones, the whole floor of the forest full of anemone-stars and constellations. . . .

[99]

To Karl von der Heydt　　　　　Meudon-Val-Fleury, Seine et Oise
April 7, 1906

In me is all the restlessness of these unbelievably blissful spring days which, like a hall that goes up several stories, reach through the whole sky; the birds are singing, already the periwinkle in the shadowy green is opening its gazing blue eye, and the scent of wallflowers fills the whole morning. And the plum trees are in bloom. And I lack nothing but that little bit of freedom to be by myself and to listen down inside myself and to consider some work of my own. Will you understand that every day I have to exercise all my common sense not to climb aboard a train and go to Viareggio, there on the coast of the Ligurian Sea, where the third part of the *Book of Hours* came into being, all embedded in the great noise of the lonely sea? So strong is the feeling in me that I could do, should do something now,—something that may perhaps never come again like this, but that cannot come here, stifled by the correspondence I must do and diverted from me through the continual qui vive of my function, through this never being able to be inwardly alone. . . . My God, I have to say that to someone, just in order to have said it, and I say it to you because you, on your journey that will quickly pile up again new and different things over this letter, can best forget it again. . . .

[100]

To Karl von der Heydt   Villa des Brillants
                              Meudon-Val-Fleury (Seine et Oise) France
                                  Wednesday after Easter 1906

I thank you for the question. Only my father could have asked like that. And I feel that I can answer you, as I would have answered him, honestly, without hesitation. I am seriously reflecting and thoroughly took counsel in myself last night: What can you do for me? Dear friend:

What I would need, according to my feeling and my conscience, is: to be able to work for myself alone for a year or two, under conditions such as I had for a while that time in Rome; alone, with only my wife in the neighborhood, who was working too, so that we did not see each other every day by any means, yet were helping each other. Without a function, almost without outside contacts. (Then the *Notebooks of Malte Laurids Brigge*, to which I have not yet returned, came into being, and other things wanted to come. But my stay had to be cut short.) I went then to my friends in Sweden who offered me everything the most generous hospitality can give, but still could not give me this, this limitless solitude, this taking each day like a lifetime, this being-with-everything, in short, space, to the end of which one cannot see and in the midst of which one stands, circled about by the innumerable.

So the time in Sweden became more a receptive time, as Friedelhausen was later, in all its legendary beauty, and as, in still another way, Meudon is now. But after all that and after certain anxious and profound occurrences that have peculiarly linked and interpreted everything that went before, a time should, must come for me, to be alone with my experience, to belong to it, to reshape it: for all that is unconverted is already oppressing and confusing me; it was only an expression of this state that I should have been longing more than ever to take upon myself, like a vocation, this spring that reached out to and touched everything: since it would have become the highest inducement for so much that is only awaiting a start. I don't believe I am fooling myself when I think that my age (I shall be thirty-one this year) and all other circumstances speak for the fact that, if I might now collect myself for my next advance, I could produce a few works that would be good, that would help me along inwardly and perhaps also pave the way outwardly for giving to my life a security which my so-far published books have not given, but which seems not quite excluded for later.

But: I cannot possibly leave Rodin now; that is just as clear to me. My conscience would not be light enough for work of my own if I went away from him like that, unexpectedly. Especially as he has been sick all these weeks and still feels tired and low and has need of my support, insignificant as it is, more than ever. I shall now have to hit upon some kind of compromise with my great longing. I am convinced that patience is always good and that nothing that in the deepest sense is justified in happening can remain unhappened. I shall some day take up and bring to an end the work for which conditions are now lacking, if it is really as absolutely necessary and organically demanded of me as I believe. I shall carry on this life with good will and absolute readiness to serve a while longer, as well as I can, and give it up some day when we have considered whether that is possible and in what way it is to happen. To think that out, slowly to think it out ahead of time for next fall perhaps, that is the only thing, dear friend, that you can do for me now. . . . But it will alter my life and my position very much if I can just hope to be able to return to my own work and task in the not too distant future. Then I shall at once have joy in the patience now required of me, imposed on me by circumstances, in a certain sense difficult but yet not hostile, by this great old Master who wants it thus. I am incessantly called and interrupted and will let matters rest for today with having spoken these few words to you: which to me has been an indescribable relief. . . .

[101]

To S. Fischer   Meudon-Val-Fleury (Seine et Oise) France
April 19, 1906

. . . A few days ago Rodin began the portrait of one of your most remarkable authors, which promises to become something quite extraordinary.

And yet hardly ever has a portrait been so much aided in its making by the subject it represents as this bust of Bernard Shaw. Not only that he stands excellently (with an energy in his keeping still and with such an absolute giving of himself to the hands of the sculptor), but he knows too how to collect and concentrate himself to such a degree in the part of his body which, within the bust, will after all have to represent so to speak the whole Shaw, that the nature of the man springs over from it with unbelievably heightened intensity, feature by feature, into the bust.

This personality of Shaw's and his whole manner makes me desirous of reading a few more of his books, of which I think I know only the *Man of Destiny*. Would sending me a few of his books be justified if I say that I am hoping to write a little thing about him (though without blindly obligating myself to it)?

I would be deeply grateful to you, you may be sure, if you would send me some of his things. I could also relay something of them to Rodin; he wants to become acquainted with Shaw's books, but since there are as yet no French translations in existence, the only source for him would, for the present, be what I could tell him of them.

Madame Shaw, who brought about the making of this portrait over her husband's head in the most charming way, is a solicitous, quietly attentive good woman, full of zeal and enthusiasm for beautiful things, hovering about her husband with all this as the spring wind plays about a billy goat.—This by way of information about your remarkable author. . . .

[*102*]

To Clara Rilke   Meudon-Val-Fleury (Seine et Oise) France
                    Thursday after Easter 1906 [postmarked April 19, 1906]

. . . The summer is moving fast. Here at least it seems to be approaching with great rapidity. Can you imagine that the Avenue de l'Observatoire is thick and green, as it was that time when, returning from Viareggio, I walked up and down there. And in the Luxembourg it is all shadow on the upper terraces, the shimmer of the girls' dresses is now more subdued, with more nuances, under the full chestnuts—: no longer in their very shiny spring-bright whiteness. And here in the garden already yesterday a blue iris opened; the strawberries are blooming, the currant bushes too I saw out there in blossom. The little new light-green heraldic eagles are set up by the round fig bushes. And now, since yesterday (after many, many summer-warm, radiant days) there is falling, day and night, a soft, quiet rain, thick, gentle, and full, as from the rose of a watering can: comme tombant d'un arrosoir, one would like to say, because that sounds and falls still darker and fuller on the ear. And the green is growing under this rain: swelling and pushing up, and here and there opening all fresh and new. . . . (And I think of Rome.)

Bernard Shaw comes out daily with his wife, we see each other often, and I was present at the first sittings and saw for the first time how Rodin tackles his work.—First there is a firmly shaped clay dummy, consisting of nothing but a ball set on something that supports it like a shoulder. This dummy is prepared for him and contains *no* armature *at all;* it only holds together by firm kneading.—He begins his work by first placing his model at a very short distance, about half a step from the stand. With a big iron compass he took the measurement from the top of the head to the tip of the beard, and immediately established this proportion on the clay dummy by lumps of clay. Then in the course of the work he took measurements twice more: nose to back of head, and ear to ear from behind. After he had further cut out the eye sockets very quickly, so that something like a nose was formed, and had marked the place for the mouth with an indentation such as children make on a snowman, he began, with his model standing very close, to make first four profiles, then eight, then sixteen, having his model turn after about three minutes. He began with the front and back views and the two full side-profiles, as though he were setting four different drawings vertically against the clay ball, then fitted half-profiles, etc., between these contours. Yesterday, at the third séance, he seated Shaw in a cunning little child's armchair (that ironic and by no means uncongenial scoffer was greatly entertained by all this) and cut off the head of the bust with a wire (Shaw, whom the bust was already remarkably like, in a superior sort of way, watched this decapitation with indescribable joy) and worked on the recumbent head, partially supported by two wedges, seeing it from above, at about the same angle as the model sitting low down a step away. Then the head was set on again and the work is now going along in the same fashion. In the beginning Shaw *stood*, often very close to the stand, so that he was somewhat higher than the bust. Now he sits right next it, exactly as high as the work, parallel with it. At some distance away a dark cloth has been hung up, so that the profiles always stand out clearly. The Master works rapidly, compressing hours into minutes, it seems to me, executing stroke after stroke at very short intervals, during which he absorbs indescribably, fills himself with form. One seems to feel how his quick, bird-of-prey-like clutch is always carrying out only one of these faces that are streaming into him, and one comprehends his working from memory after the sitting is over. . . .

Be of good cheer and earnest confidence. Should this blessed life, which indeed never does anything twice but still might come back to letting us work side by side, give us a chance once more like the one in Rome, we shall be much further ahead and more capable and will do a lot of good things. . . .

[*103*]

To Elisabeth von der Heydt   Meudon-Val-Fleury,
Seine et Oise, France
April 26, 1906

. . . Do you know, does v.d. Heydt know Shaw's works?
There is a man who has a very good way of getting along with
life,—of putting himself into harmony with it (which is already
something). Proud of his works, like Wilde or Whistler, but
without their pretentiousness, proud as a dog is proud of his
master. . . .

[*104*]

To Clara Rilke   Meudon-Val-Fleury, Seine et Oise
May 3, 1906

. . . there is no nightingale in the garden here, not even
many bird voices; on account of the hunters probably who come
by here every Sunday; but sometimes in the night I waken with
the calling, a calling somewhere below in the valley, calling out
of a full heart. That sweet ascending voice that does not cease
to mount, that is like an entire being transformed into voice,
all of which—its form and bearing, its hands and face—has become
voice, nocturnal, great, adjuring voice. From afar it sometimes
bore the stillness to my window, and my ear took it over and
drew it slowly into the room and, across my bed, into me. And
yesterday I found them all, the nightingales, and in a mild, cur-
tained night wind walked past them, no, right through the midst
of them, as through a throng of singing angels that only just
parted to let me through, and was closed in front of me and shut
to again behind me. Thus, from quite near, I heard them. (I had
been in town, to eat with passing friends of the Elberfeld von der
Heydts, and came back to Val-Fleury by train toward ten.)
Then I found them: in all these old, neglected parks (in the one
with the beautiful house whose walls are slowly falling in, as
though some artillery of time were aimed directly at them, the

one that is cut through the middle by the road and like a fruit that has fallen apart shows its interior, withered and moldy;—and a little further over in a thickly wooded stretch of park) and behind and above in the closed gardens of the Orangerie. And from the other side it came across over the walls of the old Mairie and then suddenly beside me out of a dense little garden full of hedges and lilac bushes—: came so recognizably and so interwoven with the little garden lying withdrawn into itself under the half-light night, as when in a piece of lace one recognizes the picture of a bird spun of the same threads that signify flowers and blooming things and densest superfluity. And that was noise and was about me and drowned out all thoughts in me and all my blood; was like a Buddha of voices, so big and commanding and superior, so without contradiction, vibrating so, up to the very boundary of the voice, where it becomes silence again, vibrating with the same intensive fullness and evenness with which the stillness vibrates when it grows large and when we hear it. . . .

[*105*]

To Clara Rilke   Meudon-Val-Fleury, Seine et Oise
Thursday evening [postmarked May 11, 1906]

. . . this will only be a little Sunday letter, because I have a big task: *this*, to pack up and move out of my little house into the old freedom with all its cares, with all its possibilities, with the great possession of all its hours. I am full of anticipation and happy. About how it came, there is not much to tell, and what there is to say I do not want to write. It probably had to come and it came so of itself. I bore everything, even this last period, with quiet, introspective absorbed patience, and I would probably have borne it that way for a month or two longer. But the Master must have felt that I was suffering—. And now the end has come so quickly, doubtless more quickly even than he expected, because he wants to go to the country for a while and close up the house and garden completely. So I plan to move into the city on Saturday; I have rented a room in the little hotel in the rue Cassette

(—No. 29—) in which we once visited Paula Becker, the room on the entresol under hers, that still, over the opposite wall, looks out on and tells of the presence of the green convent trees. I have rented it without obligation from week to week. There I shall now be and shall meditate upon myself and remain alone a little with what is in me. And go on, at once, getting the *Cornet* ready and arranging the *Book of Pictures*. And see the Louvre and the Cluny now and then and walk in the avenues, by now so dark, of the Luxembourg gardens toward the gray sun outside. . . .

Don't be anxious about what is to come. There are ways, and we shall surely find them and make good plans in the course of the next weeks.

[*106*]

To Auguste Rodin   Paris
   [in French]   May 12, 1906
My Master,

I cannot begin the unforeseen life you have prescribed for me, without having placed in your hands a short exposition of the facts as I most sincerely feel them to be.

M. Thyssen's letter was addressed to me, as your secretary; nor did I withhold it from you in speaking to you that very evening and first thing next morning and in then proposing to you to send the letter prepared several days before to M. Thyssen and to add a postscript relative to his German letter. If I was at fault in this matter, it is that I judged the letter of little importance, being built on a false supposition and therewith no longer valid. You thought otherwise, though I remain convinced that my point of view was excusable in regard to a letter that was not meant to take rather indelicate advantage of the implied mistake and of your absence.

M. Rothenstein's letter was the reply to a purely personal letter I had addressed to him; it was (I must remind you) as your friend that you introduced me to M. Rothenstein, and I could see nothing improper in accepting the little personal relation that had been established between your friend and me across our conversations, the more so as we had very dear mutual friends. But you no longer wished to remember that it was as a friend that you invited me to come to you and that the function into which you introduced me after a few weeks was at first only a means of procuring for a poor friend some quiet time favorable to his work. It was thus that you formulated your proposition, the morning we were walking in the avenue deliberating this possibility which made me happy in the extreme.

"You will help me a little; that will not take much of your time. Two hours every morning." Those were your words.

Moreover, I did not hesitate to give you, instead of two hours, almost all my time and all my strength (unfortunately, I haven't much) for seven months. My work has been neglected for a long time; but how happy I was nevertheless to be able to serve you, to be able slightly to lessen the preoccupations that disturbed your admirable labors.

You yourself opened your intimacy to me and I entered timidly there, in the degree that you wished it; never making any other use of that unforgettable preference than to take comfort in it deep in my heart and that other use, legitimate and indispensable to accomplishing your affairs the way you wanted under your eyes. If I felt that I ought to penetrate those intentions in order someday truly to help you, by knowing your decisions in advance, that feeling need not be blamed; it was bound to waken in one who ardently wished to relieve you and to render you fully the service you had confided to him.

Nevertheless, I have all appearances against me at the moment when you see fit to shift my sincere efforts to a basis of suspicious mistrust.

Here I am, dismissed like a thieving servant, unexpectedly, from the little house where, before, your friendship had gently installed me. It was not to your secretary that you gave those familiar quarters. . . .

I am profoundly hurt by this.

But I understand you. I understand that the wise organism of your life must immediately repel that which seems to it harmful, in order to keep its functions intact: as the eye repels the object that disturbs its sight.

I understand that, and do you remember? how well I understood you often in the happiness of our contemplations? I am convinced that there is no man of my age (either in France or elsewhere) who is endowed as I am (by temperament and by work) to understand you, to understand your great life, and to admire it so conscientiously.

(My wife, from a slightly greater distance and in another way, has a similar feeling for you. I am distressed that you did not think of her in dismissing me, not by a single word, although she (who has such need of your help) has not offended you; why must she share this disgrace of fortune into which I have fallen?)

You have now, great Master, become invisible to me, as though by some ascension carried up into skies of your own.

I shall not see you any more—but, as once for the apostles who were left behind saddened and alone, life is beginning for me, the life that will celebrate your high example and that will find in you its consolation, its justification, and its strength.

We were agreed that in life there is an immanent justice that fulfills itself slowly but without fail. It is in that justice that I put all my hope; it will one day correct the wrong you have seen fit to inflict on him who no longer has the means nor the right to show you his heart.

Rilke

[107]

To Ellen Key   29 rue Cassette, Paris VIe
                                        May 19, 1906

. . . So now: you are coming and I am very happy about it. It is true—to forestall disappointment—you must give up Rodin, at least seeing him with me. Since six days ago, I am no longer with him. At his wish I left him rather unexpectedly, serving him up to the last moment with all my powers; I would not have been able to go on doing it for long anyway, for in the end there was no time left for myself, none at all. Only it would have been difficult for me to take my departure, on the one hand without leaving him in the lurch with all the writing, on the other because of my own uncertain situation. But now that he has taken the step I have no reproaches to make myself, and must assume that all is for the best. My longing for my own things too was already great enough—; *they* shall now have their turn again; externals and the conditions of life will simply have to take on some sort of form. Things must go on somehow, as they have gone up to now.

Of the further particulars of my parting with Rodin, I cannot speak; I can only tell you, because you must know it, that I *cannot* go with you to him, and would also have to ask you, in case you see him—which I hope and desire very much—not to speak of me.

Perhaps you will go to him with Verhaeren—; what a pity: all these months I have rejoiced in this one thing, above all in this: taking you about among his things and into my little house; now everything has come about otherwise.

But please do not conclude from this that I do not feel for Rodin all that I ever felt of admiration and love; my inner relation to him is unaltered, only I can give it no outward expression for the moment, and I must leave it to time to bring about an adjustment that will again reinstate me in the rights of my feeling. —Will these circumstances keep you from coming to Paris? I hope this will not be the case. Paris is so beautiful now and I would derive so much consolation and encouragement from seeing you now and talking with you. (Tell me when you are coming and where you are going to live). . . .

[*108*]

To Baroness Gudrun Uexküll   29 rue Cassette, Paris VI°
                                      Ascension Day [May 24] 1906

. . . Several days ago now I left Rodin to come home to my own work, to myself, to all that has long been repressed. Ah, how very alien any service is if it is not one's very own, the spontaneous service that goes straight from the heart and hands toward what is greatest, if it is not service to God, without an intermediary. Now everything must slowly come to me again, the whole widely scattered herd of my tasks and labors, which has been without supervision. The *Cornet* is once more, finally, to be recast and tested tone by tone down to every echo, and the new edition of the *Book of Pictures*, which will be published with many additions, awaits its assembling. . . .

[*109*]

To Clara Rilke   29 rue Cassette, Paris VI°
                                                Friday morning [May 25, 1906]

. . . I am still far from Malte Laurids; the *Cornet* and the *B. of P.* must first be all ready for the press. And there it is, in the *Cornet*, the passage in question that holds me up. I am almost afraid, in spite of everything, it will have to stand as it is. The same superficial, unperceptive presentation is actually in the whole work (only not in the rewritten passages any longer), and that obtrudes intolerably only in the passages about the "brown maiden," while elsewhere it is hidden. Don't you think so? It is so very much a work of youth and requires much forgiveness. —The entire arrangement of the *B. of P.* also is still before me and will not be easy. . . .

[*110*]

To Clara Rilke   29 rue Cassette, Paris VI°
                                                Tuesday morning [May 29, 1906]

. . . I understand your letter as if I had written it myself, and if I did not talk about all that in mine, which you got Sunday, it is because I believe we must still have patience: you, as long as your work is going ahead and coming to a close, and I, until my *Cornet* at least and my *B. of P.* can go to press and until the moment when I feel I am somewhat organized and clear in mind and inwardly resolute. My leaving Rodin is still too close to me, there is much here I would still like to see, this seeing and this being alone must still do much in me. . . . Despite the feelings that, in me too, have become impatient, urgent, and relentless, already more than once, I think that *your* work, your beautiful and important work, must, since for the moment I am involved in none, be the gauge for us: when you have come to some stopping-place in it, let us make up our minds and act without delay. Either you come here then, have a few days with me (my last) in Paris and we go from here somewhere by the sea, or I come to W[orps]wede into your dear house, into your summery room, —and we go from there to some small, inexpensive beach. (Ah, if we could only save, and only had the knack of living on next to nothing, of holding back everything and letting go only the most necessary, unwillingly and with bad grace. Ellen Key is almost offended if she is asked for money anywhere, and incredibly distrustful of the person who takes it. As a bowler his ball, so, with her whole feeling, she keeps following her franc piece for a long time, expecting each one to make all nine. She is stingy, I notice, our good Ellen. She has probably had to be; it was her mimicry for getting by in various years. But it is not pretty to watch. Since she has been here I live in quite unfamiliar poverty whenever I am with her. We wait on the most diverse corners for the most diverse buses, we eat in a Duval in between, secretly as it were, and I suspect she gets her nourishment principally from what is set before her during some visit. This indigence is sad, but has as consequence a freedom we could well use. One can do a great deal, one can always manage this way—.)

But she is good and honest, our dear Ellen, and convinced and so touchingly untouched by all experience. With her, although she is practical, one cannot discuss practical things because she assumes, if it is a question of plans, that one mentions only those for which the means are already at hand, counted out exactly. Then she naturally says yes and amen to the fine plans. One lives within the money one has, she thinks, and makes one's plans within this enclosure (which would yield pretty poor little vegetable gardens). And also one can scarcely talk with her of inward things, because she still has certain holiday ideals and such unalloyed sentiment that with warmth promptly turns into emotion. So little can be done with that. But do not conclude from all this that I am not pleased to be with her: I am really fond of her in many ways and for much have a quite natural, spontaneous admiration. Out of an unsuccessful life she has made something happy; she has made contact with very important things, and has fallen in love with life and put her trust in life with a pure readiness and a careless serenity like the bird which "has not this care."—She will be here for a fortnight (during which I naturally do not always want to devote myself to her with complete regularity), and already the first day, the Sunday, was of course thoroughly organized. First in turn was the Louvre, in which she looks at and interprets everything in an entirely emotional way, so undisturbed in her points of view: this was really strange before the Mona Lisa, who on that day was of a forbidding haughtiness, deep and clear in the shadow and with all the blue light behind her on water courses and falls and the blue flames of the animated mountains. Before many things this reaction was banal, sometimes it was of a Goethian comprehensiveness, sometimes very inadequate, and a thing like the St. Anne withdraws utterly from such a familiar approach and treatment. The Venus of Milo, which we saw only from a distance (I finally had to go to lunch), would have been the most admirable subject for such interpretations, and down there before her curtain, she seemed to be just waiting for emotional photographs of that sort. (To me, this way of looking is of course fatal: I feel like the young dog with his nose pressed into the little bit of past one should not do in the room.) Then in the afternoon, on the way back from Jouven, Ellen was in my room for a moment (we sent a card to you). She told about Worpswede and is still very amazed at Ruth and indescribably proud of her. At four we arrived by the most various buses at Verhaeren's who, because of his annually recurring hay fever, must now avoid the country and stay on in a little attic lodging in Batignolles.

We had a very lovely hour with him and his wife to which at the end, unfortunately, came Madame G . . . R . . . , the poet's widow, of whom one very well understood her surviving him. But most remarkable was the evening of this already very long day. We saw Ibsen's *Wild Duck* at the Antoine. Excellently rehearsed with a great deal of thought and shaping-up: amazing. Naturally distorted, twisted, misconstrued in detail through certain differences of temperament. But the play itself. Thanks to the circumstance that both female characters (Hjalmar Ekdal's wife and the fourteen-year-old Gina) were simple, without French make-up, all their brilliance came from within almost to the surface. There was something very great, deep, essential. Doomsday and judgment. Something ultimate. And suddenly, the hour had come when Ibsen's majesty deigned to look upon me, for the first time. A new poet to whom we shall go by path after path, now that I know one. And again a man misunderstood in the midst of fame. An entirely different person from what one hears. And still another experience: the unspeakable laughter of the French audience (a very inferior one, to be sure) at the most delicate, most tender, most painful places, where even the moving of a finger would have hurt. There: laughter. And again I understood Malte Laurids Brigge and his northernness and his being wrecked by Paris. How he saw and felt and suffered it.—Yesterday, Monday, the most important thing was the Faillet private collection with all the most important Van Goghs and Gauguins reproduced and praised in Meier-Graefe. There is something most important there beneath arbitrariness and next to insanity. I don't yet know what. It was very remarkable. And I could take that very seriously, while a Gustave Moreau exhibition only gave me the feeling of not belonging there. So I am, after all, somewhat further along than four years ago. . . .

[*111*]

To Clara Rilke   Friday, June 1 [1906], morning

. . . now we have had a few days of bright sun again and today
there is rain, and across the way, over the wall, a light wind is
turning the leaves of the chestnut trees and acacias so that they
get and feel the rain from all sides and are shining with it. And it
is one of those rainy days that are not for the city. That one
should experience outside, to see all the darkened green, all the
meadows mirroring gray, all the beech leaves that are in motion
and more variegated in their green since the lights are no longer
there (the bright, melting, dissolving lights), leaves that have
only reflections, green that sees itself again in green, green that,
set against green, has green shadows, green that has become deep
and finally has a bottom somewhere, a bottom of green. And suddenly all the color is taken out of the scent too, as if the sun
in leaving had let it sink into the flowers. Now the leaves are
fragrant, the little beech leaves especially, and the old-fashioned
leaves of the elms and the little tipped-over leaves of the balsam
poplars are flowing slowly out into the air.—Yesterday we saw
this rain in preparation out in the country, in beech-tree paths,
over broad meadows and water surfaces, in the windows of an
old castle: in Chantilly. This was not a really royal castle, and it
isn't like one. It belonged to the Condés and it is different, more
intimate than Saint-Cloud or Versailles or Saint-Germain, ducal
only, but full of decorum and quiet, not dominating and arrogant
in its feeling, but proud in its reserve and conscious worldly dignity. From the castle (of which only a small wing is old and
good) no views out into an empire that goes up to the sky. But
within the roomy circle of trees which is or seems to be the
boundary, a spreading out, an unfolding with roads and avenues, with water mirrors and rose parquetry, with steps that,
flowing out of balustrades, seem to follow the ascending palace
like its train, with scarcely dipping meadow slopes and scarcely
rising roads, with nuances of movement, with a play of advance
and retreat, of hasty approach and withdrawal, of faltering rise

and swift fall, with this whole minuet of space that is sometimes reflected in one of the high windows and is blotted out by the sky which, out of the depths of this mirror, shimmering like mother-of-pearl, comes plunging, light gray and exaggerated, spilling over everything. Inside, a magnificence spoiled in later times. A series of pictures; little portraits of women and men, black-white-yellow on a jade green background; little Clouets, exquisite and awkwardly elegant, set on an escutcheon-blue background, Fouquet miniatures (legends of Christ and the saints) taken from the livre d'heures of Étienne Chevalier; a drawing of Rembrandt, drawings of Watteau and Prud'hon; Botticelli, Pollaiuolo, and Raphael with pictures; ornaments: among them a Benvenuto Cellini; a very beautiful, dew-bright, liquidly trembling amethyst, surrounded with brilliants, belonging to the greatest member of the house of Condé—and suddenly, looming large in a passageway, that remarkable drawing of Leonardo's for the Mona Lisa, which looks too dark on the card; its tone is that of calf's leather and is rather light against the background spottily covered with brown. . . .

[*112*]

To Clara Rilke   29 rue Cassette, Paris VI•
                                          June 14, 1906

. . . it is strange that for us beginnings perpetually all but coincide with changes. That interruptions almost always impend when the sap is rising; as with grapevines pruned too late, it pours out then and what should have been a mouth has become a wound. La vigne pleure—they said of it in Meudon in an old gardener's expression. I too have now a slight fear of moving. Being occupied with the *B. of P.* (it was sent off today at last) has brought me back, if not literally into work, at least (after an incalculable interim) into warmth, into the body temperature of my soul (to be so rudely graphic), and that is already something and something which, after long coldness, I know how to appreciate. To go on living like this without any change: much in me would like that now in spite of the fact that my room is not without its defects, etc. Now perhaps that is both possible and, in the interests of both of us, the most advisable. We are indeed in the same situation . . . so let us perhaps, each in his place, keep on doing his own work, as long as it continues and circumstances permit, without thinking of anything beyond. Then both our invitations will wait and can become effective when necessary. I haven't written there yet, but I think we could go as early as the second half of July to the Baron and Baroness von der Heydt who are already at Königs-Höhe, while the Karl von der Heydts, as far as I remember, are expecting us in August. . . . Stina Frisell has, in the meantime, gone away again with her little Karin who is now to be introduced "into life," eighteen years old and in the midst of it as she is. Stina Frisell is a dear, simple, loyal person . . . and she was wonderfully comforting beside Ellen Key, of whom scarcely anything seems to be left, she is so gnawed and eaten away by all those rat-souls that cling to her. Ah, it is really sad. How she is nothing but a little shred of old-fashioned ideals worked into a Secessionist armchair and quite delighted with her own use. How she sees and hears nothing any more, neither the human drama incessantly being unloaded upon her, nor works of art, which she analyzes like a schoolteacher without taking or needing anything from them, nor her own memories which, dissolved in her discolored activity, have lost all local color. How, with a certain propensity to take her own life seriously (that was perhaps all), she has yet made it almost ridiculous: into the life of a good aunt to all the world, who has her pockets full for those who find pleasure in sugar lumps and cheap candies, but who cannot appease the hunger of a single person with her miserable, already slightly stale fare. And how natural and right that it happened thus. One cannot desire to make something out of the ordinary (and what is more exceptional and unusual than to be able to help someone—?) into an everyday matter and into a profession. And only someone who looked at human life so little directly, so goodheartedly and, at bottom, so old-maidishly as Ellen, could fall (with such complete conscientiousness and conviction) into this error.—That is just Ellen Key. Remarkable, isn't it; almost a little weird? Oh, all these noiseless transformations of life. The being no longer this and no longer that, while one still believes one is getting to that stage. This pouring out, gently, like an upset bottle that is lying on its side and feeling quite well and yet is already as worthless as a broken one. How these gentle things simply go away if we offend them with any kind of demand; how they lack any attachment whatever, how completely unsentimental they are,—simply go away, fly off, are seen no more.

Ellen's métier is contrary to nature. But I know its charm and intoxication, which our good Ellen has perhaps felt only rarely, because she was too modest and because, alas, because she could not even give what arouses, as a reflex, this intoxication in the giver: that absolute, ultimate something which at times attracts this or that young person to us, to you or to me,—that something learned and suffered in the making of things, which is our prestige and our wealth. Some such young person will speak out to us and not know why it helps him so much. Oh that we might find the means, without stingily shutting ourselves up, of saving and keeping back. I think we must listen a great deal and attentively, then gradually we will answer more and more prudently and better and better. . . . Just think: two days ago in a studio (rue Campagne-Première) (scarcely three steps wide and three long) I read my Rodin essay to six young people. It just came about: I knew only one of them slightly (Dora Herxheimer, of whom I told you, who makes the big lions), but it was lovely and serious and warm.

How has it been in Oberneuland? I got a dear warm letter from our little girl, with rose leaves that felt like herself. It was quite well "written," in spots condensing into lines. I am so stupid that I don't know at all how to answer her nicely, but I shall write her today or tomorrow, as best I can. With rose leaves. And it strikes me that she should be the first to learn a piece of news which . . . will interest her. To you I shall only say that it is connected with the fact that soon now (in Ellen Key's book) a series of pictures of me will be published and that I myself am quite pleased with a certain alteration which I undertook for that and also for other reasons. However, enough of that, otherwise you will guess it and I would rather Ruth told you. . . .

[*113*]

To Clara Rilke   Friday morning, June 21, 1906

. . . Ellen Key left on Sunday for Switzerland; I accompanied her as far as Fontainebleau and we spent some not very profitable hours there, driven by flunkies at full speed through the castle in the midst of a Sunday pack (since E.K., with her inexhaustible receptivity, must always see everything), and passing a few afternoon hours in the big forest which, with its enormous beeches, ferns, and solitary birches in quiet glades, almost made one think of Danish forests. We were in the end wholly without contact and our mutual expressions of friendship had become mere social forms and were worked with a couple of handles like a machine. In the little station of Fontainebleau-Avon from which our trains went out in different directions at almost the same time, this situation rose of its own accord into a symbol and thus, having become real, lost its oppressiveness: just as in a poem, a situation taken up into a metaphor loses its transitory, painful and unstable quality, and becomes full of significance and inner validity, the moment it passes wholly into an image; so life provided us (or me: since E.K., accustomed and practiced in replacing all actuality with the "ideal" of the actual long since ready within her, must have noticed scarcely anything of all this—) with the kindly satisfaction of relieving us of what was unspoken in our situation through a complete expression of it. Just think, it couldn't be better done: two people on two opposite platforms, separated by a pair of tracks on which, in a while, two trains going in opposite directions will come in to take one away to this place and the other to that. My platform just a platform, with people, impatience, departure: nothing to stay for. Ellen's, almost exaggeratedly peaceful: wholly in the sun, with rosebeds, nice benches, and a certain imaginary happiness: like a little garden city. And then between us this legally prescribed impossibility of crossing—: so that really nothing had been left out or forgotten. And now that life had taken everything upon itself so literally, trait for trait, in the presence of this superior transfiguration, so finely developed with every means at hand, it was not difficult for me to look over in a friendly and open way now and then (the trains were a little too long in coming) and to return warmly the loyal and feeling gaze that encircled me from over there. With real warmth in my look. Now I understood how this old maid was only one of the many old maids who lay up memories in a room, memories and memories of memories and all only memories of one thing: of that love the once vague, mounting possibility of which had already been so exuberantly taken up by their hearts that the experience no longer needed to come at all. And all the accumulated things that always signify this one state and derive from it, from unlikely parents, from an error, from chance perhaps, have something uncertain in their look and something shy in their behavior, are themselves inclined to consider that they are not quite legitimate, while the old maid does nothing but weep over the indescribable respectability of her ancestry. Are certain people marked to fall into certain destinies, not to get beyond the type? And then if, as with Ellen, unusual power is added, resolution, perhaps also a certain desperate determination to grow out of the fate to which she dimly felt herself committed, then in spite of everything, doesn't just the same destiny result, as if it were lived in a larger room, with disproportionately extensive memories which make that nullity of experience even more evident? Perhaps the conventions of such wasted lives must be exaggerated like that in individual destinies in order to be noticed. Perhaps that is their way out: this once more becoming as tragic in the great and obvious as they often were in the minute. But how good life is. How just, how incorruptible, how not to be cheated: not by force, not by will, not even by courage. How everything remains what it is and has only this choice: to fulfill itself or to exaggerate itself. . . .

[*114*]

To Clara Rilke   29 rue Cassette, Paris VI°
                                                  Friday morning [June 29, 1906]

. . . I am thinking only remotely of the visiting journeys; though I occasionally believe it possible that they could offer us the frame and setting for very dear reunion (of the two and the three of us). . . . For the rest, I am absolutely decided to shut myself up for a certain number of hours every day, and no matter where and under what exterior conditions . . . for the sake of my work: whether it really comes now or whether I only make the appropriate gestures, unfilled. For haven't I known with such great conviction ever since Russia, that prayer and its season and its gesture passed on reverently and unabbreviated was the condition God made and that of his return to this person and that, who scarcely expected it and only knelt down and stood up and was suddenly full to the brim . . . ? So will I kneel down and rise up, every day, alone in my room, and I will consider sacred what happened to me in it: even the not having come, even the disappointment, even the forsakenness. There is no poverty which would not be fullness if one took it seriously and worthily and did not make it into an exasperation and abandon it.

For the present do not count, for this (and many other) reasons, on my coming soon. My room is good to me and keeps itself about me and the heat seems to me so unusually bearable that I haven't yet complained of it at all. To be sure, there are already really hot days (like yesterday), but toward evening, the wind comes up of itself, without rain and storm, or at least it comes at night and the next day is a beginning again and has distance before it. As long as it is so bearable I will hold out and only run the risk of change when it becomes necessary. Nonetheless, it helps me to calm and cheerfulness to feel and to have before me the possibility of coming to you, the way you have indicated.— It is to be hoped the change in diet, which may be in prospect, will not cause you any inconvenience. I believe that these things will in time prove less and less difficult for us, that in the end we shall have a joyful way of taking them as they come. I am eating at Claire's now at noon (completely vegetarian all these weeks), and in the evening drink two cups of milk in a crèmerie—: that is all, with fruit evening and morning, and it is excellent and nourishes me as easily and naturally as sap does a tree. . . . I would like to send you with this, because I cannot write more, a little poem; a little sketch from life. . . .

[*115*]

To Clara Rilke   Friday morning [July 6, 1906]

. . . I must see about something to read and hear on the Rembrandt celebration; is it connected with an important exhibition? If we could only go on from where we left off looking in Kassel and Frankfurt last year; and I think it would surely be like that; how beautiful it was before the Samson; we ought to have written down a few words then and there. Didn't you do it? Later? That was such a good day, when one apprehended and understood. And the joy in such great things happens so entirely in nuances that one cannot later say it was of this color or that. And one recalls almost nothing of it if one hasn't a few notes out of the immediate experience that might help. It is the same for me with the last year's portrait in Berlin. Looking at such things a metaphor ought to come to one, something like a little entrance of one's own through which one can always get in. It seems to me as if all that could be better if one put oneself into that state of mind of which I wrote recently, and it strikes me also that one must be able to reach and evoke it, because it is perhaps nothing but attentiveness. I tried that in the Louvre recently. I had been there a few times and it was like looking at great activity; thus things kept happening and happening there before me. And then, a short time ago, there were only pictures and many too many pictures, and everywhere someone standing, and everything was disturbing. And then I asked myself why it was different today. Was I tired? Yes. But wherein did this tiredness consist? In the fact that I let everything possible come into my mind; in that everything possible went right through me like water through a reflection, dissolving all my outlines into flux. And I said to myself: I will no longer be the reflection but that which is above. And I turned myself over so that I was no longer upside down, and closed my eyes for a brief moment and drew myself about me and stretched my contours, as one stretches violin strings, until one feels them taut and singing, and suddenly I knew I was fully outlined like a Dürer drawing, and I went thus before Madonna Lisa: and she was incomparable.—So, do you see . . . , it is this that one must sometime be able to do. Not to wait (as has happened until now) for the strong things and the good days to make something like that out of one; to anticipate them, to be it already of oneself: that is what one must sometime be able to do. And won't everything be work then? For what in that state is unfruitful? It is precious black earth in us, and our blood has only to go ahead like the plow and make furrows. Then, while we are at the harvesting, the sowing will already have started again in another spot. . . .

[*116*]

To Karl von der Heydt   Hôtel de la noble Rose, Furnes, Belgium
                                            last day of July, 1906

My dear friend, I no longer propose to be burdened by still, day after day, not having thanked you for your little letter and the fulfillment of what it had to announce. You know—: thanks with all my heart.

This last period has been confused, the leave-taking from Paris difficult and inwardly complicated. I am sitting in a strange little, old city in the midst of a Teniers kermis, my eyes full of swings and round games, my ears full of hawkers, my nose filled with the smell of beer, honey cake, and peasantry, on my tongue the dust and dryness of this activity, and the pressure of indescribable summer warmth on all my feeling. (It is in keeping with

Flemish taste to count with all five senses and to enumerate them all.)

In Furnes the tram line begins by which the whole Belgian coast is tied together from knot to knot; at intervals I am looking for the town it is to be. But most of them, alas, are already real "bains de mer" with *distractions, courses,* etc. (Heavens, where is it going to, the solitude of earth?)

[*117*]

To Countess Mary Gneisenau   Friedelhausen bei Lollar
                                                           September 11, 1906

How are we to thank you for the delightful correspondence you keep up with such unforgettable and charming tokens? This summer seems to us in retrospect almost like a fairy tale, the way it stands about your figure and behind it, enhancing it to yet deeper significance; or rather, to put it differently, opening life up to us, riches and expanse, pictures behind pictures, contacts and understandings; how much has come to us unawares through you, things real and given, and how new things are continually being given into our hands out of your letters and journals. How are we to thank you?

That Sister Marianna's letters returned to me from your hands adds to the letters themselves that by which the book had been enriched when I got it back: the equilibrium that lies in a rose like that being so inexpressibly beautiful, a rose that has slowed the joyful and princely rhythm of its prime till it became transiency, evanescence, a series of slowly descending tones.— But, as we somehow need the rose in its coming and its opening, how very necessary this is for us too, how closely this too is bound up with our hearts, and how we *cling to it:* to this faded-ness and to the tender, slightly plaintive nuances of fadedness: those yellows in the yellow, ah yes, they are in us too, and we come to find them beautiful and to rejoice in them; we come to let count everything in life's hands, in a waiting, a willing, still a little bit elementary impartiality. For fading and fadedness and giving oneself over to them is one beauty more beside the beauty of what comes and burgeons and bears, just as lamentation is a beauty, and fearfulness, and self-surrender, and futile and self-abasing entreaty, when it comes so violently, rushing on so irresistibly over a heart's declivity, as it did with the Portuguese nun: —"A wee bit small and indiscreet" it was indeed, that supplication and belittling and abasing of self in love disdained; and yet it was so rich, so creative, so very much this heart's progress and glory to have become—didn't you feel it too?—great and valid beyond its object, exhaustless and beautiful. Only in comparison with that dull and insignificant object was it wrong and unfitting to show such devotion. Gauged by the measure of the devotion itself, its object no longer exists; it has become space, and the immense ardent lamentation goes right through it and toward no one any more. And at this point it becomes manifest that it has entered again into a majesty beyond its apparent humbleness.

That is why loneliness, which so often increases their sorrows beyond number, is so suited to the lot of women: because only within this seclusion is such a transfiguration possible; this being way down deep not implicated in the suffered wrong, this inability ever to become vulgar, this intactness, is this too heavily paid for by all that women have borne? A voice is lifted, ah, a small, a weak voice in utter distress and wants only to cry out; a betrayed little heart wants to rest, two eyes seek their pasture —and no impatient straining arises from it and no distortion: the eyes look out more and more clear-sightedly, the heart grows, and already there is no longer anyone there: no one so big that he might follow the prodigious calling that goes forth from that lamenting mouth. Who can pity women that has ever seen how they grow beyond wrong and pettiness, how they are something untouched, an untapped store. Perhaps the man doesn't pass by "uncomprehending and unsuspecting," perhaps it is *they*, exalted as they are, whose fate it is, even there where they kneel before him, to grow immeasurably out beyond him. . . .

[*118*]

To Karl von der Heydt   Schloss Friedelhausen
                                           September 11, 1906

. . . Clara is thinking seriously of Berlin and wants to try transferring her Worpswede studio thither and to begin an industrious winter there. And I—I am thinking in all seriousness and hardihood of—Greece. You have indeed suggested all kinds of things to me which really appeared not much less daring, but for which no justified urge spoke in me; but now here is a country that in climate would offer everything those southern places promised, of which we thought. And besides, there are voices in me counseling this so unconditionally and honestly that I would still feel this choice to be less forced and arbitrary and finical, despite the rather more complicated trip and greater distance, and that this decision appears to me simpler, more direct, more sober than any other. What I learned with Rodin of bearing and capacity and joy: where could I better test and apply it and become one with it than in the presence of those unforgettable things back to which, up many branches, the blood of his own things goes? Should it not be of special value to write there the second volume of the little Rodin book, which is indeed to be the very next thing I begin? I feel that much in me could broaden there and that other things that were perhaps growing one-sidedly could there experience the correction and restraint that can emanate from the age-old experiences of that land. . . .

[*119*]

To Gudrun Baroness Uexküll   Friedelhausen
                                               September 12, 1906

. . . I only want to tell you today how beautiful it is here: how animated and spacious these days are, autumn days, as one must admit; but the vistas between the full trees are deep and radiant, the clouds are built up into great shapes on the horizon and if one looks up, one sees a poplar glittering against blue air. The day is already divided for one's feeling, like a bicolored flag, into cool and warm. Sun is one thing and shadow is another, and they seem to have nothing more to do with each other. Only below in the nursery garden it is still different. There it is still summer from morning to evening. There sap is still rising in the stalks and stems, and there things still confidently go on growing. There each warms the other, and an old-fashioned blanket of fragrance is lying over the asters and gilliflowers and "marvels of Peru" which stand close beside each other, holding color against color, full of simplicity and joy. All this greets you through us and so much in us joins in the greeting. . . .

[*120*]

To Countess Mary Gneisenau   Friedelhausen bei Lollar
                                                 September 20, 1906

No, there is nothing I would not like to write you about; only it seems to me so immodest and unsuitable to talk about the "person" after whom you, kindly, ask. That person is something very helpless and his growth and progress is slow and hesitant and full of relapses—; it cannot be a question of his becoming something worth talking about, rather everything depends only on how much and how completely he will be able to transpose himself into artistic matter. That is why, particularly in less good periods, I have almost no means of letting him express himself; that is why I was silent about myself, although I wish nothing more urgently than to feed the relationship between us with the best: yes, for that very reason. Moreover my recent letter was conceived as the first part of a communication the second part of which was to contain more personal matters. Then it didn't come to that: so far in advance did what came send its dismay and depression; I could only have talked of vague fear, of much sadness, of how much this gray autumn breaking in swiftly upon us frightens me with its manner and makes all the cold and hardness coming up with winter seem colossal to me, as to a little bird. Should I have written about all that?

Then little Ruth fell ill here in the unfamiliar house and all that kept working on us in the same direction. She had a few distressing days, while the illness was asserting itself; since it has become manifest, not only does most of the discomfort seem to be past, but the little girl is applying her energy and nature so bravely now to becoming well again that we really have no more reason to worry. But however quickly she may get through with it all, we must still count on remaining in Friedelhausen at least until the end of this month. This new delay is strange when one considers how very much we wanted soon to get at carrying out those decisions which even now haven't been made.

Just think (ah, how I long at heart to tell you about everything) that to the possibilities we thought we faced, a new, very tempting one was added: the renewed invitation of our present kind hostess to pass the winter with her in complete freedom for work in her villa on Capri. You can imagine that that appealed to us. We spoke much about it, but now it does seem to us that Clara would do best to choose the most courageous among all the possible decisions, the one that looks least like an evasion of what will, after all, one day have the upper hand in some form; your dear letter and everything you have already begun to do for her coming to Berlin helped her very much to this good inclination in which (as far as I can see) she is now becoming strengthened from day to day. . . .

May I too find some most courageous one among my coming decisions. Occasionally I think of going to Greece now, of writing or at least preparing there the second volume of my Rodin book and of accepting the Capri invitation for the rest of the winter. But it may still come out quite differently. At present everything seems unreal to me: one plan as well as another, and also much that is past, like the time on Wacholderhöhe which in us too has sunk into such a dreamlike haze. And which already seems distant. A distant summer. . . .

[*121*]

To Ellen Key   16 Hubertusallee, Grunewald bei Berlin
                                           November 6, 1906

. . . Off and on, by roundabout ways, I have had good news of you, and so I didn't feel entirely separated from you, although I did nothing at all to give you a visible sign of all the good greetings and thoughts that are accustomed to go to you.—I heard just now that you are well and am very happy about it.

There would be many things to say now about myself, but perhaps—so I hope—I shall be able to deliver to you personally a supplement to all that has happened.

I am for the nonce skipping everything up to the moment (a month ago now) when we arrived here. Clara (you will already have heard about it) wants to try to get pupils and commissions here and to undertake a trial winter in this (alas, so loathsome!) city. I helped her a little in the preparation for it, had myself a few steps and paths to take here besides, finally had to go in for a troublesome dental treatment which led to a great deal of distress and has so weakened me that my whole constitution is in a state of severe exhaustion which I am only now hoping to get out of again. The summer was not very good for me anyway, not as regards health, and not otherwise.—According to my inner need, I would now like best to go to Paris again, where I worked well and industriously until the first of August. But the means are lacking, so I am snatching at a kind and friendly invitation that calls me to *Capri*, where I hope to concentrate on serious work. It is the sister of Countess Schwerin who died last year (Frau Alice Faehndrich von Nordeck-Rabenau), who means to arrange a little room for me in her villa on Capri. With a heavy heart I am renouncing Paris, which was so favorable to my work, but it is of course a great joy that there is the other possibility permitting me to hope for a good winter.—So as soon as I feel a little stronger I shall travel (and indeed without stopping) to Naples in order to get very quickly to work (the last months have taken me very far away from it).

Now let me tell you at once, dear Ellen, that my friend and hostess would be *very* happy to receive you in her house on Capri. Note that down, also that I expect you there, and arrange your plans so that if in the course of the winter you go farther south, you stop off with us!

So, now I have acquainted you somewhat with everything, and now comes a request. I have already voiced it once before in similar form and am repeating it now at the present moment in all frankness. Dear Ellen, wouldn't you do me the favor *not* to let your essay on my books be published for the present *as a book?* I asked you that once before. Then you said you had promised Bard something and had nothing else suitable for him. Now this reason does not hold, since the little book has been taken away from the publishing house, and I am making use of the opportunity once more to tell you quite honestly that it would be a relief to me if the little book were *not* published, not now. It is so profoundly necessary for me now not to be shown and recommended, it is quiet and obscurity that I need above all in order to take my next steps. The essay, which is based largely on passages from letters for which no evidence as yet exists in my books, *outstrips* me in a certain sense, while on the other hand it also fixes my religious developments at a stage beyond which they have, in part, already been shifted. I have no publication now which in that sense would speak for itself, it is by no means a moment to call attention to me and I am more and more anxious to have my books speak for *themselves*—; dear and valuable as your helpful voice is to me; it has certainly had its effect too, and indeed no slight one,—but there is no reason at present for again attempting any influence. In addition the place with Fischer is a very conspicuous and exposed one in which the book would necessarily and rightly provoke considerable opposition that is unnecessary. In short: all in all: I beg you (relying on your not misunderstanding me) *not* to bring about a book edition of the essay immediately, perhaps to postpone it until some one of my future works is at hand which might then justify the publication of such a brochure, for which there is now no occasion at all. It only disturbs me to be thus exhibited now, and you are really aiming at just the opposite, aren't you?

So let us wait, please, let me work and let time do its part. You will give me the deepest joy if you respect my request. May I count on it? . . .

Duse is in Berlin. We shall see her play tonight (I hope) in *Rosmersholm*.

[*122*]

To Clara Rilke   Hotel Hassler, Naples
                              Thursday morning [November 29, 1906]

If one went (you remember) up our Strada Santa Lucia a few houses to the left, and then, instead of to the square with the fountain, out the other side—toward the sea—, there began to the right, following the curve of the shore, a street on the left side of which only the sea remained and the castle (Castello del Ovo) jutting out at the bend, while on the right it was bordered by a long line of hotels—. One of these hotels recedes a little in order to thrust out before it a whole edifice of terraces: that is the Hassler; my room with its high door gives directly on these terraces, which run out to the right of the house into a little garden, in which I am now sitting; to be sure, its last flowers (purple asters) are faded, but over a wall hangs clematis in blossom, sun lies on the sea, and behind the sun, just opposite me, beside Sorrento's foothills, is visible the contour of Capri.

The journey was really not bad; when I arrived I thought: it could go on that way for five days more, I almost wanted it to; because the feeling for the very foreign, for the unknown, was strong and decided in me. But now the trip already seems long ago, although there is nothing in between but a supper alone in the empty dining room (there seem to be only a few people here), a warm bath, a night under the zanzariere, in deep sleep, a breakfast with very pale yellow-green honey, and finally this moment here in the terrace garden while I have been writing. And five more days of travel might well have preceded it, it is so unfamiliar here: foreign in such a good way. There is the bay, now and then little silhouettes of oarsmen against it in such beautiful restraint of movement and just what makes a living creature of the boat—; sailing ships in the distance. Then the bend toward Posilipo, this whole rim as if just flung out, and to the left the protruding castle, as if in a cloak and placed against the sun like one of Rembrandt's figures against the light. And foreign the sounds; this swift trotting of little horses, this clattering turn of primitive wheels, the little bells on the horses' necks, echoing the trot once more in diminished form, cries in between, shouts, music, children's voices, and cracking whips—: everything foreign even to the cracking of live-oak fruits under my steps in the little garden.—If it could only go on, this being known by no one.—Your telegram was brought to me immediately upon my arrival; I was just washing up a little when they came with it, and right to me, actually, although I hadn't yet given my name at all. It now seems to me conceivable that I shall remain here two or three days before I sail across into the new over there: into that contour which it will behoove me to fill out. . . . The sea has already changed twenty times while I have been writing. Now I am stopping and want to look. . . .

[*123*]

To Clara Rilke   Hotel Cocumella, Sorrento
                          Friday morning [November 30, 1906]

Today I saw Naples for the first time from the sea. But I haven't yet gone to Capri, only toward it in order to stay, halfway, in Sorrento. I was expecting to see Vollmoeller and was happy about this meeting after years. But it fell through. It turned out that he had gone to Florence and would not return until April. But the villa. One approaches from behind, driving up through a thick, dark, half-grown orange grove through which little deep-laid paths go out in all directions. Then comes the country-house, with the land in front running toward the sea—one sees an arborway and at the end, the outline of a railing behind which it becomes vast and light: the sea. The road thither from Sorrento between walls, old houses with quite black entrances and interiors. Now and then overtaken by little wagons that pass breathlessly by. Above the walls, toward the sky, many orange trees at their greatest bearing, heavy, the colors pieced together like stained-glass windows. Reapers here and there. Women carrying too full baskets upright on their heads come gravely and solemnly toward one.—And ever and again this fullness of fruit against the light sky. Sometimes an autumnal live-oak in between, a great olive or, spread out over all, a solitary pine.

Even on sailing in one saw those pines opened out here and there over the flat houses that rise, terrace after terrace, up to the little piazza at the very top. There is wonderfully much nature in this architecture; arriving in Sorrento one sees even more, when one leaves Naples behind in the morning on the ship: then it takes on more and more the character of an enormous quarry that is reddish and bright on its fresh surfaces between old, steep, long-unbroken gray. The deeper-lying parts finally fade away completely into reddish mist, but the castle remains, stands, shimmers and still creates in the distance the impression of rock.— Mont Valérien (opposite Meudon) could often give this impression toward evening; or also early in the day; then even the houses of Meudon could recede or stand out like that on the opposite slopes. That is due to the *plans*. For a while then the ship gives a close view of Vesuvius, whose contours are so animated, one could tell by the look of them that they had just recently been altered again. I didn't have my glass with me. But I noticed how strangely the upper part of the mountain is marked by all the lava flows, which give this peak the character of being not yet completed. The light behaves strangely on this material and something self-illuminating results from it, so that one can a little bit imagine Fuji.

And again and from somewhat nearer I saw Capri's contour, like a signature I have already read often. I would like to show you a little of all this, . . . therefore I write these few words quickly before I go back.

[*124*]

To Clara Rilke   [Picture postcard with "Fauno con otre" (Pompeii)
dated Naples, December 2, 1906]

Was finally in the museum today. Have seen many things
again, only not the one little Pompeian tablet with the slender
figures against the sea. Little fragments, single bronzes, Orpheus,
Eurydike, Hermes; a great deal that is confirming, helpful . . .
Monday I expect to go to Capri. . . .

[*125*]

To Clara Rilke   Hotel Hassler, Naples
[December 2, 1906]

. . . Naples too, as indeed everything Italian, is more beautiful in the summer, as that time we were first here; now it has
surrendered much of its character and peerlessness, now, since,
as my barber said today: the bad weather is coming. I tried to
modify his definite expression a little, unnoticeably, in my favor;
but no, he would not let it be changed, now it would come and
there would be nothing to do about it. "Pioggia, scirocco—
eh—." And he was right. Yesterday toward evening the wind
must have shifted or it had already shifted (my sense of direction is nothing to boast of), in short, something had changed
after all the radiance that seemed so secure; the sea came on more
powerfully, rose up white on the breastworks, far out was green,
and as surface looked calm, as if grown heavy, but from across
it came a wind, an agitated something, and, over the rising city,
dazzling with the light that fell over it, piled up clouds, heedlessly, clouds which didn't fit upon each other at all, so that
empty places were left between or bits of light sky, squeezed in;
piled and piled, while the evening continued to shine on everything from over there, so that the dark became always darker and
the light more and more sudden and dazzling and the red of the
blind arcades of the Pizzofalcone (first elevation by the sea below the castle) which are built up on top of each other, dissolved

into red and redder and extreme, scarcely credible reds, which
one believed could last only a moment. All that made quite without contour, simply out of a mass, like one of those powerful
Goyas in which figures and trees and buildings and mountains
are rolled into shape with the same energy—(look at the Cucaña
(Maypole), the little picture upstairs on the very top floor of the
National Gallery, where there are also the beautiful Manet
Hunter that looks like a Turgenev, and Rodins, four or five of
them, to be seen again)—. Then came the night and brought
frightful storms; Sunday then began with a rather piercing sun,
turned to rain, wind, change; the dull primed green of the sea,
now and then the white (what white!) of a seagull fading out
against it: those are Pompeian values. It might have become clear
to us even then that a painter could come into being here with all
this; for painters do develop out of color, the real ones—and
color is here, and indeed in every gradation. At the corner of
one of the black side alleys that branch off the Via Roma (the
long, narrow main street leading up to the museum), I saw yesterday the stand of a lemonade seller. Posts, roof, and back of
his little booth were blue (of that animated blue dulling toward
green of certain Turkish and Persian amulets); it was evening,
and the lamps fastened to the back wall opposite caused everything else to stand out very resolutely before this color; even
the earth-brown of the clay pitchers with a thin coat of water
constantly gliding over them; the yellow of single lemons, and
finally the smooth, glassy, ever-turning red in several big and
little goldfish bowls. That was certainly strong, too obvious, possibly, but nevertheless well worth noticing. Van Gogh would
have gone back to it.—Perhaps I see all this because I have been
reading his letters (in the complete book edition, which I pro-
cured back in Munich and which were my favorites on the long
journey and are really beautiful, not mature in some things but
unutterably earnest, unutterably moving, and for painters really
like a good, helpful voice.) Title: Vincent Van Gogh, Letters. . . .

[*126*]

To Elisabeth and Karl von der Heydt   Villa Discopoli, Capri
December 11, 1906

I have been here a week, and that long at least I wanted to wait, so that, besides the greetings I often think in your direction, I could report to you something of what has impressed me and that not too unjust and momentary. But now I shall attempt a few impressions. There are first of all my immediate surroundings, and they are full of friendliness. The mistress of the house in a very kind way does everything for my well-being and gives me so much freedom and right to go my own way that I am able to arrange much solitude, half-days at a time and, if it becomes necessary, more. (My inner life really had been dislocated for months, I notice, and being alone provides primarily only a kind of psychic plaster cast, in which something is healing.) But nothing is so important as that; already on the long trip I felt it. There is perhaps nothing so jealous as my profession; and not for me a monk's life in the close association and isolation of a cloister, but rather I must see to it that little by little I myself shall grow into a cloister and stand there in the world, with walls about me, but with God and the saints within me, with very beautiful pictures and furnishings within me, with courts around which moves a dance of pillars, with fruit orchards, vineyards, and wells whose bottoms are not to be found. But to continue with essentials. My solitude is supported by the circumstance that the room I live in is quite separate, in a little house by itself, some fifty steps from the villa proper. For the present I am the only guest. . . . My room is simple and very congenial and already has a natural attachment to me for which I am grateful to it.

. . . no one but you knows what being completely alone, being unobserved, unseen, invisible means to me. For three days in Naples I went about with it as with a treasure in all the gloriously foreign world. . . .

And now Capri. Ah yes. I really have nothing more to learn there. Jacobsen says somewhere: "It requires so infinitely much tact to handle enthusiasm." Well, this place has got its stamp from a very ill-exercised enthusiasm; the foreigners are away, for the most part, but the traces of their stupid admiration that always falls into the same holes are so obvious and cling so fast, that even the huge storms that from time to time take the island in their jaws do not tear them away. I am always saddened in such landscape exhibitions, before this evident, prize-crowned, unassailable beauty: since it is almost too much even to pick up a stone on the path, a chestnut, a withered leaf, since even the beauty of a little, insignificant and ordinarily trivial thing (once one has recognized it) makes the heart overflow, what is one to do in such concerts of beauty, where everything is a program number and rehearsed and intentional and selected? It may be that with these picture-books of beauty one could begin learning to see and to love, but I am a little bit too advanced to say Ah and Oh before them. Rapture-spelling is far behind me and perhaps my whole life joy and life task really lies in this: that, though very much of a beginner, I am one of those who hear the beautiful and recognize its voice, even where it scarcely lifts above the noises; that I know God did not set us among things in order to select, but rather so thoroughly and largely to keep on taking that in the end we can simply receive nothing else at all but beauty in our love, our alert attentiveness, our not to be pacified admiration. And to grow in this feeling here is not the place. The name Paris must have taken shape in me under the influence of this longing, even if I had never heard it (I believe).

Truly, what people here have made out of a beautiful island is close to hideous. But that doesn't speak against them; there were in any case serious and thorough and significant people among the thousands who have collaborated here at Capri. But did you ever see that people arrived at agreeable results when they let themselves go or were active in the direction of pleasure, relaxation, enjoyment? Neither bullfights nor music halls nor any other institutions of amusement, from the dance hall to the beer garden up and down, are beautiful or pleasing or ever have been so. The heaven of which I once heard an excited preacher speak in San Clemente was replete with dubious happiness, in bad taste and boring. But in all seriousness, isn't even Dante evidence for it, whose Paradise is filled with such helplessly heaped-up bliss, with no gradations in light, formless, full of repetition, made of smiling, angel-pure perplexity, as it were, of not-knowing, of not-being-able-to-know, of pure, blissful mendacity. And the Inferno beside it. What a compendium of life. What knowing, hailing, judging. What reality, what particularization even into darkest darkness; what a meeting again with the world. From this it does not follow that suffering is more right than happiness and its surrender and expression and admission; only, so far mankind has not yet attained in bliss that depth, that urgency, that necessity which has already become accessible to it in suffering. (And therefore Capri—is a monstrosity.)

For the rest, one can see Diefenbach coming to the surface now and then, gray in gray, of those grays that old wood of wooden palings takes on under the influence of sun and rain. And Gorky has settled down here, feted by the socialists and scattering money about him. I close, dear friends, in the consciousness of having spent an evening hour with you, which I needed. . . .

[*127*]

To Countess Mary Gneisenau   Villa Discopoli, Capri (Italy)
December 15, 1906

The rose is here with me and the wreath of everlasting (Clara has contrived a careful bed for them in which they can go all over with me without suffering—) and from both, whenever I find them again, comes a reminder, a summons, no, a gentle monitory calling-by-name of a few unsayable things I must master, deep in my work. You had a great faith in me, an unconscious disposition to expect valid things of me, and what you expected of me was something you long felt must one day come.

Out of all this, out of such a remarkably wrought context comes to that wonderfully placed yellow rose, comes to that small wreath returning a little bit resignedly into itself, the power they both have over me and that superiority, at the same time that curious being-older, which enables them to accompany me as it were protectively. You should see this rose a moment. Do you still remember it? It is little altered. I would like to be able to describe it to you, and perhaps I can some day. It has become, I can express only this much at the moment, more final, more inward, more withdrawn. Its fullness has not dwindled, but the rose seems no longer filled with itself, but rather, like an Egyptian queen, all filled out with dainty and exotic delicacies, with an alien fragrance, so that it no longer has to give out fragrance itself. There is a deep repose in it; it lies on the very bottom of its name, rose,—there where the word grows dark, rose, and everything that is contained in it of movement, of memory coming and going, of swiftly ascending longing, flows away over it, up above, and touches it no more. But what there is in it of heaviness, of fate, of heaven as it were and earth, of starry night, of stillness, of loneliness (for how often was it alone and gave away beauty of its awakening, mouth of its dewy coolness, the way it could look out from itself toward evening, and the diffused, no longer to be contained pallor of its nights, gave away, gave back, to no one, to nowhere—), but what was in it of things thus unsayable, of things never taken by us and yet not lost to us, has *remained* in it, no longer imperiled now, secure, come home, as forces have come home in a talisman, collected, as we are collected in our hearts, held back by nothing, yet without inclination to stream out, quite absorbed, as it were, in the enjoyment of our own equilibrium. You should see this rose a moment. Were you to see what I am trying to evoke here, only for the little while your eyes spend over this letter, were you to see how it has retained your gesture, the movement by which your beautiful hands compelled it to lie thus (there was a little, tenderly-impatient compulsion in that), you would understand that you gave me indescribably much that time, extravagantly much, so that, my hands still all filled with this rose, I was unable later, in meeting again, to grasp anything at all. Have I let something fall? Has something broken? Your image stands before me, Countess Mary, in all the innate, lovely pride you bear so grandly and are so equal to, and for which we first began to admire you. (Ah, what a long, thousandfold admiration, how many evenings we have spent, Clara and I, enumerating your beauties, and could not find an end nor get to sleep for doing it.) And now your image stands before me just like that in the solitude (and now, please, don't be angry) that so well becomes it. If I prayed for you, I would pray for you not to break through it, this solitude, not now, not impatiently, not at any price. It is difficult, certainly; but it seems more difficult to you because you take it for an empty space, while it must be there, as space for the radiance that emanates from your figure. Was I permitted to say that? Where may you be? . . .

[*128*]

To Clara Rilke   Villa Discopoli, Capri
                                    Monday, December 17, 1906

I could read your letter (the fifth) . . . over and over again. Hearkening anew each time in my heart. . . . If Lou knew how many such letters I write to myself in thought. Long letters, with just such objections. They are all quite familiar to me. I know their faces into which I have looked for hours, I know how they come nearer and nearer and straight and blindly at me. And yet there is something new in the way they came this time, something that made me more attentive than perhaps I ever was to them. I thank you . . . for this handing on of words which merely to take, to arrange and, where you thought best, to reject, must have been laborious and exacting enough for you. . . . So that too came on top of the many, many things you are in the midst of. Came and used you, used all your strength, your memory of words, of facts, of sorrows, of the ruthless, almost desperate exaggerations by which I sometimes try to get to the very bottom of sincerity, thereby causing pain to you and to myself. You had to see all that rise up before you, with all the menace, hardness, momentary hopelessness that comes up with it, and had to find the determination, this clearheaded superiority, to set yourself above it, confronting Lou, and to defend what has so often attacked you when you yourself were without defense.

. . . With me it is like this: I am all eagerness not to miss any of these voices that are to come. I want to hear each one, I want to take out my heart and hold it in the midst of the condemning and censuring words so that it is not touched by them on one side only and from a distance. But at the same time I will not give up my hazardous, so often irresponsible position and exchange it for a more explainable, more resigned post until the last, the ultimate, final voice has spoken to me; for only in this situation am I accessible and open to them all, only in this situation shall I be found by all I am to meet of destiny, appeal, or power, only from here can I one day obey, obey as absolutely as I am now absolutely resisting. By each premature compliance with that which in the guise of "duty" tries to subdue me and make me useful, I would indeed shut out of my life a few uncertainties and the semblance of that constant desire for evasion, but I feel that thus also the great, wonderful aids that take hold in me in almost rhythmical succession would be shut out of a fore-seeable order, directed by energy and a sense of duty, in which they no longer belong. Lou thinks one has no right to choose be-tween duties and to shirk the immediate and natural ones; but my immediate and natural ones have always, even in my boyhood, been these on the side of which I keep trying to stand, and if I wished to take on others, it was not as a new task added to that first, already too great one, but because I believed I discerned in certain duties a point of support, an aid, something that would be a firm place in the instability of my homelessness, something un-shiftable, lasting, real. I didn't actually plan to do anything for the inception and existence of this reality, I thought it would come, as everything wonderful comes, out of the depths of our union, out of its tremendous necessity and purity. I really couldn't with a good conscience take on any new work, a new profession, and if I said responsibility, I meant and desired responsibility for the deepest, most inward existence of a reality dear and indestructibly related to me. And have I shirked this responsibility? Am I not trying, as well as ever I can, to bear it and, on the other hand, hasn't my longing been, on the whole, infinitely fulfilled? What does misfortune in trivial matters prove against it; how can the circumstance refute me that we must keep postponing our life together, which practically too is one of mutual support, since only with you two did my world grow into the nameless, did it begin to grow outward in those days, from that little, snow-covered house in which Ruth was born, and since then has been growing and growing, out from that center upon which I cannot narrow my attention as long as the periphery is pushing forward ahead on all sides into the infinite? But has there not only since then been a center, something immovable, a star from whose position I could for the first time determine the movement of my heaven and could name the constellations that before were but a throng? Aren't you two now the one tree in the indescribably wide plain of my journeying to which I always find my way back, toward which I often look in order to know where I am and whither I must go on? If we are living thus separated from each other by days of travel, and trying to do that which our hearts require of us day and night (are we not turning away from the difficult for the sake of the difficult? Have I not this consciousness at least for myself, as I am trying to live this lonely life?), tell me: isn't there a house about us after all, a real one, for which only the visible sign is lacking so that others do not see it? But do we not see it most clearly for just that reason, this dear house in which we are together as from the very first, and out of which we shall go some day only to step into the garden?

This orderly course, into which in minor matters we would have to be policed (I understand very well and quite seriously what Lou meant by that), have not angels already held us to it with the deep, convinced inexorability that is given to angels?

Ah, . . . you understand that I would like to make my powers and my standard measure up to big things; even as a boy, I had the feeling of being attached to great and mature people as to older brothers and sisters, for I never believed that one becomes worthy of associating with them by dealing first with the mediocre and inferior. It may often seem, therefore, as if I were living life in reverse; the majority take it on the other way round, and they also manage to rise by the ordinary up to the beginning of the extraordinary, yes, even into the extraordinary. That may hold and remain valid for them. For me, the ascent from that side was an impossibility. Spiritually overstrained and physically spent as I was from early days, I would have stuck in the beginnings of the ordinary and died one way or another. But then for the first time those powers came into play which, in lifting me over the immediate obstacles, set me at the beginning of greater and less temporal tasks, for which I had in a remarkable way become ripe and not yet disheartened. Then, in that Beyond as it were, I began my work (and of course Lou was the first person who helped me to it), not lifted away over the weight of life, but over the difficulties; there, outside of all my anxieties, I became established in the feeling to which I would never have found a way below: in the love of life, grown out of the experience, so indispensable to me, that the hostile thing is not life but myself, I myself, and with me all the rest; then I received from indescribably knowing hands the right to that devotion which, below, would have become an annihilation for me, while above, among the great powers, it became my beauty, my growth, that on which I may boundlessly rely.

And if I persevere up there where I have now spent the greater part of my mature life, am I not in the real, in the difficult, among duties? And mustn't there come a place, if only I go far enough, where above and below pass into each other as unnoticeably as also happens one day with those who have gone the other, the lower way, honestly and loyally to the end?

I feel a little like the Russian people, of whom also outsiders or persons who have become distrustful say that it must eventually be drawn out of its previous development over to the normal path of growth and must fix its eyes upon reality, in order to come to anything. And it would come to something then too, most certainly. As western people have come to something, to this and that, from one thing to another. But would it come to the one thing for which alone, beyond everything, its soul longs? I believe it would then be completely cut off from it and forever. May nobody at all then go toward this one thing, which even those who renounce it, in their very renunciation, crave so much?—

For the Russian people the "chances" do seem to have come to an end. I have one more. I know I have not always made use of all of them as I should, I have perhaps even wasted one or two, but still I accept them each time more like very great tasks and demands, and if God gives me so very many and always one more —it is not too many, so long as he believes it necessary; perhaps he will not stop, because I do understand him better and better and in the taking of these chances am making little advances, for which I would offer him my little book as proof, if he required one. . . .

[*129*]

To Clara Rilke   Villa Discopoli, Capri
                                  December 19, [1906] evening

. . . can one read a letter on Christmas Eve; but above all: how is one to write one four days ahead that can be read on that evening? I am not writing to Ruth. It is not I who should speak to her, nor is it you, although you will be beside her and will feel her fine, soft hair against your cheek when you look together into the tree that is to speak to you both, to her especially, to the dear, dear child who now, when you see her again, will already reach up a little farther on you and deeper into your hand. Look at her well when you see her again . . . see her again not only as a mother, see her also with your serious worker's eyes: then you can be quite happy. Before those eyes that evening will be complete, and if you do not let yourself be confused, it will not seem

strange and disturbing that I am not really standing beside you:
. . . indeed nothing, nothing can keep me from being about
you so that you feel me; and when I really used to be there,
there still was (except for that first Christmas Eve in Westerwede) always much of me that only reproachfully stood by, that,
if not at the last moment, yet even an hour before, would gladly
have been alone, far away, God knows where. This face that
met yours and was sometimes taken by Ruth's dear little hands
and held against a firm, warm, happy cheek, this face felt itself
so unfinished, even on that evening, and was so too. This face
ought to be in solitude, much behind its hands, much in the dark.
It ought to be there for its thoughts and from its thoughts to
look out toward no one, finding a bit of sky, a tree, a path, something simple with which it can begin, something that is not yet
too difficult for it; how often when you looked at it . . . it was
a face distraught in its unfinishedness, one that had not gone
deeply enough inward and not far enough outward, a face that
had stopped halfway, like an only partly silvered mirror, reflecting in some places, in others transparent, and you never
saw in it the greatness of your trust and the whole of your love
which it was not capable of receiving. But if it is sometime to be
given back to you better, it must be worked on for a long time
yet, night and day. For this Christmas it has not been finished.
But it is in good hands, and when it is a little farther along you
shall see it again, and then, each time, there will also be something like Christmas; each time, even in the middle of the year.

Do you remember . . . our two restrained Christmas Eves?
(the one in the rue de l'Abbé de l'Épée, the one in Rome in the
Studio al Ponte, both of which were so much less authentic because neither of us could be with Ruth, where everything turns
into Christmas of itself when the hour comes); how much we felt
even then that we must mingle our work so deeply with ourselves
that its workdays would lead out of themselves to holidays, to
our true holidays. Everything else is indeed only a schedule such
as we had in school; many, many set things and the empty places
for Sunday and for Christmas and Easter. Empty places one fills

up with something that is in contrast to the other, the fixed; and so we have still gone on accepting all those periods that came up with the calendar somewhat like vacations, finding distraction in them and always gladly putting off the end, although we already had an inkling of those holidays that spring from one's own heart, that are no contrast to the weeks that unnoticeably bring them along, and no distraction and no loitering away of vague days. Only once perhaps since we have been together did the two fall at the same time. You know when. On the twelfth I relived so strongly that indescribable feeling of Christmas which filled our lonely house then and went on increasing in it, so that one might have believed it must be reaching far out beyond it into cold days, into the long nights of Advent; that it must be visible even for those who passed at a distance, must have changed everything so that people far away came over and looked. But no one came, and what stood there was nothing but a little house, over-burdened with an enormous thick roof that seemed common-place to human beings, but of which the angels perhaps knew that it had the right measurements, those with which they measure the great space surrounding it. It was like the smallest part of that endless scale, the unit of measure, which keeps recurring and with which one can reach to the end, without adding anything else but the same thing over and over.

You know . . . what Christmas was to me in my early child-hood; even when the military academy made a hard, unbelievably malicious life, devoid of wonders, appear so real that no other reality seemed possible to me beside that undeserved one; even then Christmas was still real and was that which approached with a fulfillment that went out beyond all wishes, and when it was out beyond the very last, never even wished ones, then only did it really begin, then what had hitherto walked, unfolded wings and flew, flew till it was no longer to be seen and one knew only its direction, in the great flowing light.

And all that still, still had power over me. And in each of those years when I built up a Christmas for us or for Ruth, I rather scorned what I had built because it fell so far short of that wonder which I knew had not just grown spontaneously and unhindered in my imagination: so great, so indescribable had it always been.

And then I sat a long time on the twelfth and thought; thought of the whole deep time of grace that went through our hearts then. Felt again the evening before in the living room; the morning, the early one first, by candlelight, in which the New rose up, spreading fear like a flood and terror; then the later morning in the winter light with its entirely new order, with its impatience, its anticipation strained to the limit, which through the little, momentary and tangible fulfillments grew to ever stronger tension; then that whole steep forenoon, as if one had to go up a mountain quickly, much too quickly, and finally, in all that was uncertain, not conceivable, not possible: something real, a reality which, fabulously bound up with the wonderful, was hardly to be distinguished from it and yet real. And after that at last, spreading gradually out, a relief that was at first received like that which comes when a pain ceases, and yet was a quite different, lasting relief, as it turned out later. And then suddenly, a life on which one could stand; now it carried one and was conscious of one while it carried. What would I be without the stillness which arose in me then; what, without that whole experience in which reality and miracle had become identical; what, without those weeks of surrender in which, for the first time, I did not lose; what, without those simple services which awoke in me a readiness I hadn't known; what, without those night vigils: when the night, the winter night lay cold upon my eyes, which I closed, drawing into this closing, too, through the tendril tracery of the grape arbor, a distant star outside; when there was simply stillness, stillness of that greatest stillness that I did not yet know, while against this background, the smallest of the incomprehensively new sounds stood out clear and distinct.

Hardly ever has anyone who wasn't working kept watch so justly and with so much zeal, holding so profoundly still, as I did then, when, as I now know, work was being done on me. Like a plant that is to become a tree, so was I taken then out of the little container, carefully, while earth ran off and some light came to my roots, and was planted in my place for good, there where I was to stand until my old age, in the great, whole, real earth.

And when I thought further of the twelfth, and thought that then Christmas was coming, only that Christmas came to my mind, only the hall which was so big and so shadowy up to the bright, big tree to which you drew near for a while, quickly, with an uncertainty that was quite girlish again, more girlish than anything, holding the tiny head against your lovely face and together with it into the radiance which neither of you could see, each filled with her own life and the other's.

Then only did I notice that for me that Christmas was still there and not like one that once was and has passed, but rather like an everlasting, eternal Christmas celebration to which one's inner eye can turn as often as it needs. All at once, joy and bliss and anticipation of other Christmases had become small behind it; as if those had rather been my good, loyal father's Christmases, his anxious, provident heart's own holiday. But this was mine: all light and dark, and still, and unrepeatable. . . .

Out of all this too arose my ability for once to be alone this Christmas and yet not anxious or sad. Now I'll not write more, but shall just go on thinking, and you two will feel it. . . .

[*130*]

To Clara Rilke   Villa Discopoli, Capri (Italy)
                                          January 1, 1907

. . . This morning began so radiantly, now it is becoming a gray day; but first there was a shining as from a brand-new, never used year. And the night was a bright, distant one that seemed to rest above far more than just the earth; one felt that it lay above oceans and far out beyond, above space, above itself, above stars that looked toward its own stars out of endless depths. All that was mirrored in it and held by it above the earth and hardly even held any longer: for it was like a continual overflowing of heavens.

I thought there would perhaps be midnight Mass and went out after eleven; the streets and footpaths between the walls lay there long, like lowered outspread banners, black and white, made of a strip of wall shadow beside a strip of light; for it was the first night after full moon, and the moon stood very high in the sky and sharply outshone all the stars, so that only here and there a distant very big one flared so strongly that some darkness was formed about it. How the illumined rims of the walls dazzled, how the leaves of the olives were made entirely of night, as if cut out of skies, old, no longer used night skies. And the mountain slopes had such an air of lunar decay and towered up out of the houses like something unmastered. And the houses were dark, and where the wooden shutters had not been closed over them, the windows had the faded, translucent look of blind eyes. Finally, on the little piazza under the clock tower, there was standing a crowd of Capri youths in rendezvous. Out of a little coffee-house with red curtains, which was set into the blackest corner, came now and then the impatient rattling of a tambourine. The arch of a gate spanned a narrow street leading upward and snatched in a bit of sky with its curve and held it against the street. A step in wooden shoes clattered along by the houses, the clock began and struck the last quarter before midnight. But the church was shut, as if it had been closed for decades. And what rang out from over there, far off and yet oddly penetrating, from the olive slopes and from the vineyards, was no Christian singing. Heavy voices full of old wavering laments, long drawn out, without beginning, not as if they were suddenly starting, only—as if one's ear were unexpectedly tuned to some continuously held tone; voices seemingly fetched out again from the hearing of remote mountain-faces; voices that come into being of themselves, as though night wind were caught in the soul of an animal; long, heavy, wavering voices, calls and series of calls of a primeval natural drunkenness, dull, unconscious, more tolerated than willed, and intermittently, laughter breaking out flamelike and quickly consuming itself, short, alert, and warm as out of a summer night, and then again, moonlight; paths, walls, houses, an earth of moonlight, of moon shadow, that keeps still while with strange meaningfulness New Year's midnight strikes, slowly laying stroke on stroke: each all smooth, all spread out, foldless, as if it were to be preserved like that.

I had gone back again to my little house and stood up on its roof and wanted to see a good end in all that and to find a good beginning in myself. And now let us believe in a long year that is given to us, new, untouched, full of things that have never been, full of work that has never been done, full of tasks, claims, and demands; and let us see that we learn to take it without letting fall too much of what it has to bestow upon those who demand of it necessary, serious, and great things.

[*131*]

To Clara Rilke   Villa Discopoli, Capri
                                    January 18, 1907 (Friday)

. . . My trip back was like the back of a book cover whose title was that first morning, when I took the trip I described (a week ago today). Between the two our reunion lies like a single long light day: out of it I have so much memory of waking, so little of sleep. At the top of the title page stood the little moon-end, on the back of the jacket the beginning of a new moon, shining very bright and sharp, as I drove up evening before last from the Grande Marina. Then I intended to climb up very early on the heights of the Tiberio to see the "Oceana" once more from there; but then nothing came of it, I was too tired,— couldn't refrain, though, from climbing up later at least, in the forenoon that was warm and radiant and full of the seduction of spring. On top there stands a little santuario beside a tall-columned statue of Mary, and a young monk lives beside it; he told me he had seen the lights of a big ship in the middle of the night, and then we stood and looked southward into the glittering of the sun, in which, far away already, it must have been moving on somewhere with all its windows flashing, dazzling far and wide with its high white prow—.

I couldn't begin anything at all yesterday; I was merely continuing to live what had just been, and let myself go into the sun and be a thing shone upon among the many over which the day was passing inexhaustibly. I looked at the fig trees against the blue sea and found rosemary, which I know now—and couldn't even get to this letter, which I originally wanted to write immediately. . . .

[*132*]

To Clara Rilke   Villa Discopoli, Capri
                                      Sunday, January 20, 1907

. . . it is again a Sunday, and I am still so much in the holiday feeling of our dear reunion that it seems to me I should be calling for you in a while down there in the Villa Pagano. But when I look up, my glance falls on the opened atlas, always on the same, now familiar plate which looks like a genealogical tree representing the tremendous, long life of an ancestor, and which at the very end branches and spreads far and wide. Again and again I take a look at this stream that performs miracles, and more and more it seems to me to represent the history of the gods of that land; the mysterious, never known origin of the deity from the exhaustless stores of high-lying lakes, its long, powerful, growing course in which it always worked the same way on everything it encountered, and finally its disintegration into arms and branches, into the many lesser gods with which every culture disembogues, fades out, becomes unrecognizable.—

I have brought over the big Andrée and am deep in this remarkably unified page; I admire the course of this stream's line which, rising like a Rodin contour, contains a profusion of varied movement, recessions, and turns like a coronal suture, millions of tiny gestures with which it turns to the right and to the left, like someone who goes through a crowd distributing and sees one more person here and one more there who has need of him, and progresses but slowly.—For the first time I feel a river thus, so in its essence, so real to the verge of personification, so as if it had a destiny, a dark birth and a great, spread-out death, and between the two a life, a long, tremendous, princely life that kept everyone in its neighborhood busy, for millenniums; it was so big, so demanding, so little to be mastered. (How impersonal the Volga was by contrast, how much only an immense road through that other sublime land whose God is everywhere still in the process of becoming—.) But while I follow the holy worker of miracles on its way past names heavy with a sediment of ancient meanings, the desert, like a counterpart to its visibleness and security, rises up uncertain, without end and without beginning, like something uncreated; expanses that sometimes stand up and are everywhere, destroying the heavens with their nothingness, a tissue of ancient roads canceling each other, a sea whose ebb goes to the very bottom and whose flood to the stars, rising like wrath, incalculable, incomprehensible, not to be stemmed. When one has seen the sea and has become accustomed to the endless presence of the skies mirroring the flat earth, skies against which that earth elsewhere braces itself with the buttresses of its mountain ranges, when one has grasped a beginning of all that, there still remains this one thing, not included: the desert. You will see it. Will see the head of the great Sphinx that with effort holds itself up out of the desert's continual swell, that head and that face which men began in its shape and size, whose expression, however, and gaze and knowledge were completed unspeakably slowly and so entirely differently from our countenance. We take our inner images and place them outside us, we avail ourselves of every opportunity to shape a world, we set up object after object around our inner selves—: but here was a reality that thrust itself from without into these features that are nothing but stone. The mornings of millenniums, a people of winds, the rising and setting of countless stars, the great presence of the constellations, the glow of these skies and their spaciousness were there and were there again and again, working on it, not ceasing before the deep indifference of this face, until it seemed to gaze, until it showed every sign of a gazing at just *these* images, until it lifted itself up like the face to some inside in which all this was con-

tained and occasion and desire and need for it all. And then, at
the moment when it was full of all that confronted it, and formed
by its surroundings, then its expression too had already grown
out beyond them. Now it was as though the universe had a face
and this face flung images out beyond it, out beyond the farthest
stars, thither, where images had never yet been . . . Tell me
. . . isn't it like that? I imagine it must be like that: endless
space, space that goes on beyond the stars must, I believe, have
come into being round about this image . . .

[133]

To Elisabeth von der Heydt   Villa Discopoli, Capri
February 10, 1907

. . . I have already given up counting on the weekdays; their
program is completely taken up with what I want or should or
would like to do and of which at best only a hundred and seventy-
second part is ever carried out. But that Sunday after Sunday
passes by without my at last getting around once more to asking
about you with a few words and reporting to you with a few
others what there may be to report,—that I no longer wish to
countenance . . . I have intended to send you a little sign, if
not before, at least when there was something really good to
impart. That is now the case. Not so good, I admit, as I hoped
in time to be able to write, but still something good that closely
affects me personally and that you especially ought to know.
Namely: the *Book of Hours* is sold out (five hundred copies in
something over a year!), and we are setting about printing a new
edition, eleven hundred copies this time. That is a great, very
unexpected joy for me: and a hope: and an agreeable strengthening of my relations with the Insel-Verlag, which in this way
bestows on me more and more confidence. Since I have had this
news, I am looking a little more assured again. The last weeks
have been good and not good: according to the way you look at
it. Good: because I want for nothing; I have everything necessary and our little circle, as it has finally been rounded out, shows

me every kindness. . . . There is no longer anything casual in our companionship, we have many and interesting things to say to each other . . . not good: because, being the way I am, the talent for light, merely refreshing conversation is entirely lacking in me and every association, especially every good association, inveigles me into conversational expenditures that cause a deficit which makes itself felt in my work.

I have done all kinds of things and some that are good. But I have again stored up so very much longing for complete solitude, for solitude in Paris. How right I was when I considered that the next necessity, and how much harm I did myself when, contrary to all understanding, I half missed, half wasted this opportunity. Will it come again? On that, it seems to me, everything depends, and that is the question and worry which greatly occupies and bothers me, the more so as I myself have not yet done much about it since I have been here.

I can already foresee a little that I shall have learned much here and also done many things, but perhaps shall have brought no single work far enough along for it to be converted at once into money. So much is growing, quite organically, I feel, but very slowly, and I destroy everything if I push and hurry. To the poems in the *Rundschau* ("Orpheus, Eurydike, Hermes," etc.) new ones are being added; something like a new *Book of Hours* is beginning. But what will be ready at the end of these weeks? Not much, I fear.

So, I am working as well as I can, and you will feel, dear Frau v.d. Heydt, that this is not meant as a complaint, much rather as a short bulletin which your valued friendship surely allows me or expects of me. . . .

[*134*]

To Clara Rilke   Villa Discopoli, Capri
                                    February 18, 1907

. . . Evening has come, and I am tired because this evening's day was very beautiful, an endlessly shining, blue, soaring day, the first of its kind; one of those which in Rome too—I remember well, even at this season sometimes—surprised and overwhelmed us: one is planning this or that, something quite definite, perfectly ordinary, specified, that is a continuation of something of yesterday,—but then a day dawns that has no yesterday (still less a tomorrow), a leap day so to speak, and one notices it on waking, right away, even before looking out, as if it had penetrated one's very sleep. And besides this Antonio came in to me and with: è splendida la giornata (and at the splen . . . his smile burst open like a fruit over those south-Italian teeth). Then I already knew I would have to take a walk, a long walk; in order to distribute guilt and conscience somewhat (guilt and conscience for so frivolous a decision distracting me from my desk), I asked the Countess to go out with me, and we went up on Monte Solaro and looked at the island like birds and felt quite as if next moment we could be high above the sea too; for Monte Solaro, at its extreme peak, pressed but slightly against the soles of our feet, and what bore and surrounded one was, above all, that which belongs to the birds: that deep glittering blue which, on its front so to speak, was warm and full and mild and seemed to be lined with sea wind as with silk, when it turned over from time to time and, blowing, touched one with its underside. I am beginning to discover Anacapri, the farthermost Anacapri that lies beyond that last point we reached together. It gets very lonely and wild there and goes on like that by itself for a long time, and if one sees a shepherd that is a great deal. And the houses are left behind, and where the few stony paths can finally go no farther, there is the sea again, or rather, there is another sea, one through which Odysseus might come again at any moment, an ancient Grecian sea, beginning deep, deep down below one and out of sight. It really is here too (I read recently) that Odysseus came by, and today—from Monte Solaro—we saw lying in the Gulf of Salerno the three islands of the Sirens (strange rocks, obstructing the way, that looked as though they had once been gilded), past which, lashed to the mast and only by this coercion safe from the invertible force that came ringing across, distilled in the light wind, he sailed along, much too slowly for his safety, an infinitely long time, as it must have seemed to him. And on such days and removed from the inquisitiveness and pettiness of the foreigner's town, up there in the mountain lands of a shepherd's world, there grows upon one slowly and blurring ever and again, an inkling of that southernness of antiquity of which Uexküll wrote recently. When you come we must be up there a lot; up there you must tell, up there I will listen. By then, of course, the days that are now an exception will have become daily ones and yet, I am assured, for that reason no less lonely in those regions that are under the protection of their own remoteness and being-half-accessible (unless a hereditary something still preserves them untouched).

We were back again for lunch, but the afternoon passed rather with the echo of all that; I sat by my little house in half sunlight and walked up and down in front of it till the stars came out.— I wanted to tell you a lot more today about your words, with which you evoked the desert, the indescribable desert; . . . you will already know how keenly I felt it, how here it burst your hasty expression of it, into which it (or something of it) had been compressed, and was there before me, infinite again and unsayable, as it is. More wanted to be written to all this, but now too much new sun is vibrating in me, from today, and I cannot rightly recognize anything within me.

[*135*]

To Clara Rilke   [Capri, February 22, 1907]

. . . with a few words only I come to thank you for your letter, the fifth; I can well understand it in everything and go with you even into your sadness, that sadness so deeply familiar to me, for which one can naturally find reasons . . . and which is nevertheless only a sensitive spot in us, always the same, one of those spots which, when they hurt, can no longer be identified, so that in all the dull feeling of pain we do not know how to recognize and treat them. I know all that. And there is a happiness too, which is similar—and perhaps one must still somehow manage to get beyond both. I thought so just recently when several days in succession I climbed up into the lonely mountain slopes of Anacapri and was so happy up there, so painfully happy in my soul too. But always one lets them fall again, the one and the other: this happiness, that sadness. One *has* neither as yet. And what is one, so long as one gets up and a wind out there, a brightness, a melody of bird voices in the air can take one and do with one what it will? It is good to hear and to see and to take all that, not to be blunted by it, on the contrary: to feel it ever more thousandfold in all its variation, yet without losing oneself through it.

Once I said to Rodin on an April day that was full of spring: "how it releases one, the way one must collaborate with all the sap and exert oneself till one is tired—. Don't you know that too?" And he, who surely knew of his own accord how to take spring, with a quick glance: "Ah—Je n'y ai jamais fait attention." That is what we have to learn, to *not* pay attention to certain things; to be *too* collected to touch them with some sensitive side when one can never come close to them with one's whole being. To feel everything only with one's *whole* life; then much (that is too slight) remains shut out, but all the important things happen. . . .

[*136*]

To Gudrun Baroness Uexküll   Villa Discopoli, Capri
February 24, 1907

. . . for a week now Walter Calé's book has been here in my hands, and I haven't yet acknowledged its arrival or given you any word of thanks. I would like to have added at once to such thanks a comment on my relationship to those notebooks; but at present I have not read far enough to be able to speak in more than general terms; a vague sympathy arises in me for this man quickly and resolutely departed, but as yet—after a few poems —it is not sufficiently positive and fixed for me to be able to define it. I wonder whether here—just a fleeting thought—a person quickly matured by loneliness and doubt has not mistaken the call to understanding for the task of the artist? Whether it wasn't in this that his doom kept hidden, that which finally would no longer be moved and came forth and overpowered him? Much maturity comes together in this young man, in him the transitory—it seems to me—is transposed into the simultaneous, as in a painting: but the absence of development implied in such conditions corresponds so little with the calling—which begins every day anew, every day with nothing—of the artist, who may take neither the burden of knowledge nor the denying doubts of ignorance with him on his way, which leads him from miracle to miracle. Too quickly and too easily for an artist this man whose life was cut off masters the tasks in which one still in process of becoming slowly learns to value patience and love and devotion according to their difficulty. He remains too general; his love enters too little into the particular, into the unimportant, the unassuming, to win from them the unit of measure that already in the next greater occurs a million times. He rides too much in the express trains of thought, in the luxury trains of modern, fast, dizzy thinking, from one end of philosophy to the other. If he had only insisted more (I wish inwardly) on *walking*, walking barefoot where possible, taking in every little stone, the edge of every grass-blade, and now and then stooping over some modest find: because then I would have met him, while like this he always drives past me, impatient, restless as he is. . . .

But perhaps I feel it this way because I was rash enough to read both the introductions, which are only misleading and of which the one by his friend especially makes one feel with dismay how unalterably lonely the man was who wrote thus and thought thus and in the end wanted to do neither any more. . . .

[*137*]

To Clara Rilke   Villa Discopoli, Capri
                                                    February 25, 1907

. . . You wish me—"Spring at last," and your wish has been
immediately and very well fulfilled: even a week ago I was able
to report to you the kind of walks I am taking and with what
joy I find them. Those remote paths up there in Anacapri, those
views out on the ancient Grecian sea, the being alone beside the
little locked-up church and among the broad mountain slopes
which at one place enclose something like an amphitheater, on the
open side of which Vesuvius looks in, with the snow-mountains
standing a little back on either side—: I have often sought all
that out again in the past week, the first half of which completely
fulfilled your wish. Spring was suddenly so very much here, and
this going-into-it was so very like something important that my
conscience remained light, although I consumed many hours for
it, all the mornings almost.—This being-in-the-sun and breathing-
in-spring-sky and this listening to the little bird voices that are so
well distributed one seems to feel how in every spot in the air
that can bear, there is one, and the confirmation of the sense of
belonging that increases in one from it all: this, I think, can lead
to no losing or missing anything. And however much reason I
may have to force myself to my desk, yet again and again I go
with it, if the morning suddenly calls somewhere outside in a
way that makes one feel there must be another morning somewhere, a very big morning, the morning of the seagulls and of
the island birds, the morning of the slopes and of the inaccessible
flowers, that ever the same eternal morning that has not yet to
reckon with human beings, who blink at it dubiously, mistrust-
fully, and critically out of their before-breakfast mood. And one
need only walk for half an hour, with those quick, light, early
steps that take one so incredibly far, to have it really around one,
the sea-morning that is sure everything in it is with it and nothing against it; that in its opening its own gesture repeats itself
thousands and thousands of times, till it slows down in the little

flowers and as it were collects itself.—And with it all, I certainly feel what you wrote recently: that such spring mornings belong to a foreign spring, that my own . . . would be infinitely more cautious and hesitant and less obvious. Don't you remember how much I came to miss in Rome that spring which keeps pace with our hearts? How shocked I too was at the frivolous simultaneousness of all that blossoming, at its showiness, its impatience, corrected by nothing and so effortlessly put through? How we scorned that soon appeased nightingale, in whose badly composed song could no longer be recognized at all the yearning that we knew so well. Yes, I understood it then, and now too I know very well what you mean, and that you are right. It is possible that our nature really often avenges itself for the inappropriate alien things we expect of it, and that between us and our environment rifts occur that do not remain entirely on the surface. But why did our forebears read about all these foreign things: while they let them grow to dreams within them, to desires, to vague fantastic pictures, while they suffered their hearts to change pace, spurred on by some adventurousness, while, boundless and misunderstood distance within them, they stood at the window with a gaze that almost scornfully turned its back upon the court and the garden out there,—they quite literally conjured up that which we now have to do and, as it were, to make good. With their surroundings, which they no longer saw, they lost sight of all reality, the near seemed to them boring and commonplace, and what distance was depended on their mood and imagination. And in the process near and far passed into oblivion. So it has fallen to us not to differentiate at all between the two, to take upon ourselves and to restore both again, as the one reality which in truth is nowhere divided or closed off and which is not ordinary close around us and romantic a little further on, and not boring here and full of variety yonder. They distinguished so spasmodically in those days between the foreign and the accustomed; they did not notice how both are everywhere in densest interpenetration. They saw only that the near did not belong to them, and so they thought that what was really possessable and valuable would be abroad, and longed for it. And they considered their unconfined and inventive longing a proof of its beauty and greatness. For they still fully believed that we can fetch something into ourselves, draw it in, swallow it, whereas really we are so filled up from the start that not the smallest thing could be added. But things can all exercise influence. And they all do exercise it from afar, near as well as distant things, none touches us, all communicate with us across separations, and the ring on my hand can no more enter into me than the farthest stars can into us: only as with rays can all things reach us, and as the magnet evokes and sets in order the powers in some sensitive object, so they can create a new order in us as they act upon us. And before this insight do not near and far vanish? And isn't it *our* insight? This as provisional answer to your beautiful letter. . . .

[*138*]

To Clara Rilke
Villa Discopoli, Capri
March 4, 1907

. . . my windows and my doors are open, and I can hear how it is turning to evening outside. I recognize the stillness of this coming of evening, which is composed of many small sounds, of many verse beginnings of little bird songs, now opening up more and more like all things round about. Do you remember that from Rome? I can't help thinking often of my little house there; much in my present living resembles it, and there is always more to recognize again, now that spring is growing. It seems to me I am seeing many things a little better and more maturely and more justly than that time in Rome, and as if the years had come with things that have worked on me. Although there is no end to the unfinished places about me; indeed, there seem to be more and more of them. But it is comprehensible of course that they are becoming clearer, the more separate spots here and there come to a modelé. And patience and patience, I keep saying to myself, saying it more confidently and more modestly than ever before.

And if I stop saying it, there are now always enough things on hand persuading me with that same word.

It is remarkable how far just what we imagined and planned on a walk together in Friedelhausen when we needed comforting, is now really coming to fulfillment: that I would see Greece. For no landscape can be more Greek, no sea more filled with the expanses of antiquity, than land and sea as it is given me to see and experience them on my walks in Anacapri. Here is Greece, without the Greek world's works of art, but almost as before they came into being. The stony slopes lie up there as if all that were yet to come, and as if all the gods too were yet to be born that Greece's abundance of horror and beauty called forth. And you should hear the kind of language the people speak up there. I have never heard any so ancient on human lips. You ask them the name of the region in which you are and they tell you something big, powerful, sounding like the name of a king, of a first, early, legendary king, and you think you have already divined his name before in the storms and in the muffled swell of the heavy sea.—You see, it has fortunately proved true that there is a world up there and much reality. . . .

[*139*]

To Clara Rilke   Villa Discopoli, Capri
                                                        March 8, 1907

. . . my letter crossed your beautiful description of those evening excursions, of which I received more through the keenness of your words than you perhaps hoped to include in them in the quick jotting down. Your notes are very good and sure and positive, and when you read them again here with me, you will be surprised to see so much stored up in them. Then a lot else, completing and expanding all the rest, will find its way to them, and perhaps we can compile from the whole an Egyptian journey such as no one has ever been able to make and to tell about. Only collect many more impressions; don't think of letters that have to give information and be easily understood; keep taking in with swift capturing gestures one thing and another: something that passes quickly by, glimpses, brief flashing revelations that last a second in you under the influence of some occurrence; all the unimportant that often becomes significant through a passing intensity of our vision or because it happens at a place where it is perfected in all its fortuity and perpetually valid and of deep import for some personal insight which, appearing in us at the same moment, coincides meaningfully with that image. Gazing is such a wonderful thing, of which we still know so little; with it we are turned completely outward but just when we are most so, things seem to be going on in us that have waited longingly to be unobserved, and while they, untouched and curiously anonymous, achieve themselves in us *without us,*—their meaning is growing up in the object outside, a name convincing, strong, the only one possible for them, in which we blissfully and reverently recognize the event within us, though we ourselves do not quite reach to it, only quite faintly, quite from afar, comprehending it under the sign of some thing, strange a moment ago and already next moment newly estranged.—It often happens to me now that some face affects me like that; in the morning, for example, as they begin here now for the most part; one has already had lots of sun very early, an abundance of brightness, and if then suddenly in the shade of a street a face is held out to one, under influence of the contrast one sees its character with such distinctness (distinctness of nuance) that the momentary impression is spontaneously heightened to the symbolic. More than ever I wish for someone here who could paint; seriously paint. Just recently again. Picture to yourself: a green rectangular field, flat against the curving, deep-blue sea beside which it was set, without one's seeing the vertical drop of ancient substructions that alone separated one from the other. On this field a woman sitting, in rhubarb red and orange, another in a faded green going back and forth among the white sheets and tablecloths hung out to dry on lines and moved in most varied fashion by the wind, now hollow and drawn in, full of translucent shadow, now dazzlingly billowed out, ever and again interrupted

by the distinct blue of the sea and overflowed by the sky continually coming down over everything . . . and so forth.
Wouldn't that give P.B. pleasure? It is a real sin to write it down
in ink. Why doesn't some painter come and drive the money-
changers from the temple and do what would be so necessary and
so natural to do?

So once more then, make many notes, even if you don't read
them over (for in reading over one is unjust, and much then
seems impossible that is plainly necessary), and if you can, make
drawings of the same sort with all uncompromising directness of
the instant stroke. All this only as material we will then sift here,
discussing it and joining the natural breaks. You will see, it will
fit. Only there must be lots, so that we can really pour it out before us and reach into it. The more the better.— . . . Write
only briefly and save up for your notes and sketches. (Looking
into interiors of houses as into fruit-meat is an experience for me
from somewhere. From Rome?) Look, look, look. . . .

[140]

To Clara Rilke   [Villa Discopoli, Capri]
                                      March 11, 1907, Monday

. . . I always write it Monday, the "Oceana" letter, and it gets
to you only the next Sunday, at ten-thirty: so your cards in-
form me, which I do indeed consider as a letter (the tenth).
How lovely those cards really are, and again: how well you told
what they confirm. The avenue up to the Pyramids you evoked
in me just that way, only with everything the card can't give
besides, with the luminosity and the movement toward that luminosity. But the disposition and distribution of the whole had
arranged itself in me on your indications just as the card now
gives it. You wish "again and again, to be alone more," you say.
Yes, how much and in how little considerate a manner I would
surely wish it if I came back from such expeditions and such
things and from that market place into the dreary boredom that
looms under the influence of parlor games. . . . Our upbring-

ing is probably to blame for our managing social affairs so badly. The Heluan people, in so far as they aren't professional sitters-about (for of walking there is no question), have probably learned from childhood up to reckon with this excess of social inconveniences as with the unavoidable. That is the canvas on which they have worked their embroidery again and again. Whereas I: I did indeed really live in the little churchyard corner in the school garden, where I was safe from my contemporaries, and in the extremely unsocial environment of their ruthlessness, which like paper scissors cut one very sharp and clear out of the group picture of that unattractive throng. And later it was so again and again, and it was the little narrow room in Tante Gabriele's apartment, and each time it was a separation and singleness and an obligation to accept and somehow come to terms with it. . . . People, before they had become properly acquainted with work, invented distraction as relaxation from and opposite of false work. Had they waited, ah, and been long patient, real work would have become a little more accessible to them, and they would have come to understand that it can as little have an opposite as the world itself has one, or God or any living soul. For it *is everything*, and what is not work neither is nor is anywhere. Renan once noted down: "Travailler, ça repose." I shall put it as motto in the new Rodin volume (which I shall not begin before we have talked about Egypt). . . .

[*141*]

To Paula Modersohn-Becker   Villa Discopoli, Capri
March 17, 1907

I looked forward to your letter more than I can say. . . . I do think your life has powers, to replace and to retrieve and to come to itself at any price. And if outward circumstances turned out differently from what we thought in those days, still only one thing is decisive: that you bear them courageously and have won through to the possibility of finding within the given conditions all the freedom *that* in you needs which must not be destroyed in order to become the utmost that it can become.

For solitude is really an *inner* affair, and the best and most help-ful step forward is to realize that and to live accordingly. It is a matter, after all, of things that do not lie entirely in our hands, and success, which is something so simple in the end, is made up of thousands of things, we never fully know of what.

For the rest, just leave me to my expectation, which is so great that it cannot be disappointed. Where one expects something big, it is not upon this or that that one counts, one cannot count or counsel at all; for it is a matter of the unexpected, the unforseeable. And the slowness of a course could disconcert no one less than myself, whose daily experience is of the great units of measure by which artistic growth increases.

It only saddens me that I shall not see you again now; I think of getting to Paris soon and remaining there as long as possible. But you will already be gone then. This time I shall look for a studio and furniture, for it is to be a serious settling down to all the work there will be to do. Even the summer, about which you ask, I shall probably spend entirely there, in some corner of that tremendous solitude for which I am longing.

Here I have thought much, much of you. Such remarkable color experiences are possible here: unprecedented. And again, it is all never seen, never made; only that bad painters cover it up now and then with their backs—: that is all. Still I wouldn't have wanted to call you or disturb you. My admiration for Paris is too great for that, and my conviction that there one can become every-thing, too sincere. And then: even one's whereabouts are more an internal than an external question,—otherwise real pictures would already have had to come into the world here. . . .

P.S. Clara will soon be able to receive your greetings, when she comes through here on the return journey. Her letters are beautiful and remarkable. Just as when our grandparents traveled and wrote, and a letter was long on the way and contained much that was strange and foreign when it finally arrived. Only that everything foreign is near to us, because we apprehend it and have need of it as expression for things within.

[*142*]

To Clara Rilke   Villa Discopoli, Capri
Monday, March 18, 1907. Afternoon

. . . Thanks for everything you share with me in such a loyal way; it seems to me you are handing me the bigger half of it all. I gather so much from passages in your letters and from pictures, especially from the former, and when everything is added by word of mouth, as it arises in our talks, I shall have some sort of whole that I can remember and look forward to enjoying. . . . And remarkable, to feel this sublimely carried sphinx-head inserted into space with the whole tremendous persevering of its existence. Remarkable, so remarkable that that word recovers its literal worth for one. Again and again I am forced to think: what a world for a section in a new *Book of Hours,* in and before which to let figures rise up in all their size. And how close all that has come to me. Even should I not get there for years, how far I have already been initiated and am in contact with it all. And when I read a chapter in *A Thousand and One Nights* . . . the details I know about from you take on a life of their own, get up out of their corners, come together and form associations that look organic and viable when one heightens the conditions and dimensions of life to the colossal. The caliphs' graves had already surprised me on a recent card; but on the one enclosed this time the earlier impression is heightened to the incredible. Before I found your remarks on the back, I thought of the fruit and fruit-stone quality of those plastic cupolas, which are great sculpture, the height of plastic art with their nowhere interrupted, nowhere weakened or neglected modelé. Of them you must tell me much. How everything is indeed always *one.* When a path turns toward greatness, how one sees again and again, as one proceeds in that direction, everything else one has already known: as though there sat together at the end of it a circle of gods, silent, in quiet similarity and eternal kinship.

Your saying that you cannot draw much now, I can understand. No, how would that be possible with everything, since you

Capri. / Villa Discopoli / Italien.
am 21. März 1907

Mein lieber Hofmannsthal,

Sie werden wissen, wie sehr mich das
angeht und berührt, was Ihr Brief von
Zustimmung zu meinen Arbeiten ent=
hält; ich halte mich nicht dabei auf, es
Ihnen zu versichern. Ergänzend will ich nur
aufschreiben, daß Ihre Worte, fast wie ge=
sprochen (mit dem ganzen Schwingen, das
im Worte sein Kern) zu mir kamen. Ich
habe mich in den letzten Tagen immer wie=
der mit Ihrem Vortrag — vom Dichter und
dieser Zeit — beschäftigt, und so war ich
an Ihre Stimme gewöhnt und gleichsam da=
rauf vorbereitet, Sie wieder zu hören.

Ich war in diesen Tagen mehrmals
nahe daran, Ihnen zu schreiben. Auch das
werden Sie verstehen. Aber ich finde doch im

Augenblick, (obwohl der Eindruck, den
ich von Ihrem schönen Vortrag empfing,
mich stark zusammenfasst fort) nicht
die innere Gelassenheit zu dankbarer
Aussprache. Vielmehr will ich, ohne Sie
warten zu lassen, Ihre besondere und lie-
be Einladung beantworten, zusagend, wie
Sie denken können : völlig zusagend. Denn
in diesem Falle werden alle Gründe ungültig
die ich gegen die Publikation lyrischer Beiträge in Zeitschriften sonst anzuführen wüsste
und es treten andere entscheidende auf,
denen ich nachgebe, wenn ich Sie bitte, über
mit meiner Theilnahme ganz und gar zu
rechnen. Insofern nämlich vorbeschlossene
Dinge da sind.

 Ich glaube, ich werde Ihren Wunsch
erfüllen können, indem ich Ihnen zunächst
(im Laufe der nächsten Woche, wenn es so

lange Zeit fort) zwei Gedichte von der Art
einer, die Sie ... seinerzeit unveröffentlicht,
zur Verfügung stellte. / Die Rosenschale. /
Alkestis. / Für späterhin werde ich Stücke
aus einem Gedicht, Buch vorbereiten, der in
absehbarer Zeit zum Abschluß kommen soll.

Sie sehen, daß mir daran liegt, mei=
ne Bereitschaft auf das Herzlichste zu erweisen,
in diesem Fall, wie in jedem anderen Kommenden.

                Ihr Rilke

have your work and have to talk with and adapt yourself to everybody. I am not afraid you might bring too little with you. When you spread it out here, you will be amazed yourself at all there is. And just go on living it quietly and whole and without limitation. The weeks go so quickly here it is hard to keep up with them, and all of a sudden you will be here. But do not let yourself be disturbed by what is to come; rather, be in that which is still around you and which enters with an immeasurable past into the present that is yours. That is why I too am postponing everything I would like to tell you of myself until it can be told verbally. Only this much: while Ellen Key was here it was half decided that I will be able to go to Paris with the same opportunity offered again that I lost and frittered away in the fall. So, if everything comes as I think and am with full hope planning, I shall go from here directly to Paris and there resume my solitude and work again a year later, exactly where it eluded me when I went to Belgium. And this time I will hold out and not go away again so soon, and bring something to conclusion. I have promised the Insel-Verlag a new book of poems in time for Christmas (with all the reservations with which that sort of thing can be promised), but I would like really to carry it through and multiply the beautiful new things until they are a book, the book that must come now. That is now my concern and my confident hope, and to that my immediate living must adjust and regulate itself. . . .

[*143*]

To Hugo von Hofmannsthal   Villa Discopoli, Capri, Italy
March 21, 1907

My dear Hofmannsthal,

You will know how much the approval of my work that your letter contains concerns and touches me; I will not stop now to assure you of it. I simply want to add that your words came to me almost like spoken ones (with all the vibration that can be about words). In the last few days I had been taken up again and again with your lecture—on the poet and these times—, and so I was accustomed to your voice and as it were prepared to hear it again.

I have recently been several times on the point of writing you. That too you will understand. But for the moment (although the impression I received from your fine lecture has strongly concentrated me) I still do not find the inner calm for grateful discussion. Rather will I, not to keep you waiting, reply to your kind and special invitation, accepting, as you can well imagine, entirely accepting. For in this case all reasons I might otherwise have advanced against the publication of lyrical contributions in periodicals become invalid, and other decisive ones appear to which I yield when I beg you to count absolutely upon my participation. That is, in so far as I have finished things on hand.

I believe I shall be able to fulfill your wish when I put at your disposal shortly (in the course of the next weeks, if it can wait that long) two poems of the type of those that Bie published some time ago ("The Rosebowl," "Alkestis"). For later on I shall prepare single poems out of a cycle the conclusion of which is in sight..

You see that I am anxious to prove my readiness most sincerely, in this case as in any other that may come up.

Your Rilke

[144]

To Clara Rilke   Capri, Villa Discopoli
                                  March 25, 1907, Monday afternoon

. . . once more we are set in the midst of the storms that are jostling the spring all the way in among the many people who now belong to Capri. Remarkable was the night of the spring equinox, a moonlight night with many leaf-shadows being chased over the paths (made of white light). The scent of the wallflowers had no rest over its blossoms and suddenly found itself above quite different bushes, to which it didn't belong, and all the hard trees, prepared for sea wind, became audible again in all their hardness as their leaves turned and struck against each other. But the wind (one could see) no longer reached so far up into the night,—it was now only a stream of wind, a road of wind, above which, deep and silent, blossoming sky stood motionless, spring sky with single, great, open stars . . . The last week of March is beginning, and I am sure it will pass quickly, like all the others. This last one has left me two more things to report: This year's Insel-Almanach, which they are already preparing, will have three poems as a sample of the new book, together with a little essay on the letters of Marianna Alcoforado, with which I have again been having a good deal to do and from which the moving figure of the Portuguese nun seems to me to rise more clearly each time, like that of a Spanish madonna almost: so large and oppressive and set with stones is the habit of this love, in which her yearning face is only one little place. And Hofmannsthal wrote me a very, very kind letter, occasioned by the founding of a new weekly in which a special and fastidiously arranged lyric section will be under his charge; his intention was to tell me this and to say he would like to count quite particularly on my collaboration,—but you will see in what a kind way he knew how to express it. . . .

I am writing only this today, because, on account of the wind perhaps, I have something of a headache, with which I nevertheless have to write a few more things. . . . I already feel a little the beginning of the end here and sit before the coming weeks like one pondering how a whole garment may still be squeezed out of a tapering remnant. . . .

[*145*]

To Tora Holmström Villa Discopoli, Capri, Italy
March 29, 1907

Dear Fräulein Tora Holmström: I naturally rejoice from my heart for you, that you are going to Paris and could think of taking up your work there. I am only worried that you may want to take it upon yourself with too great energy and vehemence, together with all the tremendous thing that Paris is: for one doesn't know that till later: that Paris is itself a task, a very great, a well-nigh exhausting task, which one accomplishes without noticing it. The claim that city makes on one is immeasurable and uninterrupted. (I am grateful to it for the best I have been able to do heretofore.) That is why it doesn't help one immediately and directly in artistic activity, doesn't at first, as it were, affect the work one does,—but it transforms, heightens, and develops one continually, it gently takes from one's hand the tools one has been using and replaces them with others, indescribably finer and more precise, and does a thousand unexpected things with one, like a fairy who delights in seeing a creature take on all shapes the possibilities of which are hidden within it. When one has Paris around one for the first time, one must let it act more like a bath, without trying to do too much about it oneself: save to feel and let it happen to one. . . .

[*146*]

To Clara Rilke

Villa Discopoli, Capri
April 8, 1907 (Monday)

. . . it is remarkable how spring still keeps us waiting here; or actually, it isn't keeping us waiting; it has begun, but it is like the opening of a show: nothing has been finished. One goes from exhibit to exhibit across the worst holes and amid great disorder. (How this southern spring display always forces such comparisons upon one.) Freezing has still not been discarded and only once was the morning such that bird voices woke me: the starting in of a nightingale, who here likes best to try her skill in the early hours, as though she weren't determined, as with us, to keep vigil for her longing's sake, but at most to get up somewhat earlier than the others. Of course everything is blooming most recklessly: if it were voices instead of colors, there would be an unbelievable shrieking into the heart of the night. But in spite of the days with much rain, the air keeps letting the scent fall as if its hands were still too cold for it. Most spacious of all are the starry nights that blossom out moonless in the dark and scatter shooting stars out of sheer exuberance: some that fall quickly and suddenly and, as if they were falling into water, unexpectedly go out; burning ones that spring out of a star and, as if they had gauged their spring, into another star, and quiet ones that soar in a flat arc obliquely through the sky like birds with outspread wings, emerging between two stars, vanishing between two others, as if these skies were only something to pass through—not to stay in. Thus we saw it yesterday evening from the balcony of the studio and good Frau Nonna was quite moved to have all the magnificence before her departure. . . . She is genuinely fond of us and we are all asked, Ruth too, to settle down sometime for a while in great-grandfather's pavilion in Londorf.

. . . If the Monday letters are really still not reaching you until the next Saturday (that would be the fourteenth), this will be the last to find you in Heluan. It wishes you a good farewell, unhurried like the closing of a book which one has finished alone in the night and which, in laying the cover over the last page, one seems for a second to encompass in an indescribably broadened feeling. . . .

[*147*]

To Ernst Norlind [Capri, 1907]

. . . I can understand your desire, better than anyone. Have I not sometimes attempted Russian poems at moments when an inner experience seemed able to clarify itself only in that form. And I am still from time to time compelled to write certain things in French to be able to bring them to form at all. But in so doing I have also come to the realization that one must not yield too much to this urge, rather one must keep applying one's powers to finding everything in one's own language, to saying everything with it: for this, to which we are related even deep into our unconscious, and only this, can in the end, if we take pains with it, give us the opportunity of delineating with it, very precisely and exactly and definitely, even to the echo of every echo, the ultimate validity of our experience. The material of the writer is no more yielding than that of any other art and no easier to encompass! You won't believe how much I still feel in German like a beginner who is very far from reaching surely and resolutely for the words which each time are the only right ones. My experience and knowledge in this connection are too clear and basic to let me withhold them from you at the moment when you write of your hope and intention to publish sometime in German. The attraction a "great cultural language" has for you will also fall away when you consider how accessible the great thoughts of all languages have become to us, and how Swedish especially has been able to draw attention to itself whenever your poets have grown out beyond national significance. And it has often seemed to me that something great has only to be *thought* in order to exist indestructibly! Feeling like this, there is no sense in choosing a language because it is widespread; much rather should it be our task to reach the ultimate in clarity in that which one has. (If you knew furthermore what small prospect one has just now of finding among readers of German people who understand when one tries to write in this language of the great final things, of the most important, the ultimate, the most profound—you would not wish to grow into this language! I say this quite without bitterness; for works of art can wait: indeed, they do nothing but that and do it passionately—.)

About your new books, of which through Ellen Key I hear such very good things quoted—Bonnier's opinion namely—, I am heartily glad, dear friend. It is only too bad: Danish I read fairly easily, as I tried out just recently (Helge Rode's new drama *Morbus Tellermann*), while I can adjust myself less easily to Swedish. Nevertheless I shall naturally make an effort to read you, and all the inexpressible that passes back and forth between us will certainly help me here and there to grasp something by feeling and intuitive groping.

Besides your kind letter I have also to thank you now for what you sent: the lithograph and the photograph of your new picture.

In both I find the landscape and arrangement of space extraordinarily fine and successful; the birds aren't so convincing at first glance. I have the feeling that you often spoil your real knowledge of form and movement by a too conscious attempt at stylization. The mood emanating from these pictures is certainly very strong in spite of this, but the effect it spontaneously produces on one is again and again interrupted by a certain surprise at the bird-forms, which do not evoke movement along with their gesture. But without qualification I admire your more and more energetic mastery of space, executed with ever simpler means. . . .

[148]

To Gudrun Baroness Uexküll   Villa Discopoli, Capri
                                      April 15, 1907

. . . I have behind me a daily task I was fond of, a translation of the forty-four beautiful *Sonnets from the Portuguese* of Elizabeth Barrett Browning, the carrying out of which I owe to my hostess here. Someday a little book will come of them, and I look forward quite particularly to laying it in your hands! These English love sonnets are of a perfection and precision of expression: crystals of feeling they are: so clear, so ordered, so transparently mysterious, and grown up in such a deep untroubled place. And it was somehow possible for me to let the German version take shape in similar depths, so that the translation pleases me, the way it has succeeded. . . .

[149]

To Karl von der Heydt   Villa Discopoli, Capri
                                 May 3, 1907

. . . Perhaps it will amuse you that . . . I have seen Gorky. One evening I sat up there in his house about a round table. The sad lamp shed its light quite evenly, without bringing anyone into prominence: on him, his present wife, and a couple of disconsolate Russian men who took no notice of me. We managed to

understand each other first in Russian, of which a certain amount
returned to me under stress of the moment; later I spoke German
and Madame Gorky translated. You know my opinion, that the
revolutionary is the direct antithesis of the Russian: that is, the
Russian is admirably suited to be one, rather as a cambric handkerchief is very nice for wiping up ink, provided you completely
misuse and ruthlessly misjudge its real attributes. Add to this that
neither can I in any respect imagine the artist, obedient, patient,
fitted for slow development as he is, among the insurrectionists,
and you will understand that the preliminary conditions for our
getting on together were not exactly propitious. And this was in
general confirmed. He speaks even of art as a democrat, as a dis-
contented man, narrowly and hastily judging; with judgments
in which the errors are completely dissolved, so that one cannot
fish them out. But then he is of a great, moving kindness (of that
kindness which again and again makes it impossible for Russians
to remain artists), and it is very moving to find upon a face quite
unprepared the traces of very great thoughts and a rare smile
that breaks out of it laboriously, as though it had a hard, unre-
sponsive surface to push up through from deep down. Remarkable was the atmosphere of nameless, anonymous égalité into
which one fell as soon as one sat down at the round table. It was
like some Beyond in which these exiles were lingering, and their
eyes seemed to be turned back to the earth which is Russia, return to which seems so utterly impossible. . . .

[*150*]

To Friedrich von Oppeln-Bronikowski   Hôtel de Russie, Rome.
En route, May 29, 1907

. . . I admire Stefan George's poems, and my having met the
poet nine years ago in the Boboli Gardens belongs to my most
cherished memories.

He spoke at that time against young people publishing too soon
and too hastily, not without reference to myself; this voice
counseling patient work that expects nothing from without had

its effect, together with other earlier voices, and strengthened
me in an attitude for which I must have had the necessary pre-
disposition. If you wish to call that an influence, designate it as
such.

The effect of works of art seems to me in no way measurable.
Their influence is so much dissolved in memory and experience
and interwoven with them, that it cannot be presented separately.
According to my experience, the effect of George's poems, like
that of other serious works of art, consists in their developing
one's ability to admire and to work and obligating one absolutely
to Nature.

That is all I can say on the subject. . . .

[151]

To Clara Rilke   Hôtel du Quai Voltaire [Paris]
                                    Monday, June 3, 1907

. . . how much seeing and working differ elsewhere; you see,
and think: Later—. Here they are almost the same. You are here
again: that isn't odd, not remarkable, not startling: it isn't even a
celebration; for even a celebration would be an interruption. But
here this takes you and goes on with you and goes with you
toward everything and right through everything, through the
small and the great. Everything that was arranges itself differently, falls into line, as if someone stood there giving orders; and
what is present is in all fervency present, as if it were on its knees
and praying for you. I have already lived a long life here since
Friday morning and countless memories. You can imagine. On
Saturday (June 1) I took my first Turkish bath with complete
enjoyment and without any discomfort. It was glorious to sit in
the good warmth, for which I was of course prepared by our
warmth down there. I even wished there were some of it outside
the bathhouse; the green is far along here, but the air changeable,
cold in spots when it moves, and where it is still, insipidly warm,
so that one feels mistreated by it and by the dreadful sharp dust
one of those sudden snatches of wind tosses up; I have never found

that so bothersome as this time; (am I especially sensitive to it after all the sea air?) But what is that to the principal thing. The way everything is here again, reality right into the smallest part. You go somewhere and simply are happy and feel in the mood, and your tasks go on before you with their delicate, winged feet and linger a little and are not at all unattainable,—only very proud. Yesterday I was in Notre Dame and heard again the singing that streams into that wonderful mold and everywhere takes on its interior shape. Spent a curious hour this afternoon in the Carrière exhibition. . . . It really is singular, this work, and not at all as though one might soon shake it off. Dora has looked at studios for me that are listed at Colarossi's as "furnished": but the dirt that goes with them each time is insuperable. And I do have a horror of settling an empty studio and of time and money going in the process. So it will probably again be—rue Cassette. . . . And that will be an upper room, the one right above Paula Becker's, that looks on the little church through the chestnuts of the convent garden: that I look forward to. And then? Last year cannot come again, though much chimes in so similarly: but it will after all be a quite new one, and to that too I look forward. Today I saw Mathilde Vollmoeller at Jouven's; she was as always simple and sympathetic. And everything leaves one so gloriously in peace. . . .

[*152*]

To Clara Rilke   29 rue Cassette, Paris VI°
                                          Friday afternoon [June 7, 1907]

    . . . Here I have already been to many places again. Tuesday in the little Bagatelle Palace where there is an exhibition of women's portraits from 1870 to 1900. A wonderful Manet rewards one superabundantly for all the rest. That is a painter; he is beginning to open up to me all over again after this portrait and after the incredible "Déjeuner sur l'herbe" that I saw today in the Louvre in the newly installed Moreau-Nélaton collection. That is a painter, still, and again and again and all the more. Carrière was wrong after all and Van Gogh is something else, something inexorably obsessed with expression that bends painting to its will. With him the never before painted came in, but with Manet everything paintable. (That sounds strange; for by the meaning of painting everything actually must be paintable; yes, but it isn't yet, and Van Gogh wanted it to be, to be, to be.) At Bernheim jeune, I saw Van Goghs: a night café, late, dreary, as if one were seeing it with sleepless eyes. The way he has made the old lamplit air (by drawing circles concentrically about the hanging lamps, which seem gradually to dissolve in the room), is far from being painting any longer, but is forcibly won with colors, and it overpowers: one becomes positively old, wilted, and drowsily disconsolate before it. There are Maillols there too: very, very beautiful ones. The torso of a girl, still in clay (to be baked), which is indescribable. And at the same time another well-known Japanese collection is shortly being sold at auction which one should also see!

. . . But the difficult, the anxious is somehow still here too— indeed everything is again: as always in Paris.

Thank you for the notes written en route. Perhaps you are right in many respects. I thought so today at two pictures of Berthe Morisot: they were painted for Manet's sake, and Bashkirtseff painted for Bastien-Lepage—out of him, for his sake. What we do for the sake of God, do women always do for a man? But the human and the divine are equally unattainable: so their task could for that reason still become broad and personal and their own? And now a good Sunday to you. . . .

[*153*]

To Clara Rilke   29 rue Cassette, Paris VI°
                                             June 13, Thursday evening [1907]

. . . a variety of circumstances (unpleasant neighbors in the next room and such), which someone else would more easily conquer, is responsible for my still not being at home here and not taking Paris as it continually offers itself (extravagantly)—, but probably above all it is because I am not working. . . . Yes, the study plan is falling through, item by item, for that will come which has to come, and not that which we put on the program; let us just take what comes and has a right to come well and firmly in hand. And may it come soon, so that there will be no pauses. . . .

I was in the Jardin des Plantes all morning yesterday, looking at the gazelles. Gazella Dorcas, Linné. There are two of them and a single female besides. They were lying a few feet apart, chewing their cuds, resting, gazing. As women gaze out of pictures, so they gaze out of something with a mute, conclusive turn. And when a horse neighed, one of them listened and I saw the radiance from ears and horns about her slender head. Were the ears of those in Al Hayat just as gray (as tin to gold in relation to the tone of the other hair) with a soft, dark, ramified marking inside? I only saw one get up for a moment, she lay right down again; but I saw, while they stretched and tested themselves, the magnificent work of those hind legs: (they are like guns out of which leaps are shot). I couldn't go away at all, they were so beautiful, and exactly as I felt before your delicate photograph: as though they had only just been changed into this shape. . . .

[154]

To Clara Rilke   29 rue Cassette, Paris VI°
                                              June 19, 1907

    . . . I do not know why I am so slow this time in adapting and settling in. The neighbors are not bad, and yet it is again the Paris that consumed Malte Laurids. A student studying for his examinations for years. Then just before the tests an ailment manifests itself: his face becomes troubled over his books, the lines dance and one eyelid closes down, simply closes down like a shade whose cord is broken. This condition made him nervously miserable, and then, at the time I moved in, he was going about in his room, stamping with every turn and even late into the night, in a kind of bleary resentment, throwing things on the floor, some kind of tin things made as if for the purpose, which rolled along in order to be picked up and thrown down again and again. You know one couldn't have provided a more susceptible neighbor for this young man. How that kept me engrossed and breathless the first nights, before I knew what it meant. Alas: because I at once grasped the rhythm in that madness, the weariness in that anger, the task, the despair—you can imagine.—That ate into me a little and confirmed and occupied me in my dreadful melancholy. And a person like that, when he is at the end of his powers, takes some for himself through the wall. Instinctively,—what does it matter to him.—That is all. And now they are operating on his eyelid (the muscular exhaustion of which naturally cannot be surgically removed). But it is so in keeping with this misery to have the hospital mixing in and the clever gentlemen who for a moment are certainly taking an interest in this obstinate eyelid.—Today, I believe, he will be operated on for the second time, and then he is supposed to leave soon for home somewhere. His mother came at the worst time. To hear her step outside, ah, she had no idea how much that step had to stand by me too. One had only to hear it outside in the corridor when she came and went. One heard: a mother has a sick son—heard it as if one saw it depicted on ten bas-reliefs in various stages: that is how one heard it. . . .

[*155*]

To Julie
  Baroness von Nordeck zur Rabenau 29 rue Cassette, Paris VI⁰
                                          June 20, 1907

 . . . it is a mistake, I know, to live with such self-surrender that one is always getting lost in one's surroundings of the moment. This mistake would be more pardonable if I were already in a position to utilize it wholly for my art; but even that I do not as yet understand, and so only long and cumbersome acclimatizations come out of it, periods of transition that remove me forcibly from my fellows, without permitting me even a tangible connection with the next new thing. I am in the midst of such days. For Paris, which I admire so much and which I know I must go through as one goes through a school,—is something continually new, and when it gives one the feeling of its greatness, its almost limitless-ness, that is when it becomes really ruthless and so completely annihilates one that one must quite diffidently start in all over again with an ardent attempt at living.—Now Italy is already so far off, Capri with its good, even, sheltered days, with the house about everything that one did and thought and dreamed, so that doing and thinking and dreaming became something mild and almost noiseless—and Naples, the glorious city, princely in its layout: as if gifts had been set out along that bay, mountains of gifts for a king whose ship, the most dazzling in a retinue of ships, may appear shimmering out there at any moment—, all that is already far away. . . .

[*156*]

To Clara Rilke   29 rue Cassette, Paris VI⁰
                                     June 21, 1907

. . . I still owe you the explanation of what I meant by God himself having taken it into his hands to teach me economy. (Alas, he underestimates the difficulty in any case.) But see how he began it. It started in Naples. We were riding with Tante Alla and the Countess to the museum; I sat behind you and was on the point of paying with one lira (the fare for four people) in my hand and a ten centesimi piece which I wanted to put with it and give away too. My neighbor became interested in my hand and did not let it out of his sight; when the conductor appeared over at the edge of the bench, he took my lira with perfect calm and made me put away the two soldi, while he gave me to under-stand that it cost four times twenty-five and basta. A porter on the journey functioned similarly when I, in some desperation over the emigrants, was in the process of paying goodness knows what extra for goodness knows what transportation, and he simply fetched me back from the office (after he had patiently observed my intentions for a while) and sat me down in second class under my baggage, with sharply bent legs, as is proper. That was clear. And I have taken it to heart. I have crossed out everything, 1. carriages, 2. tea drinking, 3. buying books (alas), and still—it is more difficult than ever. Why? What a stupid clumsy person I am; all the others about me can and could do it, even Mlle. de Lespinasse, when the Count de Guibert complained to her of certain worries, answered: "Paris est le lieu du monde où l'on peut être pauvre avec le moins de privations: il n'y a que les ennuyeux et les sots qui ont besoin d'être riches." That too is clear. And nevertheless I have done a lot of calculating again these last days, and haven't arrived at understanding how it will turn out. For the present, it seems to me, I can neither stay here nor travel,—but if I can just work: wouldn't that after all be the solution?

If only one of us had a little of the practicality and shrewdness that money develops in those who know how to handle it. Ruth? Ah, better she should have the health and the security and the inner gayety which for sheer innate wealth feels no want, what with so much deciding and doing. . . .

[*157*]

To Clara Rilke   29 rue Cassette, Paris VIe
                                          Monday, June 24, 1907

. . . this morning [came] your long letter, with all your thoughts. . . . Works of art are indeed always products of having-been-in-danger, of having-gone-to-the-very-end in an experience, to where no man can go further. The further one goes, the more one's own, the more personal, the more unique an experience becomes, and the work of art, finally, is the necessary, irrepressible, most valid possible expression of this uniqueness. . . . Herein lies the tremendous help of the work of art for the life of the person who must make it:—that it is his rallying of strength; the knot in the rosary at which his life speaks a prayer, the ever-recurrent proof of his unity and trueness, but directed only toward himself and to the outer world working anonymously, unnamed, as necessity only, as reality, existence—.

We surely have no choice then but to test and try ourselves out to the extreme, but also we are probably bound not to express, to part, to impart this extreme before it enters into the work of art: for as something unique that no one else would or should understand, as personal insanity so to speak, it has to enter into the work in order to become valid there and to show the law, like an inherent design which becomes visible only in the transparency of the artistic sphere.—Two freedoms of communication there are, nevertheless, and they seem to me the utmost of what is possible: the one face to face with the thing completed and the one within our daily life itself, in which we show each other what we have become through our work and thereby mutually support and help and (in the humblest sense of the word) admire each other. But in the one case as in the other one must show one another results, and it is no lack of trust, no missing something in each other, and no excluding, if one does not display the instruments of development, which have in them so much that is bewildering, distressing, and only in its personal application valid. I so often think how insane it would have been, how destructive for him, if Van Gogh had had to share the uniqueness of his vision with anyone, had had to examine the motives with someone before he made his pictures out of them, those existences that justify him with their whole soul, that answer for him, that swear to his reality. In letters he probably sometimes thought that he needed this (although there too, he is treating largely of things already done), but scarcely had Gauguin appeared, the longed-for companion, the likeminded friend—before he had to cut off his ears in desperation, after they had both previously resolved to hate each other and at a good opportunity to send each other out of this world. But that is only one thing: felt from artist to artist. The woman and her share are something else. And a third thing (but thinkable as a task only for later years), the complication of the woman being an artist. Ah, that is an entirely new question, and thoughts bite at one on all sides if one takes only a few steps into it. On that I shall write no more today—my relationship to my "models" is certainly still false, especially as I really can't use any human models at all yet (the proof: I am not making any yet) and shall be occupied with flowers, animals, and landscapes for years to come. (The opening scene of "Alkestis" is perhaps my first reach into the world of "figures".)

You see . . . I am writing hurriedly in order to have time for other things. You will not misunderstand the haste in my handwriting: the content is not so hurried and neither is that which prompts me to write. I quite obstinately go on asking for something about the Rodin conversation; I don't know why I think that it would be valuable for me to have a little share in it. . . .

[*158*]

To Clara Rilke   29 rue Cassette, Paris VI᷉
                                          June 26, Wednesday [1907]

. . . How will it be sometime with Rodin? It is too much to write about it now, it leads too far in all directions. Also it is not time for it yet. It pains me not to be able simply to go out to see a few things again and Rodin himself. Naturally even I understand something of those objections. And yet something is not right about them; this whole emphasis that turns against what is literary and literature-ish in other arts is itself literature and emanates from littérateurs. That is suspicious; I would rather hear a plain craftsman, of Maillol's simplicity for instance, taking Rodin to task. And didn't I have with him the very experience for which you prepared me years ago: that of the immaterial, the unintentionally formed—"like the worm that makes its way in the dark from place to place——"? in a word: of the modelé? And couldn't you think him so calm and confident in Egypt before those tremendous things? But no, if I go on writing now, I must go up to the stars and down to the bottom of the sea and can leave nothing unpacified: for then what is left out? Till later.

Today there is a banquet in honor of Diriks (do you remember the Norwegian painter whom we always thought so congenial, to look at; in celebration of his being decorated with the Legion of Honor). By chance I received an invitation; I might almost have gone, but Rodin will be there, and what according to my whole feeling would have been an urgent reason for being there becomes through the circumstances just as decisive a one for staying away. Strange. Life takes pride in not appearing uncomplicated. With simplicity it would probably not bring us to all those things to which we are not easily brought. . . .

Today I sent you "registered" something unexpected. My new book. In recent days I have been copying and putting together like the girl "who still doesn't know what will come out of it all." And it almost seems to hold and bear itself and *be a book?* It is to remain in your care until we send it to the Insel. . . .

[*159*]

To Clara Rilke   29 rue Cassette, Paris VI⁰
                                             June 28, 1907

. . . I must still keep my head somewhat clear as long as the second part of my Rodin book is not written. In this, certain shifts in point of view may as yet play no part; they would destroy much that was of a simple order, and still not be familiar enough to me yet to allow of a new, equally clear and, in the deepest sense, right relationship of insights. Naturally this second part will be the present lecture, hardly or not at all changed— for it is by no means the moment to say anything new about Rodin now. But I must simply be allowed to let the lecture stand in its entirety still while I am preparing it for publication. I can still understand it fully, it seems to me, although I am already beginning to see too that many of its perceptions belong perhaps to the demands Rodin taught us to make, not to those which his work realizes in each case. But I know nothing of that as yet, and that Rodin does not "think," but rather remains within his work, within the attainable, that was just what we felt to be his advantage, his humble, patient road into reality: and I still have no other belief to put in place of this belief. One can only remain in the "realized" in art, and by reason of remaining in it, it grows and continually leads out beyond one. The "final intuitions and insights" draw near only to him who is and remains in his work, I believe, and he who considers them from afar acquires no power over them. But all that belongs so much already in the sphere of personal solutions. At bottom it does not concern us how someone manages to grow, if only he grows and if only we are on the track of the law of our own growth. . . .

[*160*]

To Clara Rilke   29 rue Cassette, Paris VI•
                                    last day of June, Sunday [1907]

What a rain; is it like this with you too, today, Sunday . . . ? I don't know, I had no intention whatsoever of going out, and yet I stand at the window and act as if the bad weather had kept me from something. Over there in the convent church behind the tall chestnuts they are singing to the organ, and from time to time one feels the rising of tones right through the noise of the falling, which makes the whole afternoon into a single long hour that heeds no stroke of the clock and simply lasts on and on, as in childhood sometimes the afternoons one spends reading, one's head between one's two fists. . . .

[*161*]

To Clara Rilke   29 rue Cassette, Paris VI•
                                    July 9, 1907 (Tuesday)

. . . Just think, here in the Luxembourg, back of the museum, in front of the ball-game courts, an enormous bed of low-growing roses has been laid out, with paths inside on which one unfortunately cannot walk; by each rose stands its name, and a few days ago I read on one of the tablets: Baronne Louise d'Uexküll. Who could that have been?

But the most beautiful is the La France bed, the floor of which is sometimes all covered with fallen petals; a bed like that I would like to have sometime, when I am old, and sit before it and make it, of words in which everything is that I then know. . . .

[*162*]

To Clara Rilke   29 rue Cassette, Paris VI⁰
                              July 12, Friday morning [1907]

. . . Don't worry about the laboriousness of my work: it is naturally bound up with the unusual circumstances which do not allow one simply to go out, to see, to hear—. But I have indeed had more time than anyone to see, to hear, to be outside. . . . Only I have forgotten much, and all my memories, which were so suddenly broken off one day, have got a crack; it goes right across them. All that makes this occupation somehow distressing. To postpone, however, would be of no use; that only makes it worse. And I have promised myself to work off all my arrears one after the other. It is the great quantity of what is not done that lies with all its weight on what wants to come out of the soil. So do not worry. Everything that is work is good and is justified, is even justified in being difficult. . . .

[*163*]

To Clara Rilke   29 rue Cassette, Paris VI⁰
                                    August 9, 1907

. . . A thousand thanks for your trouble over the new book. It is as you say: as soon as I see it in print, I shall go over several things once more from a disinterested distance, and shall still substitute for "Gazelle" and "Marionette Theater" other, less dubious things. It is a book: *work*, the transition from the inspiration that comes to that which is summoned and held fast. *What shall we call it?* . . .

Paris VIe; 29, rue Cassette.

Am 27. August 1907.

Sehr geehrter Herr Doctor,

Um Ihnen nicht alle Mühe umsonst gemacht zu haben, sage ich zu, den Abend zu theilen, wie Sie es in Ihrem letzten Schreiben vorschlagen; in der Annahme allerdings, daß das Honorar das vereinbarte bleibt (350 Mk einschließlich der Reisekosten) und daß Sie, falls der Freiherr von Gleichen-Russwurm nicht den Rest des Abends übernehmen sollte, mich verständigen, wen Sie an seiner Statt eingeladen haben.

Es interessiert mich natürlich sehr, durch Sie ein Wort über den Verlauf des "Täglichen Lebens" zu hören, (gegen welches sich ja viel einwenden läßt und thatsächlich einwendet.) Da ich die Kritiken und überhaupt gar keine Zeitungen lese, erfuhr ich so zuerst von jener besonderen Aufführung, nicht ohne ein dankbares Gefühl für Ihre freundliche Auffassung.

Ich erwarte, geehrter Herr Doctor, nunmehr Ihren Bescheid, ob die Angelegenheit als abgeschlossen gelten darf und ob wir beim 5. November bleiben können.

In vollkommener Hochachtung
begrüßt Sie:

Rainer Maria Rilke

[*164*]

To Julie
Baroness von Nordeck zur Rabenau   29 rue Cassette, Paris VI°
                                              August 10, 1907

. . . Time passes so quickly, and I have long ago given up running a race with it. More and more (and to my joy) I am living the existence of the seed in the fruit which disposes everything it has round about it and outward from itself in the darkness of its working. And more and more I see it is my only way out to live thus; otherwise I cannot transform the sourness around me into the sweetness that I owe to God from eternity.—In a word: I stand at my standing desk and nothing else. . . .

[*165*]

To Dr. Martin Zickel   29 rue Cassette, Paris VI°
                                         August 27, 1907

My dear Doctor,
    in order not to have made you all the trouble for nothing, I agree to divide the evening as you propose in your last letter; on the assumption of course that the fee remains as agreed upon (350 mks. including traveling expenses) and that, should Baron von Gleichen-Russwurm not take over the remainder of the evening, you will inform me whom you have invited in his stead.

It naturally interests me very much to get word through you of the way *Daily Life* went (against which much can be said and actually is said). Since I never read criticisms and no newspapers at all, I thus learned of that Breslau performance for the first time, not without a feeling of gratefulness for your friendly attitude.

I now await word from you, my dear Doctor, whether the matter may be considered settled and whether we can keep to November 5.

                    With high regard
                            the greetings of:
                                    Rainer Maria Rilke

[*166*]

To Clara Rilke

29 rue Cassette, Paris VI*
August 30, 1907

. . . it was on this day or on the last of August five years ago that I first arrived in Paris. I still recall exactly my arrival, the drive from the Gare du Nord to rue Toullier, the arrival there, strange and frightening right at the first moment and yet full of expectation and promise and necessity to the smallest detail. I ordered coffee, was astonished, I still recall, at the big spoon one got with it—went out across the Boulevard Saint-Michel, obliquely across it to the little post office that no longer exists, by the outer side of the Palais, where I telegraphed to you. According to my correspondence book, I wrote you then on September 2. What can I have written? So that was this Paris, as it is now, already post-summer and still pre-autumn Paris. Then I didn't really understand how the city had got into this state, this year I have seen it coming on; yes, I even feel a little as if I had helped to produce it and had myself taken the leaves from the chestnuts that are now quite empty.

. . . Have you read Sabatier's *Saint Francis* now? It is so long ago, I still know only very dimly that it was beautiful and his figure to be well felt, something always achieved somehow by the French, who know how to arrange the details so much better than German scholars, with whom little particulars are always left piled up on top of each other. I am now going almost every morning to the Bibliothèque Nationale, more for reference than for reading. Thus there came into my hands a few days ago translations of wonderfully beautiful Chinese poems of Li Tai Po and others. What poets those were. They make a sign, and things come and go; one feels them after a millennium through the late, foreign language: how light it was, how it came and went, what they evoked; and how all heaviness passed into the weightless, there to endure. . . .

[167]

To Ernst Ludwig Schellenberg   29 rue Cassette, Paris VI°
                                     September 2, 1907

. . . It is very kind of you to meet my silence with so much consideration in spite of the fact that it must seem very strange and unfriendly to you. The chief reason lies in a correspondence that far exceeds my powers; but this does not excuse me. And perhaps it cannot even exonerate me if I candidly admit that the answering of your letters was put off and could finally pass into oblivion, because all literary evaluation and discussion that my works provoke are very remote from me.

You show me so much good will that I owe you at least a few words on that subject. You have to do here with a personal feeling, a weakness, if you will, which, in admitting, I do not mean in any way to justify. I am wrong, perhaps, but I *never* read anything concerning my work. I did indeed do so years ago as a very young man, when I didn't yet know any better and was curious. Now the close relationship which I have with my work prevents me from ever again looking at a criticism. *I must be alone with my work,* and I have as little need of hearing others speak about it as, for instance, one would wish to see in print and to collect the opinions of others on the woman one loves. The correct as well as the incorrect comments some critic is able to make get between me and the work, are foreign bodies, and were it possible to assimilate them, it would seem to me a poor way out; for then what is expressed in them would always expel and replace the unconscious element in that very intimate and inward relationship which with such reticence and mystery binds the worker to his work, to its past and to the future waiting in it. This unconscious element in one's working and in the continuation of one's own path (which must not be lost) is endangered by every criticism (to my way of feeling), and it is doubtless due to my own propensities that I (personally) feel that criticism is a letter to the public which the author, since it is not directed to him, does not have to open and read.

Do not understand that by this I mean to say anything general; what I say applies only to myself, who am under discussion here since you wished it so.

Forgive me then if I make no exception even for your little book and place it unread among my books. Your very favorable disposition toward me I know from your letter which I had the pleasure of reading; for however alien and not pertinent to me much criticism addressed to the outside world may seem, still I know nothing kinder and more helpful than an expression of appreciation directed to me, meant only for *me*, which, when it falls to my share, I accept with my whole heart and hold in honor. And in thanking you for it especially, I am also thanking you for the little book that grew out of your occupation with my work. In going out, it assuredly does much for me; feel that I am not overlooking or underrating that; on the contrary, I know very well how great the influence of a convinced voice can be. I rank criticism very high; the only qualification being that where it concerns my work I can, in consequence of a certain inner organization, have no connection with it whatever.

I am writing in haste, and do not know whether I am comprehensible; but I wanted very much to be so, at least enough for you not to think me moody or ungrateful.

[*168*]

To Paul Zech   29 rue Cassette, Paris VI⁰
                                        September 12, 1907

. . . why should we not talk any more about it? I carried the article around with me a long time, read this expression and that sentence over again, and in so doing considered how dangerously close you have sometimes come. The unerring recognition of my metamorphoses through your eyes would at other times perhaps have disconcerted me; for I do not know whether there was ever enough brightness of day in my consciousness for me to live with things (of which you stated that they were corporeal) in a neighborhood as aware as though they were within me. Sometimes (this I often experience) they have gone in a feeling of dream through my restlessness and were weary of long wandering and sought a leafy hill: to linger beneath it. Furthermore one cannot always lay hold of the experience on all sides and feel out whether it may fit into the vessel of our body. We experience many things and the ups and downs of what happens with them beyond the real day. And it would be unbearable to live that way if the noisy and industrious day lay always at our door. You, to whom the weight of reality is closer by how many degrees than I feel it: desire that all glass shall be transparent. And of that I would not disapprove; yet is not the misted distance built infinitely further out into eternity? Still I would be able to fill out many of your questions. But since you also promised me that we shall meet on November 5, the living word had better help us over any contradictions. Or do you believe: that here too physical proximity would create that confusion which makes the meaning of the real unreal?

Write me a line about it. . . .

[169]

To Clara Rilke   29 rue Cassette, Paris VI⁸
                                        September 13, 1907 (Friday)

. . . never has heather so touched and almost thrilled me as recently, when I found those three twigs in your sweet letter. Since then they have been lying in my *Book of Pictures* and have permeated it with their strong stern odor, which is really only the scent of autumn earth. How glorious it is, though, that fragrance. Never, it seems to me, can the earth be thus inhaled in a single smell, the ripe earth; in a smell that means no less than the smell of the sea, bitter where it borders on taste, and more than honey-sweet where one feels it must be impinging on the beginnings of tone. Containing depth within it, darkness, the grave almost, and yet again wind too; tar and turpentine and Ceylon tea. Serious and shabby like the smell of a begging friar and yet again resinous and hearty like costly frankincense. And to behold: like embroidery, gorgeous; like three cypresses embroidered into a Persian rug with violet silk (a violet as vehemently moist as if it were the complementary color of the sun). You ought to see it. I think the little twigs couldn't have been so beautiful yet when you sent them off: else you would have said something surprised about them. By chance one of them is lying now on the dark blue velvet of an old writing box. It is like fireworks; no, just like a Persian rug. Are really all, all those millions of branchlets of such wonderful workmanship? Look at the coloring of the green in which there is a little gold, and the sandlewood-warm brown of the little stems and the break with its new, fresh, inner scarcely-green.— Ah, for days now I have been admiring the splendor of these three little fragments and am really ashamed that I wasn't happy when I was able to walk about in it, in all the profusion. One lives so badly because one always comes into the present unready, unfit, and distraught for everything. I can think back on no time in my life without such reproaches and even greater ones. Only the ten days after Ruth's birth, I think, did I live without waste; finding reality as indescribable, even to the smallest detail, as it doubtless always is.—But probably this city summer I have lived through has also made me so susceptible to the splendor of those little bits of heather coming from the array of the northern year. Not for nothing probably has one gone through a room-summer like that, where one is lodged in the smallest of those boxes, one of which always fits into another, twenty times. And one is in the very last, crouching. Heavens: how well I managed last year; seas, parks, wood, and woodland meadows: my longing for all that is sometimes indescribable. Now, with winter already threatening here. Already the misty mornings and evenings are beginning, when the sun is only like the place where the sun used to be, and when in the parterres all the summer flowers, the dahlias, and great gladiolas and the long rows of geraniums scream the contradiction of their red into the fog. That makes me sad. It brings up disconsolate memories, one doesn't know why: as though the music of the city summer were ending with a dissonance, in a mutiny of all the notes; perhaps only because already once before one had looked all this so deep into oneself and interpreted it and united it with oneself, yet without ever *making* it. . . .

[*170*]

To Julie
    Baroness von Nordeck zur Rabenau   29 rue Cassette, Paris VI*
                    September 17, 1907

I really must tell you at last how glad I was at the good news from your new work. What work could be finer than this which, like no other, needs love and absorbs it, love, which in all those little, expectant and future hearts is transformed into life, into deeds that some day will be there, into resolutions to the good, into courage, into patience, into earnest simple reality. Now they all press about you, flowers and children, almost with the same need, and how ripe and moving must the experience be for you of seeing the inner loneliness of many years rewarded through the dependence and affection of this environment that has grown to be yours. Now you will daily give and give, and the great stores of your love will not lessen thereby: for this is the miracle that happens every time to those who really love: the more they give, the more they possess of that precious nourishing love from which flowers and children have their strength and which could help all human beings if they would take it without doubting. . . .

[*171*]

To Clara Rilke   29 rue Cassette, Paris VI*
                   Sunday [September 29, 1907]

. . . What you felt with the Portuguese grape, I know so well; I am experiencing it at the moment with two pomegranates I bought recently at Potin's: how magnificent they are in their massive heaviness, still with the back-curved ornament of the pistil on top; princely in their golden rind, through which red underpainting comes through, strong and genuine, as on the

leather of old Cordovan wall-coverings. I haven't yet tried to open
them; they are probably not ripe either, for usually, I think, they
split open easily of themselves over their own fullness and have
purple-lined slits, like noblemen in full dress.—At sight of them,
desire and anticipation of foreignness and southernness arose in
me too and the charm of great journeys. But how much one really
has all that in one beforehand, the more, the tighter one shuts one's
eyes over oneself. I felt that again when I wrote the Corrida which
I never saw: how I knew and saw it all! . . .

[*172*]

To Clara Rilke   29 rue Cassette, Paris VIe
                                      October 3, 1907

   . . . if only you were sitting in my room on this cold rainy
day, which is passing unwillingly and for no one, which now at
last (as I saw at Jouven's) is filling other people too with surprise
and perplexity. Sitting with me before the Van Gogh portfolio
(which I am taking back with a heavy heart). It has done me so
much good these two days: it was the right moment. . . . You
probably wouldn't have read at all the little biographical notice
of at most ten lines that precedes the table of contents, relying
simply on your looking. It is, nevertheless, very, very factual and
yet so strangely suggestive to read. Art dealer, and when after
three years he somehow saw it wasn't that, small school teacher
in England. And in the midst of it the resolve: to become a clergy-
man. He comes to Brussels to learn Greek and Latin. But why the
detour? Aren't there people anywhere who ask neither Greek
nor Latin of their minister? So he becomes what is called an
evangelist, and goes into the coal region and tells the people the
gospel. In telling he begins to draw. And finally he doesn't notice
at all how he is growing silent and doing nothing any more but
draw. And from then on he does nothing else, even up to his
last hour, until he resolves to stop everything, because for weeks
perhaps he would not be able to paint; so it seems natural to him
to give up everything, life above all. What a biography. Is it

really true that all the world acts, now, as though it understood this and the pictures that come out of it? Shouldn't art dealers and equally so art critics really be more perplexed or more indifferent about this dear zealot, in whom something of Saint Francis too came to life again? I marvel at his swift fame. Ah, how he too had discarded and discarded. His self-portrait in the portfolio looks needy and tormented, desperate almost, and yet not catastrophic: as when a dog is having a bad time. And holds out his face, and one sees, in fact, that he is having a bad time day and night. But in his pictures (the arbre fleuri) the poverty has already become rich: a great radiance from within. And so he sees everything, as a poor man; one need only compare his *Parks*. Those too he says so quietly and simply, as if for poor people, so that they can understand; without going into the showiness that lies in the trees; as if even that would indicate partiality. He takes no sides, not the side of the parks, and his love for all that goes toward the nameless and has thus become hidden by himself. He doesn't show it, he has it. And puts it out of himself quickly into his work, into the most inward, unceasing part of the work: quickly: and no one has seen it! So one feels him in these forty pages: and haven't you after all been beside me a little and looking through the portfolio? . . .

[173]

To Clara Rilke   29 rue Cassette, Paris VI°
                                    October 4, 1907 (Friday)

. . . it is still as if one were in a wet sponge someone is tossing about. What a strange effect it can have, being thus lifted out of order! The seasons are usually just so beautiful and helpful through continuity and contrast, one can rely on them; but this time everything that began was abrupt, as though one suddenly turned over in an encyclopedia to another letter and went on reading, after something quite different, under Th or Y.

To be sure, if one were as secure in one's work as one should be, that would not disconcert one, even in conjunction with a cold: one would simply see and make things out of this state of mind. (It was a similar one in Schmargendorf which once made me, quite unexpectedly, as I remember, write the "Pages from a Stormy Night" in a single evening.) But one is still so far from being able always-to-work. Van Gogh could perhaps lose his composure, but the work was still behind the composure, he couldn't fall out of it any more. And Rodin, when he is unwell, is very close to his work, writes beautiful things on countless slips of paper, reads Plato and thinks along those lines. But I have a feeling that that is not mere discipline and compulsion, to be that way with one's work (for then it would tire one, as it has tired me these last weeks); it is sheer joy; it is the natural well-being in this one thing which nothing else equals. Perhaps one must still more clearly perceive the "task" one has, more tangible still, recognizable in hundreds of details. I do feel what Van Gogh must at a certain point have felt, and feel strongly and greatly: that everything is still to be done: everything. But I am not good at giving myself to what is nearest, or at least only in the best moments, while it is just in the worst that one needs it most. Van Gogh could make an intérieur d'hôpital and painted on the most dismaying days the most dismaying subjects. How else would he have survived. At that one must arrive and, I certainly feel, not by compulsion. Out of insight, out of desire, out of inability to postpone, considering all there is to be done. Alas, if only one hadn't those memories of not-having-worked that even now do one good. Memories of lying still and sensing one's well-being. Memories of hours waited through, turning over old illustrations, over the reading of some novel—: and such memories in heaps way back into childhood. Whole regions of life lost, lost even for the retelling, through the seduction that can still issue from their idleness. If only one had memories of work from early days: how firm the ground would be beneath one; one would stand. But this way one sinks in somewhere at every moment. This way there are two worlds *within* one too, that is the worst of it. Sometimes I go past little shops, in the rue de Seine perhaps; dealers in antiques or little secondhand booksellers or vendors of engravings with very, very full windows; no one ever goes in to them, they apparently do no business; but one looks in, and they sit reading, unconcerned (and yet aren't rich); they are not concerned for the morrow, don't worry about a success, have a dog that sits in front of them, in good humor, or a cat that makes the stillness about them still greater, as it prowls along the rows of books as though it were wiping the names off the backs.

Ah, if that were sufficient: I would sometimes like to buy myself a full window like that and to sit behind it with a dog for twenty years. In the evening there would be light in the back room, in the front everything quite dark, and the three of us would sit and eat, back there; I have noticed, seen from the street, it always looks like a Last Supper, so big and solemn through the dark room. (But this way one has all the worries, the great and the small.) . . . You know how I mean that: without complaining. And it is good this way and will get still better. . . .

[*174*]

To Clara Rilke   29 rue Cassette, Paris VI°
                              Sunday afternoon [October 6, 1907]

. . . Noise of rain and striking of hours: it makes a pattern, a Sunday one. If one didn't know it: it has to be Sunday. That is how it sounds in my silent street. But how much it was Sunday in the old aristocratic quarter through which I walked this morning. The old closed-up hôtels in the Faubourg Saint-Germain with their white-gray window shutters, the discreet gardens and courts, the grillwork gates screened close behind their bars and the heavy well-shutting entrances. A few were very haughty and pretentious and inaccessible. Those must have been the Talleyrands, the de la Rochefoucaulds, unapproachable personages. But then came an equally silent street with somewhat smaller houses, no less dignified in their quality and absolutely aloof. One of the gates was in the act of shutting; a manservant in morning livery turned back once again and looked at me attentively and thoughtfully. And at the same moment it seemed to me that only a trifle need have been different at some time, for him to recognize one and step back and hold open the door. For an old lady to be up there, a grand'mère, who was making it possible to receive her favorite grandson even at this early hour. With a smile, herself a little affectionate, the confidential lady's maid would take care of it and precede one through the draped apartments, inwardly looking back and hurrying out of zeal and out of uneasiness at having to go ahead. A stranger would understand nothing in thus passing through; but one would feel the presence of all those things filled with associations: the glance of the portraits, the faces of the musical clocks and the contents of the mirrors, in which the clear essence of this dusk is preserved. One would have recognized in a second the light salons that are quite bright within the darkness. And the one room that seems darker because the family silver at the back has taken all the light to itself. And the solemnity of it all would pass over to one and would carefully prepare one in advance for the old lady in violet white, whom one cannot picture from one time to the next, because there is so much belonging with her.

I went along through the silent street and was still in my fancies, when in the display window of a confiseur in the rue de Bourgogne I saw beautiful old silver. Pitchers with slightly drooping full silver flowers on their lids and fantastic reflections in their flaring curves.

Now it is scarcely credible that this should have been the way leading to the Salon d'Automne. But I did finally come to the gaily colored picture-mart which, much as it strives to impress, still did not dispel my inner mood. The old lady held her own, and I felt how much beneath her dignity it would be to come and see these pictures. I thought whether I mightn't still find *something* I could tell her about, and found a room with pictures by Berthe Morisot (Manet's sister-in-law) and a wall with things by Eva Gonzalès (Manet's pupil). Cézanne simply wouldn't do for the old lady; but for us he counts and is moving and important. He too (like Goya) painted the walls of his studio in

Aix with fantasies (of which there were a few Druet photographs). . .

[*175*]

To Clara Rilke   29 rue Cassette, Paris VI⁰
                                                October 8, 1907

. . . it is remarkable, after two days of Salon d'Automne, to
go through the Louvre: one first notes two things: that every insight has its parvenus, who, when they have it, become vocal,—
and then, that it is perhaps not so much a question of insights at
all, which bring up too much consciousness. As if those masters
in the Louvre had not known that color is what matters in painting. I looked at the Venetians: they are indescribably consistent in
their coloring; one feels how far it goes in Tintoretto. Almost
further than in Titian. And so until into the eighteenth century,
where they become wanting only in the use of black, to arrive
at a Manet scale. Guardi has it, of course; it was unavoidable in
the midst of the brightness, after the laws against display had
prescribed black gondolas. But he uses it rather more as a dark
mirror than as color; Manet first sets it thus on a par with everything else, emboldened to do so anyhow by the Japanese. Con-
temporaneously with Guardi and Tiepolo a woman too was painting, a Venetian, who came to all the courts and whose reputation
was one of the most widespread of her day. Rosalba Carriera. Watteau knew of her, and they exchanged a few pastels, their own
portraits perhaps, and mutually held each other in tender esteem.
She traveled a great deal, painted in Vienna, and a hundred and
fifty of her works are still preserved in Dresden. In the Louvre
are three portraits. A young woman, her face lifted from her
straight neck and then turned naïvely to the front, holds against
her low-necked lace dress a little, clear-eyed, capuchin monkey,
which below, at the edge of the half-length picture, looks out just
as eagerly as she does above, only a tiny bit more indifferently.
With its perfidious little black hands, it is reaching for hers and
by one of its slender fingers draws the delicate, distraught hand

into the picture. That is so full of one period, it is valid for all. And is charmingly and lightly painted, but really painted. A blue shawl appears in the picture furthermore and a whole white-lavender spray of stock which oddly provides the breast ornament. And seeing the blue, it occurred to me that it is that special blue of the eighteenth century which is to be found everywhere, in La Tour, in Peronnet, and which, even in Chardin, does not cease to be elegant, although there, as the band of his curious cap (in the self-portrait with the horn-rimmed glasses), it is already used quite regardlessly. (It is conceivable that someone might write a monograph about blue; from the thick waxy blue of the Pompeian frescos to Chardin and further to Cézanne: what a life story!) For Cézanne's very peculiar blue has this parentage, comes from the blue of the eighteenth century that Chardin divested of its pretentiousness and that now, with Cézanne, no longer carries with it any secondary significance. Chardin was, on the whole, the intermediary; even his fruits are no longer thinking of dinner, they lie about on the kitchen table and care nothing for being nicely eaten. With Cézanne, they cease entirely to be edible, they become such very real things, so simply indestructible in their obstinate existing. When one sees Chardin's portraits of himself, one thinks he must have been an old eccentric. How much so and in what a sad way Cézanne was, I shall tell you tomorrow perhaps. I know a few things about his last years when he was old and shabby and every day on the way to his studio had children after him throwing stones at him as at a bad dog. But within, deep within, he was most beautiful, and now and then would furiously shout something quite magnificent at one of his rare visitors. You can imagine how that would happen. . . .

[*176*]

To Clara Rilke   29 rue Cassette, Paris VI°
                                                        October 9, 1907

. . . today I wanted to tell you a little about Cézanne. As far as work was concerned, he maintained he had lived like a Bohemian until his fortieth year. Only then, in his acquaintance with Pissarro, did the taste for work open up to him. But then so much so, that he did nothing but work for the thirty latter years of his life. Without joy really, it seems, in continual fury, at variance with every single one of his works, none of which seemed to him to attain what he considered the most indispensable thing. La réalisation, he called it, and he found it in the Venetians whom he used to see and see again in the Louvre and had unconditionally acknowledged. The convincing quality, the becoming a thing, the reality heightened into the indestructible through his own experience of the object, it was that which seemed to him the aim of his innermost work; old, sick, every evening exhausted to the point of faintness by the regular daily work (so much so that he would often go to bed at six, as it was growing dark, after an insensibly eaten supper), ill-tempered, distrustful, laughed at every time on the way to his studio, jeered at, mistreated,—but observing Sunday, hearing Mass and vespers like a child, and very politely asking his housekeeper, Madame Brémond, for somewhat better fare—: he still hoped from day to day, perhaps, to reach the successful achievement he felt to be the only essential thing. In so doing (if one may believe the reporter of all these facts, a not very congenial painter who went along for a while with everybody), he had increased the difficulty of his work in the most obstinate way. In the case of landscapes or still life, conscientiously persevering before the subject, he nevertheless made it his own by extremely complicated detours. Starting with the darkest coloring, he covered its depth with a layer of color which he carried a little beyond that and so on and on, extending color upon color, he gradually came to another contrasting pictorial element, with which he then proceeded similarly from a new center. I think that in his case the two procedures, of the observant and sure taking over and of the appropriation and personal use of what he took over, strove against each other, perhaps as a result of becoming conscious; that they began to speak at the same time, as it were, interrupted each other continually, constantly fell out. And the old man bore their dissension, ran up and

down in his studio, which had bad light because the builder
didn't deem it necessary to listen to the eccentric old man, whom
they had agreed not to take seriously in Aix. He walked back
and forth in his studio, where the green apples lay about, or in
despair seated himself in the garden and sat. And before him lay
the little city, unsuspecting, with its cathedral; the city for respectable and modest citizens, while he, as his father, who was a
hatmaker, had foreseen, had become different; a Bohemian, as
his father saw it and as he himself believed. This father, knowing
that Bohemians live and die in misery, had taken it upon himself
to work for his son, had become a kind of small banker to whom
("because he was honest," as Cézanne said) people brought their
money, and Cézanne owed it to his providential care that he had
enough later to be able to paint in peace. Perhaps he went to the
funeral of this father; his mother he loved too, but when she was
buried, he was not there. He was "sur le motif," as he expressed
it. Work was already so important to him then and tolerated no
exception, not even that which his piety and simplicity must certainly have recommended to him.

In Paris he gradually became even better known. But for such
progress as he did not make (which others made and into the
bargain *how*—), he had only distrust; too clearly there remained
in his memory what a misunderstood picture of his destiny and of
his intent Zola (who knew him from youth and was his com-
patriot) had sketched of him in *Oeuvre*. Since then, he was
closed to writing of all sorts: "travailler sans le souci de personne
et devenir fort—," he screamed at a visitor. But in the midst of
eating he stood up, when this person told about Frenhofer, the
painter whom Balzac, with incredible foresight of coming developments, invented in his short story of the *Chef d'Oeuvre
inconnu* (about which I once told you), and whom he has go
down to destruction over an impossible task, through the discovery that there are actually no contours but rather many vibrating transitions—, learning this, the old man stands up from
the table in spite of Madame Brémond, who certainly did not
favor such irregularities, and, voiceless with excitement, keeps

pointing his finger distinctly toward himself and showing himself, himself, himself, painful as that may have been. It was not Zola who understood what the point was; Balzac had sensed long ahead that, in painting, something so tremendous can suddenly present itself, which no one can handle.

But the next day he nevertheless began again with his struggle for mastery; by six o'clock every morning he got up, went through the city to his studio and stayed there until ten; then he came back by the same way to eat, ate and was on his way again, often half an hour beyond his studio, "sur le motif" in a valley, before which the mountain of Sainte Victoire with all its thousands of tasks rose up indescribably. There he would sit then for hours, occupied with finding and taking in *plans* (of which, remarkably enough, he keeps speaking in exactly the same words as Rodin). He often reminds one of Rodin anyway in his expressions. As when he complains about how much his old city is daily being destroyed and disfigured. Only that where Rodin's great, self-confident equilibrium leads to an objective statement, fury overcomes this sick, solitary old man. Evenings on the way home he gets angry at some change, arrives in a rage and, when he notices how much the anger is exhausting him, promises himself: I will stay at home; work, nothing but work.

From such alterations for the worse in little Aix he then deduces in horror how things must be going elsewhere. Once when present conditions were under discussion, industry and the like, he broke out "with terrible eyes": Ça va mal . . . C'est effrayant, la vie!

Outside, something vaguely terrifying in process of growth; a little closer, indifference and scorn, and then suddenly this old man in his work, who no longer paints his nudes from anything but old drawings he made forty years ago in Paris, knowing that Aix would allow him no model. "At my age," he said—"I could get at best a fifty-year-old, and I know that not even such a person is to be found in Aix." So he paints from his old drawings. And lays his apples down on bedspreads that Madame Brémond certainly misses one day, and puts his wine bottles among them and whatever he happens to find. And (like Van Gogh) makes his "saints" out of things like that; and compels them, *compels* them to be beautiful, to mean the whole world and all happiness and all glory, and doesn't know whether he has brought them to doing that for him. And sits in the garden like an old dog, the dog of this work which calls him again and beats him and lets him go hungry. And yet with it all clings to this incomprehensible master, who only on Sunday lets him return to God, as to his first owner, for a while.—And outside people are saying: "Cézanne," and gentlemen in Paris are writing his name with emphasis and proud at being well informed—.

I wanted to tell you all this; it is related to so much about us and to ourselves in a hundred places.

Outside it is raining copiously, as usual. Farewell . . . tomorrow I will speak again of myself. But you will know how very much I have done so today too . . .

[*177*]

To Clara Rilke
29 rue Cassette, Paris VI⁰
October 12, 1907

. . . Taking walks is less difficult now than last week. How much a little moon like that can do. These are the days in which everything is about one, clear, light, scarcely indicated in the bright air and yet distinct; even nearby things have the tones of distance, are taken away and only *shown*, not set down as usually, and what has relation to space—the river, the bridges, the long streets and the lavish squares—has taken this space to itself, holds it to itself, is painted on it as on silk. You will feel what a light-green wagon can be then on the Pont Neuf or some red or other that cannot contain itself, or a placard simply on the fire-wall of a pearl-gray group of houses. Everything is simplified, arranged on a few bright real *plans*, like the face in a Manet portrait. And nothing is trivial or superfluous. The bouquinistes along the quai open up their cases, and the fresh or faded yellow of the books, the violet brown of the bindings, the green of a portfolio:

everything fits, counts, takes part, and sounds in the unity of the bright combinations.

I recently asked Mathilde Vollmoeller to go through the Salon with me sometime, in order to see beside my own an impression that I take to be calm and unswayed by literary considerations. We were there together yesterday. Cézanne prevented us from getting to anything else. I notice more and more what an event that is. But imagine my amazement when Fräulein V., trained and observing quite as a painter, said: "He sat in front of it like a dog and simply looked, without any nervousness or ulterior motive." And she said more that was very good about his method of work (which one can see from an unfinished picture). "Here," she said, pointing to one place, "this he knew, and then he said it (a place on an apple); close by it is still empty, because he didn't yet know it. He did only what he knew, nothing else." "What a good conscience he must have," I said. "Oh yes: he was happy, way inside somewhere . . ." And then we compared "artistic" things, which he may have made in Paris while associating with others, with his most individual things, in the matter of color. In the first, color was something per se; later he takes it somehow, personally, as no human being has yet taken color, only to make the thing with it. The color disappears completely in the realization of the thing; no remnant is left. And Fräulein V. expressed it very well: "It is as though laid on scales: the thing here, the color there; never more, never less than the equilibrium demands. That may be much or little, accordingly, but it is exactly what the object requires." That last would not have occurred to me; but it is eminently right and enlightening as regards the pictures. It also struck me very much yesterday how unaffectedly different they are, how little concerned with originality, sure, in every approach to thousand-sided Nature, of not losing themselves, rather of discovering earnestly and conscientiously her inexhaustibility through the manifoldness without. All that is very beautiful. . . .

[*178*]

To Clara Rilke   29 rue Cassette, Paris VI°
                                    October 13, 1907 (Sunday)

. . . it is raining again in the same way I have already described
to you so often; as if the sky had glanced up brightly for just an
instant, only to go right on reading in the even lines of rain. But
it is not to be so easily forgotten that under the turbid coating is
that light and that depth which one saw yesterday: now one
knows it at least.

I had read about your autumn right away in the morning, and
I could feel all the colors you had put into the letter changing
back in me and filling my consciousness to the brim with strength
and radiance. While I was admiring the distilled clear autumn
here yesterday, you were going through that other one at home
that is painted on red wood, as this one here is on silk. And the
one reaches through to us as well as the other; so deep at the bottom
of all change are we placed, we most changeable ones, who go
about with a disposition to understand everything and who make
of the too great (while we don't really grasp it) the action of our
hearts, so that it shall not destroy us. If I came up to you two, I
would assuredly also see anew and differently the pageant of
moor and heath, the floatingly light green of the meadow strips
and the birches; indeed this transformation, when I once fully
experienced and shared it, called forth a part of the *Book of Hours;*
but in those days Nature was still a general incitement for me,
an evocation, an instrument on whose strings my fingers found
themselves again; I did not yet sit before her; I let myself be
carried away by the soul that issued forth from her; she came
over me with her breadth, with her great, exaggerated existence,
as prophecy came over Saul; just that way. I went along with
her and saw, saw not Nature, but the faces she inspired in me.
How little I could have learned then before Cézanne, before
Van Gogh. From the amount Cézanne gives me to do now, I notice how very different I have grown. I am on the road to becom-

ing a worker, on a long road perhaps and probably just at the first milestone; but nevertheless I can already comprehend the old man who has gone on somewhere far ahead, alone, only with children after him who throw stones (as I once described it in the fragment on the Lonely). I went to see his pictures again today; it is remarkable what a company they form. Without looking at any single one, standing between the two rooms, one feels their presence joining in a colossal reality. As if those colors took away one's irresolution once and for all. The good conscience of those reds, of those blues, their simple truthfulness educates one; and if one places oneself among them as ready as possible, they seem to do something for one. One also notices better each time how necessary it was to go even beyond love; it is of course natural for one to love each of these things, when one makes it: but if one shows that, one makes it less well; one *judges* it instead of *saying* it. One ceases to be impartial; and the best, the love, stays outside the work, does not go into it, remains unconverted beside it: that is how mood-painting arose (which is in no way better than subject-painting). One painted: I love this; instead of painting: here it is. Whereupon everyone must then look well for himself whether I have loved it. That is in no way evident, and many will even declare there is no question of love. So without residue is it consumed in the act of making. This consuming of love in anonymous work, out of which such pure things arise, no one perhaps has so fully achieved as this old man; his inner nature, which had become mistrustful and sullen, supported him in this. He would certainly never again have shown his love to any human being, if he had had to love; but with this disposition, which had been fully developed through his isolated eccentricity, he now turned to Nature too and knew how to repress his love for each single apple and to store it in a painted apple forever. Can you conceive how that is and how one experiences it through him? I have the first proofs from the Insel. In the poems there are instinctive tendencies toward similar objectivity. I am also letting the "Gazelle" stand: it is good. . . .

[*179*]

To Clara Rilke   29 rue Cassette, Paris VIe
                                   October 16, 1907 (Wednesday)

. . . How human beings do play with everything. How blindly
they misuse the never observed, never experienced; distracting
themselves with that which is infinitely collected and which they
displace. It is not possible that a time, in which aesthetic demands of this sort somewhere get their satisfaction, should admire
Cézanne and grasp anything of his devotion and hidden magnificence. The dealers make a noise, that is all; and those who have
need to cling to these things could be counted on two hands, and
they are aloof and reticent.

You have only to see, of a Sunday say, the people going
through the two galleries: amused, irritated to irony, indignant,
furious. And when it comes to expressing conclusions, they stand
there, these monsieurs, in the midst of that world, with the
pathos of despair, and one hears them assert: il n'y a absolument
rien, rien, rien. And how beautiful the women think themselves
as they pass by; they recall that they have just seen themselves,
with complete satisfaction, in the glass doors on entering, and
conscious of that reflection, they place themselves for a moment,
without looking at it, beside one of those touching attempts at a
portrait of Madame Cézanne, so as to exploit the odiousness of
this painting in a comparison so extremely favorable (as they
think) to themselves. And someone told the old man in Aix that
he was "famous." He, however, knew better inside and let them
talk. But before his things one comes again upon the idea of how
mistrustful all recognition (with quite isolated, unmistakable exceptions) must make one toward one's own work. Actually, if
it is good one cannot live to see it recognized: or it is only just
half good and not sufficiently ruthless. . . .

[*180*]

To Clara Rilke   29 rue Cassette, Paris VI⁰
                                October 18, 1907 (Friday)

. . . You must have known, while you were writing, how
much good that insight of yours would do me which sprang spontaneously from comparing the blue slips with my Cézanne experiences. What you say now and warmly confirm, I somehow
suspected, although I could not have indicated how far that development, which corresponds to the immense advance in the
Cézanne paintings, is already realized in me. I was only convinced
that it is inner personal reasons that make me more observant
before pictures which a while ago I would perhaps still have
passed by with momentary interest, without returning to them
any more eagerly or expectantly. It is not the painting at all that
I am studying (for despite everything I am still uncertain about
pictures and am only with difficulty learning to differentiate good
from less good ones, and am always confusing the early with the
late). It is the turning point in this painting that I recognized because I had just reached it myself in my work or at least had come
somehow near to it, probably having been long prepared for this
one thing, on which so much depends. That is why I must be
cautious in trying to write about Cézanne, which naturally tempts
me greatly now. Not the person (I really ought to see that at
last) who takes in pictures from so private an angle is justified
in writing about them; one who could quietly confirm them in
their existence, without experiencing through them more or other
than facts, would surely be fairest to them. But within my own
life this unexpected contact, coming and making a place for itself
as it did, is full of confirmation and pertinence. Another poor man.
And what progress in poverty since Verlaine (if Verlaine wasn't
already a relapse), who under "Mon Testament" wrote: Je ne
donne rien aux pauvres parce que je suis un pauvre moi-même,
and in almost all of whose work this not-giving was, this embittered displaying of empty hands, for which Cézanne during
the last thirty years had no time. When should he have shown his

hands. Malicious glances did often find them, whenever he was on his way, and lewdly uncovered their indigence; we, however, are given to know from the pictures only how massive and genuine the work lay in them to the end. This work, which had no preferences any more, no inclinations, no fastidious indulgences; whose smallest component had been tested on the scales of an infinitely sensitive conscience and which with such integrity reduced the existent to its color content that it began, beyond color, a new existence, without earlier memories. It is this unlimited objectivity, which declines to interfere in any other sphere, that makes Cézanne's portraits so outrageous and absurd to people. They apprehend, without realizing, that he was reproducing apples, onions, and oranges with sheer color (which to them may still seem a subordinate device of pictorial practice), but when they come to landscape, they miss interpretation, judgment, superiority, and where portraiture is concerned, why, the rumor of intellectual conception has been passed on even to the most bourgeois, and so successfully that something of the kind is already noticeable even in Sunday photographs of engaged couples and families. And here Cézanne naturally seems to them quite inadequate and not worth discussing at all. He is actually as alone in this salon as he was in life, and even the painters, the young painters, already pass him by more quickly because they see the dealers on his side. . . .

[*181*]

To Clara Rilke   29 rue Cassette, Paris VI*
                                      October 19, 1907

You surely remember . . . from the *Notebooks of Malte Laurids* the passage that has to do with Baudelaire and with his poem: "The Carcass." I could not help thinking that without this poem the whole development toward objective expression, which we now think we recognize in Cézanne, could not have started; it had to be there first in its inexorability. Artistic observation had first to have prevailed upon itself far enough to see even in the horrible and apparently merely repulsive that which is and which, with everything else that is, *is valid*. The creator is no more allowed to discriminate than he is to turn away from anything that exists: a single denial at any time will force him out of the state of grace, make him utterly sinful. Flaubert, retelling with so much discretion and care the legend of Saint-Julien-l'hospitalier, gave it that simple credibility in the midst of the miraculous, because the artist in him made the saint's resolves along with him and happily assented to them and applauded them. This lying down beside the leper and sharing with him all his own warmth, even to the heart-warmth of nights of love: this must sometime have been in the existence of an artist, as something overcome toward his new blessedness. You can imagine how it moves me to read that Cézanne in his last years still knew this very poem—Baudelaire's "Charogne"—entirely by heart and recited it word for word. Certainly one would find among his earlier works some in which he forcefully won from himself the extreme possibility of love. After this devotion begins, first with small things, holiness: the simple life of a love which has endured, which, without ever boasting of it, comes to everything, unaccompanied, unostentatious, speechless. Real work, abundance of tasks, all begin only after this enduring, and he who has been unable to go that far will probably get a glimpse in heaven of the Virgin Mary, a few saints and minor prophets, King Saul and Charles le Téméraire—: but of Hokusai and Leonardo, of Li Tai Po and Villon, of Verhaeren, Rodin, Cézanne—and of God himself, they will be able even there only to tell him.

And all at once (and for the first time) I understand the destiny of Malte Laurids. Isn't it this, that this test surpassed him, that he did not stand it in the actual, though of the idea of its necessity he was convinced, so much so that he sought it out instinctively until it attached itself to him and did not leave him any more? The book of Malte Laurids, when it is written sometime, will be nothing but the book of this insight, demonstrated in one for whom it was too tremendous. Yet perhaps he *did* stand it: for he wrote the death of the Chamberlain; but like Raskolnikov he was left behind, exhausted by his deed, not continuing to act at the moment when action ought just to have begun, so that his newly won freedom turned upon him and rent him, defenseless as he was.

Alas, we count the years and make divisions here and there and stop and begin and hesitate between the two. But how very much of one piece is what befalls us, in what a relationship one thing stands to another, has given birth to itself and grows up and is brought up to itself, and we in reality have only to *exist*, but simply, but ardently, as the earth exists, assenting to the years, light and dark and altogether in space, not desiring to be at rest in anything save in the net of influences and forces in which the stars feel themselves secure.

Now someday time and peace of mind and patience must also be at hand, in order to continue writing the *Notebooks of Malte Laurids;* I know much more about him now, or rather: I shall know it when it becomes necessary. . . .

[*182*]

To Clara Rilke   29 rue Cassette, Paris VI⁰
                                          October 21, 1907

. . . But I really wanted to say further about Cézanne: that it has never before been so demonstrated to what extent painting takes place among the colors themselves, how one must leave them completely alone so that they may come to terms with each other. Their intercourse with one another: that is the whole of painting. Whoever interrupts, whoever arranges, whoever lets his human deliberation, his wit, his advocacy, his intellectual agility deal with them in any way, has already disturbed and troubled their performance. The painter (any artist whatever) should not become conscious of his insights: without taking the way round through his mental processes, his advances, enigmatic even to himself, must enter so swiftly into the work that he is unable to recognize them at the moment of their transition. For him, alas, who watches for them, observes, delays them, for him they change like the fine gold in the fairy tale which can no longer remain gold because some detail went wrong. That one can read Van Gogh's letters so well, that they contain so much speaks in fact against him, as it also speaks against him as a painter (when set beside Cézanne) that he intended this and that, knew it, had found it out; that blue summoned orange and green, red: that he, the inquisitive, secretly listening at his eye's interior, had heard such news in there. So he painted pictures on a single contradiction, taking into consideration besides the Japanese simplification of color, which sets a plane on the next higher or next lower tone, summed up under a collective value; which again leads to the drawn and outlined (that is, found) contour of the Japanese as a frame for the equalized planes: to sheer design, to sheer arbitrariness, in a word, the decorative. Cézanne too was brought by the letters of a writing painter, not a real one, that is, to express himself in reply on painters' concerns; but when one sees the old man's few letters, what an awkward attempt at expression, most repugnant to himself, they remain. Almost nothing could he say. The sentences with which he tried become long and involved, resist, get into knots, and finally, beside himself with fury, he lets them be. On the other hand, he succeeds in writing very clearly: "I believe that the best thing is work." Or: "I am advancing daily, though very slowly." Or: "I am almost seventy years old." Or: "I shall answer you through pictures." Or: "l'humble et colossal Pissarro—" (the man who taught him to work), or: after some beating about (one feels how relieved, and how beautifully written) the signature, unabbreviated: Pictor Paul Cézanne. And in the last letter (of September 21, 1905), after complaining of his bad health, simply: "Je continue donc mes études." And the wish that was literally fulfilled: "Je me suis juré de mourir en peignant." As in some old Dance of Death picture, Death reached from behind for his hand, painting the last stroke himself, trembling with pleasure; his shadow had been lying a while on the palette and he had had time to choose from the open round of colors *the one* that pleased him best; when its turn came, he would seize the brush and paint . . . there it was: he took hold and made his stroke, the only one he knew how to make.

[*183*]

To Herr von W.
29 rue Cassette, Paris VI°
October 21, 1907

I would gladly take time and quiet to do justice to your confidence down to the smallest detail; but when you hear that I am just managing to get through the last very busy days before a rather long journey, you will look with indulgence on my making the answer short. Short, not easy. For it remains difficult in any case, whether one determines to say much or little, and is an immeasurable responsibility.

Experience leads me to believe that nothing is to be learned and prognosticated from the works of certain early years, unless one is bent on a presumptuous prophecy or on circumlocutions that are so out of place in the face of artistic realizations, before which (despite all criticism) only yes and no can stand.

It makes no difference what one writes as a very young person, just as it makes almost no difference what else one undertakes. The apparently most useless distractions can be a pretext for inwardly collecting oneself; yes, they can even be instinctively seized upon by Nature to lead the examining observation and attention of an inquisitive intellect away from spiritual processes, for which it is important to remain unknown. One may do *anything;* this alone corresponds to the whole breadth life has. But one must be sure not to take it upon oneself out of opposition, out of spite toward hindering circumstances or, with others in mind, out of some kind of ambition. One must be sure to act out of desire, out of strength, courage or high spirits: to *have* to act so.

It often struck me later how much art is a matter of conscience. In artistic work one needs nothing so much as conscience: it is the sole standard. (Criticism is not one, and even the approval or rejection of others active outside of criticism should only very seldom, under unmistakable conditions, acquire influence.) That is why it is very important not to misuse one's conscience in those early years, not to become hard at the place where it lies. It must remain light through everything; one may feel it just as little as any inner organ that is withdrawn from our will. The gentlest pressure emanating from it, however, one must heed, else the scale on which one will later have to test every word of the verses to be written will lose its extreme sensitivity.

I hardly know what more to say than this, which is valid in every case. Perhaps to add the advice to take solitude seriously and, whenever it comes, to feel it a good thing. That others give you no relief lies less in your indifference and reserve than in the fact that we are really, every one of us, infinitely alone, and in-accessible save with very rare exceptions. To that one has to accommodate oneself.—

[*184*]

To Clara Rilke   29 rue Cassette, Paris VIe
                                              October 24, 1907

. . . I said: gray—yesterday, in giving the background of the self-portrait, light copper obliquely crossed with a gray pattern; —I should have said: a particular metallic white, aluminium or something similar, for gray, literally gray, cannot be shown in Cézanne's pictures. To his eye, most intensely that of a painter, it did not stand up as a color: he got to the bottom of it, and found it to be violet there or blue or reddish or green. Violet especially (a color never before opened up so extensively and in such varia-tion) he likes to recognize where we expect only gray and are content with that; then he doesn't let up but fetches out the so-to-speak wrapped-up violets, just as some evenings do, autumn evenings especially, that address the graying of façades directly as violet, so that it answers them in every tone, from light, floating lilac to the heavy violet of Finnish granite. When I made this observation, that there was nothing really gray in these pictures (in the landscapes the presence of ocher and unburnt and burnt earths is too palpable for gray to occur), Fräulein Vollmoeller pointed out to me how much, nevertheless, when one stood among them, an atmosphere of soft, mild gray emanated from them, and we agreed that the inner equilibrium of Cézanne's colors, which nowhere stand out and obtrude, evokes this quiet, as-it-were almost velvet air, that certainly does not come easily into being in the hollow inhospitality of the Grand Palais. Though it is one of his peculiarities to use chrome yellow and burning red lacquer quite pure for his lemons and apples, he still knows how to keep their loudness within the picture: all of it, as if into an ear, sounds into a listening blue and thence gets a mute answer, so that no one outside need feel spoken to or called to. His still lives are so wonderfully occupied with themselves. The often employed white cloth in particular, that miraculously soaks up the preponderant local color, and the objects placed therein, that now, each with its whole heart, comment on this and speak their minds. The use of white as a color was from the first a matter of course to him: with black it formed the two ends of his wide open palette, and in the very beautiful composition of a black stone mantelpiece with its pendulum clock, black and white (the latter in a cloth that covers part of the slab, hanging down) behave quite colorlike beside the other colors, on equal terms and as if long acclimated. (Differently than in Manet, where the black acts like the interruption of a current and yet, as if coming from elsewhere, still contrasts with the colors.) In the white cloth there brightly assert themselves a coffee cup with a very dark blue stripe around the rim, a fresh, fully ripened lemon, a cut glass goblet with indented edge and, at the extreme left, a large baroque triton shell,—peculiar and eccentric looking, with its smooth red mouth facing forward. Its inner carmine, swelling out into the light, provokes the wall behind it to a thunderstormy blue, which the gold-framed mantel mirror near by repeats once again deepened and more ample; here in the reflection it again meets with a contradiction: with the milky pink of a glass vase which, standing on the black clock, twice (actually and, a little more yieldingly, in the reflection) makes its contrast tell. Room and mirror-room are by this double stroke conclusively defined and musically differentiated as it were, and the picture contains them as a basket contains fruit and leaves: as though that were all as simple to grasp and to give. But there is yet another object there, on the bare slab, pushed up to the white cloth; for this I would like to look the picture through again. But the salon is no more; in a few days it will be followed by an exhibition of automobiles which, each with its fixed idea of speed, will stand there long and stupidly. . . .

[185]

To Clara Rilke   29 rue Cassette, Paris VI⁰
                                    October 26, 1907 (Saturday)

. . . it's no use, though enmity has already been sown among my things and they are treading on each other's heads and one is on the other's heels, I must write anyway before I go at my packing again. Yesterday almost nothing happened: there are letters and they want to be put in order; there are those things that take delight in repeatedly turning up at certain intervals, until at the crucial moment they hide and watch from somewhere how they, whom before one had wished out of the way, are being sought and needed. There are all the remarkable formations of the breakup, bastards sprung from the association of impossible objects, in a word: misery, hell; you know it. And one plays at foresight and fancies one can provide and select for indefinite future contingencies. I am fortunate meanwhile, in that Fräulein Vollmoeller (who has recently moved into a big new studio) is taking my standing desk and above all my books and housing them there, so that I won't have to consider *them* at least individually and yet through her can always have whatever I come to need in the course of the winter.

Also it doesn't get light in the room until toward ten o'clock and grows dark again by around four, so that one hardly has time to see everything that is there.

It seems to me I am oversensitive; even about the weather. But you must imagine something late. November, about the time when, in the rue de l'Abbé de l'Epée, we had already lit the stove several times, the time when one thinks of Verlaine, of how the corner of a coffeehouse seems to him a refuge, something magnificent with its mirrors covered with a tepid film of steam and smoke.

And yet, however cold and harassed one may be, one is still much too well off; if (as I have just done again, for the first time in a long, long time) one goes through the Luxembourg and in the dense, close air sees the rise of the fountains (like a woman in a Japanese print) and a dahlia that melts like a dark berry as one looks at it, and geranium-red and yellow in begonias and colors and colors (the light ones as if they had turned fluid, the dark ones on a black ground), all fraternizing with each other on gray—one is after all compensated, over and over, and can scarcely tear oneself away. . . .

[*186*]

To Clara Rilke   Hotel Erzherzog Stefan, Wenzelsplatz
Prague [November 1, 1907]

. . . will one be here someday and able to see even this, see it and say it, from one stage of existence to another? Will one no longer have to bear its weight, the immense significance it took on when one was little and it was already big and growing out beyond one; in those days it used one in order to feel itself. There was a child, and all this felt itself through him, saw itself mirrored in him large and fantastic, became haughty and ominous toward his heart. All this it may no longer be. Degraded below itself, come back again like one who has long done violence, it is somehow ashamed before me, exposed, confined, as if it were now meeting justice and retribution. But I cannot rejoice to see badly treated that which once was hard and overbearing toward me and never condescended to me and never explained to me what difference is decreed between us, what hostile kinship. It makes me sad to see these house corners, those windows and entrances, squares and church roof: humbled, smaller than they were, reduced and altogether in the wrong. And now in their new state they are just as impossible for me to master as they were then in their arrogance. And their weight has turned into the reverse of what it was, but how much, place for place, it has remained weight. More than ever since this morning I feel the presence of this city as something incomprehensible and confused. It should either have passed away with my childhood, or my childhood should have flowed off it later, leaving it behind, real beside all reality, to see and express objectively like a Cézanne object, incomprehensible so far as I am concerned, but tangible. But this way it is ghostly, like the people who belong to it and to me from earlier days and who bring us together and speak of us in the same breath.—I have never felt it so oddly, my aversion was never so great as this time —(probably because meanwhile my disposition to see and to take everything I look at with an eye to my work has greatly developed). . . .

[*187*]

To Clara Rilke   November 4 [1907], morning
                                   on the Prague-Breslau train

. . . will you believe that I came to Prague to see Cézannes? That beside your letter there was a letter from Rodin in my pocket when I drove to the lecture? (Last evening at five.) So everything comes and comes, and one has only to be there with all one's heart. First: Rodin's letter. The salutation: Cher Monsieur Rilke, at the close, greetings and quite special greetings and warm remembrances for you. The whole written by Mr. Cherny, in his polite tone, and only signed by Rodin. The contents factual, concerning an exhibition of the drawings in Vienna at Heller's, the very bookdealer's where I shall read and stay; inquiring about his reliability. But I am happy, happy. It has been so difficult just lately not to be able to get into communication with him on practical matters; this exhibition in Vienna was to be done; *Kunst und Künstler* wanted to reproduce drawings, and all I could do was admit that I was not in a position to be of the least use. Once this practical connection is established, however, I can attend to all that whenever occasion requires: which is so natural for me. You will understand that I am happy. I answered immediately, just as factually, but spoke of all the matters that had accumulated. He is just having translated for himself (so he wrote) the extract of my new Rodin work reprinted in *Kunst und Künstler* (October issue, which I am bringing along).—And Cézanne. Out in the Manes Pavilion, where Rodin's exhibition was in its day, there was (as I luckily learned in time) a show of modern pictures . . . —That and the two hours in Schloss Janovič were the best and most peaceful. Of Janovič too there would be much to tell. The carriage ride itself through the hard glazed autumn afternoon and the naïve country was so beautiful. I drove alone from the train and back to the train. And that was Bohemia as I knew it, hilly like light music and all at once level again behind its apple trees, flat without much horizon and divided up through the plowed fields and rows of trees like a folk song from refrain to refrain. And suddenly one went gliding out of all that (as if passing in a skiff through a weir) through a park gate, and park it was, old park, and came up quite close to one with its moist autumn. Until after several turnings, bridges, vistas, separated by an old moat, the castle rose up, old, its upper part bending backward as if in haughtiness, scattered over with windows and coats of arms, with balconies and oriels, set up around courts as if no one were to be allowed to see them. The Baroness, who is widowed, remained (it was All Souls' Day) in retirement; the beautiful young Baroness (who looks like a miniature that was made a year before the great Revolution, at the last moment) came to meet me on the castle bridge with her two very attractive young brothers; we went through the park, then as it was already turning dusk, through the extraordinary castle (with an unforgettable dining hall), while two menservants with heavy silver candelabra shed light into the deep apartments as into courts. So we remained quite by ourselves and (which with the shortness of time was especially pleasant) finally drank tea (there were pineapple slices with it) and were happy together, each enjoying the other. It was a little like a children's party, only that there were no grownups and one unpacked and packed the toy boxes in imagination. In the course of conversation the remarkable fact came out that Kamenitz an der Linde, the castle in Bohemia that belonged to our great-grandfather, was at another time (perhaps afterward) the property of an ancestor of these Nadhernys, a direct forebear. Prague itself was confused. Everyone wanted to have me, as though I were edible,—but once they had me, I found them not hungry and as if they had to diet. My mother took lots of trouble to do everything possible. But . . . The reading dull; again the awful old ladies, whom as a child I used to marvel at, still the same and no more amusing now that the marveling was on their side. A few littérateurs, also the same, dustier, shabbier, and more worn-out with every year, inquisitive and too kind-hearted and too easygoing to be envious. (I shall still get to dramas sometime. I am beginning to see people, even noticing the "animal faces" Ibsen saw, the snouts and sets of teeth, but am not stopping there; for only back of that does it really begin to get interesting and, over and above all aversion and antipathy, just.) . . . I first read poems from the *B. of P.*, then Christine Brahe. Then new things: except for the "Carrousel," nothing was even picked up. It all remained lying where it fell. The program will be similar everywhere. . . .

[*188*]

To Clara Rilke   Hotel Monopol, Breslau
                                    November 6, 1907, evening

Thanks for your poste restante letter. So we walk, as though side by side, in the same stiff, icy wind; for here too it is like that, clear and cold; one could easily write December.

Again my trunks are standing packed, already for the third time since Paris, and are making the *nature morte* I drew for Ruth. The Breslau evening yesterday before those many people went off well; they were better than their reputation, and it was need-less bragging to threaten me with them. They were the usual sort who subscribe to everything and want something for their money. They couldn't say they weren't getting anything. So they sat still, coughed at judicious intervals, and behaved as the better ones among them had learned to do. Some contact was even established, here and there, so that I liked reading better than in dull Prague. "The Carrousel" again found its friends. And Ivan the Terrible developed into a kind of dramatic performance that kept everyone in suspense quite far back. . . .

[*189*]

To Clara Rilke   Hotel Matschakerhof, Vienna I
                                       November 9, 1907

. . . now we are each in a big city, each seeing people and certainly being surprised a hundred times a day. It is remarkable here, with the seeing people and all; it is such that it finds me totally unprepared, not the least bit of it reaches the point of being expressible: so little can I master as yet; here is a city, an old, self-assured, individual city, lying about me, standing there with its ancient churches and groups of houses, crossing back and forth twenty times with its bridges over the too little river and its canals, streaming with people, driving with fast carriages, with carriages that turn the corners noiselessly on the asphalt, preceded by a rapid trotting, a very light ring of hoofs quickly and variously intermingled, as of bobbins in lace-making; a city in which everything is different from the way one knows it, without this differentness lying in anything visible; rather it hovers about what is here merely like a convention of old, like a still surviving tradition, orally passed on, interpreting even the most remote in a way that is intimate and somehow unexpected: speaks familiarly to it, names it, knows it, adapts itself to it, makes it popular, draws it into the habitual (while Paris leaves everything outside), associates with it as with everyday things, concerns itself goodnaturedly and loyally with it—; here is this city, and one is not able to give an inkling of what makes these old streets so special, these squares so old-fashioned, the old Hofburg with its courtyards so ceremonious and formal, the Rings so dazzling, the gardens so ample, the baroque fountains so indispensable, and the columns of the Virgin so native: and yet the coherence and the existence of it all is condensed to the point of becoming a fragrance; one feels it as in childhood one felt a bakery, a butcher shop, or a grocery store; so entirely pervaded with itself, recognizable at every point and to be grasped in every characteristic by all one's senses: here too atmosphere has come into being, environment irradiated and darkened from within, in which people are at home and which as a stranger one shares, wards off, touches, tastes with every movement.

But my evening is over too. Well. To be sure, as a result of the rapid traveling, the many intense conversations, the attentive observation of people (which is still the most difficult use of observation), I had too much blood in my head, so much that after reading the first two poems, suddenly (I had expected and hoped for it before) I felt my nosebleed coming: my precious constitution didn't realize where I was, and seized, as it has a way of doing, on this simple way out. I wasn't angry with it: what are people to it. I told the people to have patience for a while and why, went into the authors' stall, like a goat, settled myself there as always with water, wash basin, let it bleed (everyone came and said, put your head back, etc.—but I knew that the blood would then flow behind and that would be the end of my voice), so let it bleed without nervousness, came out again refreshed and read well and clearly the entire evening (as prose selection the death of Chamberlain Christoph Detlev Brigge). During the mishap Hofmannsthal came behind, spoke to me, was charming. In case of necessity I will read, he said. But fortunately it wasn't necessary. Everyone was very attentive, everyone wanted to see me, to shake my hand. Today many flowers are coming, as is in keeping with the temperament here. But the first were sent by Sidie Nadherny (who for some other reason was in Vienna for the day without my seeing her). I had the feeling that you had instructed everyone to bring me flowers for once. That I should need them. Which was the case. Right after the lecture, Heller gave me your letter. At night, home at last, I read it; it is so beautiful. I shall read it over every day. How well you feel and say all that. You dear one, who do not feel too soon; who only feel when the feeling has become mature. You can't think how good it was, at last alone in the night to know you thinking and feeling and believing all those things.

[*190*]

To Clara Rilke H. Mayreder's Hotel Matschakerhof, Vienna
[November 11, 1907]

. . . And on the same evening Heller gave me a letter from Rodin: *long* and *affectionate: All is well again.* I could hardly believe it and read it over and over. But the close of the letter leaves no doubt. It reads: "venez, quand vous êtes à Paris me voir. Des choses, des choses. Nous avons besoin de la vérité, de la poésie tous deux et d'amitié." The dear, just man who lives things so honestly from his work outward! The *just* man. I have always known that he is that, and you knew it too. He thinks affectionately of you. He tells about his drawings containing the story of Psyche. He writes that he had thought of me: that I would have to rewrite this ancient myth just as he had to draw it; it had lifted him out beyond everything he had as yet attained: "c'est l'histoire si délicieuse de la femme et de son entrée dans la vie—" Through my agency then, over sixty drawings are to be exhibited here at Heller's. They are already on the way.—The essay in *Kunst und Künstler* pleased him: "votre étude . . . je la trouve très belle de vérité—."

Better things I couldn't have written to you in the big city, in which every bit of good news is even more desirable than elsewhere! Isn't that so?

I am on the way to Hofmannsthal at Rodaun where I am lunching today. More tomorrow. . . .

[*191*]

To Clara Rilke　　　　　　　　　Zattere 1471, Venice
　　　　　　　　　(chez Mlle. Romanelli) November 20, 1907

. . . already I must add to my letter, that I think it was a good thing to come here in all this strangeness. Do you remember how great it is, how incalculable? And it is even more so now in this gray cold that makes no effort: *This* Venice seems to me almost hard to admire; it has to be learned over again from the beginning. Ashen its marble stands there, gray in the grayness, light as the ashy edge of a log that has just been aglow. And how unexplained in its selection is the red on walls, the green on window shutters; discreet and yet not to be surpassed; bygone, but with a fullness of transiency; pale, but as a person turns pale in excitement. And this not from a hotel: from a little house, with old things, two sisters and a maid; before which the water now lies, black and gleaming, a couple of sailboats in which the hawsers creak; and in an hour the full moon is bound to come across from the Riva. I am full of expectancy . . .

[*192*]

To Countess Lili Kanitz-Menar　　17 rue Campagne-Première, Paris
　　　　　　　　　　　　　July 16, 1908 (evening)

I thank you, dear friend, for having written. I have wanted to fifty times since your letter and couldn't get to it. I have so much to overcome this time, in my work I mean, and am not as vigorous as I should be. And then added to everything came this incongruous event. What is one to say, how is one to classify it?—it is always the same question. I have had to put it to myself several times in recent years. The death of Countess Schwerin and my father's death (through both of whom I experienced infinite bigness and generosity) have brought about my no longer fearing the question. Nevertheless it is hard to have it so close about one again, even in brightest day. And in this last case it is complicated by so much: who was this woman, who lived for others and yet, behind everything and without knowing or admitting it, carried within her, as though unbroached, a whole lifetime's claims: so that it could often occur to one that she was also the opposite of what she wanted to be, and both would be equally genuine and equally unreal. And finally, what sort of relationship did one have with her, in which sympathy, yes even admiration, was so remarkably matched with resistance and rejection and condemnation that one never had the courage to balance it up and carry it along as the final sum. I have moreover for a long time received the kindness she tendered to me and which finally began to be called friendship, I don't know when, more as a beautifully fulfilled legacy from the magnificent sister who preceded her than as a gift really her own: whereby I only got further and further from any insight into this personality. And now my attitude toward death is such that it frightens me more in those whom I have missed, who have remained unexplained to me or fateful than among those whom I loved with certainty while they lived, even though they shone forth only for a moment in the transfiguration of that closeness which love can attain.—Given a certain naïveté and joy in the real (which in no way depends on time), people need never have come upon the idea that they could ever lose again that with which they had truly linked themselves: no constellation stands together thus; no act performed is so irrevocable as a human relation, which indeed, in the very instant of its visible formation, goes on more strongly and powerfully in the invisible, in the farthest depths: there where our existence is as lasting as gold in rock; more constant than a star.—

For this reason I agree with you, dear friend, when you say you mourn for those "who go away." Alas, only those can go away from us whom we never possessed. And we cannot even grieve at not having properly possessed this person or that: we would have neither time nor strength nor justness for that; for even the most momentary experience of a real possession (or of a companionship, which is but double possession) throws us with such

momentum back into ourselves, gives us so much to do there, requires of us so much loneliest development: that it would suffice
to occupy us each by himself forever.—

[*193*]

To Clara Rilke   77 rue de Varenne, Paris
                                          Thursday, September 3, 1908

What you tell does not detract from the lovely flowers. They
came as though alone and had their own quality, as you yours.
And now I want to tell you that you are right in your feeling
that I had better not come. After the experiences filling these last
two days to the brim, I can't help feeling that for the future I shall
always have to decide on staying: it is decidedly the more fruitful.
Be prepared to learn of a whole lot of new things, good ones, that
is, such as are well in hand and will now have to be guided and
realized.

Rodin actually did announce himself, just after I had moved in,
came yesterday morning, spoke from his heart, without complaining, objectively. I won't let it bother me, and will be as kind to
him as I always was. It would certainly be the richest thing that
could come about if he were to need us now a thousandth as much
as we once needed him. Perhaps you feel differently for yourself.
Do so. To me it would be like a miracle if this so far-flung road,
which I pursued even into being misunderstood, where it sadly and
bewilderingly lost itself, should not only be found again but also
were to round itself out to a wide circle through his dear, earnest
need.

We sat in your high room; he went and placed and turned the
mask: it pleased him again. I read aloud to him what Beethoven
had said to Bettina Arnim: "No friend have I, I must live with myself alone; but I know well that God is closer to me than to others
in my art, I go about with him without fear, I have always recognized and understood him; I am also not at all afraid for my
music, that can have no ill fate; he to whom it makes itself intelligible must become free of all the misery with which others are

encumbered."—How he loved it. He knew it: someone had sent him the whole passage when the Balzac was exhibited. He knows all that better than anyone else, and what we discovered yesterday has lived with him for a long time already and he has children by it. And now I also see his fate, which may lie in the race. I spoke to him of northern people, of women who do not want to hold on to the man, of possibilities of love without deceit: he listens and listens and cannot believe that that exists, and yet wishes to experience it. That woman is the obstruction, the snare, the trap on those paths that are the most lonely and most blessed: that seems to him fated. To be sure, he also thinks that the sensual must so spread out and transform itself that it is equally strong and sweet and seductive at every point, in every thing. That each thing transcends the sexual and in its most sensuous fullness passes over into the spiritual, with which one can lie together only in God. But woman remains apart for him and *beneath* all that. She does not, like things, resolve into something more demanding: she wants to be satisfied and is satisfied. And so she is like nourishment for the man, like a drink which flows through him from time to time: wine. He believes in wine. And I mention the Nun to him and speak to him of all the transformed bliss here and there and of the will of the woman out beyond satisfaction; he does not believe in that; and unfortunately he has for his opinion so many saints who, it can be shown, used Christ like a bedfellow: as a sweet substitute for the masculine, as the tenderest lover that was to be had, after all in the end to be had. And against that I have my Nun again. And show how in her few letters she has grown out beyond her beloved, and knows it too. And swear that if the Count de Chamilly, cette bête, yielding to the last letter, had returned, she could not have taken cognizance of him at all, as one cannot see a fly below from the balcony of a tower. And I am inexorable and yield nothing of my Nun.

This is a situation from our yesterday's and today's conversations, a position on the chessboard which you can picture from this description. I am so happy that we have come unexpectedly to these subjects, which were probably always in the way. The moment was sure to come when he would see the miscalculation in his prodigious sums. And it testifies to the order in the world that at that very moment, when the maliciousness of this ever-recurring danger is preoccupying him perhaps because of a momentary difficulty, the man was again beside him who himself has every need of understanding and classifying it according to his wisest knowledge. He is like a god of antiquity bound to the rites traditional in him, even to those which are not meant for us and yet were necessary in the cult of his soul in order to mold him. I shall not change him. But the voice did speak beside him. It is in his reality and will not drop out of it again. And that is a great deal.

Our lunching together again today was an exception and had the following reason: Rodin will be your housemate here in your palace. He has rented all the lower rooms, the whole right corner on the ground level, with the square middle room that I wanted perhaps to take. They are rooms such as he has always wished for in vain, so much so, that he finally began to build some out there. He wants to set up many things there and to come sometimes to be with them and to look out through the stately windows into the garden, in this place where no one will find him or think he could possibly be. In my joy at all that, I went out again yesterday and bought the beautiful wooden Christopher that looks like him and gave it to him today for a good omen and said: C'est Rodin portant son oeuvre, toujours plus lourd, mais qui tient le monde. (The sweet, straight-sitting child holds a globe possessively in his left hand, and the tall old man moves along magnificently under him and has *plans*. It is a good work of the sixteenth century.) It pleased him and the interpretation pleased him, he was happy as a child and eager in taking it. To him it was a good sign.

But I still haven't come to the end of the surprises: I too am continuing to be your housemate; I have just rented the left corner under Mademoiselle Gourvitch for myself; the circular structure with two rooms and direct opening on the terrace. It is much too expensive for me, five hundred more than I should have spent: but I do want to work. I shall not travel and shall work continu-

ally, so five hundred francs must be possible to make up. Mustn't
they? And I think I shouldn't postpone it and wait until Fräulein
Vollmoeller's difficulties become acute up there. So I have a place
and will take it on in the winter. Mr. Duval will have a tremendous
amount to do to get Rodin's rooms in order, so that I shall have
to wait for mine; but for the present I am in splendor in your
rooms. I feel easy and well after these decisions, whatever comes
now will be all right. To take action is better even than doing
exercises. Moreover it is raining and behaving like autumn, as
though it were already October, but now it can be as it pleases; if
only God remains firm. Farewell, dear, and thank you for your
thought. It was certainly there in everything. Good days and
health.

[*194*]

To Clara Rilke   77 rue de Varenne, Paris
                                     September 4, 1908

Postscript to yesterday's:

There was so much, that I forgot to tell you how well I understand your joy and new interest in the fine bust of Paula Becker;
the other day I thought of it all of a sudden quite intensively,
saw it, when I discovered up on the second floor of the Louvre
collection a royal sandstone bust of the eighteenth dynasty. It
resembled it so strangely in bearing and composition and expression: it made me think how much that is big must after all lie in
your early work if such an unpredictable impression can forcibly
call it up in one, the way the mirror image one notices of an object
at once evokes that object, even if one doesn't see it.—This, in
the boundless heavens of work, is the first state of bliss: when a
much earlier thing is given back to one so that one may grasp it
and take it to oneself with a love meantime become more just.
Here begins the revision of categories, where something past
comes again, as though out of the future; something formerly accomplished as something to be completed. And this is the first
experience that sets one, removed out of sequence, upon one's

own heart-site, which is in space and is always equidistant from everything and knows rising and setting through the endless motion about it.

I am reading *Goethe's Correspondence with a Child*, that strong, most urgent evidence against him which confirms all my suspicions. You understand, that is meant according to the extreme standard, without prejudice to his universality. Malte Laurids noted about it: "Goethe and Bettine: a love is growing up there, irresistible, in the fullness of its time and right, like the tide of ocean, like the rising year. And he does not find the one gesture to direct her out beyond himself, there whither she is bent. (He is the court of highest appeal); he accepts her, magnanimously, without using her properly; chidden, embarrassed, occupied elsewhere with a love affair—."

Malte Laurids is right; but, since yesterday, I think that Rodin would in like case have failed similarly, only with a more sympathetic gesture; and how rash it is to condemn where *such* powers fail, dissolving like a little cloud where they touch on the conventions of love: without anger, without storm, without fertilizing shower over the thirsting earth—.

How magnificent this Bettine Arnim is; once I met a woman who was like that up to a point. At the time I fell into an indescribable admiration and noted down the expression about sensualité d'âme, which since Sappho has been one of the great transformations through which the world slowly becomes more real. And now I see in Bettine that this has already existed in its entirety (while Goethe stared at it and didn't believe it and felt frightened by it). What an elemental creature she is; what a transfigurer, what a storm breaking in the air of her time. How we would have loved each other, *face en face*. I should indeed have liked to answer her letters; that would have become like a heavenly ascension, without shame, before the eyes of all.

Perhaps this too shows how our ways are for the moment running counter to each other, that I am learning from this book while Buddha must wait. Don't condemn this. Please take me as I am and have trust. Ask nothing else of me, not even in your mind.

I would feel it otherwise, and it would lay itself on a part of my heart that should be guileless.

You are now going so straight toward the divine; no, you are flying toward it, over everything, in straightest flight which nothing opposes. And I have been there, always, even as a child, and am on my way walking thence and am sent out (not to proclaim), to be amidst the human, to see everything, to reject nothing, none of the thousand metamorphoses in which the extreme disguises and blackens itself and makes itself unrecognizable. I am like one who gathers mushrooms and medicinals among the herbs; one looks bent and busied with very small things then, while the tree trunks round about stand and worship. But the time will come when I shall prepare the potion. And that other time, when for its strength's sake I shall take it up, this potion in which all is condensed and combined, the most poisonous and most deadly; take it up to God, so that he may quench his thirst and feel his splendor streaming through his veins. . . .

You mustn't put me down as boastful and wordy on account of all this. It is forced out of me because I am alone and yet was not alone these last months, and a little as though under supervision. Don't be afraid—but I am so exaggeratedly sensitive, and no sooner does an eye rest on me than it has paralyzed me somewhere. I would like ever and again to know that only the constellations dwell above me, which from their distance see everything at once, as a whole, and so bind nothing, rather leave all things free in every way . . .

Good-by, dear. Have the little casts sent soon for Rodin to see here next time. It will please him. . . .

[195]

To Clara Rilke

77 rue de Varenne, Paris
September 8, 1908

I just received, my dear, such a very beautiful copy of *The Discourses;* with a black buckskin back that bears the titles on two strips of malachite-green leather. I thank Anna Jaenecke and you from my heart for this great gift; and in connection with what I wrote recently, I would like to say further: I *know* what I was getting. I opened it, and even at the first words, just the words I happened to open to, a shudder came over me, as though doors were opening into a golden hall in which there is nothing but symmetry. Why I hold back before this quiet door that is only on the latch: why this new hesitant gesture rises in me that surprises you so much?—it may be that it is happening for the sake of Malte Laurids, whom I have too long postponed. Until then I am one with him so far as I must be for keeping the necessary state toward him and the acquiescence in his going under. Too far out beyond his suffering I may not go, else I shall no longer understand him, else he will fall away and fail for me, and I can no longer give him the whole fullness of his death.

Not *my* insights do I want to limit, but his, in the orbit and direction of which I must still be able to believe. For actually, I feel now, I should have written him last year; after the Cézanne letters, that offered so close and stern an analogy, I had arrived at the contours of his figure: for Cézanne is nothing else but the first primitive and bare achievement of that which in M.L. was not yet achieved. Brigge's death: that was Cézanne's life, the life of his last thirty years. And now I understand too my being lost last year, when I was continually in the wrong place because I did not dwell upon that figure, for which nothing was lacking save my power to concentrate and organize; save for my heart to strike like a hammer against the bell-bowl of that existence, the bowl out of which vibrates, along with every Ave Maria and every Kyrie of heaven, the neighboring-tone of a crack that seeks to heal in me.—Can you imagine that?—

Now I know too that I have only one thing to beg of you two: help me, as far as you can, to quiet time, so that I can make my Malte Laurids: I can go on only through him, he stands in my way: that is why you found me dammed up like this beside your quiet stream and saw me staying behind, as if out of obstinacy, and couldn't understand it.

I don't want to move but to strike root and do this belated work this winter until into the spring; I think to myself: I must stay healthy over it, for it; *through* it, not least. Oh that you two understood it.

—Just think, near the shop in rue Notre-Dame-des-Champs a regular, very nice vegetarian restaurant has been set up, which has nothing at all of the usual shabbiness, but rather is quite clean and ample and like a new toy the children haven't yet investigated, shining as it moves. I have lunched there twice with pleasure. And right here and now let an invitation be extended to you and Anna Jaenecke for a déjeuner I would like to offer you there. . . .

[*196*]

To Elisabeth
Baroness Schenck zu Schweinsberg   77 rue de Varenne, Paris
September 23, 1908

You have done a really good work in receiving my letter, despite all its lateness, without reproach and as naturally as I needed, for a long time, to write it. Although your insight and great fairness go so far as to release me from all writing, my joy over your letter of this morning is so great that I would have to break out for myself, even from the most compactly pressed time, the quarter of an hour for a short, gratefully meant reply, in order to set it as a small, inconspicuous stone in the ring of thoughts that have formed around your news.

It is after my own heart that it should be good news, given out from a stable inner center that seeks to keep its station and its strength in the face of everything. What you say of the passing of your dear aunt accords entirely with my feeling: that we must not be sad for *her*. But as to the influence of the death of someone near on those he leaves behind, it has long seemed to me that this should be no other than that of a higher responsibility; does not the person who passes on relinquish to those who survive him the hundredfold things he had begun, as something to be carried on, if they were to any extent inwardly bound to him? In recent years I have had to master so many near experiences of death, but no one has been taken from me without my having found the tasks about me more numerous. The weight of this unexplained and perhaps greatest of all experiences, which only through a misunderstanding has acquired the reputation of being arbitrary and cruel, presses us (so I increasingly believe) more evenly and deeply into life and lays the utmost obligations on our slowly growing powers.

What a sweet turn you gave though to my own sad recollections through the glimpse of that little childhood picture, which I have looked at quite attentively. I am sending it right back to you; because one doesn't like to think of such objects out of the house and on the way.

How much childhood there is in it and how settled everything is in it, in the quiet, the so indescribable loneliness of being a child, at the time when seated on the chair one feels no floor and sits there so bravely in the very large space that begins everywhere around one and goes on and on.—It is a very sweet, significant little picture: I thank you for letting me see it.

Do continue to believe that with your feeling and with your work you are taking part in the *greatest;* the more strongly you cultivate in yourself this belief, the more will reality and world go forth from it.

[*197*]

To Rosa Schobloch   77 rue de Varenne, Paris
                                          September 24, 1908

. . . Your understanding of the situation confronting the artist is more than merely generous; it is just. You cannot possibly know how rare it is. How hard everything tries to interrupt, divert, and hinder the artistic worker from going into himself; how everything condemns him when he wants to tend and to round out his inmost world, so that one day it may be able to hold in balance and, as it were, to set on a par with itself the whole external universe, all of it, even to the stars.—And even the friends who look on compliantly at such an inner existence, how often even they, in giving, fall into the error of expecting from the creative worker a spiritual return *outside of* his work. From this I have had to suffer the more since there persists in my nature a great, almost passionate inclination toward every kind of giving: I have known, since childhood, no more tumultuous joy than to keep back nothing and to begin the giving-away with the dearest. I know that this is more a kind of instability and almost sentimental pleasure-seeking and no kindness whatsoever. For it to turn into a virtue, I must acquire the power to gather together all my giving in the one thing, the difficult, the laborious: in work. And the friends who through their selflessness and mature insight help me toward such progress I must consider my most precious and best and accordingly must lay your note with its kind and great confession among my most important documents.

I thank you for your good wishes for my further way; I do not fear the hardness of these learning years: my heart longs to be hammered and ground: if only it is *my* hardness, that which belongs to me, and not, as during so many years of my youth, a useless cruelty from which I could learn nothing. (And yet perhaps did learn,—but with how much waste of strength.)

I reciprocate once more with wishes for your winter. Dresden can certainly do and hold in readiness for you much that is pleasant.

I have seen it under three different circumstances: as a child, from the beautiful Hotel Bellevue, later for hours, going in from the Weisser Hirsch, and two years ago on the occasion of a lecture in the literary society. Each time they were not the best conditions for getting to know it. The treasure in the Green Vault I have never seen, and I remember the gallery only very fragmentarily and superficially. I wish very much to devote a few days sometime to all those beautiful objects and portraits; recently, just as your letter was brought to me, my imagination was there in the Pastel Room with Rosalba Carriera's pictures. If chance permits you to go in there sometime, think of me. Unhappy, like almost all women who in producing works of art had to make visible by force their inner intimate vocation (the works of art still not attaining the intensity of their inner experience and suffering—), she seems to me one of the most remarkable and courageous figures, the way she passes right through almost fabulous fame, unspoiled, into the blindness of her last years, at its extreme limit, with already failing sight, painting perhaps that dying St. Theresa which is held in honor in Chioggia at the house of the Abbé Bellemo and attributed through oral tradition to her. . . .

[*198*]

To Auguste Rodin
   [in French]

77 rue de Varenne [Paris]
October 16, 1908

I am just back from the Salon where I spent an hour before Greco's "Toledo." This landscape seems to me more and more astonishing. I must describe it to you as I saw it. Here it is:

The storm has burst and is falling violently behind a city which on the slope of a hill climbs hastily up toward its cathedral and on higher toward its fortress, square and massive. A light all in tatters is belaboring the earth, stirring it, ripping it, and making the pale-green fields behind the trees stand out here and there, like sleepless hours. A narrow river issues motionless from the pile of hills and terribly menaces with its black and nocturnal blue the green flames of the bushes. The startled and affrighted city rises in a last effort as though to pierce the anguish of the atmosphere.

One should have dreams like that.

Perhaps I am mistaken in clinging with a certain vehemence to this painting; you will tell me when you have seen it.

[*199*]

To Auguste Rodin
   [in French]

77 rue de Varenne, Paris
December 29, 1908

As for New Year's Day, I would almost like to avoid the word of greeting that is making the rounds, to speak to you more of my work. I must have told you again the other day that I am managing more and more to make use of that long patience you taught me by your tenacious example; that patience which, disproportionate to everyday life that seems to bid us haste, puts us in touch with all that surpasses us.

Now indeed I feel that all my efforts would be vain without it. In writing poetry one is always aided and even carried away by the rhythm of external things; for the lyric cadence is that of Nature: of the waters, of the wind, of the night. But to make prose rhythmic one must go deep into oneself and find the anonymous and multiple rhythm of the blood. Prose wants to be built like a cathedral; there one is truly without name, without ambition, without help: among scaffoldings, with only one's conscience.

And just think, in that prose I now know how to make men and women, children and old men. I have evoked women in particular by carefully making all the things about them, leaving a blank which might be only a void, but which, fashioned amply and with tenderness, becomes vibrant and luminous, almost like one of your marbles.

I would have to explain myself at length to anyone else. But you, my dear and only friend, you will know what that means.

Your joy and mine differ only in degree; yours having been for a long time blessed and stigmatized.

Also I am sure I am not mistaken in the wishes I bring you; there are at bottom few essential ones and on those, I believe, we are infinitely in accord. . . .

P.S. The chandelier fits in well with the ensemble, and on my New Year's gift table the candy box presides with its handsome blue which is still that of the eighteenth century.

[*200*]

To Countess Lili Kanitz-Menar   77 rue de Varenne, Paris
                                                January 2, 1909

Forgive me, dear friend, if I left everything so entirely to the book, and let holiday and year pass without a direct word of remembrance. It will dispose you to leniency to hear that this time the cause was really our friend Malte Laurids, whose memoirs have been claiming me intensively all these last months. Now I know so much about him and his, so many sure and remarkable tidings have reached me inwardly, that it is a joyous and difficult obligation to be there day after day entirely for his memory. Besides which, quite against my will, recent days have brought various interruptions, and the old intrusive holiday does somehow get through cracks and crannies when one wants simply to overlook it and shut it out. Perhaps weariness too accounts in part for one's letting oneself be promptly carried away and changed by a few letters and parcels and this or that outgoing thought: the same weariness of which you speak. But just think, much as this weariness often upsets me and places me in a state of uncertainty—: if I chance to look at someone who doesn't know it, who has gone on evenly in what he has once begun, I often think he achieves this only because his nature insists less honestly upon itself or because his hearing has become dulled toward it. And really we are quite well off in being kept thus inwardly informed; perhaps in this striving and being drawn back is hidden the tendency and the possibility for a life rhythm that brings us into most intimate accord with ourselves, provided only we have the patience to perceive it. Nor should failure be a disappointment for those who are beginning the ultimate and do not settle down in something of modest proportions; it is the graduated measure of our undertakings and ought not to be referred to our feelings at all nor to testify against our achievement, which after all is continually being put together out of thousands of new beginnings.

Of this and of similar and quite different things we would perhaps have spoken before your lovely fireplace. We shall do so, I hope, some day at one of my glorious high windows, when spring comes outside in the garden. Do not forget that this is one of the friendly anticipations with which I am furnishing my new year. And now a hearty good-by and take all my wishes for your new year: good ones. . . .

[*201*]

To Anton Kippenberg 77 rue de Varenne, Paris
January 2, 1909

Your so thoroughly cordial letter dictated on December 31 of the old year is one reason the more for me to hope that mine written on the same day, with its not too modest assumptions, cannot have surprised you. You understand, do you not, that a person whose strength always suffices just for one thing is at times quite bluntly and inconsiderately concerned about that one thing; especially at a moment when he is experiencing in it such singular joys and progress as my present work has been affording me all these last weeks. I could tell you so much that is fine about it. Sometimes it seems to me I could die when it is done: so to the very end do all difficulty and sweetness come together in these pages, so finally does it all stand there and yet so boundlessly capable of the transformations inherent in it that I have the feeling of transmitting myself with this book, far and surely, beyond all danger of death. Now I have only the one thing, you see, at heart: to be able to live as long as this is in process, and to be allowed to live entirely for it alone, locked in in this work and fed from without through a little sliding window, like a prisoner by whom all things, down to the humblest and most insignificant, are only now really appreciated.

And if I think so calmly of no longer existing after this work, it is because I do not yet dare at all to promise myself the fullness I am gradually achieving with it: for now I am training for myself (this is certain, even if I overestimate some other things) a massive, enduring prose, with which it will be possible to make absolutely everything. It would be glorious after that to continue or daily to begin anew with life's whole boundless task. . . .

[*202*]

To Hugo Heller   Paris, June 12, 1909

I thank you for your frank and cordial words. The destiny I attempted to relate and to lament in the "Requiem" (the inevitable fate of which you too recognized at painful proximity) is perhaps the real conflict of the artist: the opposition and contradiction between objective and personal enjoyment of the world. That is all no less dangerously and conclusively demonstrated in a man who is an artist by necessity, but in a woman who has resolved upon the infinite transpositions of the artist's existence, the pain and danger of this choice increases to an unforgettable visibility. Since she is physical far into her soul and is designed for bringing forth living offspring, something like a slow transformation of all her organs must take place in her so that she may reach a vital fruitfulness of soul.

The birth processes which in a purely spiritual way the man artist enjoys, suffers, and survives, may also broaden and be exalted into the most highly spiritual in the woman capable of artistic gestation, but in this they really undergo only a gradual intensification, still remaining, in unlimited ramifications, within the physical (so that, exaggerating, one might say that what is most spiritual in woman is somehow still body, body become sublime). Hence for her any relapse into a more primitive and narrow kind of suffering, enjoying, and bringing-forth is an overfilling of her organs with the blood that has been increased for another greater circulation.

This destiny I sensed long ago, but I actually experienced it only when it grazed me personally and stood so big and close before me that I couldn't close my eyes because of it.

Forgive me for not giving you back the book until today. I am involved in many arrears for which all the months of bad health I had to go through are to blame.

[*203*]

To Karl von der Heydt   77 rue de Varenne, Paris
                                           August 5, 1909

Need I assure you that your affectionate solicitude and whatever misgiving you wrote of was not written on water? I have
taken it to heart, and if I am not at once going in search of a
doctor, still my own will is doctoring me, better than before, into
becoming healthy and sound again. A doctor—: it is not a question of any as things stand with me. Only I myself, who know
their cause and the basis of their confusion, am able to break up
this complicated interaction of physical and spiritual depressions:
like Herr von Münchhausen of yore I must pull myself out of
the swamp by my own wig, or God will see to it at the last moment that some clever bird sets me down tenderly on better
terrain. To endure and have patience, to expect no help but the
very great, almost miraculous: that has carried me along from
childhood up; and so this time too, although the distress is lasting somewhat longer than usual, I would like not to move my
nature along by shoves from the outside, but, as one of the last,
to wait until it takes the decisive leap of itself: only then shall
I know that it was my own strength and genuine, and not borrowed or just a foreign ferment that bubbles up only to sink back
again among cloudy sediment. . . .

[*204*]

To Jakob Baron Uexküll   77 rue de Varenne, Paris
                                           August 19, 1909

. . . If I did not write . . . it was due to a succession and
combination of various hindering circumstances. Almost simultaneously with the year there began for me a period of exhaustion,
of sickliness, finally of sickness, which, though I did not stop going
about, reading, and spending regular hours at my desk, must, as I
notice more and more, have been real: for even now my best
moments are those of a convalescent, and I have a great many less

good and a lot of bad ones. But not of that. I only bring it in by way of explanation; for your letter being what it was, you might well in the long pause have been confirmed in the assumption that it somehow hit a sensitive spot in me. I liked it, as I like all your letters. Nevertheless I grant it was not easy to answer. In conversation, which you too, as I read in it, would probably have preferred, a glance, a simultaneous silence would have brought us sooner to an understanding. Confined now to the limitations of writing, all I can do is beg that you continue to consider me as the person from whom the books have come which seem to you to be in the right. Those books (the *Book of Hours* particularly) paid as little heed and had as little reference to a reader as anything I have since let go out; so that the passage in your letter where you expect of me an art that is conscious of readers surprised me. It is possible that we diverge widely here. But this is not one of the essential points. More essential, it seems to me, is that, concerning those more recent books, I can assure you of my good, clear conscience: every word, every interval between the words in those poems came into being from extreme necessity, in the consciousness of that ultimate responsibility under whose inner tribunal my work is carried out. Perhaps shortcomings in my nature or omissions to be made up for in my development are the cause of that hard objectivity and unfeeling quality of what is portrayed: perhaps more pleasing ways are conceivable: I must continue on mine, difficult as it is.

Do you not believe, dear friend, that even the *Book of Hours* was all filled with the determination in which (one-sidedly, if you will) I have been growing? To consider art not as a *selection* from the world, but rather as its total transformation into the glorious. The marveling with which art flings itself upon things (all things, without exception) must be so impetuous, so strong, so radiant, that the object has no time to think of its own ugliness or depravity. In the sphere of the terrible there can exist nothing so renunciatory and negative that the multiple action of artistic mastery would not leave it behind with a great, positive surplus, as something that affirms existence, wants to be: as an angel. In the

Book of Hours you believed in this transformation, you understood it; in the later books, however, in which He is not mentioned for whose sake it takes place, you would incline to consider as a game what is still the same great need: and what therefore must be right, not for the onlookers, but for him who suffers and longs to survive. This is more or less what I would say, dear friend, for my own justification, incidentally. For above all I would ask about you and yours and listen at length, had I at last the joy of seeing you again.

[*205*]

To Lou Andreas-Salomé   77 rue de Varenne, Paris
                                           October 23, 1909

Dear Lou, I don't want to postpone writing you any longer, and wherever you are I want to find you and talk to you for these two pages. Lizzie Gibson wrote me once that they may perhaps expect you in Furuborg: is it there that you are reading this letter, in the autumn-wood air that rises from the lake up to the comfortable country house, in which my "golden room," as it is called, often awaits me?

How was your summer, how is your autumn going: I have often thought of it.

I have been traveling around since September. First in the Schwarzwald, at the old mineral springs of Rippoldsau, where I took a kind of cure (pine-needle-air-baths, good food, but excellent the plain piny air itself and the sound and coolness of pure springs from all the hillsides: that was a big change that ought to work). . . .

These last weeks, up to about ten days ago, I have been living in Provence, in Avignon; that was one of my most remarkable journeys. Almost daily, for seventeen days, I saw the immense Papal Palace, that hermetically sealed castle, in which the Papacy, finding itself going bad at the edges, thought to conserve itself, boiling itself down in a last genuine passion. However often one sees that desperate house, it stands upon a rock of unlikelihood, and one can enter it only by a leap across everything traditional and credible. From the other bank of the Rhone, seen from Ville-neuve, the city, God knows why, made me think of Novgorod, the great, and I did not then suspect that in this landscape, a few hours further on, I would find the marvelous place that was per-haps your earliest home. Have you never heard of Les Baux? One comes from Saint-Remy, where the earth of Provence bears field upon field of flowers, and suddenly everything turns to stone. An absolutely undisguised valley opens up, and barely is the rough road inside when it closes to behind it, shoves three mountains forward, mountains slantingly piled up one behind the other, three springboards so to speak, from which three last angels, with a terrified dash, have leaped. And opposite, laid far into the heavens like stone into stone, rise up the borders of the strangest settle-ment, and the way thither is so barricaded and tumbled with the huge fragments (mountain or tower fragments, one does not know which) that one thinks one will oneself have to fly up, in order to carry a soul into the open emptiness up there. That is Les Baux. That was a castle, those were houses around it, not built, hollowed out of the limestone layers, as though people through obstinate will to dwell had there found room, as the drop that rolls first off the gutter pays no heed to where it falls and finally stays and dwells with its own kind. Those who in particular re-mained there were the first of that almost legendary race of the lords of Les Baux, which, with an eccentric in Naples in the seven-teenth century, went out uneasily, convulsively, smoking, like a candle-end that accumulates strange drippings. But from him who founded the house, in those old days, tradition came down to the last of them that he was the great-great-grandson of King Balthasar out of the Orient and the true progeny of the three holy kings. And the crazy old Marchese in Naples still used his sixteen-rayed star as a seal.

From the hard bed of Les Baux this race arose after centuries of repose. Its fame had difficulty following it, and in the turbulence of the ascent the most brilliant names were left hanging on its crown. They became lords of seventy-nine cities and villages; they were counts of Avelin, viscounts of Marseilles, princes of

Orange, and dukes of Andria and had hardly time to notice that (according to the title) they had become kings of Jerusalem. The reality of them is so fantastic that the troubadours give up inventing; they crowd to this court which they depict, and stimulated by their songs, the lords grow ever bolder and the women achieve the unparalleled beauty that became so great in Cécile des Baux around 1240 that in remotest regions they knew of her and concurred in calling her Passe-Rose—she who surpasses the roses. But in those days the first Giovanna, Queen of Naples, was the contested heiress of Provence; the family, now for, now against her, went on and on. It flung itself so high and wide that it never fell back to itself again. In Naples the court gnawed at it and the jealousy of the San Severini; it threw out only single wild shoots now, thorny shoots at the ends of which rebellions opened up, poisonous blossoms without desire for fruit, the smell of which made even the Emperor's head swim. But clinging and unspoiled as the fig tree, it got on better where it had fallen harder: in Dalmatia and Sardinia it grew robust dynasties.

At Les Baux itself, however, only governors now sat, first of Provence, then of France, after the district had fallen to the King. All their names are known and one involuntarily retains those of the House of Manville, under whom protestantism established itself in castle and city. Claude II of Manville was still protecting the Protestants when it had become dangerous to take their part: he kept a chapel for them in his palace. But already his successor was faced with the choice of leaving his religion or his post. He decided for the extreme renunciation, and with him all Protestants were driven from Les Baux. Now there were probably already Salomés among these banished souls: grandchildren or sons of the notary André Salomé, who wrote his recollections under the first Manville governor; notebooks that may have been used since and that are now (I am assured) in the safekeeping of a notary at Mouriès, Maître Laville.

Now you understand, dear Lou, at the end, the sense of my whole story, which has become so circumstantial. I was in Les Baux for a day. The distant view from up there, of which the guide told me, I did not have: it is supposed to be infinitely large and beautifully spread out and to reach all the way to the sea and to the church tower of Saintes-Maries. But the near view was the grander the more the day grayed in and closed about it. I was soon rid of the custodian, the innkeeper too, after I had lunched. And from then on I went about just with a shepherd, who said little. We just stood side by side and both kept gazing at the place. The sheep grazed far apart on the sparse ground. But now and again, when they brushed against the sturdy weeds, the fragrance of thyme came up and stayed awhile about us.

[*206*]

To Clara Rilke   Paris, November 3, 1909 (Wednesday)
    . . . last week I went to see Rodin, who is still doing his Americans and really has a series of good strong portraits there now. How good it is that he has to do people in whom Nature still keeps him very close to the job, so that he has to graze around near by, like a tightly tethered goat that has no choice farther afield. Now he has a phonograph. The Marquise winds it up, and the thing buzzes round in a circle. I was scared when I saw I was invited to hear it. But it was glorious; they have bought a few records of old Gregorian chants which nobody wants and which, outside of the dealer, only the Pope possesses. And when a castrato voice shrieked out, sobbed out a thirteenth or fourteenth century requiem, like a wind out of a joint in the world, one forgot all the absurdity of the instrument, all the stupid mechanical tones accompanying it, and even the Marquise who (said Rodin) "ouvre et ferme le robinet d'harmonie." He himself was magnificent, quite silent, quite closed and as before a great storm. He couldn't breathe for listening and only drew a little air in quickly when the violence of the voice relaxed for a few measures. I said when it was over: "C'est large comme le silence." That made him happy. "Rilke dit: C'est large comme le silence; c'est vrai . . ." he called to Mme. de Choiseul and looked quite serious and happy. Then there was singing again: howling out of the great funnel: "The

people in hell," said Rodin, "are pushing someone forward, lifting him out over themselves so that he may say what it is like where they are," and it was just about like that too and continually renewed itself in the wailing: kept having fresh breaks out of which it issued like the sap of a branch. One felt after it as after hard work physically and in one's soul, as though one should now do one's utmost, the hardest of all. It then became apparent what the Marquise is there for: to lead slowly back down from the heights, by some path of blithe declivity. Perhaps Rodin really needs that now, someone like that to go down with him cautiously and rather like a child from all the peaks on which he is always getting himself. He used to stay up on top, and God knows how and where and through what sort of night he finally got back. Now, seeing him carried away so beyond his strength, one really felt something like fear for him, and annoyed though I was, I understood that the Marquise was putting on more and more stupid records and that we had finally arrived at a music-hall waltz-whistler; and then all the silly noises of the pinched needle really were audible, and the whole thing was fit to be thrown out. But after that, through my carelessness there came another Gregorian song, a prodigious one; only in Russia have I heard anything like it; even the chants in the Armenian church were still newfangled and feeble beside that first unpremeditated music: I believe one could not endure even Beethoven right afterward. But to end now. I really must use only cards in future, otherwise I write as good rain rains: endlessly. Good-by, my dear. And do you too write only briefly, we each have so much else to do. . . .

[207]

To Elisabeth
Baroness Schenk zu Schweinsberg   77 rue de Varenne, Paris
November 4, 1909

Every time it is a joy for me to read you, and my first impulse is always to answer you immediately. And this time I shall really do so.

You really must, by disposition, be a good painter; for even in writing you use for everything you have to say pure, strong primary colors, setting each so clear and sure beside the other. And then quite apart from painting: this ability to grasp the things of life unmixed and simple in the great primary tones seems to me a happy one in other respects; for one feels that every comprehensive experience, like a crystal lens, must then reconstruct pure sunlight for you again out of all the details and set you down in the midst of its unity and warmth.

This departure of your sister, of which you are feeling the effect, touches me more closely than you can know. Why people who love each other part before it is necessary?—well: perhaps because at any moment this necessity may step forth and demand it. Because it is after all something so very provisional: to be together and to love one another. Because behind it there really waits in everyone—often admitted, often denied—the remarkable certainty that everything that reaches out beyond a mean, beautiful but by nature incapable of transcending itself, must indeed be received and borne and mastered entirely alone, as by an infinitely single (almost unique) individual. The hour of dying, which wrests this insight from everyone, is only one of our hours and not exceptional: Our being is continually undergoing and entering upon changes that are perhaps of no less intensity than the new, the next, and next again, that death brings with it. And just as at a certain point in that most striking of changes we must leave each other altogether, so we must, strictly speaking, at every moment give each other up and let each other go and not hold each other back. Does it appall you that I can write all this down like a person copying a sentence in a foreign language without knowing what most painful thing it means? That is because this fearful truth is probably at the same time also our most fruitful and most blessed. If one associates with it frequently, it loses indeed none of its hard sublimity (and if one laid oneself about it weeping,—one would not warm and soften it); but trust in its sternness and difficulty increases every day, and all at once, as through clear tears, one seems to sense the distant insight that even as a lover one needs aloneness, that one suffers pain but not wrong when it overtakes and encloses one amid a rush of emotion toward a person beloved: yes, even that only by oneself, apart, can one fully develop and to a certain extent consummate this seemingly most shared experience that love is; if only because in the union of strong affections we generate a current of enjoyment which carries us away and finally casts us forth somewhere; while for him who is enclosed in his feeling, love becomes a daily work on himself and a continual setting up of daring and generous demands on the other person. People who love each other thus call up about them endless dangers, but they are safe from the petty perils that have raveled and crumbled so many great beginnings of feeling. Since they are prone continually to wish and to expect from each other the ultimate, neither can do the other injustice through limitation; on the contrary, they perpetually generate space and distance and freedom for one another, just as in all ages the lover of God has for God cast forth fullness and power out of his own heart and established them in the depths of heaven. This illustrious Beloved has employed the prudent wisdom, yes (it cannot be misunderstandable to say it thus) the noble cunning never to show himself; so that the love of God could indeed, in individual ecstatic souls, lead to imaginary moments of enjoyment,— and yet has remained, by the nature of it, wholly and entirely work, the hardest day labor and most difficult commission.

But now measure against this love, against its grandeur and its harvest through the ages, every attempt at love that was less lonely, less desperate, if you will—more satisfied: then (no longer frightened, no, indescribably assenting, at most in happy fright) you will admit that even between human beings only this most powerful love is justified, the only one that deserves the name. Is not—only here does my circle finally close—the presentiment of such insight perhaps the reason why people who love each other leave each other—?

Forgive me, I too thought it would be an easy path, and now I have suddenly taken you up with me into high mountains where it is cold and brilliant and without familiar vegetation—. But you had asked, and I had to climb so far in order to show you my answer in the context in which alone it does not look comfortless, but (you do feel it)—good, or simply *existing* beyond all judgment, as Nature exists, who does not want to understand and yet supports us and helps us.

On the other hand, there is something else I do not know. Do you know it? How someone, a young man, a young girl, can go away to care for sick strangers? I would like to admire this very much, and I feel that one cannot possibly admire it enough. But in this conviction something disturbs me, like uneasiness, that our time should have become guilty of such incongruous resolves; isn't there something disintegrating in it which deprives many great-willed powers of their natural points of attack? You see, this affects me exactly like the circumstance that all the greatest paintings and works of art are now in museums and no longer belong to anyone. It is said, to be sure, that there they belong to everyone. But I cannot get used to all this generality; I shall never be able to believe it. Is everything that is most valuable to pass into the general like that? It is, I can't help it, as if one were to open a flacon of rose oil out of doors and leave it open: certainly its strength is somewhere in the atmosphere but so dispersed and diluted that this heaviest of perfumes must really be counted as lost to our senses. I don't know whether you understand what I mean.

Rodin, of whom you are thinking, often comes to me for an hour and then that is naturally always a very beautiful one. Nevertheless his face would not at first glance make you as unequivocally happy as even two years ago: it is sometimes tired now; it even has constellations of sadness which I didn't know in him. With this the superb life-mask becomes certainly no less great,—but it does become—how shall I express it?—more tragic, in the sense of that antique conception of the tragic whose domain encompassed even gods and heavens, but which nevertheless closed at last in the terrestrial, as a circle whose nature and eternity it is to find no way out of itself.

For you I picture it as fine that you sometimes see our Capri priest (I can say but not write his name) and so can feel pulsating across to you the vibrations of an existence serious and bent on the profound. He has probably always been rich in inner development, even in those days on Capri, and people like that, who go about in themselves sincerely, cannot disappoint. He certainly would not have written a book had he not felt it would be a necessary and good one; one that it would have been impossible for him *not* to write. So now it is there and has reality. When it will get among people is not important in comparison. That unsuppressible books are made, that they are in existence, that one can no longer consider them mere imaginings: that always seems to me the decisive point.

But now, as after an indiscreetly long-protracted visit, I must say the shortest farewell to you; forgive me for letting myself go to so much writing; weeks may easily come again when I must deny myself letters—even those I like to write—and if this one is too much for you in one swallow, put it aside and partake of it as if it were arriving little by little. . . .

[*208*]

To Clara Rilke [Paris, November 19, 1909]

. . . for this Sunday, which is called November 21, I really must write you a little letter. . . .

Well then, many affectionate wishes: that you may begin a good year of your own, one still so young, it seems to me, when I think of other people: most of them, all those one can think of and that come to mind, are old now and as if they had always been; I know none at all younger than you and Ruth.

Paris you would recognize very, very easily as it looks now: with a sudden yellow sun between seven-thirty and eight-thirty and from there on grayer and grayer, gray seen against gray and gray through gray. I just took a quick walk to the big boulevards, as long as the skies had not quite closed: it was indescribably beautiful; the city-statues at the far corners of the Place de la Concorde gave off medium tones between the fine brightness of objects and of space and the bronze centers of the two fountains, in which the shallow water moved in little wrinkly folds, to feel itself again before freezing over. The stone horses rearing up at each other at the entrance of the Tuileries Gardens looked heavy and wintry under so much opaque sky, and the trees behind them already had the violet overtone of a winter day. To the right on the "Strasbourg" the wreaths and piles of flowers took on remarkable lightnesses and darknesses that were no longer colors, and the tricolor of the little flags was now like no more than the just-made discovery of three new grays, the extreme of what, in three different directions, could be achieved in gray. The Avenue des Champs-Elysées flowed slowly and uncertainly toward the square, and if one faced about, one saw behind, as the last thing in the indefiniteness, the golden chargers of the Pont Alexandre III flinging open their wings.

This is the text, my dear Clara, to the melody of the few flowers I sent you yesterday; they come not from this region but from the neighborhood of the vegetarian restaurant, from among those one looks at every day in passing: but they are the ones now to be seen in all florists' windows, with the exception of the few plate-glass panes of the rue Royale behind which seasonless roses and spotted orchid specimens display themselves.

Among the vegetarians, practically everything is unchanged; the handsome Spaniard or Italian now and then brings compatriots worth seeing and otherwise, deep in the "Matin," follows his special régime. The monsieur was for a long time silent and ate reading, but yesterday he reopened his communicativeness and overflowed with sheer knowledge; among other things, he said: "La Théosophie c'est une mangeuse d'hommes," and explained that in detail to the girl who listened with her round, dark eyes and very hot face. You see, this too you would recognize at first glance.

The brown woman with the crutch sends you her greetings and M. Rudier wants to be remembered to you; at a street crossing recently, sheer fate drove me to a cab from which he unexpectedly held out his hand to me from the reins. So, now you

have for your birthday as much familiar Paris as I can muster.
Good-by . . . have a fine day of good, confident thoughts and
dear memories.

[*209*]

To Georg Brandes

77 rue de Varenne, Paris
November 28, 1909, Sunday

. . . since receiving your letter, I have been turning over in
my mind how I could contribute something to the spiritual short-
ening of your hospital days. Today at last something occurs to
me: it is unfortunately just another book, and a sad one at that,
but it is of such excellent craftsmanship that it can nevertheless
be somehow gladdening.

I read very little, and so I do not know whether the impression
I got from Gide's *Porte Étroite* is dependent very much upon my
state of mind, upon the reading having been an opportune exception, finally upon a certain natural affinity (on account of which
a close acquaintance brought the book to my house). But I shall
be much mistaken if the book with its intimate precision does not
give you even more pleasure than it did me, since your reading
ability will doubtless reveal to you subtleties that eluded my spelling out. Gide's means, which I had a chance to admire here for
the first time, have remarkable command of the world he sets up;
they fulfill his intentions—it seems to me—completely, and from
this there results a finely ramified assurance which nourishes the
book calmly and as it were vegetatively, even to its incommensurable borders. Also one has only to imagine how one-sidedly
Rodenbach, say, would have developed this conflict, in order to
watch with delight the greater artist who, behind the aberration,
the pathology, the fate of the individual case, allows one again
and again to discern the very great task of love, which none of us
has been able to accomplish.

I go so far as to conjecture that this book somehow steps out of
the rotation of the French conception of love and, under the influence of a deeper force of gravity, attempts a new curve of its

own into the open. But my very insignificant reading background makes me incompetent there. (Wouldn't Kierkegaard have recognized these journals and held them in honor?) . . .

[*210*]

To Anton Kippenberg   Hôtel de Russie, Rome
                                                    Good Friday [1910]

When I reflect, my dear Dr. Kippenberg, how necessary your Sundays are to you after the long week, I am touched that, after your dictation of the nineteenth, you have written this letter besides in which I recognize all the goodness that is at home wherever you are.

It was a real satisfaction for me to read your kind pages. When one has been extremely well off for a time, as I was with you, the indifferent strangeness of strange places is hard to understand; I was spoiled, I notice. But the next stage is to discover the supplies of strength and joy that have been stored up in one through being spoiled like that; for this I am now waiting patiently, it will not delay, and when it gets to that point, occasion enough appears here to enjoy and exert oneself.

I am not very well in the first place, probably forgot too that I should be coming to such a *full* Rome; even the beautiful Hôtel de Russie, which I remembered pleasantly from a few lonely summer days, is now just a loud mass of lodgings, with music and other racket, and all other places are overfull wherever one inquires; there are even emergency beds in the bathrooms, it is a disgrace, and all of it for nothing, for none of these many too many travelers sees anything, believes in what he sees, or in any way needs it.

Forgive the mood in which I have let myself go. There is another beneath it, which just hasn't found expression yet and which is all admiration. The parks, the fountains, what one remembers of it all, much as one may often exaggerate it in hankering after it, is nothing, nothing compared to their totally incommensurable existence. Perhaps too I have made some further progress in observing, as everything overwhelms me so; but, I keep think-ing, how old one must become in order really sufficiently to marvel, to remain nowhere behind the world; how much one still undervalues, overlooks, misconstrues. Heavens, how many opportunities and examples for becoming something,—and over against them, how much laziness, distraction, and half-will on our side. A lament, a lament—.

Yesterday I sent back the end of the Malte Laurids proofs (galleys), registered too (the earlier sheets, likewise, on the twenty-second). It was singularly difficult to go through this book with that object: I felt as sadly tickled as the fool of Charles the Bold when he sits and sees how they are verifying the coarse externals of his master's body. The page proof, which is here up to page 128, I shall leaf through easily, with an eye to certain passages and as one reads a book, and from there on rely on a kind Providence for everything to go through without disturbing errors. I am so very glad to see by this page proof how excellent and appropriate everything now appears on the small pages; it pleases you too, doesn't it, we really couldn't have chosen better, whichever page one looks at: it is a book, as though it had long been one, had never been anything else. Please, let me indicate in the page proof where the first volume should end; determine it yourself if possible, or, in case of doubt, give me two places to choose from.

You see, I am writing business in between the other like this for lack of inner order; actually I ought to write several times how much I wish that the mistress of the house and of the Insel may recover quickly from the irksome influenza, so often does this wish come up new and strong in me as I write. . . .

My wife seems to have something of a cold too, according to the latest news; but she has begun to read Malte Laurids and writes more of that than of her health and her circumstances. It is very fine the way she takes him from the start as an individual and accepts him and motivates his existence from away back. You two, dear friends, and this first reader: Malte Laurids is not doing badly, he is being taken thoroughly to heart. I am becoming downright eager too and impatient to face him entirely as a reader. Much will go on taking shape in me now, I think; for these journals are something like an underpinning, everything reaches farther up, has more space around it, as soon as one can rely on this new higher ground. Now everything can really begin for fair. Poor Malte starts so deep in misery and, in a strict sense, reaches to eternal bliss; he is a heart that strikes a whole octave: after him almost all songs are possible. . . .

There would be still much to write, dear friend. But it is cold, I have an east room which gets just a little faint sun of a morning in passing, and over there, beyond the afternoon wind, the hill-side now lies in full sun: I must go warm myself. . . .

[211]

To Countess Manon zu Solms-Laubach   Hôtel de Russie
                                             Rome, April 11, 1910

This is only to catch up, but still you must know how much I enjoyed your kind letter of January 23. It reached me in Berlin, where (you will remember) I never like being; among the things that come together on such rare visits, there are always some that are warm, good, yes, quite indispensable: I don't want to complain. But there are always too many then for me (who am adhering more and more to an aloof and solitary life), and Berlin hasn't the way of feeding one things one after the other; one gets everything thrown into one's house at once, one is supposed to see and accomplish everything without coming to one's senses; it is assumed that one has a freshness, an uninterrupted capability, a prompt presence of mind, which I can muster only occasionally and only way inside for my work. So in Berlin I always fare like a bad schoolboy who is behind in everything and ends by no longer grasping from his place of punishment what is going on at the blackboard.

Think how in such days your letter was bound to give me double pleasure; with it I could keep step, I became positively peaceful and happy over it.

For it too was happy. I read in and between the lines how much your beautiful work, which deals with so much reality, future, and life, is affording you joy and inner progress. On the whole I really don't believe it is important to be happy in the sense in which people expect it, but I can so infinitely understand this laborious happiness which lies in arousing by some determined work powers that themselves begin to work upon one. For anyone who conceives the task that now fills you in such a way as to experience this in the process, it must become boundlessly fruitful and joyful.

Beside these best tidings of you it was your interest in Malte Laurids Brigge and in me that did me so much good. The *Notebooks* are now concluded, I was in Germany on their account, we are in the process of printing them. Malte Laurids has, since you have not been hearing of him, developed into a figure which, quite detached from me, acquired existence and personality, and interested me the more intensely the more differentiated it became from myself. I do not know how far one will be able to deduce a whole existence from the papers. What this imaginary young man inwardly underwent (through Paris and through his memories reanimated by Paris), led so far in all directions: more and more journals could have been added; what now constitutes the book is by no means anything complete. It is only as if one found disordered papers in a drawer and just happened for the present to find no more and had to be content. That, viewed artistically, is a poor unity, but humanly it is possible, and what arises behind it is nevertheless the sketch of an existence and a shadow-network of forces astir. The moving figure of Countess Julie Reventlow is mentioned only in the passage you know, and, quite cursorily, once again. Malte Laurids has inspired me with the desire to know more of her (than he knew). You certainly know the "Letters of the Reventlow Family Circle" published by Bobé (Danish), in which she is spoken of and which also contain a reproduction of a very beautiful portrait of the Countess in her youth. In the seven or eight volumes of this work that have come out so far there are no letters in her own hand, but one more volume is in prospect which will perhaps bring some. It must mean a great deal, to have known her. . . .

[212]

To Marietta
  Baroness von Nordeck zur Rabenau   Hôtel de Russie, Rome
                                                     April 14, 1910

If it is in any way possible: put generosity to the test: forgive me for letting so much time go by over your kind letter, draw no conclusions from its having happened. I constantly wanted to thank you for your affectionate remembrance and for your not giving me up and for making me secure in the conviction that I may be allowed to read you again and again. I wish very much that from time to time a meeting might come about, friendly and delightful, as the one in Paris was, of which I often think. Your letter, which made the trip to Paris, finally found me almost in your neighborhood, in Leipzig; I shall tell you in a moment what took me there and in the end kept me quite long in Germany, but first let me go into your news: on the whole it is good, even though this wish and that (like the work with your violin in Paris) remains outside and unrealized—. I would almost like to say, do not drown it out too much with the noise of sociability, there is no harm if it goes on growing and becomes stronger and stronger. Often it is so with me that I ask myself whether fulfillment really has anything to do with wishes. Yes, as long as the wish is weak, it is like a half and needs to be fulfilled like a second half, in order to be something independent. But wishes can grow so wonderfully into something whole, full, sound, that permits of no further completion whatever, that goes on growing only out of itself and forms and fills itself. Sometimes one could believe that just this had been the cause of the greatness and intensity of a life, that it engaged in too great wishes, which from within drove forth effect after effect into life, as a spring does action upon action, and which scarcely knew any longer for what they were originally tensed, and only in an elementary way, like some falling force of water, transposed themselves into activity and warmth, into immediate existence, into cheerful courage, according as the event and the occasion geared them in. I know that I am taking your little intimation much too importantly and ponderously by loading it with so many words; it vanishes altogether beneath them; but this as an insight had somehow matured in me (perhaps in the reading of the saints' lives, with which I am much occupied, again and again), and I could not resist the little impulse to express what was somehow ready. You will know of course that it was not meant so pretentiously and seriously as it looks here. . . .

What kept me in Germany (Leipzig and Berlin especially) from the beginning of January until a few weeks ago was the final editing of a new book, the *Notebooks* of that young Dane, of which I must surely have spoken to you in Capri. They have finally come to a kind of conclusion, they are being printed now, there too life is going on. And here, about me, is Rome (which greets you), Rome which is having its blossom time, with full hanging wisteria, with thousands of new roses daily, with all its beautiful fountains that are like eternal life, serenely new, without age, without exhaustion. . . .

NOTES

Rilke was born in Prague, December 4, 1875, and died at
Valmont, near Glion, Switzerland, December 29, 1926.

G.W. stands for *Gesammelte Werke* (1927), the six-volume standard edition of collected works; *A.W.* for *Ausgewählte Werke* (1938), the two-
volume edition of selected works; *B.u.T.* for *Briefe und Tagebücher, 1899–
1902* (1931), the volume of early letters and diaries; *B.V.* for *Briefe an
seinen Verleger* (1934), the volume of letters to his publisher, all published
by Insel-Verlag, Leipzig, in the years indicated.

(The number in brackets is that of the letter, the page number that of the
page on which the reference occurs.)

[1]   p. 17   Franz Keim: Austrian poet (1840–1918), who had been a
teacher at the local high school in St. Pölten during Rilke's
days at the military school there, and to whom Rilke had
now sent some poems for criticism. The stanza

> Es sei, so wähnen edle Menschenkenner,
> Oft ein Genie dem Untergang geweiht.—
> Nein!—Schafft die Zeit sich keine grossen Männer,
> So schafft der Mann sich eine grosse Zeit!

was published in Rilke's first volume of poetry, *Life and
Songs*, 1894, most of the poems in which had by now been
written under the title "Fragment" (*Splitter*) and with "suppose" (*wähnen*) altered to "complain" (*klagen*).

[2]   p. 17   Rilke met Valery David-Rhonfeld, the daughter of an Austrian officer, in 1892. She was eccentric and Bohemian, with
her red Empire gown and white shepherd's crook, her vase
painting and short-story writing. Though she was older than
René they became engaged, remaining so until 1895. It is
difficult to judge the importance of the relationship to Rilke,
but this letter suggests that she moved him deeply at first.
She herself, however, seems merely to have played along
with him, until he slipped away and finally eluded her altogether, whereupon she became greatly piqued: her bitter
reminiscences, published after his death (C. Hirschfeld, "Die
Rilke-Erinnerungen Valery von David-Rhonfelds," in *Die
Horen*, Berlin, 1928–29, VIII, 714 ff.), picture René as an
unlovely and pathetic youth incapable of appreciating her
generous pity and love. But the fact remains that she was the
first to give him at least a measure of much needed sympathy
and encouragement, and *Life and Songs* (see notes to [1]
and [9]) is dedicated to her. This letter, not in either edi-

tion of the *Letters*, was published in Paul Leppin's brief article, "Der neunzehnjährige Rilke," (*Die Literatur*, August, 1927).

p. 18   Tante G.: Since his mother had moved to Vienna and his father's quarters in Prague were too small to house him, Rilke lived (until 1896) with his aunt (his father's sister) Gabriele von Kutschera-Woborsky.

my frustrated childhood: [7] and [44] contain further accounts of these early years and of Rilke's parents, Joseph and Phia (Sophia) Rilke. (Cf. also the chronicle section in *Letters to a Young Poet*, W. W. Norton & Co., Inc., New York, 1934.)

Primary School of the Piarists: in Prague.

Baumgarten: a park in Prague. Presumably Rilke acquiesced in his father's plan for a military career.

p. 19   the new phase of my young life: From 1886–90 Rilke attended the military school at St. Pölten and its senior branch at Mährisch-Weisskirchen, a training for which he was obviously unfitted. He often referred to this time as the worst of his life; for a while he planned to pour all its fears and agonies into a military novel, in order to free himself of them, but never got beyond a few sketches, though as late as 1920 he wrote one of his old masters that he would never have been able to live his life had he not suppressed all memory of these years. Cf. [7] and [44].

in my childish mind . . . : Rilke's mother, in her unbalanced religious fanaticism, would have the child kiss the wounds of Christ on the crucifix.

p. 20   the urge to write: A few of Rilke's early literary efforts have been preserved in the Rilke Archive at Weimar. His mother seems, if only out of vanity, to have encouraged his childish attempts at painting and composing heroic tales and verses, though his father would reprimand her for fostering such effeminate pastimes.

"The war horse rears . . . ": a line from *The Maid of Orleans* (Prologue, scene 4) often cited as an example of Schiller's rhetoric.

p. 21   bitter disillusionments and errors: Rilke's attendance at the commercial school in Linz (winter 1891–92) ended with an amorous escapade with a governess.

the period of study: Thanks to the financial assistance of his Uncle Jaroslav Rilke, Ritter von Rüliken, who was anxious that his family's only surviving male member of the younger generation should make something of himself, Rilke prepared (1892–95) for the University of Prague by a course of private lessons with examinations at the end of each semester.

p. 22   *panička:* Czech for "little lady."

René: Rilke's parents, never reconciled to the loss of their first child, a little girl, had christened him René, and not until 1897 did he begin using Rainer, the name by which Lou Andreas-Salomé (cf. note to [8]) called him because she thought it more fitting than a French name for a poet whose language was German.

[3]   p. 23   Rilke had passed his entrance examinations in July and was now studying at the University. He had been reading *Urania* by Camille Flammarion, the French astronomer (in the translation of Carl Wenzel, 1894), and now wrote Dr. Bauschinger (1860–?), author of many books on astronomy and director of, among others, the observatories at Strasbourg and Leipzig, to ask his opinion of the book.

[4]   p. 23   Bodo Wildberg: Rilke's collaborator for the third and last number of *Wild Chicory* (see note to [9]), pamphlets containing "songs, given to the people," published at Rilke's expense and left in hospitals, workers' clubs, etc. as a free gift. "For the poor everything is too expensive," read the preface, ". . . So if you would give to everyone—*then give!*"

Thiel: Peter Thiel (1870–), author of *Des Schicksals Tücke.*

[5]   p. 24   Cf. the stanza from "In Dubiis" in *Offerings to the Lares* (p. 65; see note to [9]):

Der erscheint mir als der Grösste,	He appears to me the greatest
der zu keiner Fahne schwört,	who pledges himself to no flag,
und, weil er vom Teil sich löste,	and, because he detached himself from the part,
nun der ganzen Welt gehört.	now belongs to the whole world.

[6]   p. 25   In the fall of 1896, Rilke had left Prague to continue his studies in Munich.

Baron Karl Du Prel: (1839–99), prolific philosophical writer, zealous investigator of the occult and a spiritualist, who maintained that man is a dual being whose second self appears in somnambulistic states and reaches into the Beyond.

p. 25   "Visions of Christ": These ("Christusvisionen") were not brought out as Rilke expected and have never been published. The manuscript is in the Rilke Archive in Weimar.

[7]   p. 26   Ludwig Ganghofer: novelist (1855–1920) noted for his portrayal of Bavarian peasant life.

military institution: For biographical details in this letter cf. [2] and [44] and notes.

[8]   p. 28   Frieda von Bülow: Rilke had met Baroness von Bülow, the novelist (1857–1909), known for her association with German East Africa and the work of Karl Peters, one of its founders, through Lou Andreas-Salomé.

We are reading . . . . : Rilke was spending July and August at Wolfratshausen near Munich with Lou Andreas-Salomé, her husband, and the art-historian Endell. Frieda von Bülow had joined them for a time.
Lou Andreas-Salomé (1861–1937), whom Rilke had met in Munich, was to become his closest life-long friend. A Russian by birth, and herself a writer, she is probably best known for the role she played in Nietzsche's life many years before her meeting with Rilke. Her husband, Professor Andreas, occupied the chair of Oriental languages at Göttingen.
That the Italian Renaissance kindled Rilke's imagination is evident from many sketches and stories among his early writings.

p. 29   Botticelli: cf. *The Book of Hours* (*Das Stundenbuch*, *G.W.* II, 196; *A.W.* I, 26).

So hat man sie gemalt; vor allem einer	Thus they painted her; one above all,
der seine Sehnsucht aus der Sonne trug.	who bore his longing out of the sun.
Ihm reifte sie aus allen Rätseln reiner,	For him she ripened out of all riddles purer,
aber im Leiden immer allgemeiner:	yet in suffering more universal always:
sein ganzes Leben war er wie ein Weiner,	his whole life he was like a weeper
dem sich das Weinen in die Hände schlug.	whose weeping thrust itself into his hands.
Er ist der schönste Schleier ihrer Schmerzen,	He is the fairest veil of her sorrows,
der sich an ihre wehen Lippen schmiegt,	gently pressing against her wounded lips,
sich über ihnen fast zum Lächeln biegt—	curving over them almost to a smile—

> und von dem Licht aus sieben
> Engelkerzen
> wird sein Geheimnis nicht be-
> siegt.

> and the light from seven angel
> candles
> is not victorious over his se-
> cret.

[9]   p. 29   In the autumn of 1897 Lou moved to Berlin; Rilke followed her, to continue his studies at the University of Berlin, living in a furnished room in Wilmersdorf, "Im Rheingau 8, III."

Adolf Bonz: the Stuttgart publisher who brought out two of Rilke's early short-story collections, *On Life's Way* (*Am Leben Hin*), 1898, and *Two Tales of Prague* (*Zwei Prager Geschichten*), 1899, both now in *Erzählungen und Skizzen aus der Frühzeit*, Insel-Verlag, 1928.

p. 30   Seven sketchbooks: in part preserved in the Rilke Archive.

Rilke's poetry thus far published in book form: *Life and Songs* (*Leben und Lieder*, Strasbourg and Leipzig, G. L. Kattentidt, Jung Deutschlands Verlag, 1894, not reprinted), cf. note to [2]; *Wild Chicory* (*Wegwarten*, published by the author, Prag, 1896; three issues, not reprinted), cf. note to [4]; *Offerings to the Lares* (*Larenopfer*, Prag, Verlag von H. Dominicus (Th. Gruss), 1896; now *G.W.* I, 9–102); *Dream-crowned* (*Traumgekrönt*, Leipzig, P. Friesenhahn, 1897; now *G.W.* I, 103–160).

p. 31   *Days of Celebration* (*Feiertage*): no such book was published. This is probably the collection known as *Advent* (Leipzig, P. Friesenhahn, 1898; now *G.W.* I, 161–251).

[10]   p. 31   From April to June, 1899, Rilke was in Russia with Lou and Professor Andreas. They met many eminent Russians, including Tolstoy.

Meiningen: Rilke expected to visit Frieda von Bülow at the von Bibra villa on the Bibersberg, a summerhouse of the former Princess Marie of Meiningen, which had been put at her disposal.

Florentine spring: the preceding April (1898), which Rilke had spent in Florence.

p. 32   The Iberian Madonna (or Virgin of Iberia): an ikon in the Iberian Chapel in Moscow, a copy of the original in the Iberian monastery on Mt. Athos in Greece. The reproduction, solemnly executed in 1648 with prayer and fasting by the monks and presented to Czar Alexis Mikailovitch, was borne through the streets of Moscow almost every day, until recent times, in a carriage drawn by six horses, the people bowing low as it passed. (Cf. *Stories of God, G.W.* IV, 102.)

[11] p. 32 Rilke had now returned to his studies in Berlin, living this time at Schmargendorf, just outside the city.

The Bibersberg days: The visit, with Lou, to Meiningen (see note to [10]) had lasted from the end of July till September 12. Of it Frieda von Bülow wrote: "Of Lou and Rainer I have had extremely little during this six-weeks visit. After the longish Russian trip they took (incl. Loumann [Lou's husband]), they had dedicated themselves body and soul to the study of Russian and were learning with phenomenal industry all day long: language, literature, art history, political history, cultural history of Russia, as if they had to prepare for a fearful examination. When we met at meal time, they were so exhausted and tired that *stimulating* conversation could no longer be managed."

[12] p. 33 Rilke probably met Sofia Nikolaevna Schill of Moscow, who wrote under the pen name of Sergei Orlowski, on his first trip to Russia.

the *Chaika*: Chekhov's *Seagull*. Rilke was anxious to make Chekhov's work known in Germany. He was planning a translation of *Uncle Vanya* as well, and had even interested a publisher. Nothing came of it, which may have been due to his own loss of interest, and neither translation is extant.

[13] p. 34 Tretiakov Gallery: of Russian paintings, in Moscow. Rilke also planned a series of monographs on such painters as Ivanov (1806–58) and Kramskoi (1837–87).

[14] p. 37 From May to August, 1900, Rilke and Lou (see note to [8]) were again in Russia.

[15] p. 39 In a conversation with Maurice Betz in 1925, Rilke described this second meeting with Tolstoy rather differently, indicating that the occasion may have been less comfortable than he was willing to admit, even to himself, at the time. There seems to have been considerable lack of enthusiasm not only in the Countess' reception but in the Count's as well.

Professor Pasternak: Leonid Pasternak (1862–1945), painter and professor at the Moscow Art School, through whom Rilke had met Tolstoy on his first visit to Russia.

Yasnaia: Yasnaia Poliana, Tolstoy's estate.

[16] p. 42 In August, 1900, on his return from Russia, Rilke paid a visit to Heinrich Vogeler, the painter (whom he had met in Florence in 1898), at the artist colony at Worpswede, near Bremen, and was so enthralled by the colorful countryside of

moors and canals, and by the high seriousness and stimulating personalities of the artists, that he rented a little house there for the coming winter. He felt he could learn much from these painters about "looking" (see Introduction), much that could contribute to his poetry and enhance his awareness of life. The published portion of his diary contains the best available account of his Worpswede impressions. It records many conversations and vividly describes Sunday evening gatherings when talk was lively, there was sometimes singing, and he himself was often asked to read from his poems. Here also he met the young sculptress, Clara Westhoff, who was to become his wife. She was about to go to Paris to study with Rodin. On the evening of October first, 1900, when he and Vogeler had been at her studio, Clara described to Rilke this modeling of her grandmother, as he noted in his diary for October third (*B.u.T.*, 365–367).

p. 45   Before what little figure . . . : The diary also makes several allusions to the figures of children Clara was modeling.

[17] p. 45   Paula (Modersohn-)Becker, the painter (1876–1907), was an intimate friend of Clara and Rilke. Her work, now regarded by some as the most significant to have come out of Worpswede, had as yet achieved little recognition. She married the painter Otto Modersohn in 1901, studied painting in Paris, and died in childbirth, November 21, 1907. Her death, which Rilke felt deeply, was the occasion for the "Requiem for a Friend" ("Requiem," Insel-Verlag, 1909; now *G.W.* II, 323–333; *A.W.* I, 191–201; an English translation in *Rainer Maria Rilke: Requiem and Other Poems* by J. B. Leishman, Hogarth Press, London, 1935). Cf. also [202] and note.

[19] p. 48   evening pages: Otto Modersohn later wrote (in *Rainer Maria Rilke: Stimmen der Freunde*, the little memorial volume edited by Gert Buchheit, Urban-Verlag, Freiburg, 1931), "At that time in Worpswede, filled with inner visions, I was wont, especially on winter evenings, to give free rein to my reveries with crayon and red chalk on little sheets of paper." He later presented Rilke with several of these sketches.

[21] p. 51   Heinrich von Kleist: the great dramatic poet (1777–1811), who shot himself and his incurably ill friend Frau Vogel on November 21, 1811. Rilke describes (to Princess Marie of Thurn and Taxis, December 27, 1913), how as a young man he liked to go out to Kleist's grave on the Wannsee, and quotes the first verse of a poem he wrote there in his notebook on January 14, 1898:

Wir sind keiner klarer oder blinder,	None of us is clearer or more blind,
wir sind alle Suchende, du weisst,—	all of us are seekers, as you know,—
und so wurdest du vielleicht der Finder,	and so you became perhaps the finder,
ungeduldiger und dunkler Kleist . . .	impatient and dark Kleist . . .

"Heavens," he adds, "I knew little about him and was thinking of his death, that strange one, because I only understood the strange, but now I am thinking of his life, because I am slowly beginning to have a conception of the beautiful and of the great, so that soon death will concern me no more."

[22]   p. 51   On September 27, Rilke noted in his diary (*B.u.T.*, 348–350) a similar description Clara had given him of her first winter at her family's summer home in Oberneuland, continuing: " . . . she said I would recognize it as a happy advance that there are no longer behind us joyous and sad backgrounds that alternate with indifferent regularity with the seasons. That we see sad springs and blissful autumn days full of overflow and joy, that summer days can be heavy and desolate and limitless, and that winter can touch us in our feeling like the ringing of a triangle, like silver on damask, like roses on a girl's neck . . . This enables us to live along more peacefully and in deeper understanding with Nature, that is, more spontaneously. When behind our sadness a shimmering spring flickers and moves in high clouds, then our sadness will be more moving, and great is our crimson feeling when it fashions garlands for itself of falling leaves and exhausts all the colors of October, detached from the meaning they have in their dying."

[23]   p. 53   Paula Becker's journals: *Briefe und Tagebuchblätter von Paula Modersohn-Becker* (Berlin; edition of 1920).

p. 54   Maria Bashkirtseff: Marie Bashkirtseva (1860–84), the gifted Russian writer and painter, who died at 24. Her journal (*Journal de Marie Bashkirtseff*) was first published in 1890.

p. 55   my *Stories of God*: *Vom Lieben Gott und Anderes, an Grosse für Kinder erzählt*, Christmas, 1900; republished in 1904 and in subsequent editions as *Geschichten vom Lieben Gott* (English translation by M. D. Herter Norton and Nora Purtscher-Wydenbruck, W. W. Norton & Co., Inc., 1932. Cf. note to [32]).

Dante's brow above the lily: Rilke describes (*B.u.T.*, 304) a corner of Paula's studio in which hung a mask of Dante;

against a pile of sketches rested a guitar, in front of this a lily bloomed. He often calls Paula's studio the "lily studio."

p. 56   "first twenty years": Paula speaks in her journals [p. 62] of feeling, after reading Marie Bashkirtseva's journal, that she has idled away (*verbummelt*) her first twenty years.

the Schlachtensee: a lake outside Berlin, where Paula spent some time with relatives. Her journals record (pp. 128–130) a kind of symbolic vision in which she sees eyes looking at her out of a gray veil suspended between lake and sky. These are the "eyes of longing," and when one looks into them one forgets everything in life but the "wish of one's heart" (here her love for Otto Modersohn, to whom she was not yet married). She shudders as she feels the thrall of this longing, but the sun cries out to her "Go home to your house and create. Think of the people who live about you and love you. And you will recover." She hurls her "dearest wish" into the lake and goes home to create. This vision takes on significance in view of Paula's inability to reconcile her art with her marriage. (Cf. note to [17]; also [202] and note.)

[24]   p. 56   In April, 1901, Rilke and Clara Westhoff were married, settling in a little house in Westerwede near Worpswede.

Emanuel von Bodman: South German poet (1874–   ), with whom Rilke had become acquainted in Munich in 1897.

p. 57   laws which never fail to operate: cf. in the "Book of Pilgrimage" (*The Book of Hours, G.W.* II, 245), written in Westerwede a month later:

Wenn etwas mir vom Fenster fällt	When I let something fall from the window
(und wenn es auch das Kleinste wäre),	(though it may be the smallest thing),
wie stürzt sich das Gesetz der Schwere	how the law of gravity hurls itself,
gewaltig wie ein Wind vom Meere	violent as a wind from the sea,
auf jeden Ball und jede Beere und trägt sie in den Kern der Welt.	on every ball and every berry and bears it into the world's core.

[25]   p. 58   Helmuth Westhoff: Clara's young brother, who was to become a painter.

a dear friend, a painter: "Peacockfeather," published in *Advent*, 1898 (*G.W.* I, 172), was dedicated to Emil Orlik, a friend of Rilke's youth.

[26] p. 61 Gustav Th. Pauli: (1866–1939), art historian, director of the Bremen Art Museum.

my dear ones: Ruth Rilke was born on December 12, 1901.

Michelet: the reference is to *L'Amour* by the historian Jules Michelet (1798–1874).

[27] p. 64 Paula's letter (published in her letters and journals, pp. 164–166), to which this is a reply, accuses Clara of shutting her out of her life and giving all her love to Rilke, who is in turn reproached for entirely absorbing his wife. Paula, in her journal (May 2, 1902), comments on Rilke's statement that married people should guard each other's solitude: "Are those not superficial solitudes over which one must stand guard? Do not the true solitudes lie fully open and unguarded? And yet no one penetrates to them although they sometimes wait for someone in order to wander with him through valley and meadow, hand in hand. But the waiting is perhaps only weakness, and it makes for strength that no one comes. For this wandering-alone is good and shows us many depths and shallows of which one would not become so aware with another."

[28] p. 66 Rilke had met Countess Franziska Reventlow (1871–1918) in Munich, his interest aroused by her having gone through an unhappy love affair which she later made the subject of a novel, *Ellen Olestjerne* (included in her *Gesammelte Werke in einem Band*, Munich, 1925), which Rilke reviewed in the *Bremer Tageblatt* (cf. note to [43]).

[29] p. 67 Oskar Zwintscher: the painter (1870–1916). The previous year Rilke, with his feeling for tradition, had asked him to paint Clara's portrait in order that her "first beauty," before the "second beauty of motherhood," might be preserved for their children and grandchildren.

[30] p. 67 The allowance from home was discontinued, as Rilke expected, and no prospect of lucrative literary work had yet presented itself, but he remained firm in his determination not to resort to other means of earning his bread. There was therefore no alternative for the Rilkes but separation. Clara and Ruth departed for Amsterdam to recuperate from inroads on their health, and Rilke accepted an invitation from Prince Emil zu Schoenaich-Carolath (1852–1908), himself a poet, to spend the summer on his estate, Schloss Haseldorf in Holstein, and to use freely the library and archives. Rilke must have had some acquaintance with the Prince in Prague for he speaks of him as a contributor to *Wild Chicory*.

[31]   p. 69   Rilke had known Frau Weinmann in Munich. "In the Company of the Barons" from *Advent* ("Im Kreise der Barone," *G.W.* I, 185) is dedicated to her.

          p. 70   my portrait-bust: a photograph of Clara's bust of Rilke is reproduced in *Stimmen der Freunde* (cf. note to [19]).

                    Vicomte de Vogué: Eugène Melchior, Vicomte de Vogüé, French critic, author of *Le roman russe*.

          p. 72   new book of poems: the *Book of Pictures* (*Das Buch der Bilder*, Berlin, Axel Juncker, 1902; *G.W.* II, 9–169).

[32]   p. 73   Friedrich Huch: (1873–1913), novelist, a cousin of the great writer Ricarda Huch.

                    a perpetual embarrassment: cf. in *Stories of God*, "You see, I immediately become embarrassed when I have to talk to children. That isn't bad in itself. But the children might lay my confusion to the fact that I feel I am lying . . . And since the truthfulness of my story means a great deal to me—" (*G.W.* IV, 40–41).

          p. 73   the subtitle: this was dropped in the subsequent editions of the book. Cf. note to [23].

                    the monograph: a series of essays on the Worpswede painters—Mackensen, Modersohn, Overbeck, am Ende, Vogeler—published under the title *Worpswede* (with 122 illustrations; Bielefeld und Leipzig, Verlag von Velhagen und Klasing, 1903; Introduction reprinted in *A.W.* II, 221–242).

          p. 75   the book on Rodin: *Auguste Rodin* (published by Julius Bard, Berlin, 1903, as the tenth volume in Muther's series of illustrated monographs, with eight illustrations. This is the first part only. The third edition, Marquardt & Co., Berlin, 1907, contains also the second part. Cf. [159] and note. Republished by Insel-Verlag, 1913, with 96 illustrations selected with Rodin's approval. Now, without illustrations, *G.W.* IV, 295–418. An English translation published by Jessie Lemont and Hans Trausil, Sunrise Turn, Inc., 1919, has long been out of print but is to be reissued shortly by the Columbia University Press). That Rilke's interest in Rodin antedated his acquaintance with Clara, who was a pupil of Rodin, is evident from a conversation with her recorded in his diary on September 21, 1900 (*B.u.T.*, 320–322). A later entry (November 17, 388–391) shows that Rilke was preoccupied with Rodin long before going to Paris and that the ground was well prepared for this most fruitful contact.

                    Muther: Richard Muther (1860–1909), the art historian, editor of *Die Kunst*.

[33] p. 76 Arthur Holitscher: (1869–1941), novelist and essayist, a friend of Munich days.

For Rilke's feeling about Rodin's life, cf. *Auguste Rodin* (*G.W.* IV, 300): "for us it is as if it had passed many hundreds of years ago. We know nothing of it."

Niels Lyhne: by J. P. Jacobsen (cf. [60] and note).

[35] p. 77 In August, 1902, Rilke had come to Paris alone, while Clara remained to break up the Westerwede house, planning to leave Ruth with her parents and follow him as soon as possible. "There is no doubt about it:" he wrote Clara (in French!), "I am in Paris, although the corner where I live is full of silence. I am all expectancy: what will happen?" He was staying in the little hotel in Montparnasse which he was later to make the address of Malte Laurids Brigge of the *Notebooks.* His evenings he kept for reading, writing, reflection, solitude; but by day he explored the city, visiting and revisiting the Louvre, Notre Dame, the Luxembourg, the Cluny, writing to Clara his impressions of the sculpture and painting that interested him. Even in the first days he began to feel Paris as a "big, strange city," populated with "legions of sick, armies of dying, nations of dead." And he felt that all this would become endurable only if it could somehow relate itself to Rodin, who was after all his chief reason for coming to Paris.

p. 78 C'est une main . . . : It is a hand like this, holding a piece of clay with . . . it's a creation, that is, a creation.

p. 79 exposition at the Pont Alma: the World Exhibition of 1900 at the Pont de l'Alma in Paris.

La Prière: Rodin's "Prayer."

Porte de l'Enfer: Rodin's "Gate of Hell." Cf. *Auguste Rodin, G.W.* IV, 331–338.

p. 80 "The Last Judgment": *Book of Pictures* (*G.W.* II, 80–86).

p. 81 Mme. Rodin became very nervous: How can I be everywhere? . . . Tell Madelaine. (We retain Rilke's spellings. His French was far from perfect!)

Liebermann, Lenbach: the painters, Max Liebermann (1869–1935) and Franz von Lenbach (1836–1904).

[36] p. 82 de regarder une pierre, le torse d'une femme: to look at a stone, the torso of a woman . . .

p. 83 Le modelé . . . the law and the relationship of these surfaces: cf. *Auguste Rodin* (*G.W.* IV, 309), where this is described as consisting "of infinitely many meetings of light with the object, and it became apparent that each of these meetings was different and each remarkable."

Voilà le modelé grec: That is the Greek modelé. . . . You know, it is not the form of the object, but: the modelé . . .

p. 84   Non, c'est vrai . . . : No, that is true, it is not good to form groups, friends hinder each other. It is better to be alone. Perhaps to have a wife—because one has to have a wife. . . .

Oui, il faut travailler: Yes, one must work, nothing but work. And one must have patience. . . . I have given my life to it. . . . One must find happiness in one's art.

Tolstoy's unedifying household: cf. [15].

p. 85   not to remain with the dream: "Rodin was a dreamer whose dream rose up into his hands . . ." (*op. cit.*, p. 307).

[37]   p. 85   *La Plume:* an art periodical, in 1900 devoted a special number to Rodin. Rilke was gathering material for his monograph.

[38]   p. 87   These are the days when the empty fountains
dead with hunger fall back again from autumn,
and one divines of all the bells that ring
the lips made of timid metals.

The capitals are indifferent.
But the unexpected evenings that come
make in the park an ardent twilight,
and to the canals whose waters are so slow
they give a Venetian dream . . .
and a solitude to lovers.

[39]   p. 89   wonderful pages: in *Notre Dame de Paris*, Book III, 1.

p. 90   even on his Saturday: Rodin received visitors on Saturdays in his studio at 182 rue de l'Université.

[40]   p. 90   a tiger (antique): probably the little plaster cast of a panther (Greek) mentioned in the essay on Rodin (pp. 338–339). "It's beautiful, that's all . . ."

p. 91   the woman's bust in the Luxembourg: Rodin's Peruvian Woman.

[41]   p. 92   Early in October, Clara arrived in Paris and established her-self in a studio of her own. Rilke had moved to pleasanter quarters in the rue de l'Abbé de l'Epée because his other hotel had been "too much in the midst of student life." "My room au cinquième," he wrote, "has a balcony and before it, first

gardens, then a layer of houses held together by the dome of the Panthéon. And sky and morning and evening, distance." the monograph: *Worpswede*, published by Velhagen and Klasing. See note to [32].

p. 93   my little book: the first part of the essay on Rodin.

[42] p. 94 The Rodin book finished, Rilke, emotionally exhausted and physically ill, sought the warmth and sun of Italy in Viareggio where he had spent some time in 1898. Disappointments greeted him at every turn. He could not stay at his former hotel; the presence in this one of elderly British ladies interfered with his longed for solitude. But though he found little relief from inner restlessness, he was able to write what was to become the third book of the *Book of Hours*, the "Book of Poverty and Death," in which he gave expression to much of his feeling about Paris.

[43] p. 95 *Peter Michel:* Friedrich Huch's first novel (1901), which Rilke frequently mentioned. During his Worpswede days he had contributed reviews—of books, poetry, plays, art—to the *Bremer Tageblatt* and other papers. A collection of these was published in an edition of 100 copies by Richard von Mises (*Rainer Maria Rilke: Bücher, Theater, Kunst;* printed by Jahoda & Siegel, Vienna, 1934), who quotes (p. vi) from a later letter of Rilke's: "When I write in the *Bremer Tageblatt*, I always do it rather with my tongue in my cheek and with my left hand over my mouth in addition: it gets more journalistic that way. But nevertheless read it; it is still the truth, even if very much diluted." The volume contains, among others, reviews of Mann's *Buddenbrooks*, Ellen Key's *Century of the Child*, Lagerlöf's *Jerusalem*, Wassermann's *Moloch*, as well as three discussions of *Peter Michel*.

your new book: Rilke had written Huch a long letter about his new book, *Geschwister*.

[44] p. 96 Ellen Key: Swedish reformer, feminist and writer (1849–1926), interested chiefly in the emancipation of women, problems of love and marriage, the education of children. Much impressed by Rilke's *Stories of God*, she had written the young author. They corresponded frequently, but did not meet until 1904. Rilke addressed her as "Frau" Ellen Key, though she was unmarried, because, as he wrote in an earlier letter, "Fräulein" (Miss; literally, little woman), being a diminutive, seemed not in keeping with his respect for her.

p. 97 the Bojers: Johan Bojer, Norwegian writer, and his wife.

p. 97   Wilhelm Michel's article in *Zeit* had appeared on March 21, 1903. His short monograph, *Rainer Maria Rilke*, was published by Axel Juncker in 1904.

p. 98   my family is old: For a detailed discussion of Rilke's ancestry see Carl Sieber's *René Rilke* (Insel-Verlag, Leipzig, 1932). The family history Rilke relates here is based on genealogical research undertaken at his Uncle Jaroslav Rilke's behest, but later investigations have failed to substantiate these claims to aristocratic lineage. For biographical details in this letter, cf. also [2] and notes, and [7].

p. 103   Ellen Ljunggren: a friend of Ellen Key's who was planning to go to what Rilke termed "frightful America" in order to make enough money to continue her own work.

p. 104   Georg Brandes: the Danish literary historian and critic (1842–1927).

        Juncker: Axel Juncker, at this time Rilke's publisher.

[45]   p. 105   Spanish plan: a projected trip to Spain for material for a book (never written) on Ignacio Zuloaga, the painter (1870–).

        Carrière book: On first going to Paris Rilke had planned to write on Eugène Carrière, the painter (1849–1906), as well as on Rodin, but never did so.

p. 106   letter from Rodin: acknowledging Rilke's monograph.

        Hokusai: (1760–1849). "It was at the age of seventy-three that I almost understood the form and the true nature of birds, of fish and of plants."

[46]   p. 107   *Niels Lyhne:* see note to [60]. Rilke wrote many verses of the third part of the *Book of Hours* on the fly leaves of one of his Jacobsen books.

[47]   p. 108   Rilke returned to Paris at the end of April, remaining there for two months. In July, he and Clara had come to Worpswede, where he visited Heinrich Vogeler.

        Paris: Compare these impressions with *The Notebooks of Malte Laurids Brigge* (G.W. V, 48–49, 58 ff.; in the American edition, known as *The Journal of My Other Self*, 37–39, 50–52, 62 ff.).

        military school: see [2] and notes and [7].

        Baudelaire's "At one o'clock in the morning": "At last! alone! one no longer hears anything but the rumbling of a few belated and broken-down cabs. For some hours we shall possess silence, if not repose. At last! the tyranny of the human face has vanished and I shall no longer suffer through anything but myself . . ."

p. 116   a book of prayers: poems written in Viareggio constituting Book III of the *Book of Hours* (see note to [42]). The first "prayers" were those making up Book I. (Cf. Ruth Mövius, *Rainer Maria Rilkes Stundenbuch*, Insel-Verlag, Leipzig, 1937.)

[48]   p. 116   Clara's parents lived at Oberneuland.

[49]   p. 117   St. Francis: cf. the closing verses of Book III of the *Book of Hours*, which celebrate St. Francis and his poverty (*G.W.* II, 291 ff.; *A.W.* I, 103–104); also [172] and note.

[50]   ·p. 118   Compare this letter with the monograph on Rodin.

[51]   p. 123   Il faut toujours travailler: One must always work—always —(cf. [36]).

[52]   p. 126   Hokusai: see note to [45].

[53]   p. 127   the impending journey: Rilke and his wife were bound for Rome. Clara had received a scholarship enabling her to work there, and Rilke had decided to join her for the winter, though they were not to lodge under the same roof.

p. 131   Gerhart Hauptmann: the German poet and dramatist (1862–). Rilke dedicated the first edition of the *Book of Pictures* to him (1902).

[54]   p. 133   its waters: cf. "the joyful waters of Roman days" in *Sonnets to Orpheus*, I, 10 (*G.W.* III, 322; *A.W.* I, 274; in the translation by M. D. Herter Norton, p. 35); also "Römische Fontäne" in *New Poems* (*G.W.* III, 79).

p. 134   Woodpeace: Rilke is here playing on the name of the villa (Waldfrieden = Woodpeace) in which he had lived at Schmargendorf.

p. 135   Dahlem road: Rilke used to walk on this road in his Schmargendorf days.

[57]   p. 138   Durand-Ruel: the Paris art dealer.

[58]   p. 141   Russian war: the Russo-Japanese war, 1904–5.

Garshin: the Russian writer, M. M. Garshin (1855–88), author of *Attalea Princeps*, who fought in the Russo-Turkish war of 1877–78.

p. 141   Still keenly interested in Russia, Rilke had at this time just finished his translation of the old saga, *The Song of Ygor's Regiment* (ms. in Rilke Archive. A part of the translation was printed in the *Prager Presse*, February 16, 1930, and in the *Insel-Almanach* for 1931, pp. 143–146).

[59] p. 141   Christos voskres!: Christ is risen!, the greeting exchanged by Russians on Easter Day.

Ivanov: Alexander Andreievich Ivanov (1806–58), the Russian painter, on whom Rilke at one time intended to write an essay (cf. note to [13]).

Gogol: Nikolai Vasilievich Gogol (1809–52), the great Russian writer, author of *Dead Souls*.

Easter just once: Rilke and Lou had spent Easter together in Moscow in 1899.

Ivan Veliky: the bell-tower of Ivan the Great, which contains thirty-one bells. At exactly midnight on Easter the big bell used to begin ringing, followed by all the bells of Moscow and one hundred and twenty cannon shots fired from the Kremlin, while throngs of people bearing lighted candles milled about in the street below.

p. 142   the *Zeit:* a Vienna weekly, later a daily paper.

Kuropatkin: General Kuropatkin, one of the Russian commanders in the Russo-Japanese war.

[60] p. 144   *Niels Lyhne, Maria Grubbe:* novels by Jens Peter Jacobsen, the Danish poet (1847–85). Rilke read these, as well as the "six short stories" in the Reclam edition, in German translations (cf. [73]).

p. 145   "White Princess": subtitled "A Scene by the Sea," a dramatic sketch Rilke wrote in Viareggio in 1898 and rewrote in Sweden in 1904 with Duse in mind for the leading role.

[61] p. 146   my new work: parts of the *Notebooks of Malte Laurids Brigge* were written in Rome.

[62] p. 149   Friedrich Westhoff: one of Clara's brothers.

[63] p. 153   translated fragment: Rilke had asked Ellen Key to write an introductory essay for the *Stories of God*, a new edition of which was being brought out by Insel-Verlag.

p. 154   my growing book: see note to [61].

[64] p. 157   my first Viareggio: in the spring of 1898.

p. 160   1. The "Prayers": became the *Book of Hours*. The three sections were already completed (see note to [42]) and this continuation was never carried out.

2. My new book: *The Notebooks* (cf. note to [61]).

3. and 4. None of these were ever carried out.

Thisted: the town in Jutland where J. P. Jacobsen was born.

p. 161   Kierkegaard: Sören Kierkegaard (1813–55), the Danish religious thinker and philosopher.

the big German dictionary: the *Deutsches Wörterbuch*, the pioneer work in German philology (the first volume of which appeared in 1854), begun by the brothers Jacob and Wilhelm Grimm.

p. 164   Francis Jammes: South French, Catholic poet (1868–1938), a favorite of Rodin.

the Goncourts: the brothers de Goncourt, Edmond (1822–96), who published the famous *Journal des Goncourt*, and Jules (1830–70), novelists and art historians, who specialized in studies of eighteenth-century France.

p. 165   Ellen Key's . . . big essay: "En oesterikisk Diktare," appeared in *Ord och Bild* in 1904 (XXX, Nos. 9 and 10), and in an authorized translation in *Deutsche Arbeit* (V, nos. 5 and 6, 1905–6). It was reprinted in her book *Verk och Människor* (Stockholm, 1910), and in the translation of that volume, *Seelen und Werke* (S. Fischer-Verlag, 1911), under the title "Ein Gottsucher." Cf. [121] and note.

[65]   p. 167   Thanks to Ellen Key's lectures, which had aroused interest in his writings, Rilke received several invitations to Scandinavia. Early in June he left Rome for Sweden, stopping to pay his respects to Copenhagen, the city of his beloved Jacobsen. His first destination was Borgeby gård, a castle in Skåne, the southernmost province of Sweden, where he was to spend the greater part of his six months' sojourn in the north (July to December, 1904). While the castle—owned by Miss Hanna Larssen, who also managed the farm belonging to it—lacked its original furnishings and the flavor of antiquity he loved, Rilke writes at length of his delight in the country and the farm, the fragrant meadows, the life of field and stable, the generous table that more than satisfied his vegetarian tastes.

p. 169   Brita Sophie: cf. "In einem fremden Park" ("In a foreign Park"), *New Poems*, *G.W.* III, 61.

[66] p. 170 It was the evening . . . : cf. "Abend in Skåne" ("Evening in Skåne"), *Book of Pictures, G.W.* II, 60; *A.W.* I, 115.

[67] p. 171 Petri: Egon Petri, the pianist.

p. 172 Norlind: Ernst Norlind, the Swedish painter and writer, who was also living here, and whom Rilke describes as at once monkish and Bohemian, yet a man who "has thought much and has come out somewhere in his thinking where there is wind and sky as in poems." Mr. Norlind has published an account of these days with Rilke and Ellen Key (in *Fontaine*, the French literary review published in Algiers, IV, vol. 5, no. 30, 1943).

[68] p. 173 Kappus: Franz Kappus, to whom were addressed the letters published after Rilke's death as the *Letters to a Young Poet.*

c'est de la terre en repos: it is land lying fallow.

[69] p. 174 the *Mangwa:* pictorial encyclopedia of Japanese life, published from 1812–75, for which Hokusai (see note to [45]) provided the illustrations. On his way through Germany to Scandinavia Rilke had spent a day in Düsseldorf looking at a collection of Japanese prints, perusing in particular the thirteen volumes of the *Mangwa.*

work-boughs: cf. "Der Apfelgarten" ("The Apple Orchard"), *New Poems, G.W.* III, 248.

[70] p. 175 Tora Holmström: the sister of a young zoology-student friend of Norlind's. To Ellen Key, Rilke describes her as "a dear and deep kind of person."

Hofmannsthal, George: cf. notes to [143], [150].

[73] p. 177 Hermann Bang: the Danish writer (1858–1912).

the letters Kierkegaard wrote to his fiancée: Kierkegaard's letters to Regina (Olsen) Schlegel had been published, with other papers, in *Kierkegaardske Papirer: Forlovelsen* (Gyldendal, Copenhagen) in 1904. The notebook containing Rilke's translation is in the Rilke Archive.

[77] p. 179 At the end of the summer Rilke had left Borgeby gård for Furuborg, Jonsered, near Göteborg, a country of fir woods and sea, where he stayed with a family named Gibson. He made various trips to Copenhagen where, again through the good offices of Ellen Key, he met Georg Brandes, Karin Michaelis, and the painter Hammershöj. While at Jonsered he became interested in the Samskola, Sweden's first experiment with the community school, publishing an essay

on the subject in *Die Zukunft* (XIII, no. 14, January 1, 1905; now *G.W.* IV, 221–232). He was happy here, and wrote Ellen Key that the strength and clarity of the people's souls and the melancholy and serious happiness of the autumn were working upon him and transforming him. Clara joined him here for a few weeks.

[79]   p. 180   This letter was first published in the *Vossische Zeitung* of December 25, 1927.

p. 181   Obstfelder: the Norwegian poet, Sigbjorn Obstfelder (1886–1906), whose character and writings might suggest him as a prototype for Malte in the *Notebooks*.

[80]   p. 182   Frau Lizzi: Rilke's hostess, Frau Lizzi Gibson.

Charlottenlund: Ellen Key lived here.

[81]   p. 183   Cf. the description of the ghostly burnt-down castle in the *Notebooks* (*G.W.* V, 165–167; *A.W.* II, 117–119; *The Journal*, 131–132).

p. 184   Ellen Key's . . . *Lifslinjer*: in which she made a restatement, almost a defense of her ideas. The first part had appeared under this title in 1903 (Bonnier, Stockholm); the two parts later appeared as *Karleken och äktenskapet*.

[82]   p. 184   Rilke had returned to Oberneuland in time to spend Christmas with Clara and Ruth, staying on till the end of February, 1905. His health again troubling him, he spent March and April at the "Weisse Hirsch" near Dresden, taking a cure. Here he formed a warm friendship with Countess Luise Schwerin (née von Nordeck-Rabenau), a poet in her own right, whom he was later to visit, becoming acquainted with her circle of friends, many of whom were to be among his most frequent correspondents. From the end of April he had been at Worpswede again.

Meister Eckhart: Master Eckhart, one of the great medieval mystics (1260?–1327?).

[83]   p. 186   Rilke was visiting Lou and her husband in Göttingen.

throne of Venus: cf. [54].

my "Rodin": the monograph.

the "Panther": *New Poems, G.W.* III, 44; *A.W.* I, 172.

p. 187   *Hainbund* poets: a school of young poets, admirers of Klopstock, who in the 1770's indulged in idyllic wanderings in the groves of Göttingen.

[85]   p. 187   Friedelhausen, Lollar: the home of Countess Schwerin.

the Rabenau: the family estate of Julie, Baroness von Nordeck zur Rabenau, often referred to in the letters as Frau Nonna, the mother of Countess Schwerin.

[86]   p. 188   the following letter: "Monsieur Rodin asks me to let you know that he will be happy to see you; Monsieur Rodin will expect you in Paris from the seventh of this month. Monsieur Rodin further asks me to let you know that you will be able to live with him, at Meudon, for the duration of your stay in Paris. . . . Monsieur Rodin counts on your staying with him in order to be able to talk."

[87]   p. 189   Wacholderhöhe, Godesberg: Rilke was now visiting the Karl von der Heydts (see [100] and note).

the dear gray castle: Friedelhausen.

[88]   p. 191   After a brief visit to his Paris haunts of three years before, Rilke was now installed in the tiny "Villa des Brillants" in Rodin's garden at Meudon.

[89]   p. 192   "Age d'airain": Rodin's statue, "The Age of Bronze."

         p. 193   c'est l'orme: that is the elm.

Charles Morice: poet and writer (1861–1919), founder of the periodical *Lutèce*.

         p. 194   effigy of Buddha: cf. the two poems, "Buddha" and "Buddha in der Glorie" ("Buddha in Glory"), *New Poems* (*G.W.* III, 31 and 255).

c'est le centre du monde: it is the centre of the world.

[91]   p. 194   Verhaeren: Rilke had just met Verhaeren, the Belgian poet (1855–1916), whose work he greatly admired.

[92]   p. 196   already quite a birthday: Rilke's birthday was December 4.

[93]   p. 197   Bon courage: good courage.

[94]   p. 198   the angel: cf. "L'Ange du méridien (Chartres)," in *New Poems* (*G.W.* III, 32).

"Mais vous ne savez pas . . .": "But don't you know, . . . there is always a wind, that wind about big cathedrals. They are always surrounded by an evil, restless wind, tormented by their grandeur. It is the air falling down along the buttresses, falling from that height and wandering about the church. . . ."

[96] p. 199 Troubetzkoi's: Prince Paul Troubetzkoi, the Russian sculptor, whom Rilke had met in Moscow in 1899.

p. 200 Minne: Baron George Minne, Belgian sculptor (1866–1941).

flamingos: cf. "Die Flamingos" (*New Poems*, *G.W.* III, 236).

[98] p. 201 While on a lecture tour, speaking on Rodin, Rilke had been called to Prague, to the bedside of his father, who died on March 15th. He returned to Paris early in April.

Francis Jammes: see note to [64].

[99] p. 202 Rilke had met Karl von der Heydt and his wife Elisabeth through Countess Schwerin. They were most open-handed friends, and Rilke expressed his gratitude for their many kindnesses by dedicating to them the first part of the *New Poems*.

[100] p. 203 that time in Rome: September, 1903—June, 1904.

the *Notebooks of Malte Laurids Brigge:* (cf. note to [47]), begun in Rome, but not finished until 1910.

[105] p. 209 See [106].

[106] p. 210 M. Thyssen: a writer whom Rilke had introduced to Rodin. (For this identification we are indebted to Mr. Joseph Brummer of the Brummer Galleries, who knew Rilke at this time.)

M. Rothenstein: the late Sir William Rothenstein (1872–1945), the English artist, noted for his portrait drawings.

p. 212 justice . . . will correct the wrong: In a postscript to this letter Rilke added: "I shall tell my relatives and friends (especially my great friend Ellen Key who is arriving in Paris in a few days) that it is to return with all my powers to my own work that I have left you." And in a further note on the same day: "Once more *all* my farewells which the circumstances do not permit me to express. Most affectionately as always yours." (Cf. *R. M. Rilke: Lettres à Rodin,* edited by Georges Grappe, Emile-Paul Frères, Paris, 1931.) The breach with Rodin was healed a year and a half later (see [187] and [190]).

[108] p. 213 The Baroness, née Schwerin, was the wife of Baron Jakob J. Uexküll, the naturalist. The first edition of *The Love and Death of Cornet Christopher Rilke* (Axel Juncker Verlag, Berlin, Leipzig, Stuttgart, 1906), the dramatic poem

written in Schmargendorf in 1899, first published in 1904 (in *Deutsche Arbeit*, IV, i, October), and which he was now revising, was dedicated to her. (Now in *G.W.* IV, 5–34; *A.W.* II, 309–322.)

p. 214   *Book of Pictures:* the first edition was published in 1902.

[109]   p. 214   the passage in question: Section XI of the *Cornet*.

[110]   p. 215   Duval: well-known chain restaurants in Paris.

p. 216   the bird which "has not this care": the recurrent motive (based on Matt. *VI*, 24–34) of Kierkegaard's "Anxieties of the Heathen," constituting Part I of the *Christian Discourses* and the first of which is "The Anxiety of Poverty." Dr. Walter Lowrie in his translation of the *Discourses* (Oxford University Press, 1939) renders the phrase: "This anxiety the bird has not."

St. Anne: Leonardo's painting of St. Anne with the Virgin and Child. Ellen Key had mentioned it in an essay on madonnas, and Rilke had told her (in a letter of January 29, 1903) that when he and Clara saw the picture they thought of her.

Jouven: restaurant on the Boulevard Montparnasse which Rilke frequented.

p. 217   Madame G . . . R . . . : the widow of Georges Rodenbach (1855–98), Belgian writer, author of *Bruges la Morte* (1892).

Meier-Graefe: Julius Meier-Graefe (1867–1935), the art historian and writer.

[111]   p. 218   Rilke had gone out to Chantilly with Ellen Key, the Bojers, and Paula Becker.

p. 219   greatest member of the house of Condé: Louis II, Prince de Condé (1621–86), called "le grand Condé."

[112]   p. 219   La vigne pleure: the vine weeps.

p. 220   Königs-Höhe: the estate of Baron August and Baroness Selma von der Heydt in Elberfeld.

Stina Frisell: Rilke speaks elsewhere of spending some quiet hours, before and after his reading in the Samskola in 1904, at the beautiful house of Stina Frisell (presumably the wife of Erik Frisell, a prominent industrialist) in Göteborg.

Secessionist: at that time the modern school of art.

p. 221   Dora Herxheimer: sculptress, one of the friends who contributed reminiscences of Rilke to the little volume *Rainer*

Maria Rilke, Stimmen der Freunde (edited by Gert Buchheit, Urban-Verlag, Freiburg im Breisgau, 1931).

Ellen Key's book: the essay on Rilke (see note to [64]) was about to appear in book form. See note to [121].

p. 222   a certain alteration: Rilke had shaved his goatee.

[114]   p. 225   a little poem: "Portrait of my Father as a Youth" ("Jugendbildnis meines Vaters"), *New Poems, G.W.* III, 69.

[115]   p. 225   Rembrandt celebration: in Amsterdam, 1906, the tercentenary of Rembrandt's birth.

p. 226   stretched my contours . . . : cf. "The Founder" ("Der Stifter," *New Poems, G.W.* III, 48):

Vielleicht war dieses alles: *so* zu knien	This perhaps was everything: to kneel *like this*
(so wie es alles ist, was wir erfuhren):	(the way what we have experienced is everything):
zu knien: dass man die eigenen Konturen,	to kneel: so as to hold one's own contours,
die auswärtswollenden, ganz angespannt	that would strain outward, all close-hitched
im Herzen hält, wie Pferde in der Hand.	in one's heart, like horses in one's hand.

[116]   p. 226   Rilke had come for a few weeks to the Belgian coast, where he was shortly to be joined by Clara and Ruth.

p. 227   Furnes: cf. the little essay, "Furnes" (*G.W.* IV, 239–252).

[117]   p. 227   Countess Mary Gneisenau: poet and author, whom Rilke had met through Countess Luise Schwerin.
Countess Schwerin had recently died. Rilke, Clara, and Ruth were staying at Friedelhausen, her home, as guests of her sister, Frau Alice Faehndrich.

Sister Marianna: the young Portuguese, Marianna Alcoforado (1640–1723), a Franciscan nun, whose letters to her unfaithful lover, the Marquis de Chamilly (Rilke refers to him as the Count), Rilke had translated (first published in the *Insel-Almanach* for 1908; now as *Portuguese Letters, G.W.* VI, 103–148). An English translation by Donald E. Ericson of the original letters, which were first published in Paris in 1669, has recently been brought out under the title *The Portuguese Letters* (Bennett-Edwards, New York, 1941).

[120]   p. 231   our present kind hostess: Frau Faehndrich (see note to [117]).

[121] p. 233 now comes a request: Rilke's entreaties seem to have had at least a temporary effect, for the essay was not published at this time. See note to [64].

Bard: Julius Bard, the Berlin publisher.

the place with Fischer: in the *Neuer Rundschau*, published by Fischer.

[122] p. 234 Rilke was stopping in Naples on his way to Frau Faehndrich's on Capri.

zanzariere: mosquito net.

[123] p. 235 Vollmoeller: Karl Vollmoeller (1878–   ), poet and sportsman, now living in this country.

p. 236 *plans:* planes of composition.

[124] p. 237 seen many things again: The Rilkes had been in Naples for four days in June, 1904.

Orpheus, Eurydike, Hermes: the poem of this title had been written in that year, and Rilke had read it aloud at the evening gathering in the Samskola in Sweden in November.

[125] p. 237 "Pioggia, scirocco—": "Rain, sirocco—."

p. 238 the Cucaña: by Goya, in the National Gallery in Berlin. Rilke had described his impressions on first seeing this picture in a letter to Clara (July 5, 1905).

Vincent Van Gogh, Letters: the German edition (edited by Margarete Mauthner, Cassirer, Berlin, 1906).

[126] p. 241 Diefenbach: the painter, Karl Wilhelm Diefenbach (1837–1913).

Gorky: Maxim Gorky (pseudonym of A. M. Pyeshkov), the Russian novelist (1868–1926). Rilke writes elsewhere (December 14, 1906): "Diefenbach is still here, and everyone had become accustomed to his caprices just as they are in process of getting used to Gorky, who allows himself to be feted as an anarchist but, agreeably enough, at the moment occasionally throws money instead of bombs among the people, in heaps."

[129] p. 248 rue de l'Abbé de l'Epée: in Paris. Rilke lived at No. 3 for some months in the winter of 1902–3.

Studio al Ponte: the little house on the bridge in the garden of the Villa Strohl-Fern in Rome, in which he had lived in 1903–4.

[131] p. 253 Clara, on her way to Egypt to join Baroness Knoop, had stopped to visit her husband.

My trip back: from Naples, where he had seen Clara off in the "Oceana," the steamer plying between Naples and Egypt.

[132] p. 254 this stream: the Nile.

the big Andrée: the general atlas of Richard Andree.

like a coronal suture: cf. the essay, "Urgeräusch" (*G.W.* IV, 285–294; *A.W.* II, 274–280), translated into English by Carl Niemeyer in *Rainer Maria Rilke: Primal Sound and Other Prose Pieces* (The Cummington Press, 1943).

[133] p. 256 *The Book of Hours: Das Stunden-Buch* had been published by Insel-Verlag in 1905, with the dedication: "Laid in the hands of Lou." Of it, Rilke wrote (to Georg Simmel, August 26, 1908): "It is the only one among my older books that does not give way under me, that builds a strong calm spot and helps me along like something that was long before me and is more than just myself."

p. 257 poems in the *Neue Rundschau:* In the issue for November, 1905 (XVI, 11) had been published Three Poems in Prose: "Graves of the Hetaerae" ("Haetaeren-Gräber"), "Orpheus. Euridyke. Hermes," "Birth of Venus" ("Geburt der Venus"), later included in *New Poems*, Part I (now *G.W.* III, 96–98, 99–102 (also *A.W.* I, 181–184), 103–106). At the time, Rilke wrote Fischer, the publisher, that these were among the few things that stood up under his own judgment.

something like a new *Book of Hours:* This collection was to become the first part of *New Poems*.

[134] p. 258 Antonio came in . . . with: "the day is splendid."

the three islands of the Sirens: cf. "The Isle of the Sirens" ("Die Insel der Sirenen," *G.W.* III, 123–124).

[135] p. 260 Rodin's comment: "Ah—I never noticed."

[136] p. 260 Walter Calé: young German poet, who committed suicide (1904) at 23. A collection of short stories, poems, etc., was published after his death (5th–6th printing, Berlin, 1920).

[139] p. 267 P.B.: Paula Becker.

[140] p. 267 the "Oceana" letter: see note to [131].

p. 268 Tante Gabriele: see note to [2].

p. 268   the new Rodin volume: the second part of the essay on Rodin. The motto, "To work rests one," was not used.

[142] p. 271   a new book of poems: *New Poems*. Part I was published in December, 1907, Part II in 1908.

[143] p. 271   Hugo von Hofmannsthal: (1874–1929), the Austrian poet. The facsimile of this letter here reproduced is taken from that in the First Edition of the *Letters*.

p. 272   your lecture: Hofmannsthal's lecture on the poet and our time, "Der Dichter und diese Zeit," published in the *Neue Rundschau*, March, 1907 (now in *Die Berührung der Sphären*, Berlin, 1931, 42–71).

"The Rosebowl," "Alkestis": were published in *Morgen* (July–December, 1907, No. 14, September 13, 1907; now *G.W.* III, 110–113, 103–106; *A.W.* I, 188–190, 185–188), a weekly for which Hofmannsthal acted as poetry editor and to which he had asked Rilke to contribute.

Bie: Oskar Bie, writer on music, an editor of Fischer's *Neue Rundschau*. For the poems he published see note to [133].

[144] p. 273   three poems as a sample: "The Carrousel," "Abisag," "The Panther" (now *G.W.* III, 80–81, 17, 44; the first and last also *A.W.* I, 173–174, 172) appeared in the *Insel-Almanach auf das Jahr 1908*, together with the essay on the Portuguese nun's letters (cf. note to [117]).

Spanish madonna: Many figures in the pardon processions Rilke had seen in Belgium were of seventeenth-century Spanish origin.

Hofmannsthal: see [143] and notes.

[146] p. 275   Frau Nonna: see note to [85].

Londorf: see [85].

[147] p. 275   Ernst Norlind: see note to [67]. In reply to a request that he criticize a poem Norlind had written in German, Rilke begins by commenting, in substance, that as the poem lacks the feeling of the German language it can never really live.

p. 276   Bonnier: the Stockholm publisher.

[148] p. 277   a daily task: the translation of the *Sonnets from the Portuguese* of Elizabeth Barrett Browning, on which Rilke had worked with his hostess, Frau Faehndrich (Insel-Verlag, 1908; now *G.W.* VI, 5–50; *A.W.* II containing only nos. 6, 35, 39, 22). Cf. [74]. In 1912, Rilke still sees "no prospect of learning English"!

[149] p. 277 Gorky: see [126] and note.

[150] p. 278 Friedrich von Oppeln-Bronikowski was preparing a lecture on Rilke (delivered before the *Literaturhistorische Gesellschaft* of Bonn, July 6, 1907).

my having met the poet: Rilke had met Stefan George (1868–1933) in Florence in April, 1898.

[151] p. 280 Carrière: see note to [45].

Dora: Dora Herxheimer (see note to [112]).

Colarossi's: atelier for art students in Paris.

Mathilde Vollmoeller: see note to [172].

[152] p. 280 Bagatelle Palace: in the Bois de Boulogne.

newly installed . . . collection: of modern French paintings and drawings, collected by Etienne Moreau-Nélaton, the painter (1859–   ), was given to the Louvre in 1907.

p. 281 Bernheim jeune: Paris art dealer.

Maillol: Aristide Maillol, the French sculptor (1861–1944).

Berthe Morisot: Manet's sister-in-law.

Bashkirtseff: see note to [23].

[153] p. 282 looking at the gazelles: cf. "The Gazelle" in *New Poems* (*G.W.* III, 45). Clara had modeled some gazelles while staying at Al Hayat, a sanatorium in Heluan near Cairo, during her trip to Egypt the preceding winter.

[154] p. 282 A student: cf. *The Notebooks* (*G.W.* V, 208–209; *A.W.* II, 147–149; *The Journal*, 167–168).

[156] p. 284 Tante Alla and the Countess: Frau Alice Faehndrich and (presumably) her daughter, Countess Manon zu Solms-Laubach.

p. 285 Mlle de Lespinasse: Rilke was reading, "two or three each day," the *Letters* (1809) of Julie de Lespinasse (1732–76), at whose salon the Encyclopedists used to meet. Her answer: "Paris is the place in the world where one can be poor with the fewest privations; only bores and idiots need to be rich."

[157] p. 287 "Alkestis": see note to [143].

The Rodin conversation: Clara had had a talk with Meier-Graefe about Rodin, in which (as she remembered it) he had said that Rodin's "always working" had led to a broadening but not to a higher development of his art.

[158] p. 288 Diriks: Carl Edvard Diriks.

My new book: *New Poems*, Part I.

[159] p. 288 the present lecture: While acting as his secretary, Rilke made two tours lecturing on Rodin's work, the first to Dresden and Prague, the second to Berlin, Hamburg, Bremen, and Weimar. The material as drawn up and presented on these occasions he used for the second part of the book on Rodin (cf. [32] and note).

[163] p. 290 the new book: *New Poems*, I. The "Gazelle" was retained (cf. [178]; also note to [153]). The "Marionette Theater" has never been published.

[165] p. 291 Dr. Martin Zickel, the theatrical director, was at this time in Breslau. We owe this letter to the kindness of Dr. Richard von Mises; the facsimile is from the autograph in his collection. The letter concerns the Breslau evening described in [188].

Baron von Gleichen-Russwurm: Alexander Freiherr von Gleichen-Russwurm, a great-grandson of Schiller, shared the evening with Rilke.

Daily Life: Das tägliche Leben, an early drama of Rilke's in two acts, unsuccessfully performed at the Residenz-Theater in Berlin in 1901, had had a friendly reception at a special matinee performance in Breslau in May, 1907.

[166] p. 292 Sabatier's *Saint Francis: Vie de Saint François d'Assise,* by Paul Sabatier (1894).

Li Tai Po: (701–762).

[167] p. 294 your little book: Schellenberg's *Rainer Maria Rilke. Ein Essay* (Beiträge zur Literaturgeschichte, Heft 35. Verlag für Literatur, Kunst und Musik, Leipzig, 1907).

[168] p. 294 Paul Zech: author of the first full-length work on Rilke, *Rainer Maria Rilke, der Mensch und das Werk* (Wolfgang Jess, Dresden, 1930), from which this letter is taken.

[170] p. 297 your new work: a school for little children.

[171] p. 297 Potin's: Potin, the Paris grocer.

p. 298 "Corrida": *New Poems, G.W.* III, 213–214.

[172] p. 298 Van Gogh portfolio: Mathilde Vollmoeller, painter, sister of the poet, had lent Rilke a portfolio of Van Gogh reproductions which she had recently brought back with her from Amsterdam.

p. 299   poverty . . . a radiance: cf. the line "For poverty is a great radiance from within . . ." from the *Book of Hours* (*G.W.* II, 282; *A.W.* I, 96) (See also [49] and note).

[173]   p. 300   "Pages from a Stormy Night": *G.W.* II, 140–149.

This way there are two worlds: Rilke here wrote "zwei Welt," apparently thinking this an expression of Jacobsen's. It would appear, however, that Jacobsen merely used the abbreviation *To Verd.* (in a letter to Edvard Brandes, October 28, 1879) in referring to the title of his short story *To Verdener*, much as if one wrote *Two Wld.* for *Two Worlds*. Lydia Baer in her able article on *Rilke and Jens Peter Jacobsen* (PMLA, *LIV*, 4, December, 1939) bears out this view and explains how the misunderstanding arose through the German translation (Reclam edition) in which Rilke first read Jacobsen's stories.

little shops: cf. the *Notebooks* (*G.W.* V, 54–55; *A.W.* II, 40; *The Journal*, 41).

[175]   p. 303   Titian (1477–1576); Tintoretto (1518–1594); Francesco Guardi (1712–1793); Tiepolo (1696–1770); Rosalba Giovanna Carriera (1675–1757).

p. 304   Maurice Quentin de la Tour (1704–1788); Peronnet (J. B. Perronneau, 1715–1788); Chardin (1699–1779).

[176]   p. 305   Pissaro: Camille Pissaro (1830–1903), French Impressionist painter.

reporter of all these facts: Émile Bernard, *Souvenirs sur Paul Cézanne*, Paris, 1926 (cf. also Ambroise Vollard, *Paul Cézanne*, Paris, 1915).

p. 306   Zola: Émile Zola, the French novelist, a friend of Cézanne's youth, had written about him in *L'Oeuvre*.

he screamed at a visitor: "work without bothering about anybody and grow strong."

p. 307   *plans:* see note to [123].

he broke out: "Things are going badly . . . Life is frightening!"

[177]   p. 309   Mathilde Vollmoeller: see note to [172].

[178]   p. 310   a part of the *Book of Hours:* the second part had been written in Westerwede in 1901.

p. 311   the fragment on the Lonely: unpublished, probably among the manuscripts lost or auctioned in Paris during the war.

p. 311   the first proofs: of *New Poems*.

the "Gazelle": see [153], [163], and notes.

[179]   p. 312   one hears them assert: "there is absolutely nothing, nothing, nothing there."

[180]   p. 313   the blue slips: the manuscript pages of *New Poems*.

Verlaine, who under "My Will" wrote: I give nothing to the poor because I am myself a poor man.

[181]   p. 314   "The Carcass": "Une Charogne," in *Fleurs du Mal.* Cf. *The Notebooks* (*G.W.* V, 89; *A.W.* II, 64; *The Journal*, 69).

p. 315   Saint-Julien-l'hospitalier: the legend of this title in Flaubert's *Trois Contes* (1877). Cf. *The Notebooks* (*G.W.* V, 90; *A.W.* II, 64; *The Journal*, 69).

the death of the Chamberlain: in *The Notebooks* (*G.W.* V, 15–21; *A.W.* II, 12–17; *The Journal*, 9–15).

Raskolnikov: the protagonist in Dostoievsky's *Crime and Punishment*.

[182]   p. 317   And in the last letter: "So I am continuing my studies."

the wish that was literally fulfilled: "I swore to die painting." Overtaken by a violent rainstorm while sketching, Cézanne, carrying his heavy equipment, collapsed by the roadside with a chill. He died a week later.

[184]   p. 319   the self-portrait: The catalogue of the Salon d'Automne of 1907 (which included the retrospective memorial exhibition of Cézanne's works) lists a self-portrait from the collection of Auguste Pellerin, Paris, and from Rilke's description of the background this would appear to be No. 286 in Venturi's *Catalogue raisonné* of Cézanne's works, from the 1873–76 period (not 1879 as suggested in the original edition of the *Letters*, whose editors did not have access to the Salon catalogue).

p. 320   in the very beautiful composition: The still life Rilke here describes would appear to be "La Pendule noire" ("The Black Clock"), 1869–71, at one time in the collection of Baron Kohner in Budapest, now in that of Mr. Edward G. Robinson, Hollywood (Venturi, No. 69).

[185]   p. 321   my packing: Rilke was about to leave for a tour covering Prague, Breslau, and Vienna, speaking again on Rodin and also reading from his own poems.

p. 322   rue de l'Abbé de l'Epée: see note to [129].

[186]   p. 322   The feeling Rilke here expresses about Prague reminds one of a passage about Copenhagen in *The Notebooks* (*G.W.* V, 189–190; *A.W.* II, 134–135; *The Journal*, 151–152).

[187]   p. 323   Mr. Cherny: Rodin's secretary.

               Heller, the bookdealer: see note to [190].

           p. 324   the extract of my new Rodin work: from the second part of the Rodin essay (see notes to [32] and [140], in *Kunst und Künstler*, Jahrg. VI, Heft I, October, 1907, pp. 28–39).

           p. 325   Kamenitz an der Linde: see note to [44].

               B. of P.: Book of Pictures.

               Christine Brahe: from *The Notebooks* (*G.W.* V, 31–47; *A.W.* II, 24–35; *The Journal*, 24–35).

               "The Carrousel": see note to [144].

[188]   p. 325   the Breslau evening: see [165] and note.

           p. 326   Ivan the Terrible: in "The Czars," III, from the *Book of Pictures* (*G.W.* II, 99; *A.W.* I, 124).

[189]   p. 327   the death of Chamberlain Brigge: see note to [181].

               Sidie Nadherny: Baroness Nadherny (see [187]).

[190]   p. 328   Heller: Rilke had been invited by the bookdealer, Hugo Heller—the first in Vienna to arrange such lectures and exhibitions—to give a reading in the small room at the back of the store.

               It reads: "Come to see me when you are in Paris. So many things, so many things. We have need of truth, of poetry, both of us, and of friendship." Cf. [106] and note.

               the story of Psyche: "it is the story that is so delightful of woman and of her entrance into life—." In a letter to Rodin of this same date, Rilke wrote: "I am approaching the same subject from afar having recently done some small things on the Portuguese Nun . . . on Duse, on Madame de Noailles. . . . I am not sufficiently advanced to dare go further. I shall do so some day."

               The essay: (the extract alluded to in [187] and note) "your essay . . . I find it in truth very beautiful."

               Hofmannsthal: Rilke met Hofmannsthal for the first time on this visit to Vienna.

[191] p. 329 chez Mlle Romanelli: Rilke was staying at the Romanelli's. His letters to Signorina Romanelli have been published by Aeschlimann, Milan, but because of wartime conditions have not yet reached this country.

This Venice: As a young man Rilke had found Venice the "strangest of all wonders. . . . Venice! I gaze and gaze and am like a child. Am in accord with everything." (Postcard to Wilhelm von Scholz, March 30, 1897.)

[192] p. 329 From the end of November, when he left Venice, until the middle of February, 1908, Rilke was in Oberneuland with his family; after which he moved about, visiting friends—Berlin, Rome, Naples, Capri, Florence—not returning to Paris, or to any kind of sustained work, until May, 1908.

this incongruous event: the occasion of this letter was the death of Frau Faehndrich, the sister of Countess Schwerin.

Countess Schwerin . . . and my father: both had died in 1906, in February and March respectively.

[193] p. 331 On September first Rilke had moved into the Hôtel de Biron at 77 rue de Varenne, into Clara's temporarily vacant studio from which, on her return, he moved to other rooms in the same building. A little later Rodin also set up a studio there, at Rilke's suggestion. It is now the Musée Rodin. Among other occupants were the actor de Max, the writer Jean Cocteau, and Isadora Duncan, who used one of the rooms for dance rehearsals.

p. 332 the Nun: the Portuguese Nun (see [117] and note).

Count de Chamilly: see note to [117].

p. 333 and said: It is Rodin carrying his work, which grows heavier and heavier, but which holds the world.

plans: see note to [123].

[194] p. 335 *Goethe's Correspondence with a Child:* a remarkable book of letters, reminiscences, and hymns to Goethe, by Bettina (Brentano) von Arnim (1785–1859).

Malte Laurids: cf. *The Notebooks* (*G.W.* V, 239–241; *A.W.* II, 170–171; *The Journal,* 192–194).

Buddha must wait: see note to [195].

[195] p. 336 *The Discourses: The Discourses of Gautama Buddha.* With her friend Anna Jaenecke, Clara was reading Karl Eugen Neumann's translation (Munich, 1907), which she had sent Rilke.

[196] p. 338 your dear aunt: Baroness Schenck zu Schweinsberg, whom Rilke had met on Capri, was a niece of Frau Faehndrich. Cf. [192].

[197] p. 340 Weisser Hirsch: Rilke had taken the cure here in 1905.

Green Vault: famous collection of jewels and objets d'art in Dresden.

Rosalba Carriera: cf. [175] and note.

[198] p. 341 The "View of Toledo" by El Greco which Rilke describes is in the Metropolitan Museum of Art in New York.

[201] p. 344 Anton Kippenberg: director of the Insel-Verlag and Rilke's publisher. (This letter is taken from *B.V.*)

this work: *The Notebooks of Malte Laurids Brigge* (cf. notes to [47], [61], [100]).

[202] p. 345 Hugo Heller: cf. [190]. We are indebted to Dr. Richard von Mises for a copy of this letter (first published in the *Berliner Tageblatt*, no. 563, Friday, November 29, 1929).

the "Requiem": see note to [17].

you too recognized: Heller's first wife, also a painter, had died in childbirth.

[204] p. 346 Jakob Baron Uexküll: see note to [108].

[205] p. 348 Lizzie Gibson: Rilke's hostess at Furuborg, Jonsered, in Sweden, in 1904.

[206] p. 351 The Marquise: later the Duchesse de Choiseul, an American woman who at this time had a great influence on Rodin.

(said Rodin): "opens and shuts the harmony tap." . . . "Rilke says: it is as wide as silence; that's true . . ."

[208] p. 357 he said: "Theosophy is an eater of men" . . .

[209] p. 358 Georg Brandes: (1842–1927), the Danish literary critic, whom Rilke had met in Scandinavia.

Rodenbach: Georges Rodenbach (cf. note to [110]).

[210] p. 359 The long work period in Paris had ended, its fruits *New Poems II* and *The Notebooks of Malte Laurids Brigge*. Rilke had been visiting his publisher in Leipzig, busy with the dictation of the manuscript of the latter. He was now under way again, beginning with a month's sojourn in Rome. (This letter is taken from *B.V.*)

p. 360   the fool of Charles the Bold: cf. *The Notebooks* (*G.W.* V, 228–232; *A.W.* II, 162–163; *The Journal*, 183–186).

[211]   p. 362   Countess Julie Reventlow: cf. *The Notebooks* (*G.W.* V, 183, 289; *A.W.* II, 130, 205; *The Journal*, 147, 234).

LIST OF CORRESPONDENTS

(The numbers refer to the Letters)

Andreas-Salomé, Lou, 14, 47, 49, 50, 51, 52, 53, 54, 57, 58, 59, 61, 64, 73, 77, 81, 205

Bauschinger, Dr. Julius, 3
Becker, Paula, *see* Modersohn-Becker, Paula
Bodman, Emanuel von, 24
Bonz, Adolf, 9
Brandes, Georg, 209
Bülow, Frieda von, 8, 10, 11, 20

David-Rhonfeld, Valery, 2
Du Prel, Karl Baron, 6

Fischer, S., 101

Ganghofer, Ludwig, 7
Gneisenau, Countess Mary, 117, 120, 127

Heller, Hugo, 202
Heydt, Elisabeth von der, 103, 126, 133
Heydt, Karl von der, 90, 99, 100, 116, 118, 126, 149, 203
Hofmannsthal, Hugo von, 143
Holitscher, Arthur, 33, 55, 74, 93
Holmström, Tora, 70, 76, 145
Huch, Friedrich, 32, 43

Kanitz-Menar, Countess Lili, 192, 200
Keim, Franz, 1
Key, Ellen, 44, 48, 56, 60, 63, 107, 121
Kippenberg, Anton, 201, 210

Modersohn, Otto, 19, 41
Modersohn-Becker, Paula, 17, 21, 23, 27, 141

Nordeck zur Rabenau, Julie Baroness von, 155, 164, 170
Nordeck zur Rabenau, Marietta Baroness von, 212
Norlind, Ernst, 147

Oppeln-Bronikowski, Friedrich von, 150

Pauli, Gustav, 26

Reventlow, Countess Franziska, 28
Rilke, Clara, 16, 18, 22, 30, 35, 36, 37, 39, 40, 42, 45, 46, 65, 66, 67, 68, 69, 71, 72, 75, 78, 80, 83, 84, 85, 86, 88, 89, 91, 92, 94, 95, 96, 97, 98, 102, 104, 105, 109, 110, 111, 112, 113, 114, 115, 122, 123, 124, 125, 128, 129, 130, 131, 132, 134, 135, 137, 138, 139, 140, 142, 144, 146, 151, 152, 153, 154, 156, 157, 158, 159, 160, 161, 162, 163, 166, 169, 171, 172, 173, 174, 175, 176, 177, 178, 179, 180, 181, 182, 184, 185, 186, 187, 189, 190, 191, 193, 194, 195, 196, 198
Rodin, Auguste, 34, 38, 106, 198, 199

Schellenberg, Ernst Ludwig, 167
Schenck zu Schweinsberg, Baroness Elisabeth, 196, 207
Schill, Sofia Nikolaevna, 12, 13, 15
Schobloch, Frau Rosa, 197
Schwerin, Countess Luise, 82, 87
Solms-Laubach, Countess Manon zu, 211

Uexküll, Baroness Gudrun, 108, 119, 136, 148
Uexküll, Baron Jakob, 204

W., Herr von, 183
Weinmann, Frau Julie, 31
Westhoff, Clara, *see* Rilke, Clara
Westhoff, Friedrich, 62
Westhoff, Helmuth, 25
Wildberg, H. von Dickinson, 4, 5

Young Girl, to a, 79

Zech, Paul, 168
Zickel, Dr. Martin, 165
Zwintscher, Oskar, 29